Managing Work and 'The Rest of Life'

Forschung und Praxis zukunftsfähiger Unternehmensführung

Herausgegeben von Stephan Kaiser

Band 4

Cornelia Ulrike Reindl

MANAGING WORK AND 'THE REST OF LIFE'

The Role of Formal and Informal
Demands and Resources for the Work-Life
Conflict of Professionals

Bibliographic Information published by the Deutsche Nationalbibliothek
The Deutsche Nationalbibliothek lists this publication in the Deutsche Nationalbibliografie; detailed bibliographic data is available in the internet at http://dnb.d-nb.de.

Zugl.: Eichstätt, Kath. Univ., Diss., 2012

Cover Design:
© Olaf Gloeckler, Atelier Platen, Friedberg

ISSN 2190-7501
ISBN 978-3-631-62523-1
© Peter Lang GmbH
Internationaler Verlag der Wissenschaften
Frankfurt am Main 2013
All rights reserved.
PL Academic Research is an Imprint of Peter Lang GmbH

www.peterlang.de

Für H.H.R.

DANKSAGUNG

An dieser Stelle möchte ich meinen Dank an die vielen Personen richten, die zur Entstehung und Fertigstellung der vorliegenden Dissertation beigetragen haben. Zunächst möchte ich mich besonders bei meinen Gutachtern Prof. Dr. Stephan Kaiser und Prof. Dr. Max Ringlstetter für deren kontinuierliche Unterstützung und Mühe, konstruktive Kritik und wertvolle Begleitung in meinem Promotionsstudium und bezüglich der vorliegenden Dissertation bedanken. Mein Dank gilt weiterhin dem erweiterten Prüfungsausschuss, Prof. Dr. Joachim Genosko und Prof. Dr. mult. Anton Burger für interessante und kritische Fragen in der Disputation. Für den Weg zur und durch die Promotion haben mich insbesondere zwei Menschen ermutigt und bestärkt, Dr. Melanie Germ und Dr. Monika Nisslein. Ich danke all meinen Kollegen des Lehrstuhls ABWL, Organisation und Personal für uneingeschränktes Interesse und Freude daran, wissenschaftliche Fragen zu diskutieren, deren Offenheit für interdisziplinäre Forschung und besonders deren unkomplizierte Unterstützung wann immer sie nötig war. Meine tiefe Dankbarkeit gilt meinen Freunden und besonders meiner Familie und meinem Partner für Geduld, Vertrauen, Motivation und Respekt und vor allem uneingeschränkten Rückhalt für mein Studium und meine Dissertation.

Die vorliegende Untersuchung entstand im Rahmen des Forschungsprojektes "Innovative Konzepte der Personal- und Organisationsentwicklung in Beratungsorganisationen – IPOB" (www.consulting-innovation.de), angesiedelt an der Kath. Universität Eichstätt-Ingolstadt, Wirtschaftswissenschaftliche Fakultät Ingolstadt, Lehrstuhl ABWL, Organisation und Personal. Das Projekt wurde gefördert vom Bundesministerium für Bildung und Forschung (BMBF), dem Deutschen Zentrum für Luft und Raumfahrt (DLR) sowie dem Europäischen Sozialfonds (ESF).

TABLE OF CONTENTS

INDEX OF ABBREVIATIONS AND SYMBOLS

ANOVA	Analysis of variance
AMOS	Program used for covariance-based SEM (Analysis of Moment Structures)
AVE	Average variance extracted
bWLC	Behavior-based work-to-life conflict
CFL	Cross-factor loadings
DC status	Dual-career status (both partners working full-time)
df	Degrees of freedom
e.g.	For example (lat. exempli gratia)
f^2	Effect size (PLS)
F	F-value testing significance within ANOVA
GoF	Goodness-of-Fit Index for PLS models (Tenenhaus et al., 2005)
HRM	Human Resource Management
HRD	Human Resource Development
i.e.	That means / In other words (lat. id est)
INIuse	Use of work-life balance initiatives
INIavailability	Availability of work-life balance initiatives
KMO	Kaiser-Meyer-Olkin Criterion
LF	Law firm professionals (sample)
LISREL	Program used for covariance-based SEM (Linear Structural Relationship)
M	Mean
MC	Management consultants (sample)
MD	Mean difference
N	Sample size
p	Significance level
PCA	Principal component analysis
PLS	Partial Least Squares analysis
Q^2	Stone-Geisser criterion indicating predictive validity of PLS models
R^2	Determination coefficient in regression analysis and PLS modeling
SD	Standard deviation
SEM	Structural equation model(ing)
sWLC	Strain-based work-to-life conflict
tWLC	Time-based work-to-life conflict
WLB	Work-life balance
WLC	Work- life conflict
WLIM	Work-life integration management
β	Standardized regression coefficient
r	Pearson product-moment correlation coefficient
λ	Path coefficient in the measurement model
γ	Path coefficient in the structural model
ρ	Composite reliability
α	Cronbach's Alpha indicating measurement reliability

LIST OF TABLES

LIST OF FIGURES

INTRODUCTION

Reconciling Work with 'the Rest of Life' – A Particular Challenge for Professionals?

As work constitutes an essential part of most individuals' lives today managing the work-life interface has become a major challenge for employees. Demographic changes towards an aging workforce and the increase of employed women along with the subsequent increase of dual-career couples have rendered the traditional family pattern of male breadwinner / female homemaker obsolete and initiated the discussion about balancing work and family. But with ever longer working hours and increasing global competition, the question is no longer about 'who cares for the kids'. Ample research evidence has shown that multiple role responsibilities (employee, spouse, parent, etc.) are likely to collide which leads to so-called work-life conflict, i.e. challenges associated with successfully reconciling all life spheres. Work-life conflict is associated with a variety of negative outcomes: stress, physical and psychological health complaints, decreased well-being, etc. (Byron, 2005; Eby et al., 2005). Beyond the individual level, these outcomes harm organizations in terms of *decreased employee commitment* (Ahuja et al., 2007; Allen, 2001; Aryee et al., 2005, Casper et al., 2002; Chang, 2008; Dex & Scheibl, 2001; Smith & Gardner, 2007), *lower job satisfaction* (Boyar & Mosley, 2007; Bruck, Allen & Spector, 2002; Judge et al., 1994; Rice et al., 1992; Saltzstein et al., 2001; Thomas & Ganster, 1995), *increased absenteeism* (Boyar et al. 2005; Dex & Scheibl 2001; Galinsky & Stein 1990; Halpern 2005a; van Steenbergen & Ellemers, 2009) and *higher intent to leave the organization* (Ahuja et al., 2007; Greenhaus et al., 2001; Haar, 2004).

That employers react to these challenges becomes visible in their corporate communication, for example on firm websites, appearance of 'work-life balance' success stories in managerial journals,[1] firms' interest in scientifically examining work-life dynamics themselves[2], and their participation in scientific publications (e.g. Riester & Dern, 2010), and the attractiveness of certificates and audits attesting work-life or work-family friendliness to the company (e.g. von Kettler, 2010: Audit Beruf & Familie®). The insight that employee productivity and subsequently organizational success relies heavily on employee satis-

---

1   Cf. Friedman, Christensen & DeGroot (1998); Hewlett & Luce (2005); Perlow & Porter (2009).

2   Cf. large-scale empirical research on work-life issues conducted at IBM (Hill et al., 2004; Hill et al., 2006; Hill et al., 2007).

faction with their integration of work with other life spheres is illustrated by Brint Ryan, co-founder and chief executive officer (CEO) of Ryan LLC:

> "[...] We started experiencing in 2007 a rapid increase in the loss of talent. And I'm not talking about just general talent – I'm talking about the stars. The tipping point for me was when one of our brightest and shining stars came into my office and said, 'Brint, I love this company. I love my work here, and here's my resignation.' I was shocked! She told me, 'I want to start a family and it's not conducive to the very rigid set of rules that you have at the company for me to be able to do that' " (Galinsky & Matos, 2011, p. 273).

One branch where such work-life challenges are particularly obvious are professional service firms (PSFs). Their work culture is characterized by an 'always-on ethic' (Perlow & Porter, 2009, p. 102), excessive work hour volumes and long periods of work away from home (O'Mahoney, 2007). At the same time, *professional service firms* (PSFs) as providers of highly-specialized and complex services depend on a committed, healthy, and efficient workforce as their most critical strategic asset (Kaiser & Ringlstetter, 2011; Løwendahl, 2005; Maister, 1993). Professionals who pursue a highly demanding career path in the knowledge industry are likely face high sacrifices on behalf of their personal life spheres. It seems that many professionals, in order to advance and succeed in the 'up-or-out' career system of PSFs (Kumra & Vinnicombe, 2008), (have to) make work the central focus of their lives. On the other hand, the strong centrality of work for professionals may as much be a virtue as a pressure as they have invested considerably in their education and seek a career that is associated with many opportunities for further learning and development. A central paradigm of work-life research - the existence of and conflict among separate life roles - might therefore righteously challenged asking 'Does life begin at the office exit?': with the work role being so salient the question arises whether work-life integration is an issue for professionals at all. However, researchers argue in favor of an option of 'having it all' contending that particularly highly qualified individuals strive to lead a life where they pursue a challenging career and at the same time 'have a life' (Burke, 2009; Sullivan & Mainiero, 2007).

Of the demands in PSFs' daily work, particularly extremely long working hours and frequent business travel make the experience of work-life conflict likely. PSFs are also well-known for expecting highly motivated work behaviors and extraordinarily high engagement from their workforce. These informal time demands are engrained in organizational culture in terms of expectations to work extremely long hours as well as an unspoken requirement to put work first (Williams, 2007) and slower or halted career advancement if work-life balance initiatives were used (being taken as a sign of not putting work first). As a function of these demands work-life conflict is highly probable among professionals.

In recent years PSFs have started to acknowledge the changing needs and employer criteria of young professionals that continue to shift towards high priorities in both work and nonwork spheres, as expressed in the popular slogan of 'working to live, or living to work' (cf. also Burke, 2009). In order to remain attractive employers, many firms in recent years implemented a number of interventions to address the needs of a new 'having it all' workforce. The effectiveness of such arrangements, which primarily comprise care services and temporal working pattern adjustments (part-time, flextime, etc.), in reducing conflicts among work and personal life was shown in a number of empirical studies and doubted in others. Additionally to so-called work-life initiatives researchers argue that companies should provide an encouraging climate where management, supervisors and peers are supportive of the idea of fostering work-life balance in general. The notion that a work-life friendly culture is a prerequisite for effective initiatives was shown, among others, by Peper et al. (2011) and Thompson et al. (1999).

While these demands and resources were tested in a number of organizational contexts, we do not know how they affect the work-life dynamics of professionals in PSFs which can be counted towards 'extreme jobholders' as described by Hewlett and Luce (2006). Additionally, conflict among work and nonwork was so far largely conceptualized as work-family conflict excluding all individuals without family obligations (Casper et al., 2007). The present examination focuses on work-*life* conflict in order to draw a broader picture of dynamics among work and personal life. In sum, these aspects raise a number of questions which represent the central focus of the present dissertation:

- To what extent is the experience of challenges in reconciling work and personal life spheres (work-life conflict) an issue for professionals in highly demanding work environments such as PSFs?
- How do the demands that professionals put up with impact their work-personal life dynamics?
- Are resources offered by organizations in assistance of their professional workforce useful for solving problems at the work-life boundary?
- Are there specific types of professionals, e.g. with regards to gender, age, or organizational tenure, that are in particular need for organizational resources / that are particularly affected by organizational demands?

More specifically, a review of relevant literature on HRM and work-life interactions has revealed a number of research gaps as well as deficits in practical knowledge on managing work and personal life of professionals. From a research point of view, it is unclear what we mean by work-'life' research as studying conflicts of integrating work and family only captures a part of 'life' and excludes all individuals without proximate family responsibilities (Casper et al., 2007). Additionally, assessment of work-life/family interactions is highly diverse and yet frequently does not pay tribute to the complexity of work-personal life dynamics. One measurement that does is the concept of Greenhaus and Beutell (1985) who suggest a concept of time-based, strain-based and behavior-based work-life/family conflict. Time-based and strain-based conflict has been assessed in numerous studies while the behavior-based conflict dimension is usually neglected. Although it is argued that the majority of research on work-life/family dynamics has been conducted with professional samples (Casper et al., 2007), there still seems to be a need for further research on this complex and highly diverse workforce. Particularly jobs in PSFs which can be characterized as 'extreme jobs' (Hewlett & Luce, 2006) are a highly interesting field of study as these knowledge workers on the one hand do extremely demanding jobs and on the other hand are willing to do so because they love what they do. Hence, the present doctoral thesis wants to contribute to work-life research in a number of ways:

- Shed light on the dimensions and types of work-'life' conflict that professionals experience in order to undermine the notion that work-personal life reconciliation should not be reduced to 'work-family';
- Extend research about interactions of organizational demands and resources as predictors of work-life conflict within a context of professionals with particularly high job demands;
- Extend work-life research about professionals in highly demanding work environments in a German context;[3]
- Investigate work-life conflict in terms of the three-dimensional conflict conceptualization of Greenhaus and Beutell (1985) into *time-, strain-, and behavior based work-to-life conflict* as suggested by Michel et al. (2010), which is highly adequate to understand the specific character of conflict that professionals experience enabling differential implications for theory and practice;
- Extend methodological approaches of work-life research by applying a *PLS path modeling approach to studying work-life conflict antecedents,* a very powerful method of analysis which has been used very rarely in the work-life research arena.

Additionally, this doctoral thesis wants to contribute insights for HRM practitioners, organizational leaders and employees themselves in several ways:

---

3   The vast majority of work-life research is U.S. based (Casper et al., 2007).

- Examine *work-life instead of work-family conflict* in order to draw conclusions that are generalizable to a greater number of professionals than it was done in previous work-life research by not focusing "only on married or partnered couples with children at home unnecessarily restricting its applicability and generalizability" (Kreiner, 2006, p. 487);
- Extend understanding of the role of organizational demands and resources for the work-life conflict of professionals in order to *more effectively manage existing problems, identify strategies to deal with work-life conflict* and subsequently *maintain and improve employee performance and productivity* – from an organizational and from an individual perspective;
- Separately investigate the *role that specific work-life initiatives play for the work-life interface* allowing implications on the usefulness of such initiatives which have in turn implications for the cost-effectiveness of offering such policies;
- Shed a closer look at subsample differences which allows drawing conclusions concerning the *impact of formal and informal organizational demands and resources for various groups* within the professional service firm.

Above and beyond, the aim of the present doctoral thesis is to examine the impact of formal and informal organizational demands and resources on the work-life conflict of professionals working in PSFs.

Structure of the Present Dissertation

In the attempt to address guiding questions the present thesis is structured as follows. *Part I* constitutes the theoretical background and framework for a subsequent empirical examination. First, the relevance of work-life dynamics for the individual and the organization is explored in order to underscore the importance of successful work-life reconciliation from both perspectives. Next, the toolbox of work-life research is outlined including a brief introduction of theoretical roots of this area of research and major concepts under examination (work-life/family conflict, work-life/family enrichment, etc.) (section 1). The subsequent paragraph introduces 'professionals' as an occupational category (section 2). Characteristics of professionals in a more general sense are introduced briefly followed by a more detailed examination of the specificities of professional service firm employees and their likeliness of experiencing work-life conflict. Section 3 briefly introduces theoretical approaches to examining formal and informal demands and resources and then presents a review of empirical results regarding their impact on the work-life interface with particular focus on professionals. The impact of formal demands (work hours, business travel) is examined as well as the role of formal resources, i.e. work-life initiatives. Further, the role that informal demands and resources play for the work-life interface is investigated along guiding questions outlined previously. From these insights a set of hypotheses and research questions is developed. In *Part II*, this set of hypotheses is empirically tested using a professional sample. Specifically, within a sample of 794 professionals (252 management consultants and 552 law firm professionals) the role of organizational antecedents is investigated with a PLS (partial least squares) structural equation modeling approach. Additionally to overall modeling results, subsample effects with regards to subbranch (management consultants vs. law firm employees), life role priority, gender, age, parental status, relationship status, dual-career relationship status, tenure, and job level are examined in order to allow differential implications with respect to specific target groups within professional service firms. *Part III* is dedicated to discussing obtained results and critically reexamining conceptual and methodological issues including a number of limitations. Finally, the most important insights and implications of the present thesis are summarized including ideas for developing, implementing and evaluating effective work-life integration management (WLIM) in organizations.

I. THE WORK-LIFE INTERFACE OF PROFESSIONALS: CHALLENGES OF INTEGRATING WORK WITH 'THE REST OF LIFE'

Satisfactory arrangement of life spheres commonly referred to as 'work-life balance' concerns individuals, organizations, and societies alike. Changing dynamics of work and their impact on nonwork domains on the societal, organizational and individual level have given rise to exponentially increasing research efforts investigating antecedents, outcomes and interactions at the work and personal life border. Database research looking for studies in this field (cf. Figure 1) illustrates that not only on the organizational agenda but also in research work-life issues are "the name of the game" (Ostendorp, 2007, p. 187). Different disciplines deal with the challenges of reconciling work and nonwork domains, contributing to different perspectives and theoretical and empirical facets of work-life research as it is today. *Sociological approaches* investigate the work-life interface from the perspective of different social groups (gender, race and cultural origin, social class, etc.) (e.g. Crompton & Lyonette, 2006; Gerstel & Sarkisian, 2006). A *legal perspective* deals for example with equality concerns and legal matters of corporate policies (Still & Williams, 2006). An *economic* point of view approaches work-life research with questions about labor division, paid vs. unpaid work and the related question of what is understood by 'work' in general, consequences of female full-time employment and career orientation and related macroeconomic and socio-political issues (Drago & Golden, 2006; Kastner, 2004a). Primarily taking an individual perspective, *psychological disciplines* such as social psychology and organizational/industrial psychology provide a large body of empirical research about the causes and consequences of achieving satisfactory integration of work and nonwork domains and the role of corporate and governmental work-life balance initiatives (Thompson et al., 2006). Being a central authority of work-life research, *management research* focuses on employees' work-life interface in relation to increasing and sustaining organizational performance and success. Concepts such as reduced employee commitment and turnover intention are investigated together with the development of strategies for avoiding such undesired outcomes. Needless to say, the overlap of these approaches, particularly psychological disciplines with those of management research in studying the work-life interface is considerable and filtering out contributions 'unique' to one discipline is hardly possible.[4] While the interdisciplinary character is exactly what makes research in this area so intriguing, the proceeding section briefly illustrates the relevance of work-life integration challenges in more detail from a management research perspective as

> "[t]he topic of work-life has evolved into one of the most significant business issues of the 21st century. Rooted in the history of women's rights and equal opportunity in education and the workplace, the notion of work-life has shifted in focus from solely a woman's concern to a workforce management issue" (Harrington & Ladge, 2009, p. 148).

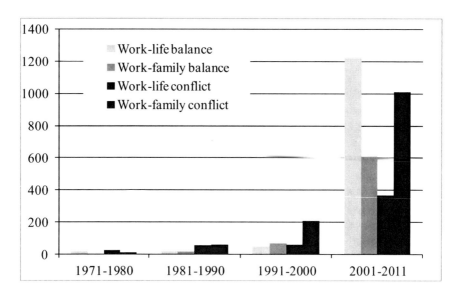

Figure 1. Development of scientific publications on work-life research (1971-2011)[5]

---

4   Most researchers operate in the fields of psychology/sociology and management re-
     search (Casper et al., 2007) and the interdisciplinary character of work-life research is
     strongly reflected by journals commonly addressed in the field: *Journal of Vocational
     Behavior, Journal of Applied Psychology, Journal of Occupational and Organizational
     Psychology, Personnel Psychology, Gender, Work & Organization, Human Resource
     Management, Human Relations, International Journal of Human Resource Manage-
     ment, Journal of Managerial Psychology, Journal of Organizational Behavior, etc.*

5   The database research was conducted using the databases Business Source Complete,
     Psychology and Behavioral Sciences Collection, PsycINFO, and PSYNDEX with the

Considerable attention has been paid to *work-life dynamics from an organizational versus an individual point of view*. Why and whether organizations care about employee work-life concerns has been vividly discussed in the last decade, from the perspective of solving problems within the organization, such as loss of talent and turnover (e.g. Thompson et al., 1999), maintenance of employee satisfaction and commitment (e.g. Ahuja et al., 2007), avoidance of absenteeism and management of employee health (e.g. Allen et al., 2000; Halpern, 2005a) to challenges from the organizational environment, such as demographic changes (e.g. Dievernich & Endrissat, 2010; Farnsworth-Riche, 2006) and changing employee values towards a life where both work and 'the rest of life' play an important role (e.g. Blyton & Dastmalchian, 2006; Hochschild, 2000; Lewis, 2003). One branch where challenges of integrating work with personal life seem to be particularly salient but hard to address are professional service firms (PSFs). They are notorious for their demanding work practices and yet represent an attractive career option for young professionals as they enable a fast career track and represent an environment of high work diversity and organizational learning. PSFs are also renowned for only recruiting the best in class and are therefore highly attentive of the current trend of 'work-life balance' as a strategy of attracting talent. Hence, PSFs represent a highly relevant field for studying the work-life interface because a) work demands are high excessive work hour volumes and long periods of work away from home are commonplace (O'Mahoney, 2007), b) intrinsic motivation of young professionals to stand up to the challenge and promote their career by engaging in such highly-demanding work environments is high (Alvesson, 2000), and c) in order to attract and maintain high potentials, PSFs provide their workforce with a set of resources, such as sabbaticals and flexible work options, which are usually communicated on corporate web sites. It is therefore an intriguing question whether for professionals in PSFs, difficulties in integrating work with personal life is an issue at all and if so, how organizational demands affect these difficulties and how organizational resources are able to buffer them.

It is the aim of the present section to span a theoretical framework for studying the work-life interface of professionals in a PSF context with specific attention to the role of organizational demands and resources. First, the relevance of studying the work-life interface from an organizational perspective is discussed including *triggers and outcomes at an individual, an interpersonal and an organizational level* also taking into account aspects of the *organizational environment* (1.1). Often-voiced concerns about what we mean by 'work-life bal-

search mode 'Find all my search terms' limited to scholarly (peer reviewed) journals on April 5, 2011.

ance' (e.g. Eikhof et al., 2007) are addressed subsequently by presenting a brief summary of approaches to studying work-life dynamics and outlining why and how exactly the present examination focuses on the construct of *work-life conflict* (1.2). The occupational category of professionals is examined more closely (2.1) with special attention to characteristics of professional service firms (2.2) and what these characteristics mean for professionals' work-life interface (2.3). A literature review on the impact of organizational demands and resources on the work-life interface with particular focus on professionals represents the heart of Part I. Following theoretical considerations of Holt and Thaulow (1996) a distinction is made into formal and informal demands and resources (3.1). Formal organizational demands that are particularly prevalent in PSFs are long work hours and frequent job-related travel (3.2.1). Work-life initiatives (WLB initiatives) such as flexible work options and leave policies are discussed as formal(ized) organizational resources (3.2.2). Informal demands and resources are first and foremost rooted in organizational culture, namely normative demands (time demands, a negative career impact resulting from using WLB initiatives) and support (from the management, supervisor and/or co-workers) as a resource (3.2.3). Insights from previous studies result in a set of hypotheses together representing a research model (3.2.4). In order to pay tribute to the diversity of individual needs and situations, subsequently the state of the art of research about work-life dynamics related to a number of demographic, work and personal life characteristics (subbranch, life role priority, gender, age, marital and relationship status, tenure and job level) is presented briefly (3.3) followed by a comprehensive summary of the major points from this part of the thesis.

1. Relevance and Methodology of Studying the Work-Life Interface

In order to span the theoretical framework of the present examination first the relevance of work-personal life interactions in the context of organizational and HR development are outlined. On the level of the individual (or intrapersonal level), successful work-life integration is relevant first and foremost for maintaining psychological and physiological health and well-being, for dealing with sources of stress and preventing related negative outcomes, and for employee motivation and satisfaction. At a group or interpersonal level, work-life dynamics affect issues of social justice and diversity, social support and cooperation and can also be a trigger for extrarole behavior and corporate citizenship. From the point of view of the organization, satisfactory work-life integration of employees can be associated with higher satisfaction and commitment and subsequently lower turnover intention. Furthermore, it has been shown that firms benefit from attentiveness to work-life integration in terms of higher employee and firm performance as well as in terms of corporate communication and competitive advantages in recruiting talent. All these issues are discussed in further detail first (1.1) followed by a brief examination of what exactly is meant by work-life integration (1.2). The 'toolbox' of researching the work-life interface contains social role theory as the very foundation on which several directions of research are built, including positive interactions among work and nonwork spheres in terms of work-life enrichment and negative interactions in terms of work-life conflict. The section closes by outlining why in the current examination the conflict perspective is put in focus and how exactly work-life conflict is understood in order to lay the foundation for subsequent investigations.

1.1 Work-Personal Life Interactions in the Context of Organizational Development and Human Resource Management

At first sight, the reconciliation of life spheres appears to be a personal issue in terms of successful individual time management, priority setting, and a general ability of managing personal goals and obligations. But findings and reflections of management literature underline the crucial role of organizations as both facilitators and stakeholders in employee work-life integration. As illustrated in Figure 2, individual, organizational and environmental issues concerning the work-life interface are intertwined environmental factors, such as societal developments influence the way organizations deal with work-life balance within the organization. The individual representing the main focus of attention in work-life research impacts the organization in two ways: a) unsuccessful reconciliation of life spheres results in negative outcomes for the individual which also affect the organization, and b) changing expectations towards an employer challenge recruiting and retention strategies as well as human resource management practices. The following pages briefly outline the relevance for organizations to care about work-life conflicts of their (potential) employees.

1.1.1 Individual Work-Life Challenges and Related Outcomes

The individual is in the center of attention in nearly every work-life study. Obviously the challenge of managing multiple life responsibilities and interests is to a large extent associated with individual-level outcomes. Not achieving what is commonly referred to as 'work-life balance' has been related to a number of undesirable outcomes for the individual. The most frequent outcomes at the individual level are psychological and physical health impairments and reduced well-being, increased levels of stress, and reduced motivation and satisfaction.

1.1.1.1 Health and Well-Being

Intense research efforts are dedicated to examining how working conditions that create work-life conflict affect individual health and well-being. In a meta- analysis Sparks, Cooper, Fried and Shirom (1997) found support for the notion that over proportionately long working hours have undesirable effects on employee psychological and physiological health. Burke and colleagues demonstrated in a number of publications how long work hours and work intensity negatively affect individual health (Burke, 2003, 2004; Burke & Cooper, 2008b).

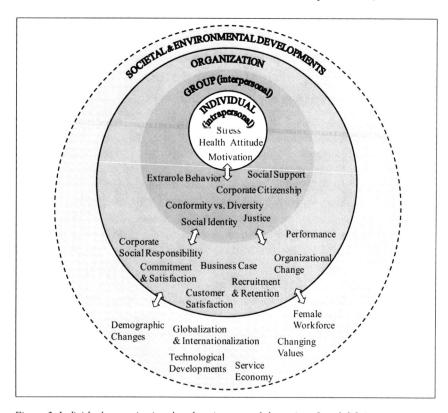

Figure 2. Individual, organizational and environmental dynamics of work-life issues

Successful work-life integration has been associated with reduced physical and psychological complaints such as burnout (Bianchi et al., 2005; Peeters et al., 2005) and depression and substance abuse (drugs, alcohol) (Frone et al., 1993). Frone et al. (1997) provided longitudinal evidence for the link of work-to-life conflict with depression, physical health complaints and hypertension and the link between family-to-work conflict and greater alcohol consumption in a study of employed parents. Short-term and long-term illnesses as a result of work-life conflict were also reported among top managers (Stock-Homburg & Bauer, 2007) and meta-analytic data support the notion that work-life conflict is strongly related to negative health outcomes (Allen et al., 2000). In other words, successful work-life reconciliation should reduce the likeliness of severe illnesses that result from job demands such as working long hours, pressure, and the experience of stress created by the struggle for balance among different life spheres.

1.1.1.2 Stress

Work-life conflict is very often associated with general feelings of stress which in turn result in undesirable physical and psychological health outcomes. A large body of literature suggests that reducing work-life/work-family conflict results in decreased stress perception and thus avoidance of negative health outcomes, even more so for professionals (Allen et al., 2000). Results of an examination of 'IT road warriors' (Ahuja et al., 2007) – IT professionals who spend most of their workweek away from home at client sites – demonstrated a positive relationship of work-family conflict with work exhaustion, i.e. perceived conflict was related to higher work exhaustion. Work-family conflict created by juggling family and job duties was identified as a key source of stress as these IT road warriors worked at distant client sites during the week. Data from married professional women in dual-career families in Singapore (Aryee, 1992) as well as further international data (Kinnunen & Mauno, 1998; Lu et al., 2009) widely confirm the buffering effect that successful work-life integration exerts on job-related stress.

1.1.1.3 Motivation and Satisfaction

Satisfactory arrangement of work, family, leisure, and other life roles has also been associated with *motivational outcomes*. Successful integration of life roles was for example shown to relate to higher satisfaction, in the areas of both work and personal life (marriage, family) (Adams et al., 1996; Mauno & Kinnunen, 1999; Netemeyer et al., 1996). Aryee et al. (1999) demonstrated that lower and middle managers that perceived conflict between life roles were less satisfied with their work and family lives (cf. also Bedeian et al., 1988). Perlow and Porter (2009) reported similar results from an investigation at an international consulting firm: after more predictable work schedules and days off work had been introduced into the previously very unpredictable schedules, management consultants experienced both higher work and non-work role quality. Data of Hewlett and Luce (2006) suggest that employees with extreme work demands who reduced their work hours or took some time off were more satisfied with their life domains although reducing hours was perceived difficult. Comparative evidence indicating how conflict between work and personal life are unfavorably linked to job, life and overall satisfaction was found in different samples of professionals (*health professionals*: Thomas & Ganster, 1995; *executives*: Judge et al., 1994; *dual-career professionals*: Duxbury et al., 1996; *IT employees*: Chang, 2008); two meta-analyses further support these findings (Allen et al., 2000; Kossek & Ozeki, 1998). It has also been argued that work-life balance is associated with higher *subjective well-being*. Greenhaus et al. (2003) examined professional accountants' work-family balance and quality of life with the finding that individuals who spent comparatively more time on family than work experienced higher quality of life than individuals who engaged in both life domains equally and who engaged more in the work domain. Bedeian et al. (1988) examined a similar sample with comparable results: work-family conflict was related to lower overall life satisfaction and marital satisfaction among accounting professionals. Achieving a desirable level of engagement in both work and non-work domains was largely shown to yield positive outcomes for the individual with regards to health and motivation (cf. Bruck, Allen & Spector, 2002; Rice et al., 1992). That successful work-life reconciliation yields benefits for the individual is an intuitive and well-researched phenomenon. Individual characteristics, personality and life stage do influence the perception of work-life conflict and related outcomes but in general everybody strives for an individually shaped solution of reconciling work and non-work roles to fit each one's specific needs. If this is achieved, individuals are more likely to perceive a high quality of life in all domains, experience less health impairments and feel less stressed. How these positive outcomes of avoiding work-life conflict also benefit the organization is discussed in the next paragraph.

1.1.2 Organizational Perspectives Related to the Work-Life Interface

The primary concern of organizations is to sustain and maximize organizational success. Hence, at first sight it is not obvious why organizations should bother about how their employees arrange work obligations with the rest of their lives. It seems to be an acknowledged fact that, particularly in today's knowledge-based economy, employees are a central asset of organizations and their effectiveness (Kaiser & Ringlstetter, 2011). Kossek and Friede (2006) argue that

> "[r]esources such as talent can become a competitive advantage when the resource is not easily imitated; under this perspective, an organization's work-life policies enhance organizational performance due to their role in adding value to the firm" (p. 616).

Particularly professional service organizations have an interest in maintaining a workforce that is satisfied, motivated and healthy. Organizations that fail to invest in employee motivation, satisfaction, and commitment risk undesirable individual-level outcomes which impair employee and organizational productivity. Work-life issues are entangled with organizational interests at the interpersonal, i.e. group or team level affecting human relations and cooperation, as well as the organizational level affecting aspects of human resource management and further aspects of strategic interest to the organization. At the interpersonal level work-life issues are linked with aspects of social justice and diversity, cooperation and social support, extrarole behavior and corporate citizenship (1.1.2.1 – 1.1.2.3). Besides the level of direct interpersonal interaction, an organization is concerned with work-life issues at a more universal level as reflected in corporate human resource strategies and further areas of strategic importance as illustrated by James P. Secord, President and CEO of a large U.S. publishing company:

> "Whenever the topic of employee-friendly practices arises, the question 'Why?' seems to follow closely. Why even care? The answer is amazingly simple: Positive employee practices lead to success" (Center for Ethical Business Cultures, 1997, p. 29).

Taking care of employees' work-life issues impacts job satisfaction and commitment, both being central factors for employee retention, for firm productivity, business case and shareholder value and last but not least affect successful recruiting, organizational communication and affect organizational change processes (1.1.2.4 – 1.1.2.6).

1.1.2.1 Social Justice and Conformity vs. Diversity

Social justice and diversity concerning work-life issues matter primarily with respect to equal treatment and equal opportunities for all employees. This should include virtually every employee as the defining character of equal opportunities is neither to privilege selected employees nor to provide one-size-fits-all solutions but to equally respect all employees' needs and potentials. That women are less likely to reach the top of the organizational career ladder is commonly acknowledged (e.g. Kumra & Vinnicombe, 2008; Lyness & Thompson, 1997), reasons are often sought in the dynamics of work-life integration. When women become mothers their careers often come to a halt and, as discussed by Williams, are marginalized in organizations despite their willingness to work and continue their career. Particularly in high performance environments mothers with young children are perceived as unable to meet "all-or-nothing workplace" norms (Williams, 2007, p. 383). Organizations are in reality often unable or unwilling to meet the needs of highly-qualified women who decide to have children. While men still more likely correspond to the picture of the 'ideal worker', available 24/7 and puts work first (Kinnunen et al., 2005), an emerging issue for research and organizational practice alike is that more and more fathers decide to take greater family and child-rearing responsibility and make use of alternative work arrangements (Burnett et al., 2011). Thus, the work-family challenge is more than ever of concern for managing gender diversity in the organization. With more women in full-time employment, demographic changes and predicted shortages of skilled workers, organizations are asked to make their policies of equal treatment and social justice a reality. Besides, claims are raised by a number of researchers for not considering only 'work' and 'family' as life domains because such a focus excludes all employees without direct family obligations and essentially reduces these challenges to the problem of child care. Casper, Weltman and Kwesiga (2007) argue in favor of an organizational culture that supports nonwork obligations of all types and of all employees, regardless of their family situation. In other words, all employees should feel equally included in the company, receive equal opportunities and promotions, be equally eligible for benefits including a repertoire of benefits that address different needs, receive equal respect for nonwork spheres, and be object to equal job expectations (Casper et al., 2007). Although it is usually argued that parents face disadvantages and exclusion, for example when it comes to career advancement, Casper and colleagues argue that single childless employees can also face marginalization as they may be considered less established and mature. It has further been pointed out that despite the fact that many newcomers and young professionals are unattached and childless, for them also the consideration of nonwork concerns is an important factor in choosing an employer and a career path (Na Ayudha & Lewis, 2011; Sturges & Guest, 2004). Equal consideration of all employees' needs is associated with high identification towards the organization and the development of a social identity where employees perceive themselves as part of the same 'we' (Alvesson, 2000). Additionally, considering all employees' concerns equally strong increases perception of fairness as pointed out by Nord et al. (2002) who report that childless employees felt disadvantaged because they had to back up employees with children.

1.1.2.2 Cooperation and Social Support

Work-life concerns also affect the interpersonal level with regards to *cooperation* and *social support*. Researchers suggest, that feeling supported by colleagues and supervisors is associated with reduced work-life conflict (Major et al., 2008; Thompson & Prottas, 2005). Findings of Wallace (1997) emphasize the importance of collegiality: the negative effect of work overload on the work-life interface was found to be buffered by co-worker support. On the other hand, employees who work on a regular schedule have to cover up for those who are on reduced-load, work from home or are on leave, as pointed out by Litrico and Lee (2008). Peer pressure, for instance with regards to making use of work-life benefits, can also be a particularly salient concern in high performance environments such as professional service firms (PSFs). Professionals who leave early or work on alternative schedules are frequently object to "jokes" and stigmatization (Fuchs-Epstein et al., 1999; Williams, 2007).

1.1.2.3 Extrarole Behavior and Corporate Citizenship

Satisfactory reconciliation of life spheres furthermore fosters *extrarole behavior* and *corporate citizenship*. Lambert (2000) suggests taking advantage of work-life benefits is related to helping co-workers. In her study, the more useful employees under examination perceived the company's benefits in terms of supporting them and their families, the more likely they were to submit suggestions for improvement, voluntarily attend meetings on quality methods, and assist others with their job duties. The findings support the basic premise of social exchange theory as applied to the workplace, that positive actions of an organization propel workers to reciprocate in beneficial ways (van Knippenberg & Sleebos, 2008). Osterman (1995) observes that in situations with a certain amount of mutual trust and commitment, more general investments on behalf of the employer may be rewarded with greater employee effort. It is further proposed that convergence of values and expectations of employee and employer encourage extrarole behavior (Chatman, 1989). This perspective of mutual engagement and responsibility is summarized under the concept of corporate citizenship. Harrington and Ladge (2009) pointed out that work-life balance programs are often integrated in the corporate citizenship strategy of high-profile firms because a favorable view of the organization is first and foremost impacted by how organizations treat their workforce.

1.1.2.4 Satisfaction, Commitment and Turnover

Employees who are happy with their job and feel committed towards their employer are more likely to remain in the organization they work for, a reasoning indicated by the meta-analysis of Meyer et al. (2002). *Undesired turnover* is cost-intensive for organizations with regards to the recruiting of new employees, losses in productivity until vacancies are refilled and lost investments on human resource development (HRD) for those employees leaving the firm. According to Thompson, Beauvais, and Lyness (1999) who studied a sample of professionals, supportive work-family culture explained close to 14% of additional variance of employees' intention to leave, i.e. the better supported they felt the less inclined they were to seek a more attractive employer. Being their key asset, for PSFs the professional workforce is of crucial strategic importance (Kaiser & Ringlstetter, 2011) and even organizations that operate under an up-or-out practice will, in order to retain their competitive advantage, try to avoid losing employees that hold important knowledge, strategically important competencies and close client relations (Connor et al., 1999; Wright & Kehoe, 2009). Several researchers suggest that work-life conflict has a detrimental effect on *organizational commitment*. For some sample findings, Ahuja et al. (2007) showed that conflict between work and family among IT professionals was negatively associated with organizational commitment ($r = .32$, $p < .01$). Allen (2001), who interviewed 522 employees from different branches and organizations, demonstrated that those employees who experienced less work-family conflict were more committed towards their organization. In a German management consulting sample, Kaiser et al. (2010) found that high work-to-life conflict was associated with reduced affective (i.e. emotional) commitment. Similar results supporting the link between high work-life conflict and lower organizational commitment were obtained in further studies (Aryee et al., 2005, Casper et al., 2002; Chang, 2008; Dex & Scheibl, 2001; Smith & Gardner, 2007) supported by meta-analytic results (Kossek & Ozeki, 1999). How much an individual's attitude towards the organization matters was also shown by Carr and colleagues (2008). They indicated that for individuals who view work as being more central to their lives, the negative relationships between work-family conflict and organizational attitudes and also employee intent to turnover is lowered. Studying the reasons of private-sector organizations for adopting work-life policies, Osterman (1995) reported that firms operating with high commitment or high performance work systems are particularly likely to adopt such initiatives (cf. also Berg et al., 2003; Eaton, 2003; Kossek & Friede, 2006). Results that give evidence to a negative relationship between work-life conflict and *job satisfaction* are equally numerous (Boyar & Mosley, 2007; Judge et al., 1994; Rice et al., 1992; Saltzstein et al., 2001; Thomas & Ganster, 1995).

1.1.2.5 Employee Productivity, Firm Performance and the Business Case

Organizational work-life support has also been discussed as a booster of organizational key figures: improved *employee performance and productivity* and higher *share price value*. If employees' work-life concerns are a cause for negative health outcomes this is obviously associated with absenteeism, which is related to costs for the organization. Several papers report that work-life friendly firms which offer adequate initiatives and epitomize a supportive culture benefit in terms of reduced absenteeism among employees (Boyar, Maertz & Pearson, 2005; DeGraat, 2007; Dex & Scheibl, 2001; Galinsky & Stein, 1990; Halpern, 2005a). Van Steenbergen and Ellemers (2009) found this link in a longitudinal study: work-life integration was positively associated with lower sickness absence as well as better physical health and higher objective *job performance*. Organizations that foster individual work-life reconciliation hence benefit in terms of increased individual productivity. Thompson et al. (1999) put it this way:

> "By *not* fostering a more balanced work-family life for employees, organizations are contributing to tensions in the employees' personal lives, the repercussions of which affect employees' ability to concentrate and be productive and creative on the job" (p. 393).

Bloom and van Reenan (2006) found that positive work-life outcomes are entangled with better management, i.e. well-run firms in the sense of a supportive management are both more productive and offer better conditions to their employees. Access to work-life benefits valued by employees was positively associated with employees' perceived organizational support and affective commitment towards the organization as well as with reciprocation in terms of higher task and contextual performance. These results occurred regardless of actual *use* of work-life programs. That the perception of benefit availability can be sufficient for achieving positive effects on employee commitment was also shown by Smith and Gardner (2007). Poelmans and Beham (2008b) pointed out that work-life programs, such as working part-time can be related to higher coverage and better scheduling for the department because employees can adjust their schedules to their work and nonwork sphere needs and organizations can plan ahead. Performance and productivity are hard to measure, particularly in professional work as the output is very often intangible. If we think in terms of increased concentration and focus, as well as reduced stress and related illness symptoms and lower absenteeism, it becomes clear how satisfactory work-life integration positively impacts professional employees' performance. Morris, Storberg-Walker and McMillan (2009) developed a complex evaluation system named Organization Development Human-Capital Accounting System (ODHCAS)[6] in

---

6   The authors suggest to evaluate effectiveness of work/life interventions by monitoring and measuring effects of firm performance; talent compensation, recognition & re-

order to assess the effect of work-life interventions on *firm performance* objectively, having identified this link as the most "understudied aspect in the w/l literature" (p. 439). Although their framework yet remains untested empirically, the researchers suggest to include work-life instruments as an item in the total operations costs and to incorporate them into organizational strategy in order to raise firm performance.

Caring for employees' work-life needs was also shown profitable in terms of tangible returns. Arthur and Cook (2004) argued that the implementation of work-life initiatives is associated with higher share price, particularly in high-tech industries (cf. also Arthur, 2003). Cascio and Young (2005) found support for this notion: within the 'Working Mother-100 Best Firms' stock price was significantly higher than for comparative groups of employers which the authors attribute to the offer and communication of work-life-friendly practices in these firms. Similarly, Konrad and Mangel (2000) argue that work-life initiatives yield benefits for corporations where the percentage of professional employees and of females is high and where firms invested a great deal in HRD. Kossek and Friede (2006) discuss managerial perspectives on the implementation of work-life policies: managers often regard work-life issues under a trade-off perspective where employees either act 'in favor' or 'against' the organization depending on their priorities and behavior in work and nonwork spheres. Organizations strive for maximizing employees' dedication towards the firm and avoid costs for considering their nonwork needs. Under a dual-agenda perspective, also referred to as an integrated approach it is assumed though, that a win-win outcome of considering work-personal life concerns can be achieved because the provision of resources by the organization is accompanied by increased dedication and attachment towards the organization (cf. Kossek & Friede, 2006; Lambert, 2000). Three principles for achieving mutually beneficial outcomes of work-life integration management are suggested by Friedman, Christensen and DeGroot (1998): 1) clarify individual and business priorities, 2) establish a culture that values employees as "whole people" (p. 120), and 3) continually experiment with the organization of work seeking approaches that enhance both employee and firm performance. It is further proposed that with these three principles, being referred to as the 'leveraged approach', supporting work-life needs adds value to the organization. "Not only do the three principles seem to help people live more satisfying personal lives, but they also help identify inefficiencies in work processes and illuminate better ways to get work done", is what

---

wards; talent performance, management, appraisal & evaluation; talent conservation; human capital strategic planning; talent acquisition, talent allocation; talent citizenship, and talent development.

Friedman et al. (1998, p. 129) report from their field studies. Besides the employer-employee relationship, it is postulated that work-life supportiveness is associated with increased *customer satisfaction* (Hyland & Jackson, 2006; Lewis & Cooper, 2005). As clients are satisfied when products and services are of high quality, an increase in work process efficiencies as a result of effective work-life integration management which avoids absenteeism and maintains employee productivity is also in the interest of the client.

1.1.2.6 Internal and Outward Communication, Recruiting and Organizational Change

The implementation of work-life integration management in organizations is also related to outward communication and image trying to transfer a picture of a people-friendly organization and an employer of choice for young professionals and high potentials (Kossek & Friede, 2006). Although researchers rarely consider this facet, at closer sight it may often play an essential role in organizational decisions pro work-life programs. Additionally, organizations must adapt to work-life challenges in order to respond to environmental changes as discussed under an organizational change perspective. With regards to *recruiting*, organizational conditions for integrating paid work with the rest of life are becoming a more and more prominent factor in employer choice, particularly in the face of the 'war for talents' and demographic change (Barnett & Hall, 2001; Dex & Scheibl, 2001; McDonald & Hite, 2008; Sanders et al., 1998). Dex and Scheibl (2001) identified recruitment advantages among the primary reasons for implementing work-life interventions. Professional employees were shown to be ready to accept a lower income if they are able to cut down their hours (Barnett & Hall, 2001). A study among young professionals by PricewaterhouseCoopers (2010) found that work-life balance is a number one criterion of employer choice for 36% of the participants. In a focus group approach McDonald and Hite (2008) evaluated ideas about career success among young professionals: one of the major characteristics of a successful career mentioned was the ability to devote adequate time to education, community, friends, and family. Concurrently, Carless and Wintle (2007) found in a study of young, inexperienced job seekers, that WLB initiatives such as flexible policies increase applicants' perceptions of organizational attractiveness. Loughlin and Barling (2001) conclude from their research that today's young professionals "may be less willing to make sacrifices for the sake of their jobs" (p. 545) and Hewlett and Luce (2006) notice that the "next generations of management – the so-called Gen X and Gen Y cohorts – seem less enamored of their jobs than baby boomers" (p. 58). It is frequently argued that a critical variable is choice. Having control over one's working pattern seems a nuclear characteristic of how employees benefit from flexible work-life arrangements (Anderson & Kelliher, 2009). The focus of to-day's workforce shifts more and more towards leading a balanced life that in-volves both success in the professional sphere and a fulfilled personal life (Sanders et al., 1998)[7]. With changing individual values of wanting both work and personal life, and family constellations shifting towards dual-earner and dual-career couples, facilitating work-life integration has become a criterion and an instrument for recruiting and retaining "a top-quality workforce" (Konrad & Mangel, 2000, p. 1226). The HRM market has picked up this trend as in the last decade a number of certifications and evaluation tools have emerged that certify a firm as family-friendly (e.g. von Kettler, 2010: Audit Beruf & Familie®; Cascio and Young, 2005: Working Mother-100 Best Firms).

Last but not least initiatives in the work-life arena can be understood as an organizational adaptation to environmental changes and demands. Three para-digms with respect to *organizational change* in the work-life arena were pro-posed by Lee, MacDermid and Buck (2000): accommodation, elaboration and transformation. Organizations must accommodate to changing employee needs and values that result from for example from demographic changes. These ac-commodations may be fostered by governmental schemes and incentives that encourage the implementation of alternative work arrangements (Poelmans & Beham, 2008b). The *elaboration* paradigm designates the development of work-life solutions involving employees and managers actively in the development process, similar to the suggestions made by Friedman et al. (1998) who propose to implement a culture of setting and evaluating employee and employer priori-ties. The third area of organizational change proposed by Lee and colleagues (2000), *transformation*, involves the major cultural change towards new work-ing patterns. Such a cultural change is not only rewarded by higher trust, emo-tional commitment, and employee morale (Hyland & Jackson, 2006; Lewis & Cooper, 2005) but is also likely to result in higher efficiency and productivity. A practical example is the culture of how performance is measured in an organiza-tion. It has been discussed back and forth that commitment and productivity of employees are hard to assess, particularly in knowledge-intensive businesses, and thus are in many corporations measured in terms of presence at the work-place (Munck, 2001; Simpson, 1998; Ulich & Wiese, 2011). A major *transfor-mation* for many organizations would be a shift from presenteeism and face-time culture towards a culture where performance is really measured by outcomes.

---

7   In their study of junior and senior high school students, Sanders and colleagues (1998) found that the vast majority of participants scored in favor a balanced life priority (M = 6.10; 1-7 scale) as compared to a career priority (M = 3.83) or a family priority (M = 2.71).

Not only does this aspect address issues of social justice and better work climate because all employees are evaluated in equal terms. Setting performance standards and priorities, as suggested by Friedman et al. (1998), organizations may detect inefficiencies that were so far hidden behind the masque of being there and available 24/7.

Above and beyond, the issue of work-life integration can also be subject to organizational change processes. Particularly professional service firms like to position themselves among the most rapidly changing and highly innovative of organizations but although many of them even do their own research in the work-life arena (e.g. Coffman & Hagey at Bain & Co. 2010; Pricewaterhouse-Coopers, 2010; Kienbaum, 2010), the question has yet to be answered whether 'true' organizational change in favor of more balanced lives of employees is a reality in organizations (Mohe et al., 2010).

In the present section a brief summary was presented of how organizational issues at the interpersonal and the general level are entangled with individuals' work-life dynamics. Social justice and diversity, cooperation and social support as well as corporate citizenship were discussed at the interpersonal level and commitment and employee retention, firm-level and employee performance, as well as communicative aspects relating to recruiting and organizational change were linked to the organizational context as a whole. The next section displays an array of societal factors and developments that affect the organizational environment and which trigger what has lastly been discussed, organizational change.

1.1.3 Societal and Environmental Developments Affecting the Work-life integration management of Organizations

Besides intra-organizational issues, a number of developments from the organizational environment affect the way organizations are challenged to deal with the border between work and nonwork spheres of employees. Among them are changes in the demographic structure towards more and more elderly employees and people in retirement, increasing female employment, first and foremost in high-level jobs, and the affirmation of an increasing invasiveness of work in our modern life.

1.1.3.1 Demographic Changes and Female Labor Force Participation

The most notable and prominent developments that affect organizations are the rise of female employment and demographic changes resulting in a 21st century workforce composition that has become very diverse. Female employment increase entails the rising number of employed mothers as well as dual-earner/dual-career couples[8] becoming a prevalent form of modern spousal relationships; demographic changes comprise the development of an overall older workforce as well as, according to demographic extrapolations, an overall decline in the number of workers versus an increase in retirees (Badura & Vetter, 2004a; Dievernich & Endrissat, 2010; Farnsworth-Riche, 2006; Harrington & Ladge, 2009; Michalk & Nieder, 2007).

In Germany, from 1994 until 2009 the percentage of *females participating in active employment* rose by nearly ten per cent, from 60.9 to 70.4 (OECD, 2010). In international comparison, male participation rates fell slightly during that period (1994: 81.4 %; 2009: 80.2 %), Germany noted a much smaller increase in male employment (1994: 79.8 %; 2009: 82.2 %) than in female employment. In 2005, six out of ten females and nine out of ten males were employed according to the German Federal Statistical Office (2006). It should be noted, however, that the rise in female workforce participation goes along with an increase of part-time employment (OECD, 2010). Although the percentage of part-time employed males has also been increasing, the clearly higher share of part-time work is made up by women (OECD, 2010)[9]. As Blyton and Dastmalchian (2006) note, the typical dual-earner couple is a part-time working female and a full-time employed male. Nevertheless, with rising education and qualification levels supported by political gender equality efforts, women increasingly pursue full-time employment. Especially highly qualified women who have invested time and effort in a career are willing to postpone or neglect the starting of a family in favor of a challenging job position (BMFSFJ, 2010a). This entails an increase of dual-career couples, where both partners pursue a highly challenging job above and beyond the necessity of "earning a living" (Abele & Volmer, 2011; Major & Germano, 2006; Neault & Pickerell, 2005; Rapoport & Rapoport, 1969). This development has particularly fuelled the debate about governmental and organizational policies supporting dependent care, i.e. childcare and eldercare arrangements and the adjustment of working time and volume as well as leave policies that address men and women alike (BMFSFJ, 2010b;

---

8   In contrast to dual-earner couples where both partners are employed part-time or full-time, dual-career relationships are described as "a relatively new partnership constellation [...] where both partners are highly educated, have a high upward career orientation, and work full time in a demanding job" (Abele & Volmer, 2011, p. 173).

9   In virtually every country that was included in the OECD 2010 survey, the largest part-time share was made up by prime-aged women in 2010 with the smallest percentage in Finland, Sweden and Denmark (35-40%) and the largest percentage in Germany, Italy, Belgium, Austria and Luxembourg (65-80%) (OECD, 2010).

German Federal Statistical Office, 2006; Gault & Lovell, 2006; Hardy & Ardnett, 2002; Zedeck & Mosier, 1990).

Another important change in the workforce demographics that triggers interest in work-life issues is the *Ageing Society* as a result of rising life expectancy and decreasing birth rates. According to statistical extrapolations, in 2050 20.7 per cent of the American population will be sixty-five and older (Marks, 2006), in Germany from today until 2030 this group of individuals will augment by one third up to 22.3 million (German Federal Statistical Office, 2011). This leaves the job market with a lack of qualified employees also discussed as the 'war for talents' (Chambers et al., 1998; Gardner, 2002; Michaels, Handfield-Jones & Axelrod, 2009). An additional implication of this demographic trend is that more work is left to less people. At the same time employees have to care for their elderly parents and relatives which may entail partial or complete withdrawal from the job. Again, this calls to action governmental and corporate policies to deal with this challenge, such as flexible working and eldercare arrangements (Galinsky & Stein, 1990; Kossek et al., 1999).

1.1.3.2 The 'Work Creep': Increasing Invasiveness of Paid Work in Modern Life?

Whereas the increase in female employment is traditionally the most prominent explanation for rising interest in work-life questions, in recent decades another dimension of the discussion emerged that has been referred to as the 'work creep' (Milliken & Dunn-Jensen, 2005). Work today is the sphere where we invest the lion's share of our time and energetic resources (Blyton & Dastmalchian, 2006; Hochschild, 2000; Lewis, 2003). This is a push-and-pull development insofar that, on the one hand, the work sphere has become more demanding in terms work hours, volume, location, and complexity. In general, work demands have been increasing during the last decades. Especially individuals in highly qualified jobs work longer hours and take work home (Blyton & Dastmalchian, 2006; Brett & Stroh, 2003; Burke & Cooper, 2008b; Hewlett & Luce, 2006; Milliken & Dunn-Jensen, 2005). Major reasons for changing work demands which lower work-life boundaries are sought in 24/7 availability and mobility of work locations as a means of new communication technologies, rising pressure as a function of global competition, and changes in work orrganisation through the rise of the service industry and knowledge-based work. Blessing and curse with regards to the work-life interface is the *development of new communication technology*, such as portable computers, cell phones, smartphones, etc. (Harrington & Ladge, 2009; Major & Germano, 2006). These technological tools are discussed within work-life research as 'blessing' in the context of flexible work arrangements enabling work from home and as 'curse' with regards to increasingly blurred boundaries between work and nonwork spheres (Messersmith, 2007; Wharton, 2006). Even though increasing opportunities to communicate with work, family, and friends can be worthwhile, communication devices lower the boundary between work and nonwork domains which can be associated with negative outcomes depending on how individuals cope with blurred boundaries. While those who prefer to integrate work and nonwork spheres profit from low boundaries, those who prefer a stronger segmentation of roles may find it difficult to cope with being accessible anytime (Kossek, Lautsch & Eaton, 2006). *Global competition*, boosted by technological development (Lewis, Rapoport & Gambles, 2003) is another trigger for fundamental changes in today's work situation. Creating and maintaining a competitive advantage virtually always entails reducing costs and increasing and fastening productivity. In response to global competition organizations are adopting innovative approaches that change the nature of organizations. Innovative organizational types such as virtual organizations, network organizations, high-performance work team organizations, etc. (Blyton & Dastmalchian, 2006) impose new and usually higher demands on employees in terms of flexibility, task variety and the speed for accomplishing tasks. Pressure imposed on employees rises and less people have to do more work in shorter time, so time devoted to work tends to increase (Major & Germano, 2006). Employees are expected to be highly flexible in terms of time and location rendering the challenge of integrating work with other aspects of life even more complex (McKenna & Richardson, 2007; for work-life challenges of flexpatriates cf. Mayerhofer et al., 2011). Another development is the *rise of the service industry* and 24/7 economy (services and/or available staff 24 hours a day for seven days a week). In order to remain globally competitive organizations must extend their operating hours which, however, does not necessarily entail flexible work hours or a second shift. Changes from a production-based to a knowledge-based industry also entail problems of performance measurement because outputs are largely intangible. As a function of this development organizations are often characterized by a culture of 'presenteeism' or 'face time'[10] (Munck, 2001; Simpson, 1998; Ulich & Wiese, 2011). As the daily output of knowledge workers is hard to measure people's productivity and commitment to the firm are evaluated by the time they spend at their workplace (e.g. emails answered at 10 p.m. and later), the major reason for the development of today's long work hours cultures

---

10   'Face time': Hooks and Higgs (2002) define it as "schedule and location to work based on being present when and where immediate supervisors work" (p. 107).

(Bunting, 2004; Burke & Fiksenbaum, 2008; Hewlett & Luce, 2006; Porter & Perry, 2008).

On the other hand, it seems that the role of work in individuals' lives has changed and employees are willing to invest a considerable amount of time in their job because they attach social recognition to it, a trend which Moldaschl and Voß (2002) describe under the notion of 'subjectivation of work'. Besides being pushed to spend increasing amounts of time and energy at work, *work is increasingly becoming a central factor of people's identity*, as also illustrated by Lewis (2003) who questions provocatively whether 'post-industrial work' is the 'new leisure' (p. 343). With rising education levels work becomes a place of social recognition and self-realization by providing, according to Lewis, Rapoport and Gambles (2003), an instance of engaging in "meaningful relation-ships with others" (p. 825). Wallace (2006) investigating generational differ-ences between so-called Baby Boomers and Generation X[11] among lawyers did not find differences in work commitment: however, for Baby Boomers work commitment was related to extrinsic rewards whereas for Generation X work commitment was related to intrinsic rewards indicating that to some extent work does reinforce itself. This transition is in part explained by the shift from an industrial towards a knowledge-based economy and the personalization of knowledge and talent (Blyton & Dastmalchian, 2006). Knowledge and expertise as central resources in this 'new economy' are attached to the individual and render the knowledge holder less substitutable; knowledge holders in turn need the organization as a context to apply their knowledge. As this development applies for men and women alike traditional gender role distributions of female homemaker and male breadwinner are levered out as today's young women have reached the same and in some fields even higher education and qualifica-tion levels than their male counterparts and are increasingly determined to over-come the 'glass ceiling' (Cheung & Halpern, 2010; Kumra & Vinnicombe, 2008; Lyness & Thompson, 1997) seeking self-realization and fulfillment in the work sphere. Along with the postulated dominance of work in individual's lives, boundaries between work and other aspects of life become increasingly blurred with work usually drawing on non-work time (Hochschild, 2000; White et al., 2003). From a practical as well as a scientific point of view solutions are sought and evaluated, how individuals can negotiate these boundaries and satisfactorily reconcile work and the rest of life.

---

11   According to Wallace (2006), Baby Boomers include men and women born between
      1946 and 1964 and Generation Xers include individuals born between 1965 and 1980.

While work increasingly becomes a characterizing dynamic of our identity, there is at the same time an observable *value shift towards more time for personal life* and family (Lewis et al., 2007). However, the general trend appears to be in favor of a 'having it all' rather than making a choice (Ezzedeen & Ritchey, 2009; Friedman, 2000). German young females for example do want both a career and a family, though with a 'career first' attitude and the family phase is very often postponed to a time where they have established their career (BMFSFJ, 2010b). The wish for high engagement in responsibilities and activities in work *and* personal life often results from *too much* work, as Sullivan and Mainiero (2007) notice:

> "Some individuals, tired of the fast-paced corporate grind, are getting off the fast
> track or declining promotions in order to spend more time with friends and family or
> to focus on self-development" (p. 239).

Their statement highlights that personal life is valued beyond family; individuals wish to lead a fulfilling life in all domains (cf. also Izzo & Withers, 2001). These changing workforce values are of course mirrored in high potentials' expectations towards the organization.

The previous section served to clarify the linkages that make work-life interactions an issue for organizational practice and management research. It was shown how individual outcomes and needs are related to organizational outcomes as well as how this network is impacted by dynamics of the social environment. It has become clear that it is not only worthwhile but necessary for organizations to be sensitive of work-life integration challenges of their employees in order to sustain long-term organizational success and particularly to maintain a motivated and high-performing workforce as well as access to high potentials. In order to span a framework for understanding these work-life integration challenges the forthcoming section sheds a closer look at the concepts and theoretical approaches behind managing demands and interests from multiple life spheres.

1.2 The Toolbox of Researching the Work-Life Interface

While 'work-life balance' has become a buzzword in print and online media in the context of the challenges of today's life, research in this area circles around a number of terms which all attempt to describe and examine a reconciliation of life domains. Different research approaches and perspectives are represented by various terms: *work-family conflict* is based on the assumption that the work and the family role compete for resources with negative individual outcomes if a satisfactory distribution of resources fails to be achieved. *Work-family enrichment* focuses on the positive and enriching effect the work role has for the family role and vice versa. Without common consensus is *work-family balance* which often serves as a generic term for describing a lack of conflict and / or successfully achieved enrichment. Then, research is also concerned with whether to take a narrow focus by investigating the work-family dichotomy or to extend the perspective towards further life roles while accepting the setback that the *'life'* component is not clear-cut. The subsequent paragraphs give an overview of the conceptual toolbox of work-life research, providing the theoretical basis for further investigation of the work-life interface of professionals in Part II.

1.2.1 Theoretical Foundation of Work-Life Research: Social Role Theory

While work-life research has its roots in various disciplines, the most fundamental and widely acknowledged theory underlying the study of interactions between work and personal life is social role theory. Collier and Callero (2005) describe social roles as

> "cultural objects that are assumed to be real, objective, meaningful features of the social world [...] and are recognized, understood and shared with varying degrees of specificity and knowledge of the culture" (p. 47).

Another frequently cited definition describes a 'role' as "a set of activities, which are defined as potential behaviors" (Kahn et al., 1964, p. 13). Ashforth and colleagues (2000) argue that in our modern lives the number of potential roles an individual is involved in has increased, also as tasks that were once performed informally, such as dependent care or social engagement, are now more strongly represented by clear-cut formal roles. The often claimed increasing complexity of our lives manifests itself in terms of an increase of role demands and responsibilities as each role is not only associated with specific behaviors but even more so by a set of expectations.

Initially, social role theory is applicable to an endless number of contexts, as each individual is involved in multiple roles which each entail a set of obligations and responsibilities. Previously outlined societal and demographic changes together with the approximation of once distinct gender role responsibilities gave rise to the discussion of role interactions in the realms of work and family (Barnett & Gareis, 2006). In the literature several mechanisms are discussed concerning the interaction between work and nonwork roles (Figure 3): segmentation and integration, spillover, compensation, role strain, resource drain and role conflict, and enrichment and facilitation.

1.2.1.1 Segmentation and Integration

Segmentation hypothesis ranges among the first approaches taken in work-family research (Geurts & Demerouti, 2003; Zedeck & Mosier, 1990). This approach is consistent with the traditional view that work and family are separate domains characterized by impermeable boundaries with men operating in the work domain and women operating primarily in the family domain (male breadwinner - female homemaker model) (Clark, 2000; Staines, Fudge & Pottick, 1986). The division of work and non-work domains and keeping family matters out of work and vice versa is obviously still the preferred model of many employers because then responsibility for managing work-life borders stays outside organizational responsibility. But besides new information and communication technology facilitating constant accessibility (through internet, mobile phones, etc.) the employment of qualified women and dual-earner couples with children strongly call the feasibility of the model of separated life domains into question. Geurts and Demerouti (2003) highlight that segmentation "does not occur naturally, but may be the result of workers' attempts to prevent work activities from intruding in their family life" (p. 282). A related, yet more flexible approach to studying work-family interaction mechanisms is the segmentation-integration continuum affirming that individuals dispose of a set of resources and preferences which impact their way of dealing with role demands in a more segmenting way. Individuals with a tendency to exclude family matters from work as much as possible are characterized as segmenters, individuals who tend to deal with work and family issues as they occur are integrators (Ashforth, Kreiner & Fugate, 2000; Clark, 2000; Marks & MacDermid, 1996; Nippert-Eng, 1996). Morris and Madsen (2007) define integration as

> "a holistic strategy including effective and efficient coordination of efforts and energies among all stakeholders sharing interest and benefits from workers able to fulfill and transition between their personal, work, family, and community obligations" (p. 442).

Ashforth et al. (2000) highlight the potentially low contrast between roles as well as the flexible and permeable boundary among roles. Low contrast between roles indicates that the role identities of a person are similar in different roles, i.e. an individual's role as a manager at work is potentially similar to the parent at home. Flexible and permeable boundaries are enforced through advanced communication technology (Major & Germano, 2006; Milliken & Dunn-Jensen, 2005; Valcour & Hunter, 2005) as well as flexible work arrangements which break the 9-5 work hour pattern (Roth & Zakrzewski, 2006). Although flexible and permeable boundaries may also have negative effects on individuals, researchers argue that they can facilitate and encourage equal attentiveness and connection with different roles without causing role conflict (Ashforth, Kreiner & Fugate, 2000; Clark, 2000). It must be noted that the term *work-life integration* is also used to refer to a successful reconciliation of life spheres in general to avoid using the term 'balance' which indicates a 50:50 relationship of work and family. Among others, Parris et al. (2008) argue along this line suggesting to speak of 'work–personal life integration' instead.

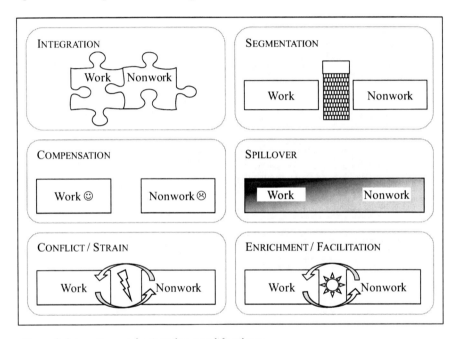

Figure 3. Interaction mechanisms between life spheres

1.2.1.2 Spillover

Spillover models assume a similarity between issues at work and issues in the family (or other non-work domains). Behaviors, attitudes, emotional states and moods can 'spill over' from one domain to another and accordingly affect either those individuals who are experiencing the mood themselves or other people in the respective domain (Geurts & Demerouti, 2003; Zedeck & Mosier, 1990). Spillover also includes the transmission and impact of experiences from one domain to another, e.g. exhaustion in the family domain can be caused by work fatigue (Rothbard & Dumas, 2006). Studies on spillover investigated the dimensions of both negative and positive spillover (e.g. Williams & Alliger, 1994; Grzywacz & Marks, 2000; Kinnunen et al., 2006). Positive spillover is associated with work-life enrichment: positive experiences in the work domain enrich family/personal life and vice versa. Negative spillover is associated with a negative impact of one role onto the other. An example is alienation which is taken from work (e.g. monotonous factory work) into the family or other life domains leading to "energy deficits" (Zedeck & Mosier, 1990, p. 241) or lethargy in personal life. A similar approach called *congruence theory* postulates similarity between work and other domains by means of a third factor (e.g. negative affectivity) which affects both domains (Edwards & Rothbard, 2000; Frone, 2003).

1.2.1.3 Compensation

The general idea of compensation approaches is that deficits in one life role are compensated in another. A lack of rewards in the work role may be associated with pursuing rewards in the family or other domains (Geurts & Demerouti, 2003). Individuals whose partner fails to acknowledge their engagement at home may increase time and energy invested in work. The compensation approach assumes that an individual's involvement in roles is complementary, i.e. if work involvement is high (e.g. due to high work satisfaction) family involvement is low. Thus the compensation model postulates a negative relationship between constructs in two roles (Rothbard & Dumas, 2006) in contrast to the positive relationship theorized in spillover hypothesis. Involvement can change regarding attention devoted, time invested and importance imputed regarding a less rewarding role (Edwards & Rothbard, 2000; Morris & Madsen, 2007). Compensation can result in role accommodation: individuals find greater satisfaction in one role and hence reduce participation in less satisfactory roles.

1.2.1.4 Role Strain, Resource Drain, and Role Conflict

Resource drain refers to the transfer of limited available resources (e.g. time, attention, energy) from one life domain to another which is associated with scarcity of this resource in the domain of origin (Frone, 2003). In practical terms this means that for example time resources spent in the work domain results in scarce temporal resources in nonwork spheres or, strong temporal engagement in the family domain is associated with scarcity of time for work and career development. According to Morris and Madsen (2007) the remaining amount of resources can become insufficient, depleted, or both, so that the potential for stress, fatigue, and burnout syndrom increases. In line with the resource drain approach is the *role strain hypothesis* which assumes that the juggling of competing resources is related to strain (Geurts & Demerouti, 2003). The role strain hypothesis postulates that „responsibilities from different, separate domains compete for limited amounts of time, physical energy and psychological resources" (Grzywacz & Marks, 2000, p. 112). This phenomenon is also referred to as scarcity hypothesis implying that a person's amount of time and energy is limited and an increase of the number of roles or of the responsibility within one role can thus be associated with increased role conflict or role strain. Negative consequences of role strain such as decreased well-being, stress symptoms, depression and so forth can be situated in both the workplace and nonwork domains. Goode (1960) who describes role strain as „the felt difficulty in fulfilling role obligations" (p. 483) postulates that not being able to fulfill expected role obligations, i.e. having the feeling of role strain, is normal for every individual. All individuals accordingly strive for adjusting their role demands to a bearable load by applying different strategies such as changing/eliminating membership in less salient roles or modifying one or more demanding roles to fit their individual capacity (Goode, 1960). Similarly *conflict theory* affirms an incompatibility of work and family roles in terms of participation. Taking responsibilities in one role can interfere with participating in another which can create negative effects for the individual that in turn can be undesirable for the employing organization (Greenhaus & Beutell, 1985). Among other studies, Grant-Vallone and Donaldson (2001) reported a negative correlation between work-family conflict and positive well-being based on longitudinal data. Reviews and meta-analyses have widely confirmed the association of work-nonwork conflict with negative outcomes for the individual and the organization (Allen et al., 2000; Byron, 2005; Eby et al., 2005; Kossek & Ozeki, 1998).

1.2.1.5 Enrichment and Facilitation

Consistent with the emergence of 'positive psychology'[12] (Diener et al., 1999; Seligman & Csikszentmihalyi, 2000) and 'positive organizational scholarship'[13]

---

12   Positive Psychology is a psychological paradigm in which, contrary to previous approaches that mainly focus on mental disorders and malfunctioning, pursues questions about human functioning, well-being and 'happiness' with the aim of preventing disorders in the first place. This direction is generally attributed to U.S. psychologist Martin Seligman who together with Mihaly Csikszentmihalyi, pioneer of research on 'flow' experiences functioned as guest-editors for a very prominent special issue of the journal *American Psychologist* on positive psychology (Seligman & Csikszentmihalyi, 2000). Meanwhile, researchers such as Ed Diener long before pioneered this research paradigm by studying antecedents and outcomes of subjective well-being (Diener et al., 1999).

(Cameron et al., 2003a; Kaiser & Ringlstetter, 2006) perspectives on the work-life interface were amplified towards positive interdependencies between work and nonwork which authors speak of as enrichment or facilitation. The positive interaction of work and personal life is much less researched and scientists have only recently started considering 'positive' perspectives, i.e. facilitation or enrichment of life roles. Frone (2003) notes that the relationship between work and nonwork domains should not singularly be described by the absence or presence of conflict: a comprehensive view of the work-life interface should consider positive interactions as well. Work-family or work-nonwork facilitation means that experiences in one sphere enhance the quality of other life domains. The basic idea of enrichment (also: enhancement) is that energy is not limited as postulated by resource drain and role strain hypotheses. Instead, energy is an expandable quantity (Barnett & Gareis, 2006). Carlson and her colleagues (2006) argue that enrichment and facilitation are distinct in the way that enrichment focuses on improving an individual's role performance and facilitation describes improvements on system functioning. This implies that enrichment has rather temporary effects that are concentrated on the individual. Facilitation in turn can also affect co-workers, family members and other role-related individuals. Greenhaus and Powell (2006) propose an affective enrichment interaction, i.e. positive emotions emerging in one domain positively impact other life spheres, and an instrumental path where skills and competencies acquired in one domain provide advantages in other domains. It was shown that enrichment and conflict are not mutually exclusive but two different perspectives (e.g. Rothbard, 2001). Individuals can experience life roles as conflicting, e.g. in terms of time spent in each life sphere and enriching at the same time, e.g. in terms of mood and emotions. From a study including 221 managers Kirchmeyer (1993) concluded that for both professional men and women "the benefits of multiple domain participation did seem to outweigh the burdens" (p. 545). Although the

---

13   Positive Organizational Scholarship (POS) represents a new direction of management research which draws on insights from positive psychology in order to improve our understanding of and promoting of human and organizational performance and excellence (Ringlstetter, Kaiser, Müller-Seitz, 2006a). POS research examines primarily on dynamics that are "typically described by words such as excellence, thriving, flourishing, abundance, resilience, or virtuousness (Cameron et al., 2003a, p. 4). A 'positive management' is for example characterized by promoting flow experiences, i.e. a state of complete absorption in a task which is enabled by a fit between individuals' skills and demands, and by a HRM which fosters employee well-being, e.g. by a targeted selection of employees, responsible corporate management of employee health and assistance with employees' integration of work with personal life (Frey et al., 2006; Kaiser & Ringlstetter, 2006).

participants in this case experienced interference between work and nonwork domains, the positive effects of involvement in work and nonwork were larger. Along this line of argumentation participation in nonwork activities (childcare and family, community work, recreational activities) may support and facilitate work activities and vice versa.

1.2.2 Work-Family and Work-Life Conflict

The previous paragraph outlined different mechanisms of how work and personal life can interact. The present study focuses on work-life conflict following the model of Greenhaus and Beutell (1985) according to whom three forms of conflict between work and nonwork roles exist: time-based, strain-based, and behavior-based conflict. The decision to focus on a *conflict* perspective and choice of the Greenhaus and Beutell taxonomy is based upon a number of theoretical considerations which are presented in the subsequent paragraphs together with an explanation for only investigating the work-to-life conflict direction.

1.2.2.1 Three Dimensions and Two Directions

As already mentioned, the underlying idea of the role conflict perspective is that different role demands of a person are incompatible and the experience of incompatibility is related to feelings of dissatisfaction and stress. The most frequently cited definition of this conflict concept was pronounced by Greenhaus and Beutell (1985) who describe work-family conflict as

> "a form of interrole conflict in which the role pressures from the work and family domains are mutually incompatible in some respect. That is, participation in the work (family) role is made more difficult by virtue of participation in the family (work) role" (p. 77).

The authors propose that conflict between work and nonwork occurs in three dimensions: *time-based, strain-based and behavior-based conflict*. As a limited resource *time* devoted to one life sphere cannot be devoted to another life sphere creating conflict. According to Greenhaus and Beutell (1985) time-based work-family conflict can occur as time pressures from one sphere a) make it physically impossible to meet demands of another role, or b) create a preoccupation with the work (family) role, when one is physically present in the family (work) role. Typical predictors of *time-based work-family conflict* are work volume and work schedule flexibility as well as marital status, number of children and employment situation of the spouse (Boyar, Maertz & Pearson, 2005; Reynolds, 2005). *Strain-based work-family conflict* refers to the experience of role interference by means of strain symptoms such as tension and fatigue evolved in one life domain that make it difficult to fulfill demands in another domain, for example as a consequence of low social support (Casper & Buffardi, 2004; van Daalen et al., 2006). Finally, if behaviors associated with one role interfere with behaviors in another role we speak of *behavior-based work-family conflict* (Peake & Harris, 2002). Behavior-based conflict occurs when acting strategies developed in one life domain interfere with role requirements or desires in another domain, e.g. postponing or canceling a vacation because of an important project at work. As this threefold taxonomy appears plausible and is more fine-grained than other operationalizations, it was applied by a considerable number of researchers (e.g. Bruck, Allen & Spector, 2002; Carlson, 1999; Chen et al., 2009; Kelloway et al., 1999; van Daalen et al., 2006). The majority of studies however focus on either time-based or strain-based models or both of them together. Empirical results on the behavior-based conflict type are rare. Madsen (2003), for example, found that teleworkers experience significantly less time-based (work-to-family) strain-based (both work-to-family and family-to-work) and behavior-based work-(to)family conflict as compared to employees who did not telework.

Although unidirectional approaches were also investigated in the past, the bidirectional dimension of work-family conflict, i.e. that work can interfere with family (*work-to-family conflict*) as well as family roles can interfere with work roles (*family-to-work conflict*) is widely acknowledged and has been researched extensively. Byron (2005) showed in her meta-analysis that both conflict direc tions have different antecedents. Job-related sources tend to have a stronger impact on work-to-family conflict and family-related antecedents influence family-to-work conflict more strongly. A considerable number of studies, attempting to enlighten the interplay of organizational antecedents with the work-life interface, focus on the work-to-family conflict direction assuming that work-related factors are more strongly related to this direction of conflict (e.g. Frone et al., 1997; Thomas & Ganster, 1995; Thompson et al., 1999).

1.2.2.2 The Work-Life Dichotomy: Does 'Life' Begin at the Office Exit?

The vast majority of publications in this research area focus on the dichotomy of work versus family. However, the narrow focus of this perspective has been criticized. Besides changing views of 'family' with increasing numbers of single parents and single individuals with eldercare responsibilities (Parasuraman & Greenhaus, 2002), Casper, Weltman and Kwesiga (2007) argue in favor of an approach that also includes individuals where family is not the dominant life role besides work. The authors suggest a measure for a singles-friendly work culture in terms of equal work opportunities, equal work expectations, and equal access to work-life benefits. They further underscore the importance of social inclusion which was in their study directly related to turnover intention and affective commitment. Similarly, Lewis (2003) noted that since the 1990s work-life debates have shifted towards a work-'life' paradigm aiming at being more gender neutral and inclusive of all individuals who face more than one role responsibility in their lives. Leisure (also of childless couples and singles) and other nonwork activities are being considered more frequently now (Frone, 2003). Thus, terminology and methodological operationalizations were extended from work-to-family conflict to work-to-life conflict based on the assumption that the basic distinction between the two conflict directions applies even more to the work-nonwork distinction. What exactly 'life' refers to is about as diverse as the existing number of studies that examine work-'life' interactions. Gröpel and Kuhl (2006) as one example refer to areas of work/achievement, contact/relationship, health/body and meaningfulness of life including religion and culture. Similar examples of life role conceptualizations include differentiations into four areas – work, family, community, and self (Friedman, 2008a), or six spheres – leisure, community, work, religion, and family (Carlson, Kacmar & Williams, 2000). Aryee (1992) suggests three types of conflict: job-spouse, job-parent, and job-homemaker conflict. Other researchers have taken the approach of leaving the nonwork category blurred by referring to work-nonwork or work-home interactions (Beauregard, 2006; Dikkers et al., 2004; Fisher et al., 2009; Geurts & Demerouti, 2003). It becomes clear in the debate that scientists are aware of the fact that individuals' lives consist of more than work and family yet find it difficult to determine clear-cut nonwork areas. According to Guest (2002) however it is not necessary in most investigations to do so. Work-life balance, he states, is "a misnomer [that] serves simply as a convenient shorthand for work and the rest of life" (Guest, 2002, p. 262), and in the majority of studies individuals and their subjective experience of life role reconciliation is of interest: therefore it is considered of only secondary importance to what exactly the 'life' component refers to.

Another critical thought must be dedicated to the fact that a *work-life* dichotomy implies that 'life' does not include work. Lewis, Rapoport and Gambles (2003) argue that the work-life terminology

> "implies work is not part of life, ignores the distinction between paid and unpaid work and suggests unpaid care work is just a part of the non-work area of life. Furthermore, it implies that work and the rest of life are in some way antithetical or mutually exclusive, which fails to capture how skills transfer between the different aspects of life" (p. 829).

Although the terminology of work versus life in itself may be viewed critically, the work role is for the majority of individuals the most time-consuming sphere and is most likely to interfere substantially with other areas of interest or obligation. Besides, the work role is not as clear-cut as it may initially seem because work in the sense of paid employment is an elastic term as well (e.g. working from home). If work beyond paid employment is considered (housework, caring for dependents, etc.) it likewise becomes a blurred construct (Guest, 2002).

The present research follows the suggested broader view of the 'life' domain by studying work-(personal)life conflict instead of work-family conflict bearing in mind the shortcomings of this dichotomy and terminology. For professionals work is usually an integral part of their life and it is therefore appropriate to take a dichotomous approach that in the first place leaves the category of nonwork spheres open to each individual's subjective perception and situation.

1.2.2.3 Work and Personal Life Dynamics: An Operational Definition of Work-Life Conflict

As outlined in the previous paragraphs there are numerous ways of making interactions among work and personal life manageable for research purposes. For the present study which investigates work-life interactions among professional employees it is highly appropriate to follow the most widely used approach and operationalize the challenge of reconciling work and personal life with the *paradigm of conflicting roles*. This decision is based upon three major thoughts:

The fact that the conflict paradigm is the most widely researched operationalization of work life interactions can be taken as an indicator that roles competing for limited resources, i.e. role conflict, is the most salient interaction. This paradigm does not rule out other interactions among life spheres such as enrichment and facilitation. Existing research shows that these interactions have distinct antecedents and outcomes and are supplementary rather than mutually exclusive. Individuals may perceive conflict between work and personal life, e.g. in terms of time available for activities in these spheres, and at the same time find that the positive mood they gain from their satisfactory personal (work) life, spills over to their work (personal life) domain and makes them a more cheerful worker. It is argued here however, that conflict is the major problem faced by all employees who want to 'have it all' in the sense of pursuing a career and at the same time leading a satisfactory life beyond work. Taking the route most traveled further yields the opportunity to draw on a large volume of existing research about the work-life interface. Hence, concepts presented in this thesis are based on a large well-established research basis. This enables comparisons of results with previous findings and avoids drawbacks that occur in exploratory research approaches. The final reflection that led to the decision of focusing on the conflict perspective concerns the specific group of interest with respect to the work-life interface. The extraordinarily high work volume of professionals together with their intrinsic work interest as experts and specialists is likely to leave little space in their lives for anything else but work. Therefore the notion that work collides with other domains of life – if there is an interest in having a fulfilled personal life as well – is likely to be a problem particularly for professionals. The existence of positive spillover and enhancement effects regarding work-personal life interactions of professionals are not completely ruled out here, yet it is assumed that conflict is a major issue for linking work and personal life and is associated with undesirable outcomes.

It was further decided to apply the *threefold operationalization of conflict* based on the thoughts of Greenhaus and Beutell (1985) for studying the work-life interface of professionals. The differentiation of perceived conflict in terms of time, psychological strain and actual behavior represents three facets that are distinct in their nature and have distinct outcomes and implications for conflict management. The threefold taxonomy is applied in the present thesis because of three reasons: Firstly, the consideration of three different types of conflict pays tribute to the fact that interactions between work and personal life are complex. A differentiated look at various appearances of conflict is necessary to draw sensible conclusions and enable differentiated implications. Above and beyond, the current approach made use of the differentiation into time-based, strain-based and behavior-based work-life conflict in order to further develop this taxonomy in two ways. For one thing, this operationalization has so far largely been tested only in terms of a work vs. family conflict interaction. The present study broadens its focus by applying the differentiation in terms of work vs. personal life conflict hoping to add insights to the study of work and personal life beyond the family focus. Additionally, the behavior dimension has to date yielded inconsistent results and therefore has often been excluded from previous studies (Allen et al. 2000; Chen et al., 2009; Rotondo, Carlson & Kincaid, 2003; van Daalen et al., 2006; Wallace, 1997). In the present thesis the behavior dimension is reanimated by tailoring the operationalization of this construct specifically to the 'behavior' that the professionals studied here are likely to exert. Finally, the current approach represents a reaction to calls for more research about this threefold taxonomy as expressed in the meta-analyses of Ford, Heinen and Langkamer (2007) and just recently of Michel and his co-authors (2010Lastly, the present dissertation focuses on one only direction in which conflict can occur: the *work-to-life conflict direction*. This decision was made frequently in previous research for comprehensible reasons. Methodologically, observing a number of antecedents or outcomes of a three-fold concept with additionally two conflict directions requires an enormous sample size to maintain statistical power which is often limited by sample sizes below the necessary margin.

Theoretical considerations strengthen the decision to *focus on work-to-life conflict*. The two directions in which conflict between work and personal life can occur were shown to have different antecedents as demonstrated in the me-

ta-analysis of Byron (2005) and should thus be considered as different constructs. There is no theoretical necessity to study both directions simultaneously,
hence whether to study the conflict direction from work towards personal life or
vice versa strongly depends on the specific insights researchers are interested in.
Thompson, Beauvais and Lyness (1999) argue in favor of studying the work-to-
life conflict direction in the context of the usefulness of work-life initiatives and
the role of a supportive work environment for work-life experiences. Regarding
life-to-work conflict there is not much, organizations can do. Understanding
how aspects of work affect personal life gives the organization a scope of action
to manage work-life conflict and negative outcomes. As in the present research
the organizational perspective and the question how organizations can support
employees' work-life reconciliation is in the center of attention, it is more interesting how this sphere impacts personal life.

In short, in the present doctoral thesis work-life conflict is studied in terms
of time-based, strain-based and behavior-based work-to-life conflict. *Time-
based work-to-life conflict* refers to conflict by means of time spent with work-
related activities and demands, first and foremost work hours, which collides
with time spent on activities and responsibilities outside work. These may be
activities with the family and / or partner, housework, caring for a sick parent
just as well as hours spent on sports and recreation, catching up with friends or
personal education. *Strain-based conflict* refers to the psychological component
of conflict, the notion that individuals experience stress and tension because of
problems in arranging work and nonwork spheres. Strain-based work-to-life
conflict thus describes the experience of tension because work demands impede
an individual's capacity to expend more time and energy in areas of personal
life. The previous two dimensions describe a more passive experience of conflict
whereas *behavior-based conflict* clearly has an active component: Individuals'
behaviors in one domain conflict with performance or resources available with
respect to another domain. Behavior-based work-to-life conflict occurs for example if an individual delays, cancels or terminates a personal holiday because
of responsibilities calling from the work domain. Such situations likely occur in
professional occupations where client contacts are highly frequent and
knowledge and available actions are strongly personalized. The present study of
professionals' work-life interface is based upon this threefold differentiation as
it best represents the distinct tensions faced by professionals with regards to the
reconciliation of their life spheres. It was outlined earlier why dynamics of work
and personal life spheres are of relevance for the organization. Further the
toolbox of research in this arena was unpacked presenting the different approaches and constructs underlying studies about life role reconciliation and its
respective antecedents and outcomes. Finally, a working definition of work-life

conflict was presented that forms the foundation for the empirical examination in Part II. In the forthcoming section the group of employees that were so far loosely referred to as 'professionals' is more closely examined.

2. Professionals as an Occupational Category of Particular Interest for Work-Life Research

When talking about professionals we have a rather nebulous idea in mind which attributes characterize these people and their jobs. The current section sheds a closer look at the members of this occupational category. First, general definitions and characteristics are examined, focusing then on the specific group of professionals who work in professional service firms (PSFs). How jobs of business professionals are characterized by heavy workloads and 'extreme' job demands is discussed further, leading to the question whether and why PSF employees are particularly eligible to work-life conflict.

2.1 In Search of a Definition of 'Professionals'

Many employees are referred to as such and there exists no widely accepted definition for 'professionals' (von Nordenflycht, 2010). Some occupational groups are named so without reference to professional norms or a validation of this label. In numerous studies the sample is described as consisting of 'professionals and managers' (e.g. Thompson et al., 1999). Others are indeed professionals according to traditional definitions without being referred to as such and are rather described with their professional field (physicians, lawyers, professors, etc.). Again in other cases, the occupational field is in the process of professionalization, attempting to establish and institutionalize their employees' status as professionals. Greiner and Ennsfellner (2010), for example, describe this process for management consultants. As a first step in the attempt to describe 'professionals' as a specific workforce, we can take a look at the definition of sociologist Eliot Freidson (1987) who described 'professions' as

> "(…) occupations especially distinguished by their orientation to serving the needs of the public through the schooled application of their unusually esoteric knowledge and complex skill" (p. 19).

The underlying notion of this description is that professionals are characterized as holding expertise in a specific field and thus are specialized in a certain discipline. Traditionally members of long-established professions are referred to as professionals such as judges and lawyers, university professors, clergymen, physicians but also dentists, architects, engineers and in recent decades for example accountants (Bürger, 2005) and management consultants (von

Nordenflycht, 2010). Løwendahl (2005) gives a list of qualitative attributes which characterize professionals in a general sense (p. 28):
- Members of a highly professionalized occupational group,
- Higher education,
- Emphasis on application and improvement of knowledge,
- Respect for professional norms of behavior, including altruistic problem solving for the client, affective neutrality and the limitations of professional expertise, and
- Respect for and willingness to participate in peer reviews and sanctions.

May, Korczynski and Frenkel (2002) add another important aspect: professionals are usually highly committed to their tasks and to the solution of complex problems indicating high intrinsic motivation. Along with this goes their pursuit of personal development and ongoing professional challenge (Konrad & Mangel, 2000). Bürger (2005) further discusses that being a professional is not necessarily tied to being member of a profession in the traditional sense. In a similar vein Greiner and Ennsfellner (2010) describe the professional as

> "any employee engaged in work predominantly intellectual and varied in character as opposed to routine mental, manual mechanical, or physical work; involving the consistent exercise of discretion and judgment in its performance; ... requiring knowledge of an advanced type ... customarily acquired by a course of specialized intellectual instruction and study in an institution of higher learning." (p. 73f.)

These authors also outline high standards of excellence – professionals as experts – and advanced education and training as core features of professional employees. Based on these thoughts and previous elaborations (Løwendahl, 2005; von Nordenflycht, 2010; May et al., 2002) professionals are within this thesis considered as *individuals with high education, specialized expertise and general process knowledge who use their competencies to solve complex problems and who are highly committed towards their profession and their organization*. These characteristics enlighten a little the blurred picture of professionals as an occupational category but this is probably as far as general descriptions take the researcher and in order to establish a more clear-cut picture of 'the professional' one must refer to a specific context or branch. One such branch are professional service firms (PSFs), which have been defined as

> "as those [organizations] whose primary assets are a highly educated (professional) workforce and whose outputs are intangible services encoded with complex knowledge" (Greenwood et al., 2005, p. 661).

First and foremost the primary input and output of PSFs is knowledge, primarily in the sense of providing specifically tailored solutions for a the complex problem of a client (Starbuck, 1992). As such, PSFs are characterized by a dependency of the client on the firm and a dependency of the firm on its 'human assets', the professional employees (Greenwood et al., 2005; Kaiser & Ringlstetter, 2011). In his taxonomy of knowledge-intensive firms von Nordenflycht (2010) proposes a distinction between classic or regulated PSFs and neo-PSFs (consulting, advertising). The classic PSF as it is described is characterized by high knowledge intensity, low capital intensity and a professionalized workforce such as law firms or accounting firms. The neo PSF, e.g. management consulting, is characterized by high knowledge intensity and low capital intensity and to a lesser extent by a professionalized workforce. However, according to Greiner and Ennsfellner (2010) management consulting is in the process of professionalization, which is for example demonstrated by the establishment of professional associations such as the International Council of Management Consulting Institutes (ICMCI) or the recent emergence of university programs that focus on business consulting.[14] Subsectors of PSFs are described by Ringlstetter, Kaiser and Bürger (2004) and Scott (2001):

– Service providers in the fields of management and IT consulting
– Commercial legal advisory
– Audit, tax and accountancy advisory
– Market research
– Recruitment, placement and personnel services
– Marketing and communication; and
– Investment banking.

2.2 Characteristics of Professional Service Firms and Implications for their Workforce

PSFs are characterized by a number of features that are unique to this type of organization. Among them are a highly educated and specialized workforce whose knowledge work is the major source of profit, the pyramid-shaped promotional structure, and a high client-service orientation that leads to extreme weekly work volumes.

---

14   As a German example, the University of Oldenburg offers a Master of Arts program focusing on business consulting in association with the University of Applied Sciences Emden/Leer (www.master-mc.de/index.php /home.html) since 2006. The University of Applied Sciences Furtwangen (HFU) offers a Master of Science program "Business Consulting" with duration of three semesters (www.hs-furtwangen.de/fachbereiche/ wi/english/studiengaenge/business_consulting_master).

2.2.1 PSFs as Providers of Specialized and Complex Services

In contrast to basic and routine services, professional services are characterized by complexity in terms of sub services or processes, a certain length of the productive process (usually several months or longer), the involvement of a number of highly-skilled individuals in the development process, a non-standard and tailor-made character of the service, and heterogeneity with respect to the sub products and services provided for the client (Bürger, 2005). The fact that such a professional service can only be provided by a highly-knowledgeable and highly-specialized (team of) professional(s) renders a major attribute to this type of product: intangibility (Greenwood et al., 2005). Von Nordenflycht (2010) speaks of an "asymmetry of expertise" (p. 158) where the professionals are experts whereas for the clients as non-experts it is hard to judge the quality of the professional service. This leads to uncertainty on behalf of the clients because they can often only assess product and service quality after the service was finished or not at all (Bürger, 2005; Ringlstetter & Kaiser, 2007; Lorsch & Tierney). The difficulty of assessing the professional services' value together with the client-specific customization of the product is the major reason for the fact that the working pattern of professionals, particularly of consultants, is organized very much around clients' needs and wishes. This includes the visibility of professional service providers at the client site. Visibility and presence at the client premises give clients a feeling of tangibility of the service in terms of, colloquially spoken, 'there are people from FirmX here who sort things out'. Very often firms deal with complex and also delicate projects where the firm gets the feeling of lacking transparency of the professional service. The consequence for the professionals' working pattern is that in many PSFs the larger part of a workweek is spent at the client site with regular overnight stays in hotels. Classically, of five work days per week four are spent at the client site with three nights away from home and 'office day', usually Friday, spent at the PSF office located near the residence of the professional (Perlow & Porter, 2009). It is also common practice that professionals are on international assignments for several weeks or months without returning home in-between (Mayerhofer et al., 2008). Obviously this type of job only appeals to a workforce that is 'up to the challenge' and that associates individual benefits in exchange for their engagement in terms of further professional development – firms usually invest a great deal of developmental efforts in their professionals (Alvesson, 2010), compensation and highly attractive earnings (O'Mahoney, 2007), highly interesting and diverse projects, and the opportunity of building a professional network that boosts their further career opportunities.

2.2.2 Professionals: The Critical Assets of Professional Service Firms

The most distinctive characteristic of PSFs is knowledge intensity; further features are low capital intensity and a professionalized workforce (von Nordenflycht, 2010). The fact that expertise knowledge is the central product of PSFs and this expertise knowledge is tied to the knowledge holder results in a specific set of demands for the professional. These demands are best summarized associated to the three core resources of PSFs being *knowledge, reputation* and *relational resources* (Greenwood & Empson, 2003; Ringlstetter & Bürger, 2003). *Knowledge* is a central resource of PSFs in two connected senses: it is the essential input for and at the same time the main ingredient of the product itself (Gmür, Kaiser & Kampe, 2009). In both senses the central actor is the professional who holds the knowledge and creates the product. Therefore the professional can be considered "the crown jewel of knowledge-producing entities" (Kor & Leblebici, 2005, p. 980) and is not easily substituted, which simultaneously increases the professionals' obligation and value towards the employing PSF. Employee turnover in PSFs is nearly always a loss of capital. *Reputation* is the confidence capital of PSFs and the foundation for their recruitment strategy, their client acquisition strategy and their pricing of services *(*Greenwood et al., 2005*)*. The professional in this type of business represents a central figure in the creation and maintenance of this reputation, reason enough for the firm to attempt high organizational commitment within its workforce (Wallace, 1995). *Relational resources* as another critical resource of PSFs are very often tied to professionals as individuals (e.g. shown by clients demanding to work with a specific professional or team only) and if professionals leave the firm in favor of a more attractive employer it is likely that important relational resources are also lost to the PSF (Løwendahl, 2005).

The dependence of PSFs on these resources underscores the fact that the professional employee is the central asset of professional service firms. Konrad and Mangel (2000) state that professionals are "a critical resource because of their tacit knowledge, their expense, their recent scarcity, and the transferability of their skills" (p. 1227). The firm depends on its human capital with its knowledge in terms of its service product and critical resources and therefore has a strong interest in maintaining and maximizing the professional's productivity and effectiveness. The somewhat paradox implication of this fact is that PSFs demand a great deal from their professionals in order to maximize firm profit and at the same time must maintain long-term performance and preventurnover or sickness absence and are thus inclined to care for their well-being, job satisfaction and motivation. Greenwood et al. (2005) summarize the importance of the professional for PSFs:

> "The professional workforce [...] constitutes the critical asset of the PSF because it embodies, operates, and translates the knowledge inherent in the firm's output, and, it is the basis of the firm's relationships with clients who often follow professionals if they change firms. PSFs are thus critically dependent on their ability to recruit, retain, and motivate professionals who are highly mobile. The managerial challenge is to design an organizational form that will achieve these goals" (p. 663).

2.2.3 The Career Path in Professional Service Firms

The traditional career path of business professionals, particularly in professional service firms requires full-time employment with a considerable investment of extra work hours (Connor, Hooks & McGuire, 1999). The corporate hierarchy in PSFs is structured in a triangle-shaped way with newcomers at junior level, usually straight from business schools, making up the largest part.

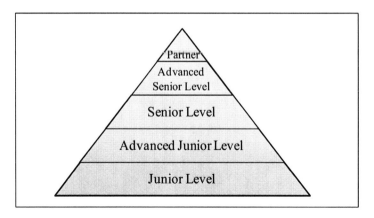

Figure 4. Hierarchy levels typical for most professional service firms
(Author's design based on Kaiser & Ringlstetter, 2011, p. 9)

'Juniors' are primarily occupied with operative project tasks, whereas a smaller number of experienced professionals, making up the middle of the pyramid, co-ordinate and manage projects. A relatively small group at top level, usually partners, is primarily concerned with retaining clients and acquiring new projects (Kaiser & Ringlstetter, 2011). The career path in PSFs is characterized by continuous career advancement also referred to as *up-or-out* principle (Connor, Hooks & McGuire, 1999; Kumra & Vinnicombe, 2008). Professionals are expected to steadily advance in the organizational hierarchy, slow or no advancement usually results in 'mutually agreed' layoff. Hence, intended turnover which serves to sort the wheat from the chaff, makes work in these organizations highly demanding as for those who do want to advance, it implies long hours, many nights away from home due to travel, and high pressure to succeed. Thus, employees in PSFs are only likely to advance if they put work 'first' in their lives.

2.3 Professionals and the Work-Life Interface

After introducing key features of PSFs and related demands in the previous paragraphs, here the professional working pattern is linked more closely to experiences concerning the work-life interface. After briefly outlining prominent features of professionals' jobs that make them particularly eligible for the experience of work-life conflict two different perspectives are discussed that illustrate the complexity of the research field: professionals face extensive work demands which are likely to interfere with spheres outside work yet they are at the same time ready to invest a lot in their interesting and exciting job and their career. Professionals are thus on the one hand a workforce that can be described within the framework of 'extreme' jobs suggested by Hewlett and Luce (2006) making them predestined for experiencing high interference of work with other life interests. On the other hand professional work is considered highly rewarding, both extrinsically and intrinsically. It may therefore be argued that work-life balance is not an issue for professionals at all.

2.3.1 Triggers of Professionals' Work-Life Conflict

Two major characteristics of the nature of professional work are particularly associated with work-life conflict: high levels of flexibility and accessibility together with extremely high work volumes. Not only as a function of the development of mobile technologies has today's work in general become much more *flexible* (Duxbury, Higgins & Thomas, 1996; Major & Germano, 2006; Mayerhofer et al., 2008; Porter & Perry, 2008; Valcour & Hunter, 2005). Rather than working in an office building many professionals work from a 'mobile workplace', e.g. using notebooks in a hotel room or temporarily at a client site. Jackson (2005) suggests that mobile technology use can be beneficial for integrating work with personal life, stating that "just as work and home are becoming portable, so are relationships becoming more virtual and 'anytime anywhere' " (p. 140). Yet despite potential positive effects, e.g. for communicating with 'home', technological devices primarily increase the professional's availability for work-related issues. As Ahuja and colleagues (2007) state from their study of IT road warriors, the use of mobile technology cannot substitute face-to-face interaction with family members. Hewlett and Luce (2006) report from their study with U.S. employees that for two thirds of the respondents, technology was found helpful for doing their job well but more than half also experienced that mobile technology lengthens their work day and enables work to encroach into their nonwork spheres. Most PSF professionals are expected to be *accessible* 24/7 for their employer and even more so for the client (Hewlett & Luce, 2006; Major & Germano, 2006). Hooks and Higgs (2002) investigated characteristics of the workplace environment in professional service firms with the finding that the crucial factor impacting professionals' work schedules are client-related factors. According to the authors, particularly the business hours of the client impact the work schedule of professionals. The fact that professional work is not necessarily bound to one physical workplace further leads to a blurring of invisible boundaries between work and non-work domains (Kossek et al., 2006). Work-related tasks are taken home (or to the hotel) to be completed after dinner, even more so because professionals perceive their work not only as a functional necessity but as a pursuit of personal interests (Brett & Stroh, 2003). Consequently professionals frequently deal with work-life issues in an integrative manner, i.e. boundaries between work and other life domains are rather permeable: work tasks are completed at home; family responsibilities can be to some extent bee organized during the workday if this does not interfere with important work-related activities (Hooks & Higgs, 2002). This can be both blessing and curse: many professionals have the opportunity of choosing where and when to work and thus can take this as an advantage in their work-life integration management. On the other hand it becomes more difficult to draw the line between life spheres and concentrate 100% on the responsibilities of one domain. This also means that, as work from anywhere is possible, availability for work matters is extended to non-work domains, particularly as workload steadily increases and work is rarely 'done' at the end of the day. Again, new information and communication technologies may well make interaction with beloved ones easier when on work-related travel, however the intrusion of work into the spheres of personal life are disproportionately higher: a client inquiry received at 11 p.m. is likely to be considered important enough to deal with it immediately compared to requests of a family member received during the work day. Hooks and Higgs (2002) found in a study of 1055 professionals of various PSFs that client issues were the most important reason for immediate voice mail response. Many responses occurred outside professionals' work schedule as "working from home [and thus outside office hours] appears to be an established phenomenon for professional services firm employees" (p. 108). Overall, the major consequence of increasing flexibility and accessibility of professional work is an increase of hours spent with work activities and consequently less time available for the pursuit of responsibilities outside work.

It is argued, that with increasing global competition the *workload* taken by a single employee has steadily been increasing during the last decades. Hewlett and Luce (2006) refer to a tendency that "more responsibility falls on the shoulders of fewer individuals" (p. 52) (cf. also Brett & Stroh, 2003; Higgins & Duxbury, 2005). Messersmith (2007) reports that IT projects are increasingly staffed on a 24/7 basis, a schedule that used to be reserved for emergencies and times of high workload only. Now the majority of projects appear to be approached with light speed leaving employees with extreme workloads and aggressive deadlines requiring night shifts, work on weekends and workdays of 12 hours plus. At the same time, due to the internationalization of markets and the influx of highly qualified females into the workforce, competition for top quality positions has become fiercer. With simultaneously declining job security "winner takes it all"-rules seem a powerful incentive to work incrementally more than one's rivals (Hewlett & Luce, 2006). Besides actual work volumes, most PSFs are characterized by a strong *long work hours culture*. Within the legal profession for example it is stated that "among elites [i.e. the law profession] the work-family conflict is primarily a problem of excessive work hours and an expectation that work always comes first" (Willams, 2007, p. 384). Time, as stated by Fuchs Epstein et al. (1999) becomes "a proxy for dedication and excellence" (p. 22). Again, probably the strongest reinforcing factor for this high investment culture is the *strong client focus* in PSFs. Meeting clients' needs is the top priority of PSFs and strongly ingrained in the working culture of firms (Litrico & Lee, 2008). Of course organizations in the PSF sector are also spoiled by their high attractiveness and popularity as an employer among young professionals. Believing employer attractiveness statistics[15], PSFs so far do not suffer from a lack of job applicants which seems to be giving them leeway for maintaining highly demanding work practices.2.3.2 Curse or Blessing? Extreme Working Conditions versus Intrinsic Rewards

2.3.2 PSF Professionals as ‚Extreme' Jobholders

Many professionals can be described by the majority of characteristics of ‚extreme jobs' suggested by Hewlett and Luce (2006, p. 51):
– Availability to clients 24/7,
– Fast-paced work under tight deadlines,
– Work-related events outside regular work hours,

---

15   In 2010, among the 10 most attractive employers for graduates and young professionals in Europe identified by the market research institute trendence, four were PSFs of the type referred to in the present thesis, primarily operating in the areas of accounting and consulting (N.N., 2010).

- Unpredictable flow of work,
- Responsibility for profit and loss,
- Large amount of travel,
- Physical presence at workplace at least ten hours a day,
- Large number of direct reports,
- Responsibility for mentoring and recruiting,
- Inordinate scope of responsibility that amounts to more than one job, and
- Working excessively long hours on a regular basis

It is reported that working patterns corresponding to these characteristics are on the rise (Brett & Stroh, 2003) with major reasons sought in increasing 'war for talent' in search for the best young professionals (Michaels, Handfield-Jones & Axelrod, 2009), 'war *of* talent', i.e. competition of career aspirants for the best jobs available (Bürger, 2005; Chambers et al., 1998; Guillaume & Pochic, 2009) as well as technological changes towards being available and ready to work anytime and anywhere (Chesley, 2006; Duxbury & Smart, 2011; Hyman & Baldry, 2011; Valcour & Hunter, 2005). Taking an individual perspective, Hewlett and Luce (2006) found that the major reasons for choosing an extreme job are the intellectual challenge of the tasks and their entailed opportunity for extending competencies and career-related development, considerable compensation and benefits, a stimulating team, and recognition and respect for their work – aspects that describe a large share of professional employees.

The job profile and related demands of professionals in PSFs likely correspond to the description of 'extreme jobs' introduced above (Hewlett & Luce, 2006). Bente Løwendahl, expert for the strategic management of professional service firms (2005), underscores that "the workload is extreme" (p. 57). Particularly with regards to workload and work hours PSFs are well-known for demanding a great deal of their professionals and 'work them to the bone'. Specific demands further depend on the structure and focus of each PSF subbranch. Job-related travel may occur frequently in consulting firms as clients require on-site presence for process monitoring, task-related analyses or implementation support. Law firm professionals are likely to face long work hours as well but not travel as much, as the larger share of their work is conducted in the firm's office and client-firm interactions are based more strongly on data exchange with less frequent face-to-face interactions. Nevertheless, it is obvious that due to their job structure and the immense work demands particularly in terms of time and required flexibility, professionals working in PSFs are a group of particular interest for work-life research because they are, colloquially spoken, bound to have no such thing as a 'life'.

2.3.3 'What Balance? My Job is my Life!' – The Intrinsically Motivating Character of Professional Work

Besides the perspective of extreme jobs which is connoted by a 'too much' of work, there is another side of the coin: extraordinary engagement and dedication of professionals towards their job may also be a matter of personal choice rather than external pressure. In their examination of managers' motives to work excessively long hours Brett and Stroh (2003) found support for the 'work at its own reward'-hypothesis, work hours being significantly related to job involvement and intrinsic satisfaction. From qualitative data studying reduced-schedule professionals and managers, Buck and colleagues (2000) found that "for some, working full-time carried a notion of professionalism, pride, commitment, and accomplishment" (p. 31). In the American bestseller *The Time Bind* Arlie Hochschild (2000) also discussed the issue that work life can be more satisfying than home life which has received some empirical support (Brett & Stroh, 2003; Hewlett & Luce, 2006). Eikhof, Warhurst and Haunschild (2007) argue along the same line stating that work, contrary to 'home' is a place of intellectual expression and personal achievement, an issue which, according to the authors is usually completely neglected in work-life initiatives and by work-life policy makers (i.e. that it is the stimulating character of work due to which intrinsically motivated employees would never dream of using policies to reduce their work volume). Thus, despite the pressure imposed on professionals, very often these individuals work long hours because they *want to*.

An explanation for the stimulating character of work is sought in knowledge work, as "it is probably not wrong to assume that more knowledge work means that people simply like their jobs more" (Hewlett & Luce, 2006, p. 55). Jobs in the professional area are perceived as qualified, challenging, and intellectually stimulating as well as implying a high degree of work morality and job commitment according to Alvesson (2000). The workplace frequently is a place of intrinsic reward and social recognition, particularly if work tasks are non-routine, complex tasks requiring highly sophisticated skills and expertise, as is the case in most professional jobs, associated with feelings of uniqueness and being irreplaceable (Brett & Stroh, 2003). Especially for women, as Hewlett and Luce (2006) found, receiving recognition for their work seems to be a major factor for loving their job. But also power and status associated with the job contributes to the highly salient role of work in professional people's lives:

> "Many professionals are wearing their outsize work commitments on their sleeves; they consider their over-the-top efforts – and often voluntary sacrifices and risks – a reflection of character" (Hewlett & Luce, 2006, p. 53).

Buck et al. (2000) emphasize that today many individuals evaluate themselves and define their identity upon work achievements further illustrating the link between success and identity. The view of seeking fulfillment in work-related success is challenged by Whittington et al. (2011) who plead for defining success in all domains of life. Nevertheless, the tendency of work as an identity-creating factor is strengthened by the observation that the workplace evolves into being the center of individuals' social contacts, replacing civic organizations, social engagement and nonwork associations (Hewlett & Luce, 2006). This development is a consequence of extremely long hours spent at work minimizing time and energy for establishing connections outside work. Additionally, long work hours may be reinforced by a malfunctioning marital and family life. A positive correlation of hours worked and family alienation was for example found in a study of Brett and Stroh (2003) corresponding to the compensation hypothesis (cf. 1.21.3), i.e. deficits in one domain are compensated in another. Lack of rewards in the family/spousal role is associated with pursuing rewards in the work domain, hence, as observed by Hochschild (2000), home has become a source of stress and guilt and work has become the place where professionals receive social recognition and approval. The feeling of having a high status in the organization or more generally, the highly salient role of work is likely to increase work-to-life conflict and spillover as, for example, the stimulating and rewarding function of work for some individuals makes it harder to cut down work hours (Brett & Stroh, 2003; Hewlett & Luce, 2006). Similarly individuals with high responsibility jobs often find it hard to reduce working hours in practical terms: "Employees who are already putting in long hours have few degrees of freedom available to make these adjustments" (Blair-Loy & Wharton, 2004, p. 260). Professionals' work-life integration – often perceived as vocation or destiny – thus can in many respects not be treated with the same standards of work-life research and practice as in other occupations (Litrico & Lee, 2008; Wharton & Blair-Loy, 2006). Hence, a frequently neglected issue in the debate about satisfactory work-life integration is that "containing work rather than reforming it also distracts attention from an important potential source of life satisfaction: work itself" (Eikhof et al., 2007, p. 331).

In sum, this paragraph discusses the importance of taking both perspectives into account: Extreme work demands can be associated with stress and strain, yet they may also be self-imposed because of the intrinsic value of an interesting job or the unattractiveness of social environments outside work. Concerning the question whether work-life conflict matters for professionals we must consider a more fine-grained perspective by taking a look at individual life role values, age, gender and other individual characteristics. Although the 'work at its own reward' hypothesis has received some support, generally existing research argued more strongly in favor of the extreme jobs hypothesis and its implication to reduce excessive work because of negative outcomes associated with overwork. The finding of Casper et al. (2007) that 68% of research papers in the work-life field are based on professional samples strengthens the perception that particularly high-level employees have problems reconciling their life spheres satisfactorily.

2.3.4 What is a 'Personal Life' of Professionals All About? A Research Question

Notwithstanding the question whether work-life conflict (and balance) is an issue for professionals at all, an important question is what we mean by the 'life' component of professionals' work-life conflict (cf. Part I, 1.2.2.2). We do know a lot about the challenges and the character of the work domain of professionals, work represents a domain that is relatively clear-cut by its tasks, time, location, etc. The 'life' component of work-life conflict is rather obscure because of its 'multi-facet' character. For two reasons, it is worthwhile to examine more closely the character of professionals' work-*life* conflict: firstly, research in general has so far neglected a closer look at the 'life' component of work-life conflict, and, secondly, defining what we refer to if we speak about work-life conflict will help us interpret research findings, e.g. on the effectiveness of work-life initiatives in reducing work-life conflict for professionals with different individual needs and resources. Therefore, as a prerequisite for examining factors that impact work-life conflict, the following research question will be examined in the present study:

Research Question 1: *Which life spheres and conflict types does professionals' work-life conflict refer to?*

Preceding sections worked out characteristics that characterize professional employees with the finding that one major consensual characteristic of professionals is their specific expertise making professional service firms a prime context of studying professionals. It was also discussed that professionals in PSFs are likely to face extremely demanding work conditions making it challenging for them to reconcile work and personal life spheres. With the ultimate goal of a better understanding and better management of professionals' work-life conflict, in the following section a review of empirical evidence of major demands and resources that professionals face with regards to their reconciliation of life spheres is presented.

3. Formal and Informal Organizational Demands and Resources of Professionals and their Impact on the Work-Life Interface

As discussed previously PSFs expect a great deal from their professionals in terms of work volume, flexibility, and engagement. However, by working their employees to the bone firms risk losing their crucial assets. While resources to buffer these demands are vividly communicated and offered by many PSFs it is unclear whether such initiatives really have a noticeable effect.[16] Therefore, the interplay of demands imposed on professionals and at the same time the resources professionals dispense of for ameliorating challenges at the border of work and other life spheres is of particular interest.

A considerable number of researchers previously examined such interactions, some of them suggesting complex frameworks of antecedents and outcomes. In order to provide a review of existing research evidence on the interplay of organizational demands and resources with regards to the work-life interface the following section is structured as follows. Briefly, a number of frameworks and general approaches to the study of work-life related demands and resources are outlined (3.1). Then, a comprehensive review of findings on demands and resources which are particularly salient in the context of professional service firms (3.2) is presented. Specifically, a close look is shed at the role of work hours and job-related travel – representing formal demands – on work-life conflict (3.2.1). Findings on formal resources, i.e. work-life initiatives, are presented accompanied by an evaluation of initiatives offered specifically in PSFs (consulting firms) (3.2.2). Following existing research, informal demands and resources are discussed under the general term of organizational culture (3.2.3). With particular focus on the professional context, existing findings are reviewed and summarized on the interaction of work-life issues with perceived organizational support (1), and organizational hindrances (2), such as a negative career impact resulting from initiative use and organizational time demands which are necessary for career advancement. Each section closes with a hypothesis on the expected interaction of the construct under review with work-life

---

16   In the research project "Innovative Concepts of Personnel and Organizational Development in Consulting Organizations (IPOB)" located at the Catholic University Eichstätt-Ingolstadt, virtually every PSF employee we spoke to about the research aim of investigating work-life balance issues in this environment highlighted the importance of the topic while expressing visible doubts that 'such thing' as work-life balance was possible in their profession.

conflict among professionals. In the attempt to achieve more fine-grained results section 3.3 reviews research findings under a 'diversity' perspective: responding to the frequent claim of previous studies – work-life solutions should more strongly consider the individual situation – research findings on the work-life interface of professionals are reviewed with specific focus on PSF subbranches, life role importance, gender and age, as well as family characteristics (marital and dual-career status, children) and job characteristics (tenure and job level).

3.1 Research Perspectives of the Interaction of Demands and Resources

In order to span a framework for examining formal and informal organizational demands and resources with regards to the work-life interface of professionals first a brief look is taken at a number of different approaches which chose a similar direction. Specifically, it is outlined why demands versus resources are examined and why it makes sense to take a closer look at formal and informal aspects.

3.1.1 Demands versus Resources

A number of research approaches explicitly suggest that job demands and job resources interact in predicting organizational and individual outcomes. One of them is the so-called Job Demands-Resources (JD-R) model proposed by the research team around Bakker, Demerouti and Schaufeli (Bakker & Demerouti, 2007; Demerouti et al., 2001). According to the researchers, job resources refer to those

> "physical, psychological, social, or organizational aspects of the job that are either functional in achieving work goals, reduce job demands and the associated physiological and psychological costs, [and/or] stimulate personal growth, learning and development" (Bakker & Demerouti, 2007, p. 312).

Within this definition the authors include the buffering dimension of resources but additionally stress the fact that job resources are 'important in their own right'. Further, it is outlined that such resources can be drawn at different levels, from macro level (organizational support) via interpersonal level (team climate) to micro level, i.e. the individual and / or the task (perceived level of participation, task characteristics, etc.). Initially, the JD-R model was used to examine how job demands and resources impact burnout (Bakker, Demerouti & Euwema, 2005; Bakker, Demerouti & Schaufeli, 2005). It was suggested that job demands increase the likeliness of burnout whereas job resources are indeed related to desirable outcomes for the organization, such as extrarole behavior. Several studies examined work-life dynamics explicitly under a JD-R approach

(Mauno et al., 2006; Schieman et al., 2009; Wallace & Young, 2008). Mauno et al. (2006) examined three work- and organization-related resources, i.e. job control, family supportive climate, and organization-based self-esteem. Time-based and strain-based work-to-family conflict represented job demands. Employees with higher job control and supportive climate experienced a smaller impact of work-family conflict on well-being and job satisfaction suggesting that these resources can buffer the negative effects of work-family conflict on other outcomes. Schieman and colleagues (2009) examined a large-scale sample for differences in work-family conflict as a function of social status as well as the differential impact of demands and resources. Besides the outcome that higher social status was associated with higher levels of conflict, their major finding was that the effect of job pressure on work-nonwork interference was substantially mitigated by control over one's pace of work as a resource. Wallace and Young (2008) examined how productivity is impacted by family de-mands and resources and organizational family-friendly climate. Among law firm lawyers it was found that fathers – who were more productive than non-fathers – benefited strongly from family resources. Female lawyers' productivity was lower if they were mothers because of family demands (household chores).

Further empirical investigations studied interactions between demands im-posed from the organization and resources to mitigate these demands without explicitly referring to the JD-R model (e.g. DiRenzo, Greenhaus & Weer, 2011; Nelson et al., 1990; Valcour, 2007; Voydanoff, 2004, 2005a, 2005b). Among female professionals, Nelson and colleagues (1990) examined the interaction of a set of demands – politics,[17] career progress, and work-home conflict – and organizational policies acting as resources for mitigating these demands. They were able to show that resources indeed acted as buffers, i.e. cushion the nega-tive impact of demands among these women. Demands were associated with undesirable outcomes, i.e. reduced satisfaction and strain symptoms. Valcour (2007) examined demands in terms of work hours, and job complexity and re-sources in terms of control over work time. Work hours were significant predic-tors of call center representatives' (lower) satisfaction with work-family balance. Time control acted as a buffer, participants with low time control and high work volume were less satisfied with their work-family balance than those with high control. Job complexity was related to higher satisfaction with work-family balance but did not moderate the relationship with work hours. DiRenzo, Greenhaus and Weer (2011) also took a demands-resources approach in order to

---

17   With 'politics' the researchers refer to practices within the organization that decide upon
      career advancement and relate to issues that were elsewhere mentioned as the 'glass
      ceiling' effect (Lyness & Thompson, 1997).

examine differences in work-life dynamics with regards to job level. They assessed work hours and general demands of the job (i.e. the requirement to work very hard). Rresources were measured in terms of job autonomy, family-supportive culture and supportive supervision. The researchers found that higher level employees were more strongly affected by work demands but at the same time benefited more from work-related resources in terms of lower work-family interference. Voydanoff (2005a) suggested three types of demands: time-based demands (e.g. work hours), strain-based demands (e.g. pressure), and boundary-spanning demands (i.e. an unsupportive organizational climate). All three were shown to positively affect work-to-family conflict. Further, she provided support for the favorable impact of work resources (time off for family responsibilities, supportive work-family culture) in a large-scale U.S. study (Voydanoff, 2005b). Incorporating community as a role context beyond work and family into the framework added insights about further social demands and resources: community demands were related to higher levels of work-family conflict and community resources were associated with higher work-family facilitation (Voydanoff, 2004).

Regarding work-life integration challenges of professionals in PSFs there are a number of obvious job demands (long work hours, high flexibility and travel requirements) and not so obvious demands which are engrained in organizational culture, such as the practice of demonstrating commitment by working excessively long hours. At the same time PSFs provide resources - work-life initiatives - to address and buffer these demands which are often communicated on their websites for recruiting purposes (e.g. Booz & Company, 2011; Capgemini, 2010). Therefore, it is particularly interesting to examine a demands-resources framework regarding work-life conflict of professionals in PSFs.

3.1.2 Formal versus Informal Demands and Resources

Several theoretical and empirical papers in the work-life arena explicitly distinguish demands and resources according to their character of being formal, i.e. based on some kind of policy or agreement between employee and employer, or informal, i.e. implicitly endorsed notions or 'dealing with things'. The formal/informal distinction is discussed by Holt and Thaulow (1996) specifically with regards to workplace flexibility. The authors refer to formal flexibility arrangements as "precisely detailed arrangements agreed upon in advance between employers and employees" (p. 82), whereas informal practices are referred to as "the unwritten rules, or workplace culture, which govern what is practice and what is permissible in the workplace" (p. 83). It is also pointed out that informal practices may either enable or limit formal arrangements. The thoughts of Holt and Thaulow referring to the concept of workplace flexibility can be extended towards the whole set of demands and resources which impact work-life dynamics: both demands and resources can be formal and informal in their character. Work-life benefits of all types are usually formalized in some way in the form of a written policy, often based on legislation (parental leave policies, etc.). If unwritten, policies are at least formalized in terms of a common agreement which applies for a certain group of employees or for the whole organization, such as the practice of flexible working hours. Informal resources, such as social support, are in contrast usually not formally agreed upon and in many cases not even consciously noticed by employee and employer. The same pattern applies for formal and informal demands. Demands such as work hours are usually based on some kind of agreement: even if an 80-hour workweek does not appear in employment contracts, employees in positions where such schedules are common know what to expect and are thus free to decide for or against such a job. Likewise travel requirements are usually based on a more or less formal agreement, e.g. by explicitly communicating extensive job-related travel obligations in job offers. An 'always-on' ethic (Hewlett & Luce, 2006) that is required in order to advance in a firm or being 'sanctioned' with slower or halted career advancement if work-life policies are used, are practices of informal character which again operate on an implicit level. Previous papers in the work-life area made such a distinction into formal/informal demands/resources with interesting findings. Anderson and colleagues (2002) found in a national sample of various employees in the U.S. that informal organizational practices were stronger predictors of work-family conflict than formal initiatives (dependent care and schedule flexibility). Similar results were provided by Burgess et al. (2007): formal programs to facilitate work and family balance had only limited potential to promote work-life integration of employees in (six) Australian organizations. Informal arrangements as well as informal managerial support proofed important in realizing satisfactory solutions of managing work and nonwork roles. An example for the impact of informal practices is the stigmatization of employees on part-time schedules through 'jokes' – which clearly is a lack of informal support – as described by Fuchs-Epstein and colleagues (1999) and Williams (2007).[18]

The distinction into formal and informal organizational demands and resources is also made in the present thesis. While demands and resources of both types are expected to affect work-life dynamics, the general expectation is that

---

18   Williams (2007) for example reports from a female lawyer being continuously asked
      which days she works long after she had returned to working full-time.

informal resources play a more important role in the PSF context because the culture in this branch is strongly characterized by the picture of the 'ideal worker' who is male and career-centered (Williams, 2007).

3.1.3 Patterns of Interaction of Demands and Resources: Person-Organization Fit

Individuals dispense of resources for coping with demands put upon them and at the same time have a set of needs related to the work-life interaction which are to a greater or lesser extent satisfied by the organization. The HR perspective of interacting needs and resources of individuals and organizations is reflected in the theory of person-organization (PO) fit. Its core ideas are pronounced by organization research scholar Chris Argyris who stated that

> "Organizations are characterized by particular types of climates and that these climates played an important role in the attraction and selection of employees [i.e.] companies hire people who are the 'right types'" (cited in Kristof-Brown and Jansen, 2007, p.123).

Compatibility of individuals with their social organizational environment (Caplan, 1987) was first and foremost researched with respect to value congruence. Chatman (1989) underscores the impact of a strong organizational culture on individual adaptation:

> "[...] When a person with discrepant values enters an organization characterized by strong values, the person's values are likely to change if that person is open to influence" (p. 343).

Fit was also discussed in terms of needs-supplies fit (employees needs are addressed by organizational supplies) and, in studies about employee recruitment, demands-abilities fit (organizational demands are met by potential employees' abilities) (Edwards & Shipp, 2007). These types of person-organization fit are described at different levels of the organization: between individuals and co-workers, supervisors, subordinates, as well as individuals and social groups, i.e. work groups, departments or the company as a whole. The degree of congruence between the employees' and organizations' values was shown to predict satisfaction and commitment better than either the employee's or organization's characteristics alone in a series of studies (Da Silva et al., 2010; Kristof, 1996; O'Reilly et al., 1991). In their meta-analysis Verquer, Beehr and Wagner (2003) found support for the notion that PO fit is associated with reduced employee turnover and increased satisfaction and commitment. The person-organization fit framework links to questions of work-life research: several researchers made fruitful attempts to theoretically and empirically associate characteristics of the work-life interface with the notion of compatibility of individuals and their environment / organization (Chen et al., 2009; Edwards & Rothbard, 1999, 2005; Kreiner, 2006; Lobel, 1992; Voydanoff, 2005c). Lobel (1992) discusses person-organization fit as value congruence and congruence of expectations in terms of work-life issues. In order to achieve fit she suggests evaluating the extent to which family and work expectations and rewards promote balance or imbalance. Mismatch (or misfit) may occur in terms of either unwillingness to adapt or inability of individuals to meet the values and expectations of the organization. From an organizational point of view, this relates to the image of an 'ideal' worker who in PSFs is characterized as work-centered, hard-working, highly committed and ever-accessible and responsive to firms' matters (cf. Barnett, 2004; Mescher, Benschop & Dooreward, 2010; Williams, 2007). Edwards and Rothbard (1999) in a large-scale quantitative study assessed fit regarding autonomy, relationships, security, and segmentation preference for both work and family, as well as the relationship of fit with work and family satisfaction, anxiety, depression, irritation, and somatic symptoms. Among other findings they reported that employee physical and psychological well-being improved if employees and organizations converged in their work-family value sets. Rothbard, Phillips and Dumas (2005) investigated fit between individuals' desires for integration or segmentation (keeping life spheres apart versus integrating them over the day or week) and their access to policies under the assumption that more policies may not always be better in terms of job satisfaction and organizational commitment. Using data of 460 employees they found that desire for greater segmentation moderated the relationship between available organizational policies and individuals' satisfaction and commitment. Respondents who preferred stronger borders between work and personal life were more satisfied and committed to the organization when they had greater access to policies which allowed segmentation instead of integration. Kreiner (2006) investigated how work-home conflict, stress and job satisfaction is affected by the interaction between an individual's work-home segmentation preference and the level of segmentation that is actually perceived to be provided by the workplace. Results demonstrated that integrating work and home is not per se the best strategy to ameliorate role conflict and stress: whether segmentation or integration is the strategy of choice strongly depends on specific individual preferences, i.e. whether individuals prefer to either integrate or segment life domains and whether they dispose of resources for following their preferred strategy. Chen, Powell and Greenhaus (2009) examined the linkage between congruence in individual work-family boundary management preferences (segmenting vs. integrating life domains) and respective work environment supplies in a sample of management employees. Congruence between desired behavior and organizational support was related to lower time-based and strain-based work-to-family conflict and stronger positive interaction between work-to-family (positive) spillover. Practically, this implies that conflict between work and life can be reduced by convergence of individual preferences to segment or integrate work and private life with supplies of the work environment to meet these preferences (i.e. fit).

These results underscore the importance of fostering PO fit with regards to work-life matters. In the present examination PO fit issues are taken into account particularly by examining different subgroups which potentially differ in their needs with regards to the work-life interface. While in the empirical study congruence between individual and organizational determinants will not be tested directly, PO fit serves as a framework for interpreting findings related to the different subgroups under examination. Professionals at a younger age, in their first years of employment, and at the beginning of their career may for example be more strongly inclined to invest their total energy in their job while employees at older ages have different work-life needs. Parents are likely to differ in their needs from childless professionals. Individual resources may also be a differentiating characteristic: having a partner may be associated with greater support and thus buffer the impact of work demands on the experience of work-life conflict. Potential groups of interest and their specificities concerning the dynamics of organizational demands and resources within the work-life interface will be discussed later in more detail (Part I, 3.4).

3.2 Organizational Demands and Resources and Professionals' Work-Life Conflict: a Review of the Literature

In times of increasingly flexible careers and high job demands, employees are finding it challenging to integrate work with the rest of their lives. However, although there are few direct comparisons of professionals and non-professionals with respect to their work-life interfaces, it was argued previously that business professionals, specifically professionals employed in PSFs are particularly prone to the experience of obstacles in reconciling work and personal life. Work demands were shown to be major if not the central predictors of work-life conflict. Following Voydanoff (2005a), general work strains are often associated with spillover, such that effects of one domain are transmitted to another domain through mechanisms of stress, negative emotions or energy depletion. As discussed previously (Part I, 2.2) *formal demands* such as extremely long working hours and high flexibility requirements which are typical in the professional context represent potential creators of work-life conflict.

Also *informal organizational norms* prevalent in firms impact the way how organizations and individuals deal with work-life challenges. Whether initiative users are threatened by negative career outcomes and whether career advancement potential is measured in terms of presence at the workplace is usually culturally endorsed and also affects individuals' decisions about their work-life strategies. As pointed out earlier, organizations are increasingly becoming aware of the potentially harmful outcomes of employees' work-life reconciliation struggles and are starting to provide *organizational resources* in order to deal with this issue. Individual and organizational resources were described by Stock-Homburg and Bauer (2007) as

> "[…] conditions that support the manager in achieving and sustaining a good balance between work and personal life. If a manager can meet his/her work demands with adequate and sufficient resources, a high work engagement is possible" (p. 30).

Formal resources, i.e. work-life initiatives are usually implemented within a HRM benefit framework. *Informal resources* are recently being considered more strongly by work-life research but not so, as it seems, in organizational practice.

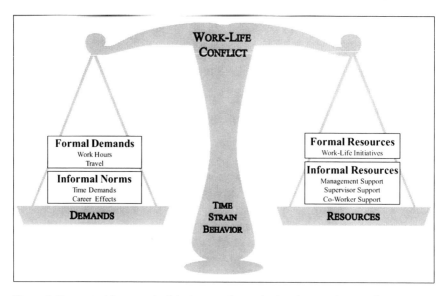

Figure 5. Conceptual framework of the impact of organizational antecedents on the time-, strain, and behavior-based work-life conflict of professionals

The basic assumption of the conceptual framework underlying the present thesis (figure 5) is that if PSFs demand a lot from their employees but want to maintain their highly-skilled workforce they must also provide resources that enable these professionals to cope with these demands. Under examination are factors that impede and factors that enable the achievement of work-life 'balance' or, in scientific terms, the avoidance of time-, strain-, and behavior-based work-life conflict. The subsequent paragraphs build a foundation for this endeavor by reviewing research evidence on the work-life interface of professionals focusing on *formal organizational demands* (work hours, job-related travel), *formal organizational resources* (work-life policies: dependent care initiatives, temporal and spatial initiatives, and secondary initiatives), and organizational culture which provides *informal organizational resources* (managerial, supervisor, and co-worker support) and at the same time represents *informal organizational demands* (time demands, negative career impact as a result of making use of work-life initiatives).[19]

3.2.1 Formal Organizational Demands: Work Hours and Job-Related Travel

3.2.1.1 Long Work Hours

It is generally agreed upon that business professionals work disproportionately long hours. Weekly work hours of 50 to 60 or more are often rather the norm than the exception (Blair-Loy, 2009; Brett & Stroh, 2003; Hewlett & Luce, 2006; Perlow & Porter, 2009; Schor, 1998). A look at how long exactly the professionals in the studies under review work reveals that weekly work hours range from 37.90 (male and female managers, studied by Taris et al., 2006) to 59.68 (top managers of a large-sized Swiss company, studied by Jacobshagen et al., 2005). Obviously there are large differences in the range of professionals' work hours, although visibly most professional samples work on average between 45 and 55 hours weekly (cf. Appendix A, Table A.5). Following Brett and Stroh (2003), "there seems to be little question that well-educated managers and professionals are working extremely long hours, especially those working in large corporations" (p. 67).

Not only as a function of the development of the *24/7 economy*, working times of professionals do not comply with a 'classic' 9–5 pattern (Burke, 2009).

---

19   Note that this literature review is not exhaustive but rather concentrates on major studies in the field which were identified within the research project "Innovative Concepts of Human Resource and Organizational Development in Consulting Organizations (IPOB)" situated at the Catholic University Eichstätt-Ingolstadt. During three years of research a large body of literature was identified and for the current review again complemented with relevant studies using the databases BusinessSourcePremier, PsychInfo, and Psyndex on EBSCO-Host.

Professionals work overtime on a regular basis perceiving 50 to 60 hour work-weeks as standard full-time employment, refrain from using their vacation time (or work during holidays), and work during the lunch break (Brett & Stroh, 2003; Burke, 2009; Messersmith, 2007; Williams, 2007). The fact that professional work is to a large extent *knowledge work* has implications for the amount of work hours. As working devices are becoming portable, work can be done from virtually anywhere and anytime and thus often happens to be 'out of sight, out of mind' of supervisors and co-workers. Particularly in PSFs as the "knowledge engines for business" (Lorsch & Tierney, 2002, p. 15), knowledge-based output is intangible and hard to measure – with the implication that work is never finished at the end of the work day. This has rendered 'face time' a primary indicator for productivity, job commitment and performance (Milliken & Dunn-Jensen, 2005; Brett & Stroh, 2003). In their prominent study of law firm professionals, Fuchs Epstein and colleagues (1999) argue that "excellence and commitment [are measured] not only by productivity and competence but by the number of hours logged and its visibility to colleagues and managers" (p. 4) and so time becomes "a proxy for dedication and excellence" (p. 22). Besides demands imposed on behalf of the organization reasons for excessively long work hours are also sought in the individuals themselves. *Workaholism* and *work addiction* are commonly known phenomena particularly among highly qualified employees (Brett & Stroh, 2003). Individuals with "an unforced addiction to incessant work activity" (Golden, 2009, p. 107) may be regarded as enthusiastic. Bonebright and colleagues (2000) examined work-life conflict among 'enthusiastic' and 'non-enthusiastic' workaholics with the finding that the latter group experienced significantly more work-life conflict and less life satisfaction than non-workaholics. Enthusiastic workaholics, who also experienced higher work-life conflict than non-workaholics, at the same time were more strongly satisfied with their lives than non-workaholics and non-enthusiastic workaholics. This leads us again to the question whether professionals really have a problem reconciling their life spheres which was discussed extensively in previous sections.

Whichever specific situation applies for an individual, personal time and energy are limited resources and will always be associated with priorities and trade-offs. The conservation of resources (COR) theory suggested by Hobfoll (1989, 2001) states that the trading of resources is a natural reaction to stress in order to achieve and maintain a state of balance and satisfaction. Resources are "those objects, personal characteristics, conditions, or energies that are valued by the individual or that serve as a means for attainment of these objects, personal characteristics, conditions, or energies" (Hobfoll, 1989, p. 514). Transferring these thoughts to the potential damage of overly long work hours on individuals, although work may be rewarding and fulfilling to a proportion of professionals research principally indicates that the larger share of professionals will try to limit the trade-offs of a demanding job.

While Major, Klein and Ehrhart (2002) pointed out that surprisingly little research examined the direct *impact of work hours on work-life conflict*, available evidence largely unites in the finding that with rising work hours, levels of pereived conflict among work and personal life increases. Madsen (2003) confirmed the positive relationship between number of weekly work hours and time-based work-family conflict for teleworkers, not so though for non-teleworkers. In an international study including five European countries the amount of work hours per week was the strongest predictor of work-family conflict (Crompton & Lyonette, 2006). Frye and Breaugh (2004) found that the number of work hours was significantly positively related to work-family conflict, however with a comparatively small path coefficient ($\lambda = .05, p < .05$); Frone (2000) reported a respective correlation of $r = .20$ in a U.S. sample of over 6,000 workers. In a large-scale study in the Netherlands contractual work hours and overtime hours were positively related to work-family interference (Geurts et al., 2008). A recently published meta-analysis suggests an average correlation of work time demands (including direct measures of work hours) of $\rho = .30$ with work-to-family conflict from 81 included studies (Michel et al., 2010).

With regards to professionals specifically, results consistently give evidence to the impact of work hours in increasing work-family conflict (Aryee, 1992; Batt & Valcour, 2003; Kossek et al., 2006; Jacobshagen et al., 2005; Judge et al., 1994; Nielsen et al., 2001; Taris et al., 2006; Thompson et al., 1999; Wharton & Blair-Loy, 2006; Wallace, 2009) (cf. Appendix A, Table A.1). A cross-national study among managers and professionals based in the United States, London, and Hong Kong indicated that "for every additional hour worked, the odds that a respondent will express concern about the effect of long hours on his or her family and personal lives increase by seven per cent" (Wharton & Blair-Loy, 2006, p. 426). Swiss top managers who work on average 60 hours weekly were shown to experience work-family conflict as a function of work hours (Jacobshagen et al., 2005). Batt and Valcour (2003), in a sample that consisted of 71 per cent managers and professionals, found that long work hours were related to increased work-family conflict for women. This association was also reported in an investigation of married professional women in dual-career families in an Asian context (Aryee, 1992). Among professionals and managers (Thompson et al., 1999), senior managers (Gutek et al., 1991), U.S. executives (Judge et al., 1994), business professionals (Nielsen et al., 2001), lawyers (Wallace, 2009), and teleworking professionals in Fortune 500 companies (Kossek et al., 2006) were found to experience higher levels of work-family conflict as a function of excessive work hours. Taris et al. (2006) found that overtime was associated with higher levels of work-family conflict among male and female managers in a Dutch retail organization. Major, Klein and Ehrhart (2002) who studied Fortune 500 enterprises' employees demonstrated that work time significantly predicted time-based work interference with family and indirectly affected psychological distress. In this examination, together with work overload and organizational norms (expected time spent at work), work time predicted 39 per cent of the variance in work interference with family. Of the studies reviewed here, only in the investigation of Cinamon and Rich (2002a) who studied the work-life interface of Israeli computer workers the number of work hours was not significantly correlated with work-family conflict. A very closely related stream of research examined work overload, a primary cause of excessive work hours (Brett & Stroh, 2003), and its impact on work-personal life integration. Consistent with findings on work hours, work (over)load was found to be positively associated with increased work-family conflict among IT road warriors (Ahuja et al., 2007), public accountants (Greenhaus et al., 1997), and law firm professionals (Wallace, 1997).

In summary, prior research strongly supports the notion that excessive work demands and first and foremost long work hours are related to conflict between work and personal life as extreme work hours can simply take away time for nearly anything else. As work is the domain in which full-time professionals spend most of their available time, due to their engagement and willingness to high-perform (Kofodimos, 1990) such conflict occurs primarily from work to family and not vice versa. Almost exclusively, researchers who studied the impact of work hours on the work-life interface focused on the work-family dichotomy with a few rare exceptions. Aryee (1992) investigated three types of conflict with the finding that weekly work hours were significantly related to higher job-spouse conflict, job-parent conflict, and job-homemaker conflict. Results from a sample of Australian university administration employees suggest that work hours are related to the more general concept of work-personal life interference (Hayman, 2009). Day and Chamberlain (2006) report from female police officers and nurses that work flexibility and the number of work hours predicted job-parent conflict but not job-partner conflict.

In the present study the work hours $\rightarrow$ work-life conflict relationship is examined differentially in terms of time-based, strain-based and behavior-based conflict. Additionally, it is appropriate and interesting to examine the 'formal' measure of actual (self-reported) work hours as compared to culturally and informally expected time spent at work (cf. 3.2.3). For the present empirical examination it is postulated that:

Hypothesis 1a: *(Long) Work hours are positively related to time-based, strain-based, and behavior-based work-to-life conflict.*

3.2.1.2 Job-Related Travel

On top of excessive work hours, flexibility is a requirement of most of today's highly qualified jobs which often entails the readiness to travel frequently (Kofodimos, 1990; Mayerhofer et al., 2008). In some professional jobs travel is inherently part of the working pattern, e.g. if the location of the employer differs from the location of the actual task. This is the case in many project-based jobs where the work location changes with every new project (e.g. Ahuja et al., 2007). Professional service firms very frequently operate this way, especially consulting organizations. Professionals spent the larger share of their workweek at the client site and are usually only in their employing firm's site on office (Fri)day. Job-related travel is bound to collide with interests and responsibilities located in other life spheres for various reasons. Time and energy are limited resources and the more time is spent working and traveling, obviously less time is available for other activities. If employees experience this disproportionate amount of time spent at work as a strain, they may try to change this undesirable state, e.g. by quitting their demanding job (Shaffer et al., 2001). This notion goes in line with the conservation of resources theory (cf. previous section) suggested by Hobfoll (1989, 2001). Traveling is time-intense, but particularly in professional jobs, hours spent on the train, at the airport or on the plane, are often not acknowledged as working time. Mayerhofer, Müller and Schmidt (2008) interviewed flexpatriates on how they deal with the challenges of their job: one flexpatriate indicated the wish "that times traveling are, at least in part, recognized as working times […]; you often spend up to 20 hours a week on transport and this is nowhere registered" (p. 109). Hence, professionals whose work is associated with frequent travel face a double burden: they are involved in highly complex tasks with high workload and tight deadlines and on top of that, they spend a considerable amount of time on transportation. Ahuja and colleagues (2007) argue that companies try to reduce traveling times by staffing projects with employees close to the region of the client, while exactly the contrary was indicated by former management consultant Joe O'Mahoney (2007). He unravels the tough working conditions in PSFs and describes the immense traveling demands stating that "home, for many [of his colleagues], became little more than an abstract notion" (p. 290). Although Welch and Worm (2006) pointed out that job-related international travel can also be a treat for employees in the sense of novel experiences and lifestyle, it does seem that negative outcomes which particularly affect work-life issues (separation from the family, stress, health issues, etc.) by far outweigh the benefits.

Surprisingly little research exists on how *job-related travel affects the work-life interface*. Although intuitively the frequency and lengthiness of business travels are likely to increase work-life conflicts, few studies have taken a look at the direct effect of travel requirements on these dynamics. Working in multiple time zones and frequent travel are listed as characteristics of extreme jobs (Hewlett & Luce, 2006) but except for the small body of literature on flexpatriates (e.g. Mayerhofer et al., 2011) for whom 'travel' is usually long-term, there are very few studies that investigate the impact of frequent travel on work-life conflict. Drawing on descriptive data, Stock-Homburg and Bauer (2007) rated travel among one of the top four factors that created work stress in a sample of top managers. Hooks and Higgs (2002) examined the work environment of accountants and the mobility of their work. They found that particularly the partners being the highest organizational rank in PSFs report working from nonstandard locations, especially on weekends. Five studies which investigated work-life conflict among samples characterized by high travel frequency were identified (Ahuja et al., 2007; Batt & Valcour, 2003; Shaffer et al., 2001; Shaffer & Joplin, 2001; Westman et al., 2008). Ahuja et al. (2007) studied IT road warriors (including 54% females) who usually spend four days at the client site and Friday at home to do paperwork. Although no direct effect of travel was tested, they found that perceived work overload, presumably created at least partly by the additional requirement to travel to and from the client site at least once a week, predicted 24% of the variance of work-family conflict. The experience of conflict was related to work exhaustion and reduced organizational commitment which in turn increased the likeliness of leaving the organization. Shaffer et al. (2001) examined work-family conflict, dimensions of support, and commitment among expatriates with various nationalities. Work-family conflict occurring in both directions increased the intention to return early from their international assignment. Interestingly, the researchers found that high organizational commitment even exacerbates this effect, i.e. highly committed expatriates who experience work-family conflict are more likely to return home early than not so committed expatriates. Shaffer and Joplin (2001) represent the only study to date where job-related travel is directly related to increased work-family conflict, of altogether two studies that investigated this association. The authors found that business travel was associated with high levels of time-based work-life conflict among expatriates living in Hong Kong who worked in various occupations. Longitudinal support for the problematic impact of job-related travel on the work and personal life interface was further provided by Westman and colleagues (2008). Sixty-six international business travelers answered questionnaires three times: before, during and after their business trip. Men experienced relatively stable levels of work-family conflict at all three stages of the trip whereas for women conflict was lowest during the trip and highest afterwards. Further, the researchers found a reciprocal relationship of work-family conflict and burnout. In a study of dual-earner white-collar employees no association between business travel and work-family conflict was detected (Batt & Valcour, 2003).

While there are few direct results on the relationship of job-related travel and work-life conflict, existing evidence as well as logic reasoning suggests a positive association. Particularly in professional occupations where workload and pressure tend to be continuously high, business trips are highly probable to represent an additional demand. As professionals usually are informed about the requirement of travel in their jobs – and thus travel is to some extent based on a formal agreement between employee and employer – in the present study travel frequency is examined as a formal organizational demand. It is postulated here that job-related travel is a major formal organizational demand which increases the perception of work-to-life conflict among professionals:

Hypothesis 1b: Job-related travel is positively related to time-based, strain-based, and behavior-based work-to-life conflict.

3.2.2 Formal Organizational Resources: Corporate Work-Life Initiatives

Employee benefits in the form of corporate policies and initiatives are a central component of the strategic human resource management of an organization (Dulebohn et al., 2009; Ringlstetter & Kaiser, 2008). Among these benefits, firms offer a variety of initiatives that target employee needs with respect to work-life integration (Harrington & Ladge, 2009). *Work-life initiatives* are

"Policies, programs, practices, and benefits that are intentionally designed to promote healthy integration, balance, enrichment, harmony, and facilitation in the interface between the domains of work and life, while also alleviating or ameliorating the bidirectional stressful demands, conflicts, and tensions between the work and life domains. [...] Work-life interventions enable individuals to experience greater and more optimal work-life situations (e.g., balance versus conflict), enabling them to unleash levels of human expertise for maximized levels of performance" (Morris, Storberg-Walker & McMillan, 2009, p. 421).

This description underscores the notion that work-life benefits pursue the specific aim of optimizing employees' work-life interactions in order to attain the strategic goal of maximizing their performance. Within the typology of re-

wards in corporate HR benefit systems described by Ringlstetter and Kaiser
(2008) work-life initiatives can be located among monetary benefits (e.g. financial childcare support) while the majority of them range among intangible benefits, specifically in the design of the work task (e.g. volume), the workplace (i.e.
working from home) and work time (i.e. temporal flexibility, etc.). Even though
these policies and their level of formal implementation vary, a set of initiatives
is available in virtually every company, not least because a number of such policies (e.g. parental leave) are based upon governmental regulations (Crompton &
Lyonette, 2006). Prevalent forms of corporate work-life initiatives are flexible
work arrangements (regarding time and location), leave policies, childcare and
eldercare services and general resource services (Frone, 2003). In order to find
out which type of initiative is most helpful for employees, attempts have been
made to categorize them from a scientific point of view resulting in different
schemes of WLB initiative types. Thompson, Beauvais and Allen (2006) distinguish organizational policies according to their structural character into time-
based strategies, information-based strategies, money-based strategies, and direct services. *Time-based strategies* include flexible work schedules such as job
sharing or part-time arrangements and leave programs such as parental leave,
sick leave or childcare/eldercare leaves. *Information-based strategies* focus on
providing relevant information about support groups, seminars related to work-
life balance (e.g. time management trainings), relocation assistance or preretire-
ment planning. Zedeck and Mosier (1990) count providing information to employees to the most cost-effective option for a company. *Money-based strategies*
provide workers with financial help, e.g. regarding health or care insurance,
childcare arrangements and adoption assistance (Thompson, Beauvais & Allen,
2006). Money-based initiatives in a wider sense can also refer to leaves and
rehiring strategies (Zedeck & Mosier, 1990; Harrington & James, 2009) such as
rehiring arrangements after parental leaves or leaves associated with further
education (PhD, MBA, etc.). *Direct services* are provided directly by the company such as childcare, eldercare, holiday and vacation programs for employees'
children, before/after school programs as well as fitness centers and concierge
services (Thompson, Beauvais & Allen, 2006). Other classifications were made
trying to structure the variety of corporate work-life policies. Dikkers et al.
(2004) differentiate only two categories, flexible arrangements (e.g., flextime,
telecommuting, and part-time work) and dependent-care arrangements.
Poelmans and Beham (2008b) suggest that initiatives consist largely of 1) flexibility policies with respect to time vs. location, 2) leave arrangements, 3) care
provisions, 4) supportive arrangements such as information services or work-
shops and seminars, and 5) conventional provisions (e.g. compensation benefits). Kossek and Friede (2006) also differentiate in terms of flexibility of work-

ing time and place, as well as support with care responsibilities and informational and social supports (hotlines, support groups).

While all these classifications are important in their own right, the majority neglect policies that are aimed at anything else but the reconciliation of the work and family domains. For an exception Poelmans and Beham (2008b) also list wellness and stress management programs among their supportive arrangements, but the vast majority of research works does not include initiatives that reach beyond the work-family facet of work-life reconciliation. Additionally, work-life initiatives are investigated at a very general level; neither are specific characteristics of a branch taken into account nor the potential needs of certain occupations (e.g. shift workers or flexpatriates). In the subsequent paragraphs work-life benefits are examined more closely which specific focus on PSFs. First of all, based on a qualitative analysis of PSF websites, a classification of work-life initiatives is suggested, including those benefits aimed at balancing life spheres in a more general sense but specifically within this organizational context. Secondly existing research evidence is reviewed with respect to the usefulness of such work-life arrangements for meeting challenges at the work-life border, taking particularly professional samples into focus.

3.2.2.1 Work-Life Initiatives in Professional Service Firms

A considerable number of young professionals who start working in PSFs soon make their decision for or against the sacrifices on behalf of other life spheres that seem necessary in order to foster their career. Hence, career systems incorporate a certain level of calculated employee turnover. Connor, Hooks and McGuire (1999) state that "there has been some degree of acceptance that fairly significant turnover (i.e. 20% or more annually) is inherent in the profession" (p. 155). In the meantime, due to increased specialization, technological advancements (e.g. automated by computers) which minimize the new-entry staff needed, and changes in workforce demographics leading to an aging population and a shortage of professionals[20] PSFs are increasingly determined to reduce undesired turnover (Connor, Hooks & McGuire, 1999). Attempts to do so include a stronger appreciation of employees as 'intellectual capital' that is worth retaining in order to serve clients' needs and entail the establishment of changing recruitment strategies and retention benefits (Werr & Schilling, 2010). Employee recruiting, likely more strongly than employee retention, frequently draws on the issue of work-life balance. Ostendorp (2007) pointed out that among the major reasons for implementing and communicating work-life benefits are marketing purposes. Likewise, Thompson (2008) suggests that organizations offer

---

20   Cf. Part I, 1.1.

work-life programs "for public relations, to increase likelihood that the company will be perceived as a caring organization, worthy of a 'top 100' list of 'family-friendly' companies" (p. 227). Most large and medium-sized firms present a work/life section on their websites with flagships, mostly working mothers, how well the company serves their employees' needs (cf. Figure 6).

There is limited evidence with regards to the actual availability and use of corporate work-life policies in PSFs. Dikkers et al. (2004) report frequent usage of flexible work hours, home office, and part-time in a consulting firm sample.[21] In a study within the German consultancy context so-called office day, educational programs, home office, and trading-off overtime hours for leisure time as well as health and recovery initiatives and sabbaticals were frequently used benefits (Kaiser et al., 2010).

Figure 6. "I made my decision in favor of a demanding job. Not against my life" – Recruiting
advertisement (Source: Booz & Co, 2011)

---

21   Altogether the use of the following six initiatives was examined: flexible working
      hours, working from home occasionally, part-time work, telecommuting, financial
      child-care support, and parental leave (Dikkers et al., 2004).

Drawing a more objective picture of the work-life initiatives offered in PSFs, a qualitative analysis of the web sites of consultancies was conducted[22] within the research project "Innovative Concepts of Personnel and Organizational Development in Consulting Organizations (IPOB)" which specifically investigates the role of work-life balance in this type of organizations. Consulting organizations were chosen according to the Lünendonck index[23] published in 2007, a regular analysis of the consultancy market producing a list of the top 25 German consulting organizations with respect to their annual sales and number of employees. Each of these firms' websites was searched thoroughly for information on how the company deals with work-life issues. Most of this information was found in the 'career' section, i.e. on the sites aimed at attracting new employees. The procedure of this qualitative approach was deductive and inductive at the same time.[24] Deductively, it was tried to retrieve initiatives that are well-known from the work-life literature, such as flexible work and care arrangements. However, in the attempt to keep the scope of this examination open towards initiatives which reach beyond reconciling work and family, every initiative found on web sites was listed serving as a basis for categorizing the search results inductively (Table 1).

The majority of findings were grouped into 'primary' work-life initiatives summarizing all benefits that are more closely linked to the idea of solving existing conflict between work and personal life including flexible work arrangements, dependent care arrangements, home office, office day, and free choice of residence. The remaining initiatives were grouped as 'secondary' initiatives because they do support individuals in their work-life integration and yet reach beyond this issue: coaching and mentoring, health and recovery initiatives, and support for educational programs. It was expected from anecdotal evidence that supportive services such as laundry or postal services would also be found, but this was not the case.

---

22   Web sites were examined for work-life issues by search functions and by scouring primarily the recruitment section. Other sections, such as press and communication and corporate culture were searched thoroughly, too.

23   Lünendonck GmbH is a market research institution specialized on systematic marketing research, analysis and consulting in the fields of information technology, consulting, and highly qualified service providers (http://www.luenendonck.de).

24   A deductive strategy develops a set of assumptions based on existing research or a theoretical basis which are tested empirically, whereas an inductive strategy deduces categories directly from the material under observation without reference to theory. Only in the subsequent interpretation existing findings and theories are considered (Mayring, 2000). An inductive strategy has also been referred to as "open coding" in the grounded theory methodology (Strauss, 1987).

Table 1. Work-life benefits offered in the top 25 German management consultancies according to their websites

'Primary' Work-Life Initiatives	No.[a]	'Secondary' Initiatives	No.[a]
Temporal (Flexible) Work Arrangements		*Coaching & Mentoring*	16
Reduced Work Schedule	7	*Health and Recovery Initiatives*	2
Short-term Flexible Work Hours	7	*Support for Educational Programs (MBA, etc.)*	15
Long-term Flexible Work Hours	2	*Supportive Services (Laundry Service, etc.)*	-
Dependent Care Arrangements			
Childcare Services and Support	5		
Eldercare Services and Support	2		
Home Office	4		
Office Day	5		
Free Choice of Residence	2		
Leave of Absence / Sabbatical	11		

[a] Number of firms that offer this initiative.

Note, that this analysis can only be an illustration of the work-life integration management strategy communicated by the largest consulting firms in Germany. The finding that firms promote a set of initiatives on websites gives us no idea about the actual use of these initiatives in the company. At the same time the fact that for nine companies out of twenty-five no initiatives and no work-life section were found on their web sites does not indicate that they do not offer any initiatives. It only means they do not communicate this issue online. What we can deduce from this brief analysis however, is a picture of the strategies (professional service) organizations use for managing work-life challenges – at least for recruitment purposes. It was observed that those firms which explicitly communicate work-life initiatives do not differ largely regarding the sets of initiatives they offer. However, values in Table 1 should not be interpreted quantitatively because firms may consider an initiative suitable for promoting work-life integration and therefore communicate it while other organizations may not. Office day for example is the practice that usually on Friday professionals work at the firm office they are assigned to, contrary to the first four days of the week where most consultants work at the client site.

Although the web analysis only provides a hint on the availability of work-life initiatives in consulting firms, it gives us a valuable idea of the way this topic is dealt with in PSFs. Some of these initiatives may be organizational reality, others rather a communicative rhetoric (Mohe et al., 2010). First and foremost, initiatives that were identified in this paragraph will be used in Part II in order to examine the effects of the use and availability of work-life initiatives on work-life conflict in a PSF context. As a further prerequisite for empirical research it is necessary to obtain a clear picture of existing evidence of the effects of work-life interventions on the work-life interface.

3.2.2.2 Work-Life Initiatives and their Impact on Work-Life Conflict

The central question here is of course whether work-life initiatives are really useful for promoting work-life balance and related personal and organizational benefits. A first hint to the usefulness of work-life initiatives are the results of meta-analyses. Four publications systematically reviewed existing empirical evidence (Kossek & Ozeki, 1998, 1999; Baltes et al., 1999; Mesmer-Magnus & Viswesvaran, 2007). In their meta-analysis focusing on effects of work-family conflict on job satisfaction, Kossek and Ozeki (1998) note with surprise that most studies focus either on the conflict-satisfaction relationship or on the link between using work-life initiatives and job satisfaction. Research about reduced levels of work-life conflict as a result of initiative use was scarce to that point. In their review one year later, Kossek and Ozeki (1999) discuss four studies that did investigate the impact of policy use with two findings in favor of reduced conflict (Kossek & Ozeki, 1999). Baltes and his team (1999) meta-analytically examined the effects of flexible and compressed workweek schedules on work-related outcomes. They found positive effects of flexible schedules on productivity, job satisfaction, and absenteeism. Compressed workweeks had favorable effects on supervisor performance ratings and job satisfaction. Again however, no findings were reported with regards to direct effects on conflict between work and personal life. An interesting finding was that generally positive effects of flexible and compressed schedules did not apply for managers and professionals, as had been hypothesized *a priori*. Baltes et al. argue that this is the case because for professionals a comparatively large scope of flexibility is inherent in their schedules, compared to other blue- and white-collar employees. Mesmer-Magnus and Viswesvaran (2007) meta-analytically examined effects of family-friendly work environments on work-family conflict with the finding that flexibility policies and dependent care are indeed related to reduced WFC. Particularly initiatives that increase flexibility were found to assist employees in their integration of work and family needs. However, the authors did not differentiate among subsamples, initiatives were assessed on a relatively general level (summed scores), and the number of correlations (i.e. studies) which were ana-lyzed does not exceed ten (nine studies in the case of 'overall WLC' measures, five studies in the case of flexibility → work-to-family conflict, and three in the case of dependent care → work-to-family conflict). For these reasons also the meta-analytic results of Mesmer-Magnus and Viswesvaran have to be interpret-ed with caution.[25]

Generally it must be noted that the majority of quantitative studies uses summed scores of used or available initiatives (Kelly et al., 2008) which makes it difficult to infer the actual benefit of one individual initiative. Qualitative studies tend to focus more specifically on one or few initiatives but due to their small scope their generalizability is very limited. Furthermore, initiatives largely refer to the rather traditional idea of supporting work-life integration in terms of work and family. Benefits that touch a broader scope of the work-life interface, e.g. recovery or individual development were rarely examined in past research. While particularly PSFs like to position themselves among 'people-friendly' and 'family-friendly' firms, for example by acquiring certifications in this area (von Kettler, 2010), evidence on the actual use of these initiatives and their effect on work-life reconciliation is scarce. In the proceeding section effects of initiative availability and use of benefits that are also available in PSFs on professionals' work-life dynamics are examined in more detail.

Dependent Care Initiatives. The point of view that 'work-life balance' means having both a successful career and a satisfactory family life put child-care arrangements in the center of attention. Moreover, demographic change has added the necessity to think about care arrangements for elderly relatives and parents. While dependent care arrangements are more pertinent than ever in the landscape of organizational work-life benefits, organizations seem to be reluc-tant in communicating respective initiatives. Besides the fact that these policies only address a certain part of the workforce, professionals in need of childcare and eldercare arrangements are unlikely to be top of the list of the 'employees of choice' because care arrangements are expensive and responsibility for depend-ents entails an amount of incalculable risk for the employer, e.g. absenteeism due to a sick child. The observation that many professionals start their career in a PSF and quit into a more settled job after a number of 'all-in' years further explains the marginal consideration of dependent care arrangements in these environments. Supportive of this notion, in a recent study of management con-

---

25 Presumably Mesmer-Magnus and Viswesvaran (2007) excluded a number of major studies due to their search strategy. They searched the database PsychInfo but did not search within the database BusinessSourcePremier, a major scientific database that also includes a large number of publications within the work-life arena.

sultants, childcare was among the least used initiatives (Kaiser et al., 2010). It was further shown that many professionals have a homemaking spouse and are thus not concerned with the issue of childcare or eldercare at all (Abele & Volmer, 2011; Bacik & Drew, 2006). Nevertheless organizations and also PSFs offer a set of dependent care arrangements, from support with finding adequate arrangements, the rare case of on-site kindergartens and/or nurseries, to emergency care arrangements. Limited empirical evidence for the effectiveness of this type of benefit can be found in the existing research. A review of Eby and her colleagues (2005) pointed out that satisfaction with childcare (and not the offer of childcare itself) decreases work-life conflict. Berg and colleagues (2003) reported that access to childcare referral services was positively associated with work-family balance in a large-scale sample, while in a sample of business professionals this effect was not found (Taylor, Delcampo & Blanchero, 2009). O'Driscoll et al. (2003) surveyed managers with regards to the use of four dependent care initiatives (summed with the use and availability of further six initiatives) with the finding that benefit availability was not associated with work-family interference but benefit use was significantly associated with reduced work-to-family interference. In a Dutch sample, levels of work-home interference were significantly reduced for users of subsidized childcare, but these inferences were based on small correlations only (Dikkers et al., 2007a). Unfortunately, the fact that most studies worked with summed scores impedes more detailed inferences about the effectiveness of specific dependent care benefits. But due to the findings mentioned here, it is likely that employer-sponsored childcare does not play a large role for the work-life dynamics of professionals, additionally bearing in mind that managers and professionals dispense of sufficient resources for affording private childcare to suit their needs (O'Driscoll et al., 2003).

Temporal Work-Life Initiatives. The most prominent and frequently available initiatives that focus primarily on the temporal dimension of work are flexible work arrangements, reduced schedules, and leave policies, such as sabbaticals. Several types of initiatives offered in organizations focus on the *flexibilization of working time* without changing the total volume of contractual hours. Such initiatives can be short-term oriented, i.e. giving employees the flexibility to choose the starting and ending times of their work schedule (Sutton & Noe, 2005), often referred to as flex(i)time or trust-based flextime. Flexible initiatives based on a long-term perspective usually operate with time-saving accounts that can be used for longer vacation time and paid leaves (Deller, 2004) or for compressed work weeks (Baltes et al., 1999). These flexibility initiatives allow employees to self-control their work schedule to a larger or smaller extent, depending on business requirements as well as the personal situation. Business requirements are an important but often neglected issue as organizations may also use flexible schedules to suit primarily their needs. Trinczek (2006) argues that companies use flexible schedules as an elastic instrument for dealing with changing work volumes, and, as work hours become harder to measure in flexible arrangements, result in a general increase of working hours. Hence, flexibility policies are not necessarily aimed at ameliorating employees' work-life interface, though they did in a number of studies: *use* of flexibilization policies (Hill et al., 2001; Russell, O'Connell & McGinnity, 2009; Shockley & Allen, 2007) as well as their *availability* (Hayman, 2009; Smith & Gardner (2007) were demonstrated to be related to reduced levels of work-family conflict. With regards to professionals, findings that suggest better balancing of life domains as a result of initiatives equal the amount of those results which do *not* support such an effect. Managers reported that using benefits, including flextime, reduced their work-to-family interference (O'Driscoll et al., 2003), the same was found in a sample of Israeli computer workers and lawyers (Cinamon & Rich, 2002a). Taylor et al. (2009) reported that the *availability* of alternative work arrangements (and dependent care supports) was not related to reduced levels of work-to-family conflict. Data of financial consultants concurrently indicate that the *use* of such initiatives does not affect work-to-family conflict (Dikkers et al., 2004). In a sample of U.S. managers and professionals, the initiative access → work-family conflict association became insignificant when the perception of a family-friendly work culture was also considered (Thompson et al., 1999). Among public accountants it was found that the availability and use of flexible work arrangements lowered the relationship between work-family interference and job satisfaction, i.e. those accountants who were able to use or did actually use flexibility policies were more satisfied with their jobs even though they perceived work-family conflict (Pasewark & Viator, 2006). Another temporal work-life initiative is a *reduced schedule* or part-time work which is more frequently used by women than men (Dikkers et al., 2004; Fuchs-Epstein et al., 1999; Hill et al., 2006; Kossek et al., 1999; Poelmans & Beham, 2008b). The time volume associated with part-time varies and is usually adaptable to the individual needs of employees. Whereas the traditional part-time model comprises half of the standard working time, in recent years more individualized models are becoming available, such as reducing hours to 60 or 80 percent (Lee et al., 2002) or a 60-hour schedule of both partners together (Hill et al., 2006). Associated with part-time employment is the policy of *job sharing* where usually two employees work on the same job position, task or project (Deller, 2004; Rustemeyer & Buchmann, 2010; Sutton & Noe, 2005). It is argued that in job sharing options accomplishment is often larger than in the case of one full-time worker doing the same job (Kossek et al., 1999). However, researchers and theorists showed that working part-time is particularly associated with slower or halted career advancement. Fuchs Epstein et al. (1999) state that lawyers who work part-time "are challenging [a] key part of the profession's traditional culture; they have become 'time deviants' who are flouting the time norms of professional life" (p. 4). Additionally, in highly demanding work environments such as professional service firms, a reduced schedule may signify working 'only' 40 to 50 hours per week, as illustrated by Williams (2007):

"Typically, a part-time schedule in a law firm is the traditional full-time schedule of other workers – a forty hour workweek – as opposed to the new full-time schedule of law firm lawyers – a sixty or eighty hour workweek" (p. 384).

Existing research within professional samples of different character suggests that reduced schedule options have limited success for solving problems at the work-personal life frontline. Dikkers et al. (2004) found no effect of work-life initiatives that included part-time on work-family interference. Although benefit usage was associated with reduced work-to-family interference in the study of O'Driscoll et al. (2003), the summed score measure does not allow inferences on the specific effect of part-time work. Van Rijswijk et al. (2004) did find an association among part-time and work-to-family interference in a sample of part-time and full-time employed mothers of various occupations. In a large U.S. firm, Hill et al. (2006) tested the success of the dual-earner 60-hour workweek where each partner works on a 30-hour schedule. Sixty-hour couples indeed reported significantly lower levels of work-to-family conflict as well as higher job satisfaction showing how IBM successfully manages to retain highly qualified and highly specialized professionals (cf. also Hill et al., 2004). In a qualitative study of reduced-load professionals and managers, the striking majority of participants (91%) reported being happier and more satisfied with the balancing of their life spheres than they were on full schedule (Lee et al., 2002). Note however, that these professionals still worked on average on a 70 per cent schedule, which is probably an equivalent or still longer workweek than the average employee. While attesting usefulness to reduced schedules as a work-life benefit, Lirio et al. (2008), drawing on qualitative data, emphasize the crucial role of the supervisor in advocating the support and protection of part-timers from career consequences and stigmatization (cf. also Kossek et al., 1999; Williams, 2007). Litrico and Lee (2008) further note that, if a good combination of flexibility on the one hand and planning and structure on the other hand is achieved, reduced-load arrangements yield great benefits for both the organization and the individual's work-life reconciliation. Barnett and Hall (2001) reason along the same line argueing that among other alternative work arrangements reduced schedules are " 'currencies' [that] also help to hold the talent once it is hired" (p. 195). Traditional and innovative at the same time is the so-called *sabbatical* or *leave of absence*, a break from work that can be unpaid, partially of fully paid, based on an agreement of returning to work in the leave-warranting organization after a period of several months (up to one year) (Carr & Li-Ping Tang 2005; Deller, 2004). The more traditional and common version of this policy is parental leave (Hardy & Adnett, 2002) typically used by mothers but increasingly also by fathers or both parents together. A more open and innovative form of leave is not dedicated to parental responsibilities (or medical issues, cf. Allen and Russell, 1999). Often as a part of the HR benefit system in larger corporations and professional service firms, after some years of dedicated work employees can take a time-out to pursue personal projects such as a long-desired round-the-world trip in order to recharge their energy and return to work fully motivated and elated (Poelmans & Beham, 2008b). Among other firms, a large German consultancy offers this type of program including parental leaves, leaves aimed at personal development and MBA or PhD programs that are supported by granting a leave, all part of its 'time away from work' program (Rustemeyer & Buchmann, 2010). Very little research evidence exists on the usefulness of these leaves on the work-life interface. Batt and Valcour (2003) who examined the availability of a set of initiatives including leaves in a mainly professional sample found no effect on work-home interference. Dikkers et al. (2004), who also worked with a summed score of initiatives, did not find significant results of initiative use on work-family conflict. In a similar study though (using governmental employees, manufacturing workers, and financial consultants), Dikkers et al. (2007a) reported that parental leave was associated with reduced work-home interference ($r = .08; p < .05$). That taking a leave can be associated with negative career consequences was shown by Judiesch and Lyness (1999). In their study of nearly 12,000 managers of a financial services organization, lower salary increase and (temporarily) lower performance ratings were consequences of initiative use. Similar results were obtained by Allen and Russell (1999) regarding the use of parental and medical leaves. Slower or halted career advancement and lower compensation can be explained by Human capital theory and the loss of value of the human resource after the time away from work. In other words: "less allocation of energy to the workplace results in less accumulation of human capital" (Judiesch & Lyness, 1999, p. 643). Hence, leaves may represent a valuable and in the case of parents a necessary intervention. Yet whether leave policies reduce work-life conflict effectively must be evaluated by further research. In sum, the temporal initiatives most well researched are flexible work hour options and part-time work. Meanwhile, leave policies and sabbaticals are not so well researched despite their attractiveness for a large audience (parents, young professionals aiming at a round-the-world trip, and basically any individuals with time-consuming personal life projects). Neither flexible or part-time policies nor leaves or related initiatives are completely convincing in terms of usefulness of these initiatives as empirical results are highly diverse and hence do not allow general conclusions which arrangement is better or worse.

Initiatives Focusing on the (Work) Location. The prototypical initiative for spatial flexibility is working from home also referred to as 'home office', telework or telecommuting. Additionally, as shown previously, office (Fri)day and free choice of residence are frequently promoted as corporate work-life benefits in this area. According to Poelmans and Beham (2008b) telework is most appropriate if work is "information-based, predictable, and portable, and/or requires a high level of privacy and concentration" (p. 54). Positive effects of telework were found in previous research. At a large international technology corporation, individuals who used home office arrangements reported higher levels of work-life balance together with higher job motivation and intent to stay in the organization (Hill et al., 2003). At the same time they were as productive as employees in the traditional office venue. Teleworkers of various occupations were shown to experience significantly lower strain-based and behavior-based work-family conflict than nonteleworkers (Madsen, 2003). Full-time professionals of a high-tech firm who accomplished about half their workload from home experienced lower levels of work-to-family conflict (Golden et al., 2006). Kossek, Lautsch and Eaton (2006) did not find a significant association between using telework and work-family conflict in a professional sample. It is argued that home-based work is likely to increase problems regarding work-life reconciliation as employees find it difficult to draw a line between work and nonwork and are likely to work longer hours than employees in traditional office venues (Poelmans & Beham, 2008b). Duxbury, Higgins and Thomas (1996) noted increased levels of role overload and interference of individuals who adopted computer-supported supplemental work at home. Working from home, according to Hooks and Higgs (2002), is an established practice in professional services firms, both during regular business hours and 'on top' of the regular schedule. Despite this observation, Rustemeyer and Buchmann (2010) consider home office an adequate *temporary* solution, e.g. in times of sick family members, while strengthening the point that in client-centered work such as management consulting, permanent home-based work is not a realistic option. Above and beyond, it must be noted that working from home may not in all cases be aimed at improving work-life balance but rather serve the need to get work done if the workload is high, an issue discussed by Dikkers et al. (2004) and Hyman and Baldry (2011). Two other options that were identified within PSFs' responses to work-life issues are *office day* and *free choice of residence*. Office day is a common practice particularly in consulting organizations, where professionals work at the client site four days a week and do their paperwork and catch up with colleagues on Friday at the local office they are assigned to (Ahuja et al., 2007). A similar option that some firms offer is the freedom to choose where to live. Whereas relocation is often the prerequisite for attaining an attractive job, some consultancies advertise their goodwill and support by offering to pay for nationwide travel expenses to and from the job wherever professionals choose to live. A medium-sized German consultancy illustrates this policy as follows:

> "It is equally important that our employees are also able to focus on their personal lives. And a fundamental aspect of this is an employee's home environment. This is why our company structure is designed to allow our employees to live in whichever part of Germany they please, in Hamburg or Berlin, Munich or the Rhine-Main region near our Frankfurt office. We pay all employees' travel expenses between their home and the office. This way, they can retain their social environment while benefiting from an exciting, challenging and international working environment" (d-fine GmbH, translated from German).[26]

To date no research exists on these policies. As the local office is usually closer to the employees' residence than the client site, the office day practice may alleviate part of the stress associated with business travel and thus positively impact the work-life interface. It was shown that job-related travel and relocation is associated with trade-offs on behalf of personal life (Galinsky & Stein, 1990; Mayerhofer et al., 2008) and working near one's residence at least one day per week might indeed have mitigating effects on work-life conflict. Addressing the work-life interface from a more long-term perspective, free choice of residence may also represent a useful benefit helping to maintain a local social network while pursuing an international career. Wiersma (1994) discusses the maintenance of social relations as one of several strategies for coping with work-home conflict, gently supporting the value which the freedom to choose one's location of living may yield for the individual.

Beyond Typical Initiatives. Besides previously mentioned initiatives, additional benefits were identified in the website analysis of consultancies' work-life sections. As they address the work-life interface only indirectly and in a more general sense they are referred to as 'secondary' initiatives (cf. also Mohe, Dorniok & Kaiser, 2010). Frequently offered in PSFs are *initiatives to support educational programs* such as MBAs or PhDs (Deller, 2004; Rustemeyer & Buchmann, 2010). Usually these programs are associated with a leave of ab-

---

26   Retrieved at: http://www.d-fine.de/en/karriere/balance-von-privat-und-berufsleben.html
     (last access: 2011-06-08).

sence that enables focused participation in the program, but they can also be supported financially and rewarded in terms of firm re-entry at a higher hierarchical level. While employability rises for the employee – and in terms of work-life balance the respective time-out from the job may signify a reduction of stress and thus represent a recovery period – for the firms this investment is meant to repay in terms of rising reputation by means of a highly-qualified workforce, frequently sought-after cooperation with universities, and the retention of highly-skilled professionals.[27] Another practice frequently mentioned in work-life sections is *individual coaching*; its usefulness is supported by a number of papers. In a public accountant sample Almer and Kaplan (2002) showed that having a mentor can be associated with higher job satisfaction and intention to remain in the company as well as lower emotional exhaustion. A supportive mentor was related to reduced work-family conflict of both directions in a sample of professionals (Nielson et al., 2001). Bussell (2008) argued strongly in favor of maternity coaching as a means of retaining professional women and thus avoiding 'brain drain' (p. 14). More generally, Höher and Steenbuck (2006) discuss work-life balance coaching as an adequate answer to employee stress and work-life conflicts. Surprisingly, while programs specifically aimed at *health and recovery* are also discussed in the work-life balance literature, their effectiveness in the work-life area is largely untested. Conservation of Resources (COR) theory suggests that stress reactions are a consequence of resource loss (Hobfoll, 1989) underscoring the importance of recovery or, in other words, a "circle of work and rest" (Zijlstra & Cropley, 2008, p. 222). Health and recovery programs can include on-site sports and recovery facilities, organizational health trainings or the fostering of individual-level recovery during and after work (Kothes, 2010) but also extend towards therapeutic interventions such as Quality of Life Therapy[28] (Burwell & Chen, 2008). That recovery from work-related stress entails higher vigor at work and further positive individual and organizational outcomes was extensively shown in the studies of Sonnentag and colleagues (Sonnentag, 2001; Sonnentag & Bayer, 2005; Sonnentag & Kruel, 2006; Sonnentag & Niessen, 2008). Stress-related psychological and physical symptoms such as burnout, depression and substance abuse were in turn associated with high work-life conflict (Beatty, 1996; Netemeyer, Boles &

---

27   Frequently, the participation in a firm-sponsored or supported educational program entails contractual obligation to remain in the firm for a certain period of time (e.g. two years) after the program (Deller, 2004).

28   Quality of Life Therapy (QOLT) has its origins in positive psychology and flow research (Seligman & Csikszentmihalyi, 2000) and works with a comprehensive approach addressing all areas of life (Burwell & Chen, 2008).

McMurrian, 1996) underscoring the crucial role of health and recovery initiatives particularly in stressful jobs. A fourth area of initiatives which are 'secondary' in their impact on work-life conflict is the field of *supportive services*. That services such as laundry or postal services reduce stress in nonwork roles and make more time available for recovery is intuitive, yet there is little empirical support. Aryee (1992) showed that long work hours are associated with job-homemaker conflict, a phenomenon that could likely be ameliorated with supportive services that reduce time spent on household chores. This notion is supported by empirical evidence on the strain associated with household chores (Blair, 1996; Forsberg, 2009; Fu & Shaffer, 2001; Kandel, Davies & Raveis, 1985; Shelton & John, 1996).

3.2.2.3 Availability versus Use of Initiatives – A Different Story?

A major issue in the measurement of work-life initiatives is whether actual *use* is addressed in the operationalization or whether researchers observe employees' *access* to them. Whereas actual use of initiatives generally is associated with the need to react to an acute work-life challenge, access to initiatives is a rather passive construct that relates to the perception of family-friendliness of an organization by providing respective benefits. A number of works focuses on both but usually either initiative use or availability are investigated with interesting yet inconsistent findings. A number of studies within professional contexts found that the use of (a set of) initiatives is associated with reduced experiences of interference between work and personal life among *computer workers and lawyers* (Cinamon & Rich, 2002a), *professionals employed in public and private sector organizations* (Dikkers et al., 2007a), and *professionals at IBM* (Hill et al., 2003). To my knowledge these studies outweigh the number of papers that do not find a significant interaction between initiative use and work-life conflict (Dikkers et al., 2004; Kossek, Lautsch & Eaton, 2006), although publication bias might impact this conclusion as insignificant results are very often not published (cf. Mesmer-Magnus & Visveswaran, 2007). Several research results indicate that professionals and non-professionals who perceive to have *access* to useful and usable initiatives report reduced levels of work-life conflict among *Asian professional women* (Aryee, 1992), *employees in high-commitment environments* (Berg, Kalleberg & Appelbaum, 2003), *professionals of various occupations* (Frye & Breaugh, 2004), *office-based employees* (Hayman, 2009), *male executives* (Judge et al., 1994), *teleworkers* (Madsen, 2003), and *employed women* (Shockley & Allen, 2007). Again, these studies outnumber other examinations that do not find an effect of initiative access on work-life conflict (Batt & Valcour, 2003; Allen, 2001; Taylor et al., 2009). A number of studies find that both *benefit use and availability* is associated with positive work-life experiences (Pasewark & Viator, 2006; Smith & Gardner, 2007). O'Driscoll et al. (2003) found that initiative use was negatively associated with work-life conflict while initiative availability was not. In a study of employed parents, Goff, Mount and Jamison (1990) found that making use of a childcare initiative was not related to reduced levels of work-family conflict but satisfaction with the childcare arrangements was, adding the perspective of acceptance.

Some examinations report that initiative use is related to *increased conflict* (Duxbury et al., 1996; Golden et al., 2006; Russell et al., 2009), a result that is of course contrary to the aim of work-life initiatives. These observations show the importance of a differential investigation. Positive results on initiative availability indicate that work-life benefits are also an issue for employees who are not in acute need of making use of them, such as young and flexible job newcomers. It must further be noted that some managers and professionals in customer-contact jobs may not be eligible to use certain benefits, such as job sharing or telecommuting (Thompson et al., 1999). Jobs may also be restricted to a fixed time frame (e.g. shift work, work attached to opening hours) and certain benefits are specifically targeted on certain groups only, such as dependent care arrangements (Dikkers et al., 2004).

In order to enlighten the effectiveness of corporate work-life initiatives for reducing work-life conflict in PSFs it is examined here whether the use of work-life initiatives is related to reduced work-life conflict. Additionally the effect of initiative availability on work-life conflict is investigated because as illustrated previously initiative access regardless of actual use, can be associated with decreased work-life conflict. This effect can be explained by the anticipation of individuals, that if in need, they have access to corporate work-life initiatives, a perception that reduces their feeling of work-life conflict. It is postulated that professionals who use initiatives and those who have (stronger) access to initiatives respectively experience decreased work-to-life conflict. Therefore the hypotheses regarding the impact of *formal organizational resources* are as follows:

Hypothesis 2a: *The availability of work-life balance initiatives is negatively related to time-based and strain-based work-to-life conflict.*

Hypothesis 2b: *The use of work-life balance initiatives is negatively related to time-based and strain-based work-to-life conflict.*

Work-life initiatives are usually considered to support employees in two ways, a) alleviate time pressure by means of enabling more flexible working hours/ less working hours or 'more' time in a leave arrangement and b) lower stress and psychological strain as for example parents know their children are taken care of and can thus take their work more easily. Behavior-based work-to-life conflict in the sense of 'behaving in a way that creates conflict in one domain' did not seem to fit with the idea of work-life arrangements. Rather, another behavior-based WLC item could be whether or not initiatives are used in order to arrange work and personal life better. From this perspective it was decided that work-life initiatives may be successful in alleviating time-based and strain-based WLC yet including behavior-based WLC in this hypothesis as well was not considered to be make sense.

3.2.2.4 Use of Summed Scores – Does 'a lot' really help a lot?

As mentioned before, the common practice of measuring the use and/or availability of work-life initiatives is either to observe one single initiative or work with summed scores with the underlying assumption that 'more helps more'. This procedure has been criticized (Kelly et al., 2008) and justifiably so. Dikkers and colleagues (2004) for instance found no effect of work-life initiatives when using a summed score of six initiatives in a consultancy sample, but in a larger sample which at least partially seemed to consist of the same data, effects were found when observing initiatives separately (Dikkers et al., 2007a). Largely, existing research neglects the idea that one individual initiative may be sufficient for reducing the work-life interference of certain individuals. Additionally, initiatives are not all mutually compatible. Reduced schedules can obviously not be used at the same time as a leave of absence, yet reducing working hours for some time might address exactly the needs of certain employees while a whole set of initiatives is not at all necessary to address their needs. This is most probably the case for many initiatives.

Although applying summed scores to deal with the methodological issue of low power in small sample sizes (Hoyt et al., 2006) is a common practice, it is strongly suggested to shed a differential look at initiatives in order to obtain meaningful results that are of use to organizations and individuals. Therefore, the following additional research question is raised:

Research Question 2: *Which of the* organizational work-life initiatives *offered in professional service firms are really effective in reducing professionals' work-life conflict?*

Concerning the methodology, in the present study both the summed scores of initiative use and availability are examined as well as, pursuing Research Question 2, a structural model for each single initiative is estimated (cf. Part II).

3.2.3 Informal Demands and Resources: The Impact of Organizational Culture

More than ten years ago Kossek and Ozeki (1999) critically remarked that human resource policy studies focus almost solely on formal work-family initiatives with little attention to informal workplace practices. Since then a considerable body of research has investigated the role of informal handling of work-life issues in organizations, usually within an organizational culture framework. As stated by Kinnunen et al. (2005) organizational culture is a "very complex multilevel dynamic phenomenon" (p. 88) which makes it difficult to provide a universal definition. According to Lewis (1997) organizational culture refers to

> "a deep level of shared beliefs and assumptions, which often operate unconsciously, develop over time embedded in the organization's historical experiences, are usually functional initially but may persist inappropriately" (p. 18).

These shared beliefs and assumptions guide organizational behavior (Kinnunen et al., 2005). A positive, i.e. supportive organizational culture is associated, among other outcomes, with high levels of job satisfaction, commitment and low intention to leave the firm (Allen, 2001; Amos & Weathington, 2008; Ashkanasy & Jackson, 2005; DaSilva et al., 2010; Meyer et al., 2006; Verquer et al., 2003). Frequently this set of beliefs and assumptions shared by individuals and organizations is referred to as person-environment fit (Caplan, 1987) reflecting the idea that a fit between individual (employee) and environment (organization) in terms a congruence of values of both parties are a prerequisite for a satisfied, committed and productive workforce (Bretz & Judge, 1994; Edwards & Rothbard, 2005; Edwards & Harrison, 1993; Greguras & Dieffendorff, 2009; Kreiner, 2006; Ton & Hansen, 2001). The general notion of fit with regards to the question whether an individual is comfortable with and can meet the demands of the organization and is satisfied with the resources that are provided is a generally underlying paradigm of this thesis.

A prominent description of the dimensions of organizational culture that relates to questions about informal work-life integration management was made by Schein (2004) who proposed three levels of culture manifestation: at the first (surface) level culture is reflected in *artifacts*, i.e. in objects, documents, graphics, tools used, but also demonstrated behaviors of organizational members. In PSFs this includes the specific style of documents used in client presentations or the dress code that is considered appropriate and also the set of organizational benefits. At a more abstract level *values, strategies and ideologies* are described which are often but not necessarily directly and publicly recorded. This includes "ideal worker" characteristics (Kinnunen et al., 2005, p. 93), such as the valuing of excessive work hours, or keeping personal matters out of the firm. Lastly, at the fundament are underlying *assumptions or paradigms* encompassing the "way we do things", i.e. at what time it is appropriate to leave the firm regardless of one's performance or, in a branch that is largely dominated by male values, the legitimacy for men making use of family-related benefits (Burnett et al., 2011). Among others, Suzan Lewis linked organizational culture with the work-family interface discussing Schein's description in terms of its meaning for work-personal life interactions (Lewis, 1997). Organizational artifacts are work-life initiatives, which are based on underlying values of the organization, i.e. the value of high job satisfaction and commitment among employees legitimizing the offer of such policies (Connor, Hooks & McGuire, 1999). According to Lewis (1997), "at the most fundamental level, values are underpinned by basic assumptions which, if left unchallenged, can be barriers to the effectiveness of policies or other artifacts" (p. 18). Such an assumption may be that actually making use of work-life initiatives is related to slower career advancement. Another assumption is that advancing in the organization is related to immense time devotions towards the job as a manifestation of commitment – a particularly salient issue in PSFs. Taking into account that organizational discourses are potential indicators of organizational values and assumptions (Lewis, 1997), the communication of work-life initiatives on web sites (cf. Part I, 3.2) may be regarded as an indicator of work-life balance support on behalf the organization. According to Frey et al. (2006) transparent communication is a key component of an ethic-oriented positive leadership which focuses on the strengths and potentials of individuals and organizations. As noted previously, there often is a discrepancy in this communication strategy between the availability of initiatives and actual usability. An environment that supports work-life initiatives but at the same time sanctions their use has been described as a 'contradictory culture' (Dikkers et al., 2004, p. 328). *Work-family culture* was described by Thompson, Beauvais and Lyness (1999) as the

> "shared assumptions, beliefs, and values regarding the extent to which an organization supports and values the integration of employees' work and family lives" (p. 394).

The authors identified three dimensions of organizational work-family culture: managerial support for work-family balance, career consequences associated with utilizing work-family benefits, and organizational time expectations that may interfere with family responsibilities (Thompson, Beauvais & Lyness, 1999). Similarly, Dikkers et al. (2004) suggest a two-dimensional structure, distinguishing between support and hindrance. The support dimension includes understanding and assistance of the management in general, and specifically of supervisors and co-workers in terms work-life integration. Hindrance refers to organizational norms and expectations that represent obstacles to successful work-life reconciliation. The authors mention organizational time demands and negative career consequences related to making use of corporate work-life initiatives as major hindrance aspects in organizations. The definition of Thompson et al. (1999) mainly reflects the second and third component of work-life culture according to Schein's (2004) conceptualization. The artifact component, i.e. initiatives, is usually described separately, although of course the availability and usability of corporate policies is closely linked to organizational culture. Nevertheless, it makes sense to distinguish into formal support and informal dealings with work-life issues because differential effects were shown by previous research. For example Dikkers et al. (2004) found that those employees who perceived their organizational culture as supportive did not use more work-life initiatives than those who did not. Particularly in PSFs which strongly use work-life policies as figureheads for recruiting such a differentiation is worthwhile. Whereas formal policies usually comprise a fixed set of options, informal work-life culture represents general "latitude for adjustment" (Holt & Thaulow, 1996, p. 79) addressing the needs of a larger crowd of employees. Findings that the availability rather than the use of initiatives ameliorates work-life conflict support this notion. The present thesis therefore distinguishes between formal support in terms of initiatives and informal support in terms of 'implicit' support from different organizational levels as well as organizational obstacles to work-life balance as conceptualized by Dikkers et al. (2004).

The fact that individual performance and career dedication is primarily associated with presence at the workplace is anchored in the implicit culture of numerous organizations. Many companies attempt to tread a new path here trying to overcome the culture of 'presenteeism' (Perlow & Porter, 2009). Yet organizational cultures not only set great store on employee presence but also sanction 'deviant behavior': employees who make use of policies such as leaves of absence or flexible work hours often experience a negative impact on performance ratings and promotions (Blair-Loy & Wharton, 2004; Dikkers et al., 2007a; Judiesch & Lyness, 1999; Thompson et al., 1999). Beyond negative career consequences generally imposed top-down the role of peer support is frequently underestimated (Kossek et al., 1999). In environments that epitomize an 'always-on' ethic (Perlow & Porter, 2009, p. 102), professionals have a hard time admitting interest in anything other than work. Therefore many refrain from using supportive initiatives in favor of their career advancement and social status quo (Brett & Stroh, 2003). Wharton and Blair-Loy (2006) state "employers demand that they [professionals and managers] demonstrate commitment by making work the central focus of their lives" (p. 416). It is not a secret that organizations tend to reward workaholic behavior (e.g. Porter & Perry, 2008). Joan C. Williams, Distinguished Professor of Law and Founding Director of the Center for Work-Life Law at the University of California, observes that total devotion to work is seen as integral to the definition of the *ideal worker*

> "as someone who begins employment in early adulthood and works, full time and full force, for forty years straight, taking no time off for childbearing, child rearing or anything else" (Williams, 2007, p. 381f.).

The following two sections discuss research findings with respect to two informal demands or, according to what Schein refers to as assumptions, which represent *obstacles* to work-life reconciliation and are rooted in organizational culture: implicitly expected organizational time demands and the perception of negative career consequences as a result of making use of work-life initiatives (3.2.3.1, 3.2.3.2). Further, findings are reviewed about the role of informal *resources* for work-life conflict which were also summed under the umbrella of organizational culture: managerial, supervisor, and co-worker support (3.2.3.3).

3.2.3.1 Culturally Endorsed Organizational Time Demands

Organizational time demands are described by Thompson, Beauvais, and Lyness (1999) as "norms about the number of hours employees are expected to work and norms about employees' use of time, e.g. whether or not employees are expected to take work home" (p. 394). Relating this description to PSFs, Hooks and Higgs (2002) found in their study within a PSF sample that vacation was naturally expected to include some work time. In many organizations long work hours are an indicator for employee commitment and engagement for the firm (e.g. Bailyn, 1993, Fuchs Epstein et al., 1999, Hyman & Baldry, 2011). Such cultures are characterized by prevailing 'competitive presenteeism' (Simpson, 1998) or 'face time' (Perlow, 1995). Particularly as performance is hard to measure in the knowledge-based economy, time spent at the workplace serves as a prime indicator for employee productivity and performance (Lewis & Taylor, 1996; Perlow, 1995).

As to whether time demands affect the work-life interface beyond formal demands, Thompson and colleagues (1999) discuss in their study of managers and professionals that employees who work for an organization whose culture requires prioritizing work over persona life, this is likely to be associated with work-family conflict regardless of actual work hours. A number of studies found that organizational time demands are positively related to work-life conflict (Dikkers et al., 2007a; Frone, Yardley & Markel, 1997; Fuchs Epstein et al., 1999; Higgins & Duxbury, 1992; Major et al., 2002; McElwain et al., 2005; Thompson et al., 1999; Williams, 2007). Frone et al. (1997) report from their study using a mixed sample of employed adults that work time commitment significantly predicted work-family conflict. In a sample of various employees in New Zealand organizational time demands and career damage were significantly positively correlated with work-to-family conflict, time demands (together with management support) being the strongest predictor of work-family conflict (Smith & Gardner, 2007). Dikkers et al. (2007a) found in a sample which also included professionals that a hindering organizational culture (high time demands and negative career consequences) was associated with increased work-home interference. Implicitly expected engagement for the organization was shown to predict work-family conflict in professional samples studied by Higgins and Duxbury (1992) and McElwain et al. (2005). In a Fortune 500 employee sample organizational time demands predicted work-to-family interference more strongly than actual work hours (Major et al., 2002). Williams (2007) and Fuchs Epstein et al. (1999) both investigated time norms in the context of lawyers who worked in law firms with the reasoning that particularly in these environments work time norms are very hard to overcome.

Above and beyond actual excessive work volumes, time demands implicitly expected by the organization in order to be perceived as committed and ready for the next upward step seem to substantially impact interferences between work and personal life. Particularly in the PSF context those implicit time demands are likely to be immense. For one thing this is due to the strong client focus of these firms which usually entails presence of the professionals at the client company for the largest proportion of their work time (Løwendahl, 2005). Additionally, professional service companies are often described by their culture of 'total commitment to work' (Litrico & Lee, 2008, p. 998) which is also engrained in professionals' job identity. Yet time demands seem to some extent also to reinforce themselves in a way that "the existence of a behavioral norm saying that one should work a lot is indicated by the observation that people work a lot" (Alvesson, 2000, p. 1105). Actual behavior and the norm are thus nearly the same phenomenon according to Alvesson and the reference to the norm is more a tautology than an explanation. In a similar vein, Hewlett and Luce (2006) pointed out that often professionals feel they must demonstrate that they are able to bear the challenge of long work hours by working even more hours and again reinforce this time culture. From this point of view studying the actual impact of implicit time demands on the work-life interface is a highly interesting endeavor in professional service firms.

Notably, neither of the studies under review incorporated a wider perspective by looking at work-personal life interactions and none of the studies presented data on the interaction of time-demands with the three-dimensional conflict scheme of Greenhaus and Beutell (1985). Taken together with the fact that professionals in PSFs and similar environments work excessively long hours it is hypothesized that implicit organizational time demands rooted in corporate culture are a central impacting factor for the work-life conflict of professionals in PSFs:

Hypothesis 3a: *Organizational time demands are positively related to time-based, strain-based, and behavior-based work-to-life conflict.*

3.2.3.2 "Deviant Behavior" – Work-Life Conflict and Career Advancement

Firms naturally expect from employees to make their largest possible contribution to organizational success. Although this is of course the central aim of any profit-oriented organization, there are differences with regards to the extent to which employees' nonwork concerns are understood and acknowledged. The more strongly organizations value time commitment as a demonstration of dedication, the more likely making use of available work-life initiatives that reduces time at the workplace or shifts the work environment, e.g. by working from home, is sanctioned with career outcomes such as held-off promotions or less interesting projects. Indeed it was shown in a number of studies that making use of organizational work-life initiatives is negatively associated with performance ratings and promotions and are thus more 'rhetoric' (Mohe et al., 2010) than reality. Judiesch and Lyness (1999) found that female managers who took family-related leaves experienced less promotions and salary increases and were rated lower in their job performance. Similarly, Allen and Russell (1999) experimentally tested the effects of making use of parental and medical leave on several outcomes with the finding that leave takers were less likely to be recommended for rewards such as promotions, salary increases or high profile projects than were non leave takers. Perceived career damage was found to be related to reluctant use of work-life initiatives (Smith & Gardner, 2007). In a public accounting sample, Johnson, Lowe and Reckers (2008) experimentally examined the effect of using several alternative work arrangements on career prospects. Not only did they find that initiative users were evaluated less favorably. The researchers also report that part-time work arrangements were more harmful for career evaluations than flexible schedules. Furthermore, working under a full-time flexible work arrangement was related to lower performance ascribed to the employee than in the case of 'traditional' full-time schedules – though this was found for male participants only. Lyness and Judiesch (2008) propose that career advancement potential and work-life balance are positively linked. In their study of nearly 10,000 international male and female managers, those participants who were rated higher on work-life balance by peers were rated higher on career advancement potential by supervisors compared to managers who were rated lower on work-life balance. Managers who characterized themselves as high on work-life balance were peer-rated higher on career advancement potential than managers who considered themselves lower on work-life balance. While prospects of slower or halted career advancement were anticipated to make managers and professionals use work-life benefits more reluctantly, such an effect was not found by Thompson, Beauvais and Lyness (1999).

Although there are findings that suggest a direct association between work-life conflict and the perception of negative career consequences (Anderson et al., 2002; Beauregard, 2006; Smith & Gardner, 2007; Thompson, Beauvais & Lyness, 1999), in the present thesis a negative relationship between the perception of career damage and initiative use is proposed. Taking from previous reasoning, work-life interference arises if individuals feel the need for solving problems at the work-life frontline but feel restricted from making use of organizational resources. The causal chain investigated here is therefore that negative career consequences primarily impede the use of work-life initiatives which would have the potential to reduce conflict instead of a direct impact of career consequences on work-life conflict.

Negative career consequences associated with initiative use are an issue that is highly salient for both the employee and the employer. If the use of corporate initiatives aimed at facilitating the reconciliation of work and other life spheres is impeded by corporate culture they are literally wasted money. As Thompson et al. (1999) put it

> "no matter how many and what kinds of work-family programs are offered, the culture in the organization is crucial for determining not only whether people will use the benefits, but also their general attitudes towards the organization" (p. 409).

In order to examine whether in PSFs professionals' use of formally offered work-life initiatives is really impeded by inherent organizational norms of putting 'work first' it is postulated that expected negative career consequences are associated negatively with making use of initiatives:

Hypothesis 3b: *Negative career consequences associated with making use of work-life benefits are negatively related to professionals' use of such initiatives.*

3.2.3.3 Informal Support and its Role for Successful Work-Life Reconciliation

Increasingly research approaches consider the key role of informal organizational support for dealing with work-life conflict. Among five facets of family-friendly work environments, Mesmer-Magnus and Viswesvaran (2007) meta-analytically identified a family-friendly work culture as most influential in reducing work-life conflict. Culturally inherent time norms and pressures are particularly prevalent in professional environments and Wallace (2009) underscores the relevance of a supportive organization that values employees as individuals with needs and responsibilities in and outside the work sphere in this context. Work-life related support inherent in organizational culture has been described at three different levels: managerial support, support from supervisors and co-worker support (Dikkers et al., 2004). All three were shown to act as potential resources for improving work-life integration.

Management and Supervisor Support. Whereas Thompson, Beauvais and Lyness (1999) describe organizational supportiveness under the general term of managerial support, Allen (2001) suggests differentiating between management in general and the specific direct supervisor of an employee. Management support is a more passive component that manifests itself for example in the communication of values which affect the work-life interface. Supervisors take an active role in the management of work-life questions, e.g. by allowing team members to make use of a certain initiative. An organization that is generally supportive of work-life issues might as well employ supervisors who are not so favorable towards their subordinates' concerns, for instance because they have a very strong always-on ethic themselves. At the same time supervisors in a non-supportive organization may put high emphasis on individual solutions including dealing with work-life policies. Fuchs-Epstein and colleagues (1999) illustrated such an example in their research involving law firm professionals. The authors reported a case of one specific supervisor who, against all organizational norms, is supportive and protective of his part-time lawyers by keeping track of their work hours and maintaining close contact with them in order to make them feel included in the team. *Management support,* which is also described as a general supportive work-life culture or family-supportive organizational perception (Allen, 2001), was largely associated with lower work-life conflict in different samples (Anderson et al., 2002; Judge et al., 1994; Shockley & Allen, 2007; Smith & Gardner, 2007), also among *managers and professionals* (Dikkers et al., 2004; Jacobshagen et al., 2005; Lapierre et al., 2008; Nikandrou et al., 2008; O'Driscoll et al., 2003; Taylor et al., 2009; Thompson et al., 1999; Wallace, 2009). From a sample of Swiss managers, Jacobshagen and colleagues (2005) report that a workplace climate supportive of work-life issues was related to lower levels of perceived work-family conflict. According to Dikkers et al. (2004) a supportive organizational culture favorably impacted time- and strain-based work-home interference of financial consultants. Consultants who felt supported experienced lower levels of conflict. A supportive work-life culture

was associated with less time-, strain-, and behavior-based work-to-family interference in a managerial sample (Lapierre et al., 2008). A 'humane orientation'
of the organization was associated with reduced work-family conflict among
Greek managerial women (Nikandrou et al., 2008). Taylor and colleagues
(2009) and O'Driscoll et al. (2003) provided further supportive evidence for the
facilitating effects of positive work climate on work-to-family conflict among
managers and professionals. Thompson et al. (1999) differentiated between an
overall supportive work-family culture and managerial support. In a sample of
professionals and managers, they found overall supportive work-family culture
to significantly predict (lower) work-to-family conflict while managerial support
failed to do so. Missing management support was furthermore related to higher
intent to leave the employer. These findings indicate that informal organizational demands (career consequences and time demands), which were regressed
simultaneously with management support on work-life conflict outweighed the
effect of managerial support in this case. Wallace (2009) provides positive findings for the linkage of organizational support and work-to-family conflict among
more than 1,200 lawyers who were married and working full-time. Cinamon and
Rich (2002a) are clearly an exception with their finding that managerial support
was not related to work-family conflict among computer workers and lawyers.
Overall, management support seems to be strongly associated with lower perceptions of work-family and presumably also work-life conflict.

A *supportive supervisor* was defined as a person who "is sympathetic to the
employee's desires to seek balance between work and family, and who engages
in efforts to help the employee accommodate his or her work and family responsibilities" (Allen, 2001, p. 417). Again, empirical findings of various samples
indicate that supervisor support is related to lower work-life conflict (Lapierre &
Allen; 2006; Smith & Gardner, 2007). Several publications report findings about
the crucial role of supervisor support for reduced feelings of work-personal life
conflict in the professional context (Batt & Valcour, 2003; Berg et al., 2003;
Dinger, Thatcher & Stepina, 2010; Major et al., 2008; O'Driscoll et al., 2003;
Taylor et al., 2009; Thomas & Ganster, 1995). IT professionals were shown to
experience reduced work-family conflict as a function of supervisor support
(Dinger, Thatcher & Stepina, 2010). Major et al. (2008) presented similar findings: positive leader-member exchange was related to lower levels of work-to-
family conflict among IT employees. Batt and Valcour (2003) report an association among supervisor support and work-family conflict within a U.S. sample
consisting of mainly professional employees. Berg, Kalleberg and Appelbaum
(2003) report from employees in high-commitment workplaces, that an understanding supervisor is positively associated with work-family balance. Managers
were shown to benefit from supervisor support in terms of lower work-family

conflict (O'Driscoll et al., 2003), likewise business professionals (Taylor et al., 2009). Thomas and Ganster (1995) reported further findings in support of this linkage among health professionals. Qualitative research among lawyers underscores the importance of supervisor support particularly in the case that the organization as a whole is less supportive. From the Fuchs Epstein et al. study (1999) a female part-time lawyer stated:

> "I didn't feel marginalized [...]. The company was not making a commitment to being supportive of [...] alternative career schedules – it was just this one individual, my boss, who was willing to support it and implement it" (p. 43).

Galinsky and Stein (1990) describe the role of supervisors in four fields of action: handling nonwork issues as they impact job performance, provide information with respect to organizational work-life policies, deal with work-personal life challenges flexibly as they occur, and handle these challenges fairly and without favoritism. Although Hooks and Higgs (2002) found that professional service firms are "empowered workplaces ... [that give professionals] considerable leeway to balance their personal and professional goals" (p. 121), it is argued that support from the management and the supervisor(s) is crucial for reducing work-life conflict in such challenging environments:

Hypothesis 4a: *Management support and supervisor support are positively related to time-based, strain-based and behavior-based work-to-life conflict.*

Co-Worker Support. Co-worker support was in a small number of studies also directly associated with decreased work-life conflict[29], while other studies do not find such an association. Using large-scale data, Thompson and Prottas (2005) as well as Major and colleagues (2008) suggest that co-worker support significantly predicts (reduced) work-to-family conflict. Berg and colleagues (2003) found conflict with co-workers to be associated with lower work-family balance. However, Smith and Gardner's results (2007) do not reveal a significant relationship between co-worker support and work-family conflict. While failing to support a direct relationship with work-family conflict, co-worker support was shown to buffer the negative effect of work overload on work-family conflict in a law firm sample (Wallace, 2009). While feeling backed up by peers at the workplace might be beneficial in terms of less work-life conflict, co-worker support also plays a role in the decision whether to make use of a work-life initiative as suggested by Thompson (2008). This assumption is based

---

29 For a review cf. Mesmer-Magnus and Viswesvaran (2009).

on two explanatory aspects: organizational justice and peer pressure. *Organizational justice* concerns circle around the idea that every employee has equal development opportunities and equal obligations towards the organization. In the context of the work-life interface, it was discussed that access to initiatives may be stratified and limited (e.g. Lambert & Haley-Lock, 2004; Poelmans & Beham, 2008a). Initiative use might have to be earned by working hard, e.g. in the case of sabbaticals, or a certain necessity for using arrangements has arisen which allows policy use, such as the birth of a child. Therefore, not everybody is eligible for work-life initiatives at any career stage or age. Furthermore, the perspective of non-users has largely been neglected. There are a number of studies that indicate co-worker support impacts work-life initiative use under an organizational justice perspective. Litrico and Lee (2008) qualitatively investigated how multiple stakeholders in the organizational context of professional service firms deal with alternative work arrangements. While arrangement users reported difficulties in 'really' making use of reduced load initiatives, co-workers were generally reported to be very skeptical towards users, they felt they were "an extra hassle" and they themselves were "picking up the slack" (p. 1007). According to Golden (2007) non-users of a teleworking arrangement are often confronted with decreased flexibility due to restrictive schedules (e.g. face-to-face meetings when teleworkers are in the office). Changes in the scope and volume of work, for example having to deal with unexpected requests or taking messages for teleworkers, and the perception of injustice as telework yields benefits for work-life balance which non-teleworkers do not enjoy may lead to feelings of injustice. Using data of professional employees it is further suggested that these tensions result in lower satisfaction of non-teleworkers with their teleworking colleagues, leading to a higher intention to leave the firm (Golden, 2007). The notion of organizational justice is also expressed by Casper et al. (2007) who argue in favor of a singles-friendly work culture that also respects nonwork responsibilities of employees without family obligations. Taking into consideration the potential perception of co-workers that 'reduced load' may be laid on their shoulders, informal co-worker support may very well be an important factor for employees' decision to make use of alternative work arrangements. The issue of *peer pressure* was also raised in previous discussions about initiative use. Managers, for example, whose peers make use of work-life initiatives are likely to use such initiatives themselves (Kossek et al., 1999) supporting the notion of 'social contagion' which Brett and Stroh discuss among reasons for overwork (2003). Professionals might therefore represent role models for their peers by working less hours or altering their work schedule. Lambert et al. (2008) report results in favor of this idea. Co-worker support itself was not associated with initiative use but if work-life initiatives were used in employees' workgroup, professionals were much more likely to make use of them themselves. The assumption, that "employees feel more entitled to use work-home arrangements when direct colleagues are sensitive to family responsibilities of workers and express positive attitudes toward the utilization of such arrangements" (p. 327) was also voiced by Dikkers and colleagues (2004). The culture in PSFs is described as male-dominated (Kaiser & Ringlstetter, 2011)[30] being characterized by masculine attributes such as high competitiveness and rivalry, (Simpson, 1998) and potentially a lack of role models regarding work-life issues (Kossek et al., 1999). Considering this and the previously outlined thoughts it is postulated that co-worker support is an important predictor of professionals' decision to make use of work-life initiatives:

Hypothesis 4b: *Co-worker support is positively related to professionals' use of WLB initiatives.*

3.2.4 A Research Model

In sum, the general assumption underlying this study is that organizational demands are related to increased work-life conflict whereas organizational resources can help ameliorate, i.e. decrease work-life conflict. Formally expressed demands and resources are based on some kind of common agreement that usually includes all organizational members. For example the demand that PSF professionals work long hours is known to everyone in the organization and the expectancy to fulfill this demand is clear to every organizational member. Formal organizational initiatives representing a resource are (usually) known to all members of the organization and (should be) offered to basically every employee within the firm. Informal demands and resources in turn are a facet of organizational culture which typically acts 'under the surface'. Whether and how formal and informal organizational resources discussed in the previous paragraphs professionals' work-life interface will be tested using the research model in Figure 7.

---

30   Kaiser and Ringlstetter (2011) pointed out that PSFs are for many female professionals not considered an attractive employer: "The low quota of women in professional service firms, particularly in consulting firms, often below 20%, contributes to the fact that specifically female competences is hardly used in daily business, and that women are thus more likely to feel discouraged by the „male-dominated culture" in consulting organizations" (p. 118).

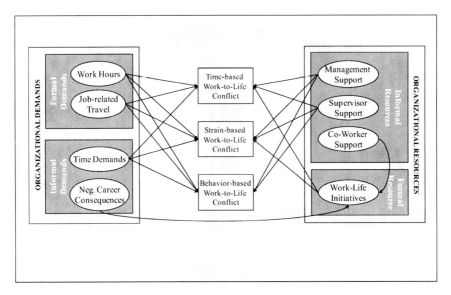

Figure 7. Research model of formal and informal organizational demands and resources related to time-based, strain-based, and behavior-based work-to-life conflict

It is adequate to examine the role of *job demands and resources* of business professionals' work-life conflict simultaneously for two major reasons: Professionals, particularly in PSFs (Løwendahl, 2005), face demands that exceed those of employees in less demanding work environments. However firms which employ professionals increasingly have a series of tools and HR programs at hand that are supposed to serve as resources in response to the effects of these demands on employees. As Stock-Homburg and Bauer state, because demands are unlikely to decrease, resources must be increased (2007). In examining demands and resources, it is also interesting to contrast those that are more *formal* in their character versus demands and resources that are *informally* rooted in the organization and thus harder to grasp and change. Holt and Thaulow (1996) point out the fact that beyond formal arrangements such as time policies or supportive initiatives informal organizational workplace characteristics they refer to as 'latitude for adjustment' (p. 79) also play a key role for managing the work-life interface. Formal initiatives refer to a set of fixed options that are usually based upon mutual agreement between the firm and its employees (Holt & Thaulow, 1996). Informal answers to work-life questions are rooted in the culture of an organization (Thompson et al., 1999).

3.3 Work-Life Diversity?! Work-Life Experiences Related to Different Work and Personal Life Characteristics

In order to enable differential conclusions and derive relevant implications for the organizational context of professional service firms in the empirical section, a closer look is shed at previous research results regarding several subgroups. Professionals may differ and yet be similar in their work-life dynamics depending on their subbranch. On the one hand, both groups work in highly-demanding work environments but on the other hand, structural work characteristics are not the same, as for example in some PSFs job-related travel may be more intense than in others. Individuals with different life role priorities, i.e. whether they favor work over nonwork spheres or not, were shown to differ in their work engagement as well as their utilization of flexible working policies (Cinamon & Rich, 2002a). Furthermore, previous studies provide a large body of evidence for work-life integration differing by age, gender, organizational tenure and job position as well as marital and parental status. A brief review of the literature on these characteristics should provide a foundation of studying these subgroups in detail in the empirical part.

3.3.1 'Endangered Species'? Work-Life Conflict in Management Consultancy and Law Firms

In Part I it was discussed why professionals in general and specifically employees in professional service firms are particularly prone to the experience of work-life conflict. Largely all publications that observe work-life issues in PSF contexts suggest that professionals in these demanding environments face challenges in integrating their overwhelming workload and time demands with personal life interests and obligations. Although it is assumed that all professionals are confronted with this issue, there may be differences depending on the PSF subbranch in at least two respects. *Structural work characteristics* differ depending on the PSF area: management consultants typically work on a 5-4-3 schedule, i.e. work five days a week of which four are spent at the clients' site with three nights away from home. Although other PSF professionals frequently travel too, it does probably not occur on such a regular basis and thus would be perceived as an exception rather than a norm. On the one hand, management consultants may perceive higher work-life conflict because of the stress associated with regular travel but they may on the other hand also be more accommodated to their journeying around the country or the world and thus be able to cope with it better than professionals who travel on a less regular schedule. Additionally, highly attractive earnings and excellent career prospects may make cutbacks on behalf personal life worthwhile. Whether these potential differences exist and whether they have implications for the work-life interface has not been empirically tested so far. Secondly, PSF professionals differ with regards to their *professional ethos* which is tied to the career path. Lawyers in a law firm or public accountants usually go through a longer and much more specific education than management consultants and are thus likely to be more committed towards their profession. Anecdotal evidence suggests that consultants who do not (want to or achieve to) become partners[31] leave the consulting firm after a number of years to work for one of its clients. Lawyers or accountants may be more likely to pursue a career within the closer scope of their branch because of their specialization and their commitment towards the profession (Hall et al., 2005). Also related to the professional ethos of the anytime working and ever available professional prevailing in many professional service branches is the stigmatization and marginalization of those who fail to conform time norms, as discussed by Williams (2007). This may be generally the case in all types of professional service firms, but there are probably differences in the acceptance of alternative work arrangements. Leave policies for example are commonly offered in the consulting area (Deller, 2004) because they are often associated with further personal and educational development. The frequent availability of this type of initiative could possibly be associated with greater openness and flexibility for employees who want to make use of work-life initiatives in general.

While professionals in PSFs are characterized by similar work characteristics and demands, it is likely that there are differences in their work-life experiences, e.g. among management consultants who are obliged to travel weekly but whose organization may be more open towards alternative schedules and law firm professionals who work more office-based in an environment where traditional values and time norms prevail more strongly.

3.3.2 'Having it all': The Importance of Work *and* Personal Life

" 'Get a life!' [...] for most of us this means spending time with our loved ones or doing things that we value – recreationally, spiritually, or in some other way that's important to us. It also means making the conscious decision to spend time or energy on those activities if that choice may have negative consequences for our economic status or career advancement. It means finding a way to make work the ally of 'getting a life' – of finding a way to overcome the inevitable conflict between two different life domains." (S. Friedman and J. Greenhaus, *Work and Family – Allies or Enemies? What happens when business professionals confront life choices*, 2007, p. 55)

---

31   Kaiser and Ringlstetter (2011) provide details about the partnership model in PSFs (cf. also Part I, 2.2.3).

It was previously illustrated that despite pressures imposed on professionals, very often these individuals work long hours because they want to. That employees 'like their jobs more' is partly seen in the stimulating nature of knowledge work (Hewlett & Luce, 2006). Many individuals define a large portion of their identity upon their professional accomplishments. While professionals do define themselves through their work to a larger extent than probably other employees (Brett & Stroh, 2003; Ladge, Greenberg & Clair, 2011), there is an observable shift towards the strong desire of a fulfilled life in all spheres (work, family, partnership, leisure, etc.) (Sullivan and Mainiero, 2007; cf. also Part I, 1.1.3).

Professionals find themselves in a dilemma between external pressures to work a lot and self-dedication to their work, particularly if they consider both work and personal life highly important (Cinamon & Rich, 2002a). Reporting from a study of reduced-load professionals and managers Buck et al. (2000) conclude that while a reduced schedule was just what some participants were looking for, others were tormented by the feeling of being unable to fully contribute to either life sphere. Many professionals and women in particular were described to feeling "torn by the desire to be successful in all areas of their lives, but unable to give full time and commitment to each of those domains" (Buck et al., 2000, p. 31). Men also are increasingly interested in taking an active role in family life as for example reported from a study of lawyers (Fuchs Epstein et al., 1999). This trend of changing values towards more satisfactory participation in personal life spheres affects organizations in the way that they must consider employee needs in order to maintain employer attractiveness and retain highly qualified professionals. Burke (2009) puts it as follows:

> "Effective and high performing organizations meet the needs of their people and the needs of the business simultaneously. Healthy employees in healthy organizations are more likely to achieve peak performance" (p. 170).

Individuals differ in how they set priorities with regards to their areas of life. Some value spending time with family and friends but still put work responsibilities first, some prefer exactly the opposite. Others again love their work and their personal life just as much and try to balance their life spheres as good as possibly. Empirically, the personal meaning or importance attached to work and nonwork roles has been associated with different outcomes. Identification with a role has frequently been conceptualized as *role involvement* in terms of psychological involvement (Frone, 2003). Among others, Frone and colleagues (1992) demonstrated that work involvement is positively related to the experience of work-family conflict. Greenhaus, Collins and Shaw (2003) suggest that balanced involvement in family and work roles leads to high quality of life because problems in one role are buffered by enjoyment in another. Others operationalised life role priorities in terms of *role salience* (Amatea et al., 1986) representing a more passive component of the same idea. In a study of Major et al. (2002) career identity salience, i.e. very high importance of the work role, was positively associated with working longer hours, though it was not related to work-life conflict. Winkel and Clayton (2010) suggest that transitions between work and family roles (e.g. answering personal e-mails at work or finishing job tasks at home) are significantly impacted by work and family role salience: professionals to whom family was of great importance were much more likely to permeate the work boundary in favor of family responsibilities (e.g. personal phone calls at work) than professionals with low family role salience. Carlson and Kacmar (2000) found that *role importance* (work vs. family) is associated with different relationships between work-family conflict and outcomes: for individuals who rate their work highly important, their job satisfaction is more strongly affected by work-related problems than for those who rate their job less important. Three profiles of *importance attribution* were compared by Cinamon and Rich (2002a), individuals with high family and low work importance, with high work and low family importance and with equally high importance of both domains ('dual' type). In their examination of computer workers and lawyers, levels of work-family conflict differed with the dual type experiencing the highest level and the family type with the lowest WFC level. The family type spent less hours at work than the other two profiles and more strongly used flexible working policies. In a recent large-scale study of employees of different occupations working in the U.S., it was found that 55 per cent of the participants were *'dual-centric'*, i.e. rated work and non-work equally important (Bourne et al., 2009). Dual-centric individuals reported significantly higher levels of satisfaction with their work-life balance together with less emotional exhaustion than those who favored work or nonwork. The authors highlight that employers should embrace this type of employee in order to remain attractive for new talents. "Navigating this sea of change", they argue, "is likely to become a strategic focus of all organizations" (p. 391).

Theoretical observations as well as empirical results indicate that individuals have different priorities in life which also impact their work-life experiences differentially. In other words, as professionals attribute varying importance to life roles they also have different needs which organizations should address if they want to maintain a diverse and yet highly-qualified workforce. The present thesis follows the typology outlined by Cinamon and Rich (2002a) and others into professionals who prioritize their work over their personal lives (*work type*), professionals who favor personal life over work (*life type*) and those who attribute equal importance to both domains (*balance type*). Contrasting these groups in the subsequent empirical investigation contributes to a deeper understanding of the role of individual values and lifestyle preferences of professionals on the perception of work-life conflict and its antecedents, an issue that was called for by Parasuraman and Greenhaus (2002).

3.3.3 'The Classics'?! Gender and Age

Typically, the two variables observed in nearly every publication in the work-life area are gender and age. The *gender* differentiation assumes that men and women have fundamentally different work-family experiences (Barnett & Hyde, 2001). A large body of papers discusses females' challenges of reconciling career and family. Often the metaphor of a "glass ceiling" (Lyness & Thompson, 1997, p. 359) is used referring to the notion that particularly women face strong barriers in their upward career movement and often do not reach the top but come to a halt at middle management. Empirical research among professionals largely supports the idea that women have a harder time reconciling work and personal life (Batt & Valcour, 2003; McElwain et al., 2005; Nielson et al., 2001; Taylor, Delcampo & Blancero, 2009; Wharton & Blair-Loy, 2006). Still, these findings are corroborated by a number of studies that do not find gender differences (e.g. Golden et al., 2006; Jacobshagen et al., 2005; Kossek et al., 2006; Thompson et al., 1999; Wallace, 1997). Dikkers et al. (2004) reported results which indicated higher (time-based) work-home interference for men than for women. Gender differences were discussed in the PSF literature by Kumra and Vinnicombe (2008) who studied the promotion-to-partner process in management consultancy. Although women become more numerous in these firms, they are fairly absent at partner level which is explained with two reasons: the competitive nature of the promotion-to-partner process where women are less aggressive and self-promoting *and* the issue of fit in the sense of "being one of us" (p. 70), which is usually based on male attributes such as competitiveness, 'gravitas', technical expertise and high ambition. The notion of an 'ideal worker' with predominantly male characteristics was also addressed by Williams (2007).

Age is the second most frequent variable typically tested in studies about the work-life interface. From a life course perspective, early career typically represents a stage where individuals invest a large amount of time and energy in their jobs in order to advance within the organization and increase their further chances on the job market. At this stage issues of work-life balance are frequently put aside in favor of career advancement (Sturges & Guest, 2004). After some years of employment the family stage cuts in and poses unique challenges and very immediate needs for work-life reconciliation solutions for both mothers (Ladge et al., 2011) and fathers (Burnett et al., 2011). In the later years of employment, spheres beyond work and family, e.g. social engagement become increasingly important. Age was shown to moderate the relationship between antecedents and work-life conflict in past research (Matthews et al., 2009). However, the majority of examinations do not find direct effects between age and work-life conflict (Batt & Valcour, 2003; Golden et al., 2006; Jacobshagen et al., 2005; Pasewark & Viator, 2006; Taylor et al., 2009; Thompson et al., 1999).

Given the intuition that work-life conflict differs as a function of gender and age and the yet ambiguous state of research, it is worthwhile to investigate whether formal and informal organizational work-life conflict antecedents exert a differential impact for men and women and different age groups. Being standard variables of observation in nearly all studies, age and gender are also examined in the present investigation in order to find out whether group differences exist with regards to work-life balance needs and experiences within the PSF context.

3.3.4 (Dual-Career) Relationships and the Role of Children

Variables of central concern to previous work-life research are personal life constellations, i.e. whether individuals are single or in a relationship and the presence of (young) children. Several studies suggest that support from spouse or family reduces work-life conflict levels (Carlson & Perrewé, 1999; Mathews et al., 2009; van Daalen et al., 2006). But interestingly, meta-analytical evidence indicates that spousal support can also be related to higher levels of work-family conflict (Mesmer-Magnus & Visveswaran, 2007). While having a partner can relief individuals from a number of strains and stresses, being in a relationship is also related to higher responsibility and less flexibility, e.g. in terms of time spent at work versus at home. Largely, there is little evidence for the notion that *being married or in a relationship* itself is a predictor of higher work-life conflict or better work-life 'balance'. Most investigations, also among professionals, found that marital (and relationship) status is not significantly related to conflict levels (Allen, 2001; Kossek et al., 2006; Lapierre & Allen, 2006; Shockley & Allen, 2007; Thompson et al., 1999; Wallace, 1997). In contrast, two characteristics of personal life were commonly found to increase conflict: being in a *dual-career relationship* and the *presence of young children* in the family. It is generally agreed upon that individuals with complex family constellations and extensive family demands, such as partners in dual-career relationships and / or parents are more likely to perceive challenges in balancing life spheres (Aryee, 1992; Abele & Volmer, 2011; Grady & McCarthy, 2008; Neault & Pickerell, 2005). Particularly for dual-career couples with children, personal life responsibilities more strongly require instant intervention and action as compared to those of singles or individuals with a homemaking spouse (Rapoport & Rapoport, 1969).

The first explicit approach for studying stress that arises from combining competing life roles in *dual-career* family constellations was done by Rapoport and Rapoport (1969). Taking a qualitative approach, they argue that dual-career couples particularly experience stress related to coping with juggling life roles as a function of the high value which they (dual-career couples) place on fulfilling work and nonwork roles well. The authors suggest dual-career couples face five major forms of conflict with managing life roles: juggling limited resources with regards to housework and childcare (overload dilemmas), discrepancies between individual and social norms (normative dilemmas, e.g. being a "bad mother"), the necessity of switching between competing role requirements (identity dilemmas), lack of temporal resources for maintaining social contacts coupled with incompatible norms of the network (social network dilemmas), and role-cycle dilemmas, i.e. problems that arise from being at a different stage in the career cycle versus the personal life cycle (for example feeling ready to start a family yet being still in the stage of building one's career). With this evaluation, Rapoport and Rapoport provide a foundation which guided most subsequent research concerning dual-career couples' strains of arranging work and nonwork demands. Further supportive evidence for higher work-family interference among dual-career professionals was observed by Higgins and Duxbury (1992). Their finding, that male professionals in dual-career relationships experienced higher levels of conflict than those in single-earner relationships was primarily explained with a

> "lack of structural flexibility of the[ir] workplace, outdated organizational policies that operate on the 'myth of separate worlds' and a lack of social support for the male dual-career role which contradicts societal norms" (Higgins & Duxbury, 1992, p. 389).

However, it was pointed out that such constellations also yield a number of advantages such as higher family budget, similar expectations and values among partners, equal opportunity for personal growth and mutual respect (cf. Abele & Volmer, 2011, for a review of the evidence). Ford and colleagues (2007), who meta-analytically investigated the relationship between work and family satisfaction and work-family conflict, found that dual-earner status can also have favorable effects. With regards to relationship status, the authors found that for individuals in dual-earner couples, their family satisfaction is less negatively impacted by work-to-life conflict than for singles or couples where only one partner is employed. Dual-earner status thus seems to act as a buffer in the respect that a satisfactory family sphere is less strongly impacted by role conflict if both partners work, for example as a function of better mutual understanding and respect. Having (small) children was associated with higher conflict in several studies, among *lawyers* (Wallace, 2009), *executives* (Judge et al., 1994), *consultants* (Dikkers et al., 2004), and *professionals* working in Fortune 500 companies (Kossek et al., 2006). Aryee (1992) further reported that parental demands were significantly related to the experience of conflict between the parental role and the job of married professional Asian woman in dual-career families. That parental responsibilities collide with job responsibilities is very intuitive and at the same time well-researched. This is particularly the case if women are highly-qualified and career-oriented because they are most likely to try to combine their career with family life instead of dropping out, as pointed out by Ladge, Greenberg and Clair (2011). While parental role responsibilities are (still) often reduced to females Burnett and colleagues (2011) discuss the difficulties of being "the flexible-yet-engaged father" (p. 168) in today's work cultures, which are still focused on the 'male breadwinner' type of employee (cf. also Williams, 2007).

The present research also examines the role of family constellations – parental status, marital status and dual-career status – because results inform researchers and policy makers on the differential needs faced by different groups of professionals.

3.3.5 'Faster-higher-further'? Tenure, Job Level, and Work-Life Conflict

Different tenure and career levels – these variables are usually correlated – were also argued to impact work-life dynamics. Higher-level jobs are associated with higher pressure, longer hours, and more intense emotional demands (Schieman, Galvin & Milkie, 2009) indicating higher potential for work-life conflict. However, it is also discussed that employees' legitimacy for making use of work-life initiatives rises with tenure (e.g. Lambert, Marler & Gueutal, 2008). Access to certain initiatives may even only be granted at a certain tenure level because they are attached to time savings accounts, e.g. leaves. Generally, tenure is *not* found to be related to higher levels of work-life conflict among professionals (Judge, Boudreau & Bretz, 1994; Lapierre & Allen, 2006; Taylor, Delcampo & Blancero, 2009; Thompson, Beauvais & Lyness, 1999; Wallace, 1997). In contrast, findings from Golden, Veiga and Simsek, (2006) indicated lower levels of conflict the longer individuals stayed in an organization. In a study of Batt and Valcour (2003) for men longer tenure was related to diminished levels of work-family conflict.

The examination of *hierarchy level* does not present a clear picture of its effect on the work-life interface. Employees from multiple organizations and industries were found to perceive lower conflict with rising job levels (Lapierre & Allen, 2006), while in a sample of professionals, management level was associated with higher work-to-family conflict (Golden, Veiga & Simsek, 2006). Thompson, Beauvais and Lyness (1999) did not find an association at all. Very recently, DiRenzo, Greenhaus and Weer (2011) brought work-family experiences at different job levels into focus using data of the 2002 National Study of the Changing Workforce (NSCW) in the United States. Under the general assumption that work-family conflicts are higher for higher-level employees, they proposed that managers and professionals experience higher conflict levels as a function of demands related to their job, i.e. excessive work hours and stressful jobs. The authors further suggested that employees at higher ranks have stronger access to organizational resources, i.e. supportive cultures, supervisor support, and higher levels of job autonomy. Specifically they argued that higher level employees would experience a stronger buffering effect of these resources on their job demands – work-family conflict relationship. DiRenzo et al. did find higher levels of work-family interference among higher ranks caused by job demands. While support for the buffering effect of job resources was found for all employees at all levels, it was indeed stronger for managers and professionals. These large-scale data therefore support the notion that work-life experiences are different as a function of organizational level.

From the point of view of PSFs it is interesting to know more about the work-life experiences, needs, and dynamics of professionals of different tenure and hierarchical levels. Longer tenure and higher job level are associated with higher responsibility. Usually, those with leadership and project responsibility arrive first in the morning and leave last at night making them particularly susceptible for work-life conflict. On the other hand longer tenure can be associated with greater access to organizational benefits. Furthermore, once professionals have reached partner status in the ownership system of PSFs (von Nordenflycht, 2010) career advancement pressure may become less salient. Additionally, the longer employees prevail in this type of organization the more accustomed they might become to the pressures and demands and cope with the workload increasingly better. In this context the potential of 'strong cultures' in changing individuals' personal values is discussed (Lorsch & Tierney, 2002). From an HR perspective, tenure and job level are interesting variables for managing the work-life interface with respect to benefits at certain career stage or tenure. Leaves of absence for example were described as attractive benefits after the first career stages (Deller, 2004). In order to enlighten work-life dynamics at different tenure and job levels the present study examines these two variables in terms of three groups respectively. Professionals with less than three years tenure, between three and six years, and those who work for their organization more than six years are contrasted in the subsequent empirical examination. Furthermore, group differences of professionals at entry to medium level, at medium level and of those who rated themselves at medium to top / partner level are examined.

3.4 Summary of Part I

In sum, Part I outlines theoretical considerations underlying the subsequent empirical study of the impact of organizational demands and resources on the work-life conflict of PSF professionals.

First, major *linkages between individuals and organizations with respect to work-life dynamics* were presented (1.1). Outcomes of work-life interference were discussed at three levels: stress, health impairments and negative motivational outcomes at the individual level, issues of social justice, diversity, corporate citizenship and social support at the interpersonal level, and the impact of negative motivational outcomes in terms of low job satisfaction, commitment and turnover intention as well as the role of effective work-life integration management on employee and firm performance together with the 'business case' and matters of corporate communication including recruitment opportunities and organizational change at the overall organizational level. Further, existing approaches to the study of the work-life interface were outlined resulting in the operational definition of *time-, strain-, and behavior-based work-to-life conflict* as the major dependent variable(s) of interest in the present study.

The next section (Part I, 2.) examined the term 'professional' from a general perspective resulting in a working description of *professionals as individuals with high education, specialized expertise and general process knowledge who use their competencies to solve complex problems and who are usually highly committed towards their profession and their organization.* While these attributes guided the selection of literature used in this thesis, characteristics of professionals within the context of professional service firms was specifically investigated. As providers of highly-specialized and complex services, the product of PSFs is largely intangible and its workforce is PSFs' most critical strategic asset. This fact results in the paradoxical situation that firms demand a lot from their professionals but also strongly depend upon them and their efficiency. As central demands in PSFs high accessibility and flexibility were outlined together with excessive workload and extreme work hours. This results in the conclusion that professionals work in 'extreme' jobs likely reducing their nonwork responsibilities and interests to a minimum. However, it was also indicated that highly-skilled employees love their job and identify strongly with their professional sphere calling into question the relevance of examining work-life balance within this workforce. This discrepancy is taken further into a discussion about the character of the 'life' component of professionals' work-life conflict which will be investigated with Research Question 1 (cf. Table 2).

Table 2. Summary of Research Questions and Hypotheses

Hypothesis 1a:	*(Long) Work hours are positively related to work-life conflict.*
Hypothesis 1b:	*Job- related travel is positively related to work-life conflict.*
Hypothesis 2a:	*The availability of work-life balance initiatives is negatively related to work-life conflict.*
Hypothesis 2b:	*The use of work-life balance initiatives is negatively related to work-life conflict.*
Hypothesis 3a:	*Organizational time demands are positively related to work-life conflict.*
Hypothesis 3b:	*Negative career consequences associated with work-life concerns are negatively related to the use of WLB initiatives.*
Hypothesis 4a:	*Management support and supervisor support are positively related with work-life conflict.*
Hypothesis 4b:	*Co-worker support is positively related with the use of WLB initiatives.*
Research Question 1: (Character of WLC)	*Which life spheres and conflict types does professionals' work-life conflict refer to?*
Research Question 2: (Usefulness of spec. initiatives)	*Which of the organizational work-life initiatives offered in professional service firms help reduce professionals' work-life conflict?*

Representing the heart of this section (3.), major literature about the *formal and informal demands and resources* was reviewed which professionals face regarding the reconciliation of life spheres. Based on conclusions of the respective paragraphs a set of hypotheses was presented (Table 2). As specific organizational demands that are to some extent formally agreed, details on *work hours* and *job-related travel* as a flexibility requirement were discussed in (3.1). Further, formal organizational resources in terms of organizational benefits for fostering work-life balance were introduced and drawing on a web site analysis among 25 management consultancies the most commonly communicated *corporate work-life initiatives* were deduced. Although PSF-specific studies are rare an attempt was made to draw a comprehensive picture of the purpose and usefulness of this set of initiatives. The effect of informal organizational demands and resources inherent in organizational culture on work-life conflict was delineated (3.2).

Time expectations and *negative career consequences* related to work-life issues were presented as the major obstacles on behalf of the organization. *Management support* and *supervisor support* were discussed as direct predictors of professionals' work-life conflict while *co-worker support* was hypothesized to impact initiative usage. Finally, section 3.3 highlighted the point that work-life experiences also depend on *characteristics of the individual situation*. Varying working patterns in management consultancies vs. law firms were discussed along with individual priorities concerning life spheres followed by the rather commonly observed variables age, gender, marital, parental, and dual-career status as well as tenure and job level. The impact of a set of demands and resources among professionals is examined in the forthcoming section using the research model outlined in Figure 5 (Part I, 3.2.4). In order to take into consideration individually different needs and resources and compare professionals' work-life dynamics from different angles subsample results are examined concerning subbranch (management consultants vs. law firm employees), three types of life role priorities (work type vs. nonwork type vs. balancer), gender, age, parental status, relationship status and dual-career relationship status, as well as organizational tenure and job level.

II. Empirical Examination of the Impact of Organizational Demands and Resources on the Work-Life Conflict of Professionals

The previous part presented a set of hypotheses resulting in a framework of three types of work-life conflict antecedents: time-based, strain-based, and behavior-based work-to-life conflict. Furthermore, two research questions were raised with respect to the character of professionals' work-life conflict as well as the usefulness of specific work-life initiatives in the PSF context. Additionally, the necessity of taking a differential look at results was highlighted by presenting certain subgroups that may be of particular interest for gaining insights about how to effectively improve work-life integration management in organizations. The research questions and hypotheses are empirically tested in the present section using Partial-Least-Squares methodology (PLS). This powerful method enables the observation of linkages in one comprehensive model. Beyond examining single interactions which is the case in regression analysis, PLS enables the researcher to test several independent (exogenous) and dependent (endogenous) variables at the same time. Hence, empirical results of such a model do not only tell us about how one variable impacts another but gives us an idea of how a set of variables interacts. Moreover, PLS is the method of choice here as this methodology is also strongly practicable in the case of small sample sizes, e.g. when certain groups are compared.

A sample of 794 professionals is examined empirically in the forthcoming paragraphs. This dataset consists of two subgroups, management consultants and law firm professionals. It was outlined at the beginning of this thesis that levels of professionalization differ for certain occupations. While lawyers are counted towards a strongly professionalized workforce with institutionalized education and standards of excellence, management consultants were argued to be yet in the process of professionalization (Greiner & Ennsfellner, 2010). For this reason and because of differences in structural job characteristics, such as travel frequency and the availability of certain work-life benefits, it is highly interesting not only to observe one group of professionals but to compare the work-life dynamics of these two occupations.

The current section is structured as follows. First, the methodology including the data collection procedure, sample characteristics and measures used in the online survey are outlined (1.1). Details about the chosen strategies for data analysis are provided with particular focus on the procedure and thresholds of hypothesis testing with Partial Least Squares (PLS) (1.2). Subsequently, re-search results are presented with regards to research questions and the hypothe-sized model. After taking a closer look at the specific character of professionals' work-life dynamics (Research Question 1) including life role priorities, conflict types, and dimensions (2.1) results concerning the hypothesized research model (Hypotheses 1-4) are presented (2.2). Herein, the measurement model is evalu-ated according to previously outlined thresholds (2.2.1) followed by an estima-tion of the structural model which includes all participants (2.2.2). In order to address Research Question 2, results of the structural model are presented which only include one WLB initiative at a time (2.2.3). Finally results regarding sub-groups representing moderating effects are displayed (2.2.4). At the end of Part II major methodological facts and empirical findings are summarized regarding the dynamics of the work-life interface of professionals obtained in this study.

1. Method

1.1 Data Collection

Data for the present study were assessed within the research project "Innovative Concepts of Human Resource and Organizational Development in Consulting Organizations (IPOB)"[32], funded by the German Federal Ministry of Research and Education (BMBF). Data were collected using an online survey[33] in German language with two sampling procedures. A snowball sampling approach (Scott, 1991) was used to address management consultants. This strategy which utilizes individuals' professional and social contacts is frequently used in management research (e.g. Eddleston, Veiga & Powell, 2006) and also in work-life research, especially in cases where sensitive data are involved (Bond & Galinsky, 2006). As firms were rather reluctant to cooperate because of sensitive data concerns, e.g. data on work hours, snowballing was the method of choice. The survey link was forwarded to potential respondents within the research team with a short introduction and the request to forward the link to other consultants. As coopera-tion could eventually be established, the survey was further distributed among altogether nine law firms.

The initial snowball sample consisted of 490 cases that accessed the survey of which 52.04 per cent completed it. After evaluating the dataset for missing values and inconsistencies, the final sample resulted in N = 242. A total access

---

32   Cf. IPOB homepage (http://www.consulting-innovation.de) for more details on the background of the project.

33   The software used for this purpose was Unipark (http://www.unipark.de).

number of 1097 was registered with regards to the law firm professionals with 51.69 per cent finished surveys. After deletion of twelve cases determined by missing values analysis the final law firm professional sample consisted of N = 552. The total dataset thus comprised 794 professionals.

1.1.1 Sample

Sample characteristics are presented in Table 3. Management consultants (MC) comprised about one third of the sample, females were clearly underrepresented, particularly in the group of management consultants (N = 49). Kaiser and Ringlstetter (2011) suggest that overall the gender distribution in the sample reflects the percentage of men and women in professional service firms, women usually making up about 20 per cent of PSF employees. The majority of respondents worked more than 50 hours per week, management consultants worked longer hours than law firm professionals (LF) and travelled more frequently in their jobs. Law firm professionals on average had longer job experience, higher job levels tending towards a position in the middle of the organizational hierarchy, and exceeded average organizational tenure of management consultants by almost one year. The major part of respondents was in a relationship or married, nearly 60 per cent of those in a relationship were in a dual-career relationship where both partners work full-time. Note that nearly 70 per cent of the females with partners were in dual-career relationships compared to 55 per cent of the males corresponding to the notion that more males than females enjoy the support of an at-home spouse (Hewlett & Luce, 2006). Less than 30 per cent of participants were parents, still with the larger share in the law firm subsample (36 per cent parents). Of those who were parents the majority had one or two children (13.7 and 11.2 per cent respectively), 27 respondents had three children and seven respondents reported having four or more children. Mean age in the total sample was 34 years.

1.1.2 Measures

Except for the measure of availability and use of WLB initiatives as well as the 'behavior-based work-to-life conflict' measure all items used in this study were based on scales established and validated in other studies. As original items were in English language items were translated into German. Items were then back-translated into English by an English native speaker in order to achieve the highest possible congruence of the German with the original version.

Table 3. Descriptive statistics of the total sample of professionals (N = 794) and of management consultants (N_{MC} = 242) and law firm professionals (N_{LF} = 552)

	M	SD	Min	Max	N	%
Weekly Work Hours	54.92	11.212	0	80		
MC	58.42	11.562	0	80		
LF	53.38	10.706	8	80		
Job-Related Travel Days / Week	1.14	1.486	0	7		
MC	2.69	1.303	0	7		
LF	.36	.806	0	7		
Organizational Tenure	4.10	3.882	0	35		
MC	3.36	2.800	0	19		
LF	4.42	4.233	0	35		
Job Level	2.75	1.266	1	5		
MC	2.60	1.123	1	5		
LF	2.81	1.320	1	5		
Job Experience	6.74	6.472	0	40		
MC	5.68	5.216	1	32		
LF	7.21	6.906	0	40		
No. of Children	.50	.889	0	4		
MC	.20	.773	0	4		
LF	.60	.916	0	4		
Age	34.15	6.704	23	67		
MC	31.12	6.762	23	67		
LF	35.50	5.477	23	55		
Gender (f / m)					241 / 548	31.0 / 69.0
MC					49 / 192	20.2 / 79.7
LF					192 / 356	35.0 / 65.0
Relationship Status (single / rel.)					153 / 639	19.3 / 80.5
MC					61 / 181	74.8 / 25.2
LF					92 / 458	16.7 / 83.0
Dual-career relationship (y / n)					375 / 261	47.2 / 32.9
MC					124 / 56	51.2 / 23.1
LF					251 / 205	45.5 / 37.1
Parental Status (non vs. parent)					554 / 229	69.8 / 28.8
MC					208 / 31	86.0 / 13.0
LF					346 / 198	62.7 / 35.9

Work-to-life conflict was assessed in three dimensions: time-based, strain-based, and behavior-based work-to-life conflict. Time-based work-to-life conflict (tWLC) and strain-based work-to-life conflict (sWLC) were measured with a modified version of the three item measures developed by Carlson et al. (2000). Items were adapted such that 'family' was replaced by 'personal life' (e.g. tWLC: "Die Zeit, die ich in meinen Beruf investieren muss, fehlt mir oft für mein Privatleben [original: My work takes up time that I'd like to spend with family/friends]"; sWLC: "Nach der Arbeit bin ich oft zu ausgelaugt um privaten Verpflichtungen nachzukommen [original: I am often so emotionally drained when I get home from work that it prevents me from contributing to my family]") (cf. Appendix B for the complete list of items). As it was decided that the behavior-based conflict items developed by Carlson et al. were not suitable for the professional context, two items were specifically created for this study: "Es kommt häufig vor, dass ich private Urlaubspläne aufgrund meines Jobs ändern muss [I often have to change vacation plans because of my job]", and "Meistens kann ich nicht genau vorhersehen, wann ich von der Arbeit nach Hause komme [Usually I cannot plan exactly when I will return home from work]". All items were measured on a 5-point Likert scale with high scores indicating high levels of conflict.

Nature of conflict between work and personal life was assessed with one item. Respondents were asked to indicate whether they experienced no conflict, low, moderate, or high levels of conflict with regards to the following five interactions: work vs. partnership and family, work vs. friends, work vs. social activities and engagement, work vs. health and recovery, and work vs. self. These categories were derived from existing attempts to describe the 'life' component of work-life conflict, specifically from the fourfold differentiation of Friedman (2008a) into work, family, community, and self as well as the work centrality measure used by Carlson et al. (2000).[34]

Life role centrality, importance and *priority* were assessed as life role salience was previously shown to impact work-life experiences. In line with Carlson and Kacmar (2000) respondents were asked to distribute 100 points among the categories also used to measure conflict type: work, partnership and family,

---

34   In their work centrality measure Carlson and colleagues (2000) further refer to the study of Whitely and England (1977). The categories were adapted here as a function of the cultural context in which they were assessed. Relying on feedback from the pre-test as well as insights gained from the life role categorization by Friedman (2008b), we replaced the previously used category 'religion' with 'time for self' and added the categories 'friends' and 'health and recovery', the latter being an area which is likely to be of particular importance for hard-working professionals.

social activities and engagement, health and recovery, and self. Further, respondents indicated how important work and personal life was to them (*importance*) in two separate questions. In another question they indicated their relative *priority* of work and personal life (i.e. "How important are your personal life and work in relation to each other?") with a 5-point Likert scale specifically created for this question.[35]

Work hours were indicated numerically by respondents. Similarly, *job-related travel* was assessed with a single question asking respondents how many nights (from zero to seven) they usually spend away from home due to travel.

Availability and use of organizational work-life balance initiatives were measured directly by providing a list of the thirteen work-life initiatives that had been identified as available in the 25 top management consultancies in Germany (cf. Part I, 3.2.2 for details). 'Primary initiatives' represent programs that are more specifically targeted at work-life balance issues and are also largely in line with initiatives tested in previous research. Primary initiatives include reduced schedule options, short-term and long-term flexible work hours, home office, office (Fri)day, leave of absence, free choice of residence, childcare, and elder-care. 'Secondary' initiatives represent programs that are also advertised in many management consultants' work-life policy but that address issues at the boundary of work and personal life and were also largely not tested in previous research. Secondary initiatives comprise supportive services, health and recovery programs, individual coaching, and support from the firm with regards to educational programs (MBA, PhD, etc.). Respondents were asked to select one of the following options: "not offered and not needed", "not offered but needed", "offered but not used", and "offered and used", similar to the procedure applied by O'Driscoll et al. (2003). For the later PLS analysis answers were dummy-coded into two variables: *initiative availability* differentiated professionals who indicated 'offered but not used' (= 1) and those who indicated 'not offered and not needed' / 'not offered but needed' (= 0). *Initiative use* differentiated between professionals who indicated that the initiative was 'offered and used' (= 1) versus all other respondents (= 0). Following the example of Dikkers et al. (2004) summed scores were calculated that represent the quantity of initiatives used, assuming that higher frequency of use or perception of access to more initiatives are associated with less conflict. Due to the previously discussed flaws of using summed scores the model was also estimated for single initiatives in the total

---

35   Note: 1 = my personal life is much more important than my work; 2 = personal life and
       work are important but primarily my personal life; 3 = both equally important; 4 = work
       and personal life are equally important but primarily my work; 5 = my work is much
       more important than my personal life.

sample and contrasting management consultants and law firm professionals. Unfortunately, for further subsample comparisons dividing the sample into subgroups and assessing single work-life initiatives would have resulted in sample sizes too small to be estimated.

Corporate work-life culture represented the dimensions of informal demands and resources and was measured with five constructs: perceived *support from management, supervisor(s)* and *co-workers* as the resource dimension and perceived *negative career consequences* and *organizational time demands* as the demands dimension. The support dimension reflects the extent to which the organization, supervisors, and co-workers are perceived to be supportive of the integration of employees' work and personal lives and the use of WLB initiatives. The demands dimension refers to the extent to which organizational values and norms (i.e. time expectations and related negative career consequences) are perceived to interfere with employees' attempt to reduce work-life conflict and respective use of WLB initiatives (cf. Dikkers et al., 2004). Items developed by Thompson et al. (1999) and refined and complemented by Dikkers et al. (2004) were slightly modified to suit the context of this study. Altogether three items were used to measure each construct of corporate work-life culture. A sample item for the support dimension is: "Meine Organisation nimmt Rücksicht auf das Privatleben der Mitarbeiter [original: Managers in this organization are generally considerate towards the private life of employees]". A sample item for the demands dimension is: "Die Arbeitszeit vorübergehend zu reduzieren wirkt sich negativ auf die Karriere aus [original: To turn down a promotion for private reasons will harm one's career progress in this organization]") (see Appendix B for the complete list of items).

Subgroups were created with respect to subbranch, life role priority, gender, age, relationship, parental and dual-career status, tenure, and job level. To examine *management consultants versus law firm professionals* as two subbranches of professional service firms the snowball sample was taken as subsample 1 and all law firm professionals comprised subsample 2. *Age* was measured numerically and dummy-coded to form four different groups: below 30, 30-34, 35-39, and 40-49. This division was made based on the assumption that individuals below age 30 would differ from individuals between 30 and 40 and again individuals older than 40 with regards to their work-life interface. The 30-40 group represented the largest group of respondents, therefore this group was split further in order to achieve more fine-grained results. Number of children, reported numerically by respondents, was dummy-coded into two groups indicating *parental status*[36] (versus non-parents) whereby parents with children older than 7 years[37] were excluded from analysis because based on existing evidence it was assumed that work-life conflict caused by the parental role would be highest for children of primary school age and younger. *Relationship status* was measured categorically with one single item asking respondents to indicate whether they were single vs. in a relationship / married. A dummy variable was created for *dual-career status* using answers to whether 1) respondents worked full-time and whether 2) their partner was employed on a full-time schedule. The combination of these two items resulted in the dichotomous variable of dual-career status.[38] *Tenure* was assessed numerically and dummy-coded to form three groups: 0-3 years (entry and orientation stage), 3.5-6 years (experienced stage) and 6.5 years and more (expert stage, advancement to partner becomes an issue). *Job level* was assessed on a 5-point scale labeled 1 = entry level, 2 = between entry and medium level, 3 = medium level, 4 = between medium and top/partner level, and 5 = top/partner level corresponding to the pyramid-shaped structure of most PSFs outlined in Part I, 2.2.3. This operationalization was chosen because hierarchy labels in PSFs and related branches differ largely by company and assessing job position on a 1-5 range was expected to yield the highest comparability of results among branches. In order to test the model with regards to differences between job levels the five categories were reduced into three categories representing 'entry to medium level', 'medium level' and 'medium to top level' in order to maintain sufficient subsample sizes of all categories.

1.2 Data Analyses

1.2.1 Descriptive Data Analysis and ANOVA

In order to examine Research Question 1 evaluating the specific character of professionals' work-life dynamics, descriptive data analyses and analysis of variance (ANOVA) were used to test for subgroup differences with regards to the three work-to-life conflict dimensions and the five work vs. personal life conflict types. Significance of ANOVA results was tested with standard F statistics and, in cases where homogeneity of variances was not confirmed, with Brown-Forsythe robust test of equality of means which does not require equal

---

36   Nparents = 180; M = 2.30; Min = 0, Max = 7.

37   Nparents of children older than 7 = 49; M = 14.67; Min = 8, Max = 33.

38   Full-time employment of both partners was taken as an indicator for a career focus of both partners, as dual-earner status is often associated with one partner working full-time and one partner in part-time employment (Blyton & Dastmalchian, 2006).

within-group variance (Janssen & Laatz, 2007). A similar procedure was applied by Dikkers et al. (2004) and Madsen (2003).

1.2.2 Hypotheses Testing with Partial Least Squares Path Modeling (PLS)

Partial least squares analysis (PLS) as it is implemented in the software SmartPLS® (Ringle, Wende & Will, 2006) was applied to evaluate the hypothesized model as well as to examine Research Question 2. Developed by Wold (1982), this methodology is considered a powerful multivariate analysis tool for testing structural models. In work-life research, this methodology was applied previously (Higgins & Duxbury, 1992). Structural equation modeling (SEM) is aimed at testing relationships in models that include latent variables. A latent variable is a construct that is not directly observable and is therefore represented by a set of measurable indicators, also referred to as manifest variables. As an example, work-life conflict is considered a latent construct and is measured by a set of items that are representative of this construct. Most psychometric variables are considered to be latent variables.

Usually structural equation modeling (SEM) is associated with techniques such as applied in the programs LISREL© or AMOS© that are based on the evaluation of the covariance matrix. Particularly in marketing science the variance-based approach used in partial least squares modeling has prevailed, deemed to be the synonym of the more econometrically-oriented analysis of variance (Jahn, 2007). Covariance-based SEM requires normally distributed data, large sample sizes, and usually latent variables have to be explained by at least three indicators. PLS, also referred to as "soft modeling" (Tenenhaus et al. 2005, p. 160), is very tolerant of distribution assumptions and small sample sizes. Indeed PLS sets no requirements with regards to distribution normality of the data (Fornell & Cha, 1994). Scholderer and Balderjahn (2005) suggest to use PLS for samples N < 100 and latent variables measured with less than four indicators, as well as for studies of rather explorative character where hypotheses are uncertain or where investigations are guided by research questions. Whereas covariance-based methods focus on testing whether and how well the hypothesized model represents the data in use, variance-based methods are more strongly focused on the determination of predictive quality of the model (Jöreskog & Wold, 1982), i.e. how well the characteristics of one construct or a set of constructs can be predicted by the characteristics of another single construct or set of constructs. Being based on regression analysis, path analysis and principal components factor analysis, PLS allows testing measurement quality of the constructs (outer model) and relationships between constructs (inner model) simultaneously, avoiding the two-step approach of evaluating measurement quality first, e.g. with factor analysis, and applying these factors in a multivariate method to test hypotheses. Interpretability of the data is made easy as the loadings of the indicators on the construct are factor loadings, the path coefficients are standardized regression coefficients and the determination coefficient R^2, indicating the amount of explained variance in the model, is interpretable in analogy to the determination coefficient of multiple regression analysis. A PLS path model consists of altogether two models (Tenenhaus et al., 2005): a *measurement model* relating the manifest variables (observable indicators/items) to a latent construct (also referred to as 'outer model'), and a *structural model* relating latent variables to other latent variables (also referred to as 'inner model').

The measurement model can be composed of either *reflective* or *formative* indicators. [39] In a reflective measurement model the latent construct is modeled as a function of its observable indicators (Christophersen & Grape, 2007), i.e. by means multiple re-testing and factor analysis a set of indicators is developed that represent the latent construct and are thus highly correlated. In the case of reflective constructs,

> "each indicator represents an error-afflicted measurement of the latent variable. The direction of causality is from the construct to the indicators; thus, observed measures are assumed to reflect variation in the latent variable. In other words, changes in the construct are expected to be manifested in changes in all of its indicators" (Henseler et al., 2009, p. 289).

In short, each manifest variable reflects its latent construct (Tenenhaus et al., 2005). All latent variables in the present study are considered reflective in nature, i.e. the manifest variables reflect the latent variables unidimensionally. [40]

---

39   The character of reflective versus formative indicators and constructs is discussed vividly and controversially in the literature. It is beyond the scope of the present thesis to outline the different perspectives in detail, for further in-depth information refer to Christophersen and Grape (2007), Eberl (2006), Fassott and Eggert (2005) and particularly Jarvis et al. (2003).

40   Formative measurement models, frequently used in marketing and consumer research, are modeled by a weighted combination of indicators, i.e. the indicators are interpreted as causing the latent construct. This implies that all identified indicators are necessary in order to represent the construct correctly, adding or eliminating indicators usually means a modification of the latent variable's meaning. An example for a formative construct is product attractiveness which can be a combination of functionality, design, price, etc. each of them impacting the higher-order construct of perceived attractiveness of the product. Correlation among formative indicator, contrary to reflective indicators, is not a necessary condition. In short, a formative latent variable is generated by a set of manifest variables (Tenenhaus et al., 2005).

The variable managerial support for example is operationalized by three items which all represent a different facet of this construct. Therefore the procedures suggested by Chin (2010), Götz et al., (2010), Hulland (1999) and Tenenhaus et al. (2005) for evaluating reflective measurement models and structural models are followed here. Variables of the structural model that act as predictors only (independent variables) are called *exogenous* variables (in the model: work hours, work-related travel, time demands, negative career consequences, management and supervisor support, availability of WLB initiatives) whereas variables that act as criteria only or as predictor of one/several constructs and criteria of (an)other construct(s) are referred to as *endogenous* variables (Chin, 2010; Ringle et al., 2006). Figure 8 displays the measurement models and the structural model including all relevant relationships.

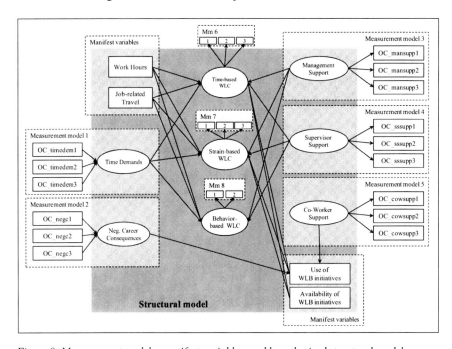

Figure 8. Measurement models, manifest variables, and hypothesized structural model

Hypothesis testing in structural equation modeling with PLS is done in two stages as suggested by Chin (1998b) and Hulland (1999): firstly, the measurement model is evaluated with regards to validity and reliability criteria; secondly, the structural model representing the set of hypotheses is estimated. The quality of the measurement model, i.e. the quality of the item sets measuring the latent constructs of interest, is observed with the following indicators (Fornell & Larcker, 1981; Hulland, 1999; Schepers et al., 2005; Tenenhaus et al., 2005) (All evaluation criteria, indicator values and thresholds of both the measurement and structural model are summarized in Table 4):

– *Content validity*. Content validity indicates the extent to which the variables of a measurement model describe their underlying construct. This quality criterion assesses whether a variable is only related to one single construct in the model and does not load significantly on several constructs, also being referred to as *unidimensionality* (Götz et al., 2010). Unidimensionality can be tested with principal component analysis (PCA). A construct is considered unidimensional "if the first eigenvalue of the correlation matrix of the block MVs is larger than 1 and the second one smaller than 1, or at least very far from the first one" (Tenenhaus et al., 2005, p.163).

– *Indicator reliability*. Indicator reliability, according to Götz et al. (2010), identifies each indicator's variance explained by the underlying construct/latent variable. More than 50% of the variance of an indicator should be explained by the construct implying that "for loadings λ of the latent constructs on the indicator variable x or y, values larger than 0.7 are acceptable" (Götz et al., 2010, p.694). Hulland (1999) suggests indicator elimination if their loadings are smaller than 0.4 for reflective measurement models.

– *Construct reliability*. Construct reliability evaluates the accuracy of a measure and the probability of random measurement error (Cronbach, 2004). Both *Cronbach's α* and *composite reliability ρ* are commonly used as indicators of construct reliability. Acceptable scores for both Cronbach's Alpha and composite reliability of scales should not be below .70 (Nunnally & Bernstein, 1994).

– *Convergent validity*. Convergent validity addresses the problem of common method variance. As it may be argued that measuring a latent construct with a number of items represents measurement with 'different methods' (Götz et al., 2010) *average variance extracted (AVE)* is a common measure of convergent validity. According to Götz et al. (2010) "AVE includes the variance of its indicators captured by the construct relative to the total amount of variance, including the variance due to measurement error" (p. 696). The value should not be lower than .50 (Hulland, 1999).

– *Discriminant validity*. Testing whether constructs that should be unrelated are indeed unrelated, discriminant validity is assessed with two metrics: a) the *square root of AVE* of each construct should exceed the correlation shared between the construct and other constructs in the model (Fornell & Larcker, 1981), and b) *cross-factor loadings (CFL)* of the measures should not exhibit

any loadings substantial in magnitude on constructs for it was not hypothesized so (Fornell & Bookstein, 1982; Hulland, 1999).

The following metrics are used to estimate the structural PLS model (Chin,
1998b; Götz et al., 2010; Ringle, 2004; Tenenhaus et al., 2005):
- *Determination Coefficient R^2 and Path Coefficients γ.* R^2 is the amount of
  variance explained by an exogenous (independent) variable, corresponding to
  R square in multiple regression analysis. The larger the determination coefficient R square, the larger is the amount of variance of the dependent variable
  that is explained by the independent variables in the model. *Path coefficient γ*
  corresponds to the standardized beta coefficient used in multiple regression
  analysis. Its significance is tested with t-statistics obtained by resampling
  methods (Bootstrapping) (Götz et al., 2010). Chin (1998a) suggests that path
  coefficients should be larger than 0.2 to speak of an interesting relationship.
- *Effect size f^2.* First suggested by Cohen (1988), effect size f^2 shows whether an
  exogenous variable has a substantial influence on the endogenous latent variable. It is obtained by calculating the structural model once with and once
  without the exogenous variable. Effect sizes of .02 are considered weak, .15
  moderate, and .35 substantial (Chin, 1998b). f^2 is calculated by hand using the
  following formula:

$$f^2 = \frac{R^2_{\text{included}} - R^2_{\text{exlcuded}}}{1 - R^2_{\text{included}}}$$

- *Stone-Geisser criterion Q^2.* The predictive quality of the model is tested with
  the Stone-Geisser test, also called 'blindfolding' (Götz et al., 2010). If the cri-
  terion Q^2 is larger than 0 the model is considered to have predictive validity
  (Chin, 1998b; Ringle 2004).
- *Goodnes of Fit GoF.* Until recently PLS modeling did not allow statements
  about overall fit of the model (Götz et al., 2010) unlike covariance-based
  SEM approaches (AMOS, LISREL). Tenenhaus et al. (2005) introduced
  GoF, being defined as the "geometric mean of the average commonality and
  the average *R square*" (p. 173). As thresholds for this *GoF* measure Schepers,
  Wetzels and de Ruyter (2005) suggest 0.1 for small, 0.25 for medium and
  0.36 for large scores.

Table 4. Summary of evaluation criteria for PLS analysis with reflective indicators

Criterion	Indicator	Threshold
Measurement Model:		
Content Validity (Unidimensionality)	*PCA loadings*	Eigenvalue > 1
Indicator Reliability	λ	Path loadings $\lambda > 0.7$ (eliminate item if $\lambda > 0.4$)
Construct Reliability	α, ρ	Cronbach's α and composite reliability $\rho < 0.7$
Convergent Validity	*AVE*	Average variance extracted (AVE) > 0.5
Discriminant Validity	*Square root of AVE; CFL*	Square root of AVE exceeds correlation shared between construct and other constructs in the model; No substantial cross-factor loadings (CFL)
Structural Model:		
Determination Coefficient	R^2	Large R^2 (ranging from $0-1$) signifies good representation of the model by the data
Path Coefficients	γ	Path coefficients $\gamma > 0.2$
Effect size	f^2	Small: 0.02, moderate: 0.15, large effect: 0.35
Stone-Geisser Criterion	Q^2	$Q^2 \neq 0$
Goodnes-of Fit	*GoF*	Small: 0.1, moderate: 0.25, large effect: 0.36

1.2.3 Assessment of Subsample Differences

Additionally to testing the impact of organizational factors on work-life conflict it was examined whether the relationships postulated in the model differ for various subgroups, specifically subbranch, life role priority, gender, age, relationship status, parental status, dual-career status, tenure, and job position. Such an analytic procedure is also referred to as moderator analysis.

A moderator is a "variable that affects the direction and/or strength of the relation between an independent or predictor variable and a dependent or criterion variable" (Baron & Kenny, 1986, p. 1174). Henseler and Fassott (2010) suggest two available procedures for variance-based structural equation modeling: "moderating effects as product terms" and "determining moderating effects through group comparisons" (p. 719). In the first technique an interaction term (exogenous variable × moderator variable) is added to the model, similar to testing moderator effects in linear regression analysis (Frazier et al., 2004). The second procedure is particularly feasible if the moderator variable is categorical in nature (as for example gender or subbranch), i.e. not continuous. The model is estimated separately for each group and differences between results of the estimation parameters are interpreted as moderator effects. Metric variables can be dichotomized by creating a dummy variable with two categories (Henseler & Fassott, 2010), for example "older than 30" and "younger than 30". In order to test subgroup effects the second procedure was applied.

2. Results

In the following sections, empirical results are presented concerning professionals' work-life dynamics in general (2.1) as well as results of estimating the structural model outlined in the previous section (2.2). From this wealth of information major findings are summarized at the end of this part (2.3).

2.1 Characteristics of Professionals' Work-Life Conflict (RQ1)

In Part I, the question was raised whether work-life conflict is an issue for professionals in PSFs at all, and which life spheres the 'life' component of professionals' work-life conflict refers to. Above and beyond, the likeliness of differences between certain subgroups was discussed, e.g. do males experience less conflict or conflict between different roles than females, and do management consultants experience higher levels of conflict than of law firm professionals because they travel more? In order to shed light to this issue a look was taken first at respondents' judgments of their life role importance, priority, and centrality. Further, frequencies as well as means and mean differences were investigated with regards to the three work-to-life conflict subscales and one variable measuring the interaction of work with other life domains, i.e. whether participants experienced no, small, moderate or high levels of conflict between work vs. family, work vs. friends, work vs. social engagement, work vs. health and recovery and work vs. time for self. Whether there are significant differences between groups with regards to time-, strain-, and behavior-based conflict as well as type of conflict among life spheres was evaluated using analysis of variance (ANOVA). As it was considered likely that subgroups in the sample, e.g. management consultants and law firm professionals or males and females differed in their judgment of life role importance and perception of conflict various subgroups were contrasted according to the following characteristics: subbranch

(MC vs. LF), life role priority, gender, age, relationship status, parental status and dual-career status, tenure, and job position.

2.1.1 Life Role Importance, Priority, and Centrality

As illustrated previously, the value individuals attach to their work and personal life spheres was assessed with three variables: respondents indicated how important their work and their personal life is to them (*importance*), how important their work and personal life are in relation to each other (*priority*) and distributed 100 points among the domains of work, partnership and family, friends, social activities and engagement, health and recovery and self (*centrality*). Mean values for the total sample and for subgroups divided by subbranch, gender, and age can be inferred from Table 5.

Work and family were clearly the most central roles in most participants' lives. The majority of respondents assigned 20 to 30 points to the work sphere and 20 to 35 points to the family and partnership sphere. Largely, respondents assigned ten to twenty points to 'friends', four to ten points to 'social engagement', eight to fifteen points to the sphere of 'health and recovery', five to fifteen points were assigned to 'self'. Asked about the importance of work in their life, 61.6 per cent judge work as important and 28.2 per cent as very important. Personal life was rated as important by 43.7 per cent and very important by 53.1 per cent. When respondents were asked whether they prioritize work over personal life or vice versa 7.1 per cent indicated that personal life was clearly more important than their work, 41.8 per cent indicated that both were important, but primarily personal life. Equal importance of work and personal life was indicated by 39 per cent. 10.3 per cent valued both but primarily work and only 1.4 per cent clearly favored work over personal life. These metrics constitute important background information for interpreting the results concerning the type of conflict experienced which was examined in the next step.

Table 5. Mean values with regards to life role centrality, importance and priority

		Complete Sample	Subbranch		Gender		Age			
			MC	LF	Male	Female	↓30	30-34	35-39	40-49
		N = 794	242	552	548	241	181	334	135	112
Life Role Centrality	Work[a]	**27.32**	26.72	27.58	27.59	26.73	26.13	27.12	28.09	27.67
	Family/ Partnership[b]	**29.60**	27.53	30.51	29.57	29.59	28.12	29.18	31.58	32.01
	Friends[c]	**14.97**	16.36	14.36	14.80	15.37	16.27	15.41	13.99	13.63
	Social Engagement[d]	**6.02**	6.24	5.92	5.99	6.13	6.50	6.13	5.27	5.85
	Health / Recovery[e]	**11.90**	12.48	11.65	11.98	11.76	12.32	12.40	11.33	10.44
	Self[f]	**10.26**	10.66	10.09	10.10	10.61	10.66	9.95	9.76	10.40
	Importance Work	**4.16**	4.22	4.13	4.16	4.17	4.20	4.12	4.15	4.21
	Importance Personal Life	**4.50**	4.57	4.48	4.50	4.51	4.54	4.55	4.45	4.47
	Priority Work vs. Personal Life[g]	**2.57**	2.57	2.57	2.60	2.52	2.51	2.56	2.54	2.62

Note. Values for centrality refer to a total of 100 points distributed over six spheres; Values for importance and priority are mean values (1-5 scale).
[a] Range 0-80; [b] Range 0-95; [c] Range 0-90; [d] Range 0-35; [e] Range 0-40; [f] Range 0-35.
[g] High levels indicate higher prioritization of work over personal life.

2.1.2 Experience of Work-Life Conflict among Professionals

Means concerning the *three work-to-life conflict dimensions*, which were measured on a 1-5 point Likert scale were $M_{tWLC} = 3.83$, $M_{sWLC} = 3.22$, and $M_{bWLC} = 3.15$ indicating that particularly time-based work-to-life conflict affects the respondents in this study. Strain- and behavior-based conflict played a smaller role although these two means still ranged above three, i.e. the central point of the scale. Resulting levels of *five work and personal life conflict dimensions* are displayed in Figure 7. Means with regards to these types ranged from 2.81 (work vs. family conflict) to 3.15 (work vs. social engagement) indicating moderate conflict levels for all types. To make more sense of these mean values it was also examined how many types of conflict were perceived moderate to high by

each individual in the sample.[41] 11.1 per cent of the professionals experienced
moderate to high levels in two types of conflict, 15.7 per cent for three types of
conflict, 23.4 per cent for four types and 35.8 per cent experienced moderate to
high levels for all conflict types. Thus, nearly two thirds of the professionals that
participated in this study felt that their work conflicts with three other spheres of
their life. This finding could serve as a first indicator that work – personal life
conflict does matter in highly demanding jobs. It must be noted though, that 31.4
per cent of respondents in the sample did not experience high levels of conflict
of either type (cf. Appendix C, Table C.2). A small portion of the sample (3.5
to 8.1 per cent) reported experiencing no conflict, yet with the highest amount in
the work vs. family conflict category. At the same time work-family conflict
was the category with the smallest percentage of respondents experiencing high
conflict (24.8 per cent). Moderate levels of conflict were reported most frequently for all conflict types ranging from 36 per cent (work vs. self) to 43.2 per cent
(work vs. health and recovery). Respondents who perceived high levels of conflict ranged from 24.8 per cent to 43.1 per cent with the highest values for the
social engagement conflict and time for self conflict. High conflict was reported
particularly with regards to work vs. social activities and engagement (43.1 per
cent) and work vs. time for self (40.5 per cent). Although these values are surprisingly high, results from the previous section should be kept in mind: the fact
that social activities / engagement and time for self were the categories with the
lowest centrality in participants' lives puts conflict levels into perspective. These
high levels of conflict despite relatively low role centrality indicate that professionals in the present sample prioritized more strongly in favor of spheres which
were central to them and made trade-offs with regards to less central areas of
their lives.

---

41   To examine whether individuals only perceived high or moderate levels in one type of
      conflict or in several, the number of values were counted for moderate and high level of
      experienced conflict per case. Thus, values range from 0 (neither high nor moderate
      conflict of any type experienced) to 5 (high or moderate conflict experienced regarding
      all types).

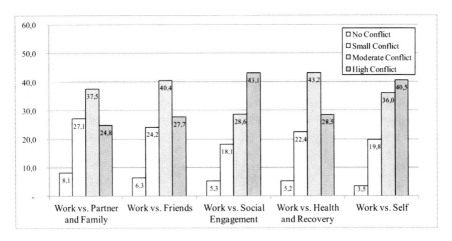

Figure 9. Examination of the types of conflict between work and several life domains

ANOVA served to further investigate whether specific subgroups differed in their experience of work-life conflict and the five conflict types. Means, standard deviations and correlations of all variables that were tested for differences with this procedure are displayed in Appendix C, Table C.3. The first subgroups of interest were *management consultants* and *law firm professionals*. Tests of mean difference revealed that respondents differed significantly by subbranch in their experience of time-based and behavior-based work-to-life conflict and with regards to the types work vs. social engagement and work vs. health and recovery. Management consultants thereby experienced higher conflict levels in each variable.[42] Time-based WLC was the most strongly experienced conflict dimension in both subsamples. Highest conflict with regards to work vs. life domains was perceived with regards to work conflicting with social engagement, however, as we have seen in the previous section respondents assigned the smallest amount of points to the 'social engagement' sphere. High conflict level may therefore also indicate that this is an area where respondents expend the smallest amount of time and energy.

Next, the experience of work-life conflict was examined with respect to *role priority* assigned to work vs. personal life. Three groups were formed using the life role priority variable (cf. Part II, 2.1.1). Individuals who indicated that personal life was clearly more important than work and who valued both but pri-

---

42   Time-based WLC: $M_{MC} = 3.93$ vs. $M_{LF} = 3.78$; Behavior-based WLC: $M_{MC} = 3.36$ vs. $M_{LF} = 3.04$; Work conflicting with social engagement: $M_{MC} = 3.30$ vs. $M_{LF} = 3.09$; Work conflicting with time for health and recovery: $M_{MC} = 3.05$ vs. $M_{LF} = 2.91$.

marily personal life were assigned to the 'life' group (N = 388). Individuals who assigned equal priority to work and personal life formed the 'balance' group (N = 93) and individuals who indicated that work to them was clearly more important than personal life and who valued both but primarily work were assigned to the 'work' group (N = 310). Mean comparisons revealed that these groups differ concerning experienced work-life conflict in a number of ways. Higher time-based and behavior-based WLC were experienced by the 'life' type compared to the 'work' type. Above and beyond, 'balancers' experienced the highest level of behavior-based WLC ($M_{balance}$ = 3.34; M_{life} = 3.21; M_{work} =3.01). The 'life' type group indicated significantly higher conflict between work vs. family and work vs. time for self.

Gender and *age* differences were further examined. Males and females did not differ in their assignment of importance, priority, and centrality of life roles as shown in the previous paragraph (Table 5). The only significant difference revealed by ANOVA was that females experienced significantly higher strain-based WLC than males ($M_{females}$ = 3.37; M_{males} = 3.14). Other than that, mean values of the WLC experiences of men and women in the sample were surprisingly similar. Regarding age, ANOVA results revealed a number of significant mean differences among age groups. Time-based WLC was highest at age 30-34 (M = 3.96) differing significantly from participants at age 40-49 (M = 3.67) who experienced the lowest levels of tWLC within this comparison. The same constellation was observed for strain-based WLC (M_{30-34} = 3.37 vs. M_{40-49} = 3.01), for work conflicting with family (M_{30-34} = 2.92 vs. M_{40-49} = 2.65), work conflicting with 'friends' (M_{30-34} = 3.04 vs. M_{40-49} = 2.65), and work conflicting with social engagement ($M_{under\ 30}$ = 3.27 and M_{30-34} = 3.27 vs. M_{40-49} = 2.88). These findings suggest that age plays a role for the experience of work-life conflict with the overall tendency of highest levels of conflict at a younger age yet after the first years of work experience.

It has been suggested in previous research that having a *partner* (often assessed as being married) and the *presence of children* as well as the *employment status of the partner* affect the experience of work-life conflict. ANOVAs were therefore conducted contrasting work-life conflict experiences of single individuals versus individuals who were in a relationship or married, parents versus nonparents and respondents in a dual-career relationship versus those without dual-career status. The only difference between singles versus individuals in a relationship was that the latter perceived stronger work-time for self conflict. Interestingly, nonparents experienced higher levels of time-, strain-, and behavior-based WLC than parents. Furthermore nonparents' mean level of work conflicting with 'family' and with 'friends' was higher than average conflict levels experienced by parents. This finding may be explained by the fact that nearly 80 per cent of the parents in the sample had a partner who was not in full-time employment, whereas the majority of non-parents were in a relationship where both partners worked full-time. Note however, that in both subgroups the majority of participants worked on a full-time schedule (93.5 per cent of the non-parents; 82.9 per cent of the parents). Related to this finding, individuals in a dual-career relationship experienced higher levels of WLC with regards to all three dimensions indicating that the variable of primary interest is dual-career status since parents within the sample are largely backed-up by a homemaking partner. Individuals in a dual-career relationship also perceived much stronger conflict between work and 'friends' than non dual-career respondents (Mean difference = .79).

Finally, subsamples were compared with respect to tenure and job position. With the exception of behavior-based WLC significant differences were found with respect to all variables under examination. Individuals with longer than 6 years *tenure* suffered less conflict concerning all types and dimensions. Highest levels of conflict were experienced by individuals who worked for their organization for 3.5 to 6 years. Similar results though with less significant findings were found for the variable *job position*. Results indicate that entry and medium level professionals experience higher time- and strain-based WLC than those in advanced and top level positions (although Bonferroni post hoc analysis slightly failed to provide significant results in the case of time-based WLC). Summing up, the major findings with regards to Research Question 1 are the following:

– Professionals *do* face challenges with regards to their work-personal life reconciliation and these challenges reach *beyond the experience of work-family conflict.*
– Subgroups differed with regards to the conflict dimensions (time, psychological strain, behavior) as well as interactions between work and several life spheres (family, friends, social engagement, health, self).

These findings are a first indicator that a differential work-life integration management within organizations is needed. Results obtained up to this point also extend our knowledge about the character of conflict between work, family, and further life spheres which helps to interpret further research findings from structural modeling that are presented in the following sections.

2.2 Hypothesis Testing with PLS: Formal and Informal Demands and Resources and the Work-Life Conflict of Professionals

After taking a look at the specific character of work-life interactions of professionals the research model proposed in Part I, 3.2.4, was examined. Evaluation

of the measurement model (2.2.1) is followed by results of estimating the structural model (2.2.2). In order to answer Research Question 2, the model is further
estimated using only one initiative at a time in order to provide insights about
specific effects of work-life initiatives (2.2.3). In 2.2.4, the model is estimated
with respect to certain subgroups whose peculiar perspective concerning the
work-life interface was outlined previously (PSF subbranch, life role priority,
gender, age, family and job characteristics) (cf. Part I, section 3.3).

2.2.1 Evaluation of the Measurement Models

In order to test quality of the measurement model metrics outlined previously
are applied (1.2.2). *Content validity* of the latent variables in the model (management support, supervisor support, co-worker support, organizational time
demands, negative career consequences; time-based, strain-based, and behavior-
based work-to-life) was investigated with principal component analysis (PCA)
in order to reveal the indicators' underlying factor structure and test for
unidimensionality of the constructs. PCA extracted five factors with initial eigenvalues above 1 and three factors marginally failing to reach eigenvalues of 1.
Supervisor support, organizational time demands and behavior-based work-to-
life conflict included non-ideal factor loadings. A closer look at respective items
indicates that these loadings could be due to the specific sample of professionals
for which items may not be as adequate as they have proven in previous studies.
The fact that the factor for bWLC did not reach an initial eigenvalue above 1
was presumingly due to the fact that it consisted of only two items. The rotated
component matrix showed that all factors were clearly distinct and there were no
substantial cross-loadings. Eigenvalues of all factors were not substantially lower than 1, particularly considering the distance of factor 8 to a potential factor 9
(eigenvalues .842 vs. .642). Communalities[43] ranged between .888 and .634.
Overall, despite small restraints mentioned, the criterion of unidimensionality of
all eight latent constructs indicating high content validity can be considered to
be met.

---

43   ‚Communality‘ is the variance of a variable explained by the underlying factor and can
     range from 0 (= null variance explained) to 1 (Janssen & Laatz, 2007, p. 536).

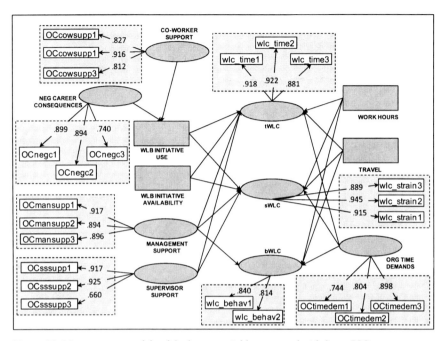

Figure 10. Measurement models of the latent variables as tested with SmartPLS

In order to assess *indicator reliability* loadings of all reflective indicators were examined. Item loadings ranged between .945 and .660. One indicator was below the threshold of 0.7 that was suggested by Götz et al. (2010). Hulland (1999) proposes indicator elimination of only loadings smaller than 0.4. After critical examination and theoretical consideration of this specific item loading (supervisor support, item 3), it was decided to keep this item within the model also taking into consideration that the loading was just slightly below the suggested threshold. All other items were kept for further analysis following methodological suggestions (Hulland, 1999) which resulted in the final measurement models displayed in Figure 10. *Construct reliability* metrics, i.e. Cronbach's α and composite reliability ρ are displayed in Table 6. All common thresholds for these criteria were met with the exception of behavior-based work-to-life conflict holding an alpha score of only .54. Because the composite reliability of this construct was satisfactory and composite reliability is considered a more accurate metric for construct reliability than Cronbach's α (Chin, 1998, 2010; Ringle, 2004) this construct was still rendered sufficiently reliable for analysis. AVE values testing *convergent validity* were all well above the 0.50 threshold suggested by Hulland (1999) (cf. Table 6). Regarding *discriminant validity*, the relevant criteria were also met. None of the cross-factor loadings exhibited substantial loadings on constructs that were not hypothesized to be related. For all indicators did the square root of AVE considerably exceed the correlation shared between the construct and other constructs in the model (cf. diagonal italics in Table 7).

Table 6. Cronbach's α, composite reliability ρ and average variance extracted (AVE) of the latent variables

Construct	No of Indicators	α	ρ	AVE
Management Support	3	.88	.85	.67
Supervisor Support	3	.79	.86	.67
Co-Worker Support	3	.83	.84	.63
Organizational Time Demands	3	.80	.84	.64
Negative Career Consequences	3	.80	.91	.76
Time-based Work-to-Life Conflict	3	.89	.89	.73
Strain-based Work-to-Life Conflict	3	.90	.98	.95
Behavior-based Work-to-Life Conflict	2	.54	.90	.82

2.2.2 Estimation of the Structural Model

Table 7 provides means, standard deviations, and correlations among model variables and subgroup variables. Evaluation of the structural model and testing of hypothesis was done by means of the metrics outlined previously. Determination coefficient *R square,* path coefficients and their significance estimated with a bootstrapping procedure (t-values) were used to test the hypothesized model.

Table 7. Means, standard deviations, correlations and square root of AVE

	M	SD	1	2	3	4	5	6	7	8	9	10	11	12	13	14	15	16	17	18	19
1 Weekly Work Hours	54.88	11.26																			
2 Job-related Travel	1.08	1.439	.337**																		
3 Initiative Availability	1.42	1.457	.148**	.208**																	
4 Initiative Use	1.70	1.467	-.099**	.325**	.033																
5 Management Support	3.12	.757	-.173**	-.063	.163**	.160**	*.817*														
6 Supervisor Support	3.41	.732	-.030	-.013	.142**	.137**	.453**	*.812*													
7 Co-worker Support	3.13	.818	-.057	.023	.162**	.137**	.543**	.572**	*.794*												
8 Org. Time Demands	3.94	.792	.212**	-.020	-.119**	-.136**	-.529**	-.275**	-.295**	*.797*											
9 Neg. Career Consequ.	3.56	.868	.037	-.203**	-.186**	-.260**	-.518**	-.309**	-.359**	.578**	*.873*										
10 Time-based WLC	3.83	.853	.269**	.115**	-.104**	-.073*	-.489**	-.255**	-.312**	.547**	.387**	*.854*									
11 Strain-based WLC	3.21	.976	.139**	.014	-.183**	-.143**	-.431**	-.261**	-.324**	.435**	.367**	.593**	*.976*								
12 Behavior-based WLC	3.13	.903	.242**	.222**	.000	-.018	-.362**	-.193**	-.216**	.383**	.257**	.460**	.384**	*.907*							
13 Gender	1.31	.461	-.237**	-.181**	-.075*	-.033	-.128**	-.111*	-.096**	.048	.052	.010	.113**	-.067							
14 Age	33.99	7.046	-.127**	-.172**	-.056	-.073*	.132**	.003	.085*	-.041	-.016	-.126**	-.117**	-.088*	-.104**						
15 Relationship Status	1.81	.395	-.009	-.015	-.027	-.026	.003	-.008	.043	-.008	.012	.000	-.034	-.035	.134**	.124**					
16 Parental Status	.50	.887	-.134**	-.112**	-.017	.050	.123**	.080*	.092**	-.076*	-.025	-.115*	-.153**	-.126*	-.173**	.554**	.208**				
17 Job Position	2.75	1.266	.036	-.013	.006	.049	.094**	.043	.105**	-.040	-.054	-.071*	-.114*	-.035	-.112*	.660**	.124**	.481**			
18 Tenure	4.09	3.884	-.035	-.086*	.036	.032	.094**	.054	.111**	-.035	-.013	-.051	-.121**	-.052	-.048	.609**	.106**	.411**	.614**		
19 Job Experience	6.77	6.460	-.147**	-.055	-.030	.020	.144**	.013	.115**	-.103**	-.094**	-.161**	-.150**	-.068	-.052	.862**	.086*	.500**	.716**	.641**	
20 Life Role Priority	2.54	.999	.101**	.028	.004	.027	.061	.027	.057	.049	-.006	-.083*	-.054	-.001	-.011	.061	-.110**	-.056	.039	.062	.066

** $p < .01$; * $p < .05$
Note. Values on the diagonal of variables 5 – 12 indicate the square root of average extracted variance (AVE).

followed by effect size f^2. The Stone-Geisser criterion Q^2 and Goodness-of-Fit indicator *GoF* introduced by Tenenhaus et al. (2005) are presented in evaluation of model fit and overall predictive quality.

2.2.2.1 Hypothesis Testing: R square, Path Coefficients and t-Values

Determination coefficient R^2 indicates the variance of endogenous variables that is explained by the exogenous variables in the model, similar to *R square* in multiple regression analysis. The determination coefficients of time-based, strain-based and behavior-based work-to-life conflict indicate a reasonable representation of the data by the hypothesized model: variables in the model explained 39.7 per cent of the variance of time-based work-to-life conflict, 28 percent of the variance of strain-based work-to-life conflict, and 24.8 per cent in the case of behavior-based work-to-life conflict (cf. Figure 9).

According to Chin (1998) *R square* values of .67 are considered 'substantial', however Backhaus et al. (2003) argue that generalizable rules of *R square* thresholds cannot be made because determining the amount of explained variance as 'high' or 'low' depends on the constructs under examination and the specific research interests.

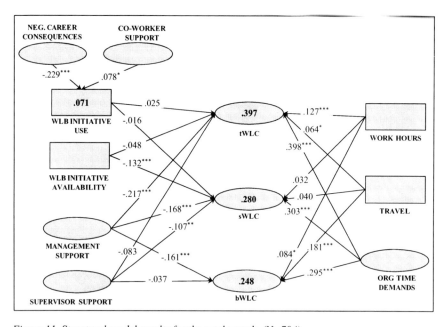

Figure 11. Structural model results for the total sample (N=794)

Considering the fact that work-life conflict is a complex construct with a potentially large number of antecedents the values of $R^2_{tWLC}=.397$, $R^2_{sWLC}=.280$ and $R^2_{bWLC}=.248$ can be considered 'moderate' in the model under examination. Path coefficients related to hypotheses are displayed in Table 8. The t-value of each coefficient was obtained by applying a bootstrapping procedure with 1000 resampling steps in order to achieve reasonable standard error estimates (Tenenhaus et al., 2005). All path coefficients relevant to initial hypothesis testing are displayed in Figure 9.

Hypothesis 1 proposed that *formal organizational demands* unfavorably impact professionals' work-life interface in terms of increased work-life conflict. Hypothesis 2 stated that *formal organizational resources*, having access to work-life initiatives and even more so making use of them, favorably impacts the work-life interface of professionals, i.e. by decreasing levels of work-life conflict:

– Hypothesis 1a and 1b stated that the number of work hours per week and job-related travel, are positively related to work-life conflict. For both time-based and behavior-based work-to-life conflict the data supported these hypotheses. With regards to work hours, all three path coefficients were positive and thus indicated that longer working hours are related to higher work-to-life conflict. Coefficients were significant for time-based ($\gamma = .127$; $t = 3.462$) and behavior-based WLC ($\gamma = .084$; $t = 2.152$), not for strain-based WLC. Hypothesis 1a thus received partial support by the data.

– Job-related travel was hypothesized to have an increasing impact on work-to-life conflict of all three dimensions as well (Hypothesis 1b). The amount of nights spent away from home due to work-related travel was positively related to time-based work-to-life conflict ($\gamma = .064$; $t = 2.005$) and behavior-based WLC ($\gamma = .181$; $t = 4.919$). No significant relationship was found for strain-based WLC. Again, Hypothesis 1b was only partially supported.

– Initiative availability (Hypothesis 2a) was negatively related to strain-based WLC ($\gamma = -.116$; $t = 3.760$), i.e. having access to work-life initiatives did have a reducing effect on the strain dimension of WLC. A relationship with time-based WLC ($\gamma = -.050$; $t = 1.695$) was found as well, though at the margins of significance. Partial support was therefore found for Hypothesis 2a.[44]

---

44 Testing an alternative model which also linked the two initiative variables to the behavior-based conflict dimension supported the assumption expressed a priori in Part I that initiative availability and use would only be related to the (passive) dimensions of work-

- Hypothesis 2b which predicted that using work-life initiatives would be related to lower levels of time-based and strain-based work-life conflict was also partially confirmed. In the data only a (small) relationship between initiative use and strain-based conflict was established. Using work-life initiatives did not significantly affect professionals' perception of work-life conflict in terms of time.

Hypotheses 3a and 3b proposed that *informal organizational demands* impact the work-life interface of professionals unfavorably, i.e. are associated with higher work-to-life conflict and lower work-life initiative use. Hypotheses 4a and 4b proposed that *informal organizational resources* impact the work-life interface of professionals favorably, i.e. are associated with lower levels of work-to-life conflict and higher probability of work-life initiative use.

- Organizational time demands (Hypothesis 3a) were indeed significantly related to time-based WLC ($\gamma = .398; t = 11.021$), strain-based WLC ($\gamma = .303; t = 8.064$) and behavior-based WLC ($\gamma = .295; t = 8.049$). Above and beyond, this construct was the strongest predictor of the three types of work-life conflict in the model.
- Perceived management support and feeling supported by supervisors (Hypothesis 4a) were negatively related to time-based WLC ($\gamma_{MS} = -.217; t = 5.596 / \gamma_{SS} = -.083; t = 1.834$), strain-based WLC ($\gamma_{MS} = -.168; t = 4.068 / \gamma_{SS} = -.107; t = 2.785$), and behavior-based WLC ($\gamma_{MS} = -.161; t = 3.695 / \gamma_{SS} = -.037; n.s.$). Except for the support $\rightarrow$ bWLC relationship, Hypothesis 4a was supported. Management support was the predictor that demonstrated the most beneficial impact in terms of reducing work-life conflict.
- Finally, it was predicted, that particularly in work environments such as PSF which are characterized by an 'always-on ethic', the use of work-life initiatives would be impacted (negatively) by negative career consequences (Hypothesis 3b) and (positively) by co-worker support (Hypothesis 4b). Both hypotheses were confirmed by the data. Particularly threatening negative career consequences were shown to prevent work-life initiative use. Co-worker support in turn was positively related to initiative use, indicating that feeling supported by peers encourages professionals' use of work-life initiatives.

---

to-life conflict (tWLC, sWLC) that are characterized by individual experience rather than action.

Table 8. Structural model results (Path coefficients and t-values)

Relationship		γ	t		Conclusion
H1a	Work Hours → tWLC	.127***	3.462	✓	H1a partially supported
	Work Hours → sWLC	.032	0.959	✗	
	Work Hours → bWLC	.084*	2.152	✓	
H1b	Travel → tWLC	.064*	2.005	✓	H1b partially supported
	Travel → sWLC	.040	1.103	✗	
	Travel → bWLC	.181***	4.919	✓	
H3a	Org. Time Demands → tWLC	.398***	11.201	✓	H3a supported
	Org. Time Demands → sWLC	.303***	8.064	✓	
	Org. Time Demands → bWLC	.295***	8.049	✓	
H3b	Neg. Career Consequences → INIuse	-.229***	6.104	✓	H3b supported
H2a	INIavl → tWLC	.043†	1.695	✗	H2a partially supported
	INIavl → sWLC	-.132***	3.740	✓	
H2b	INIuse → tWLC	.025	0.505	✗	H2b partially supported
	INIuse → sWLC	-.016*	1.958	✓	
H4a	Management Support → tWLC	-.217***	5.596	✓	H4a partially supported
	Management Support → sWLC	-.168***	4.068	✓	
	Management Support → bWLC	-.161***	3.695	✓	
	Supervisor Support → tWLC	-.083†	1.834	✗	
	Supervisor Support → sWLC	-.107***	2.785	✓	
	Supervisor Support → bWLC	-.037	.962	✗	
H4b	Co-worker Support → INIuse	.078*	2.196	✓	H4b supported

N = 794: R^2_{tWLC}=.397; R^2_{sWLC}=.280; R^2_{bWLC}=.248; R^2_{INIuse} = .071;

$^†p < .10;$ $^*p < .05;$ $^{**}p < .01;$ $^{***}p < .001$

Besides path coefficients and their significance obtained by bootstrapping, effect size f^2 is an indicator of whether an exogenous latent variable substantially impacts an endogenous latent variable. Effect sizes are presented in Table 9. f^2 was calculated for each latent variable and also for the theoretically related blocks of variables, namely work hours and travel representing formal organizational demands, availability and use of WLB initiatives representing formal organizational support and management, supervisor and co-worker support representing informal organizational support. As already mentioned, effect sizes of .02 are considered weak, .15 moderate, and .35 substantial (Chin, 1998b).

Table 9. Relative explanatory power (effect size) of the predictors of time-, strain-, and behavior-based work-to-life conflict

	tWLC	sWLC	bWLC
	f^2	f^2	f^2
Formal Organizational Demands	.038	.005	.065
Work Hours	.022	.001	.005
Travel	.005	.003	.039
Informal Organizational Demands (Time Demands)	.181	.088	.079
Formal Organizational Support	.003	.022	-
Initiative Availability	.003	.020	-
Initiative Use	.000	.005	-
Informal Organizational Support	.075	.060	.032
Management Support	.043	.022	.012
Supervisor Support	.003	.011	.001

Moderate-level effects on work-to-life conflict were only exerted by informal organizational demands ($f^2_{tWLC} = .181;\ f^2_{sWLC} = .088;\ f^2_{bWLC} = .079$), i.e. time demands rooted in organizational culture. Informal support also exerted a considerable effect on time- and strain-based WLC ($f^2_{tWLC} = .075;\ f^2_{sWLC} = .060$), particularly as a function of management support. The majority of effect sizes had to be considered small though.

Overall, effect sizes for the path coefficients explaining time-based work-to-life conflict were strongest. Initiative use and availability exerted virtually no impact in terms of effect size on time-based WLC and a small effect on strain-based WLC. Negative career consequences exerted a small effect on the use of work-life initiatives while the impact of co-worker support was fairly tiny ($f^2_{NEGC} = .048;\ f^2_{CS} = .005$).

2.2.2.2 Evaluating Model Fit: Predictive Relevance Q^2 and Goodness-of-Fit (GoF)

Predictive relevance of the model was assessed with the Stone-Geisser test applying a so-called blindfolding procedure. The values of $Q^2_{tWLC}=.314$, $Q^2_{sWLC}=.232$ and $Q^2_{bWLC}=.169$ were well above the threshold ($Q^2 > 0$) and thus, the model was considered to yield predictive relevance. Use of work-life initiatives as predicted by negative career consequences and co-worker support was $Q^2 =.067$. Calculation of a Goodness-of-Fit index as suggested by Tenenhaus et al. (2005) resulted in *GoF* = .487. Schepers, Wetzels and De Ruyter (2005) proposed GoF thresholds of .10, .25 and .36. Hence, the model was attributed good fit of the data.

2.2.3 Examination of Distinct Effects of Work-Life Initiatives

In accordance with previous studies (e.g. Dikkers et al, 2004) use and availability of WLB initiatives was operationalized by using a summed score of available and used initiatives as indicated by respondents. The advantage of this procedure is that a list of initiatives can simultaneously be evaluated with regards to their use and offer in organizations. It may be righteously criticized though that conclusions drawn from studies using summed scores with regards to the usefulness of work-life initiatives have to be considered with caution. Results about the impact of initiative availability or use do not allow inferences on the effectiveness of specific initiatives. Such detailed inferences however ought to be of immense interest for organizations because they help them decide which initiatives make sense for diminishing employees' work-life conflict and thereby achieving desirable outcomes for the organization. Particularly with regards to the fact that all initiatives examined in this study were the result of a website analysis of large consulting firms it was considered highly interesting to shed a closer look at the impact of each individual WLB initiative and its dynamics in the research model. Therefore, in order to examine Research Question 2 (cf. Part II, 3.2.2) the research model was additionally examined with regards to the distinct effect of each work-life initiative on work-life conflict (cf. Table D.1 for frequencies of initiative availability and use). The summed score of available and used initiatives was replaced by one single initiative at a time. In addition to scrutinizing primary initiatives which were comprised in the summed score, additional 'secondary' initiatives were examined as for example support for educational programs and individual coaching are also frequently presented as flagships of work-life balance solutions in organizational recruiting advertisements.

Tables 10a and b display findings for the postulated relationships of work-life initiative availability and use in reducing time-based and strain-based WLC.

Eight initiatives that were also included in the summed scores were entered
separately into the model: reduced work hour schedule, flexible work hours on a
short-term basis (flexible work hours, etc.) and on a long-term basis (work time
accounts, etc.), leave of absence (sabbatical), home office, office (Fri)day, childcare, and free choice of residence (e.g. the company bears travel expenses from
the city of residence, instead of from the office location).[45] *Short-term oriented
flexible work hours* and *working from home* had no effects on work-life conflict.
The possibility of making use of *reduced schedule, long-term flexible work
hours, leave of absence, office day* and *free choice of residence* were related to
reduced experience of strain-based work-to-life conflict. *Childcare* availability
appeared to yield the potential to reduce both time-based and strain-based WLC.
It was also found though that the use of childcare was related to higher time-
based WLC. The largest but still small effect was exerted by making use *of free
choice of residence* being negatively related to strain-based WLC. Due to the
small subsample sizes overall path coefficients were small and effect sizes were
rather tiny. Surprisingly, some connections were found with regards to 'secondary' initiatives. Availability of individual coaching and support for educational
programs was associated with reduced strain-based WLC. Respondents who
made use of support for educational programs and health/recovery initiatives
reported less strain-based WLC and users of supportive services reported lower
levels of time-based WLC than non-users. Again, path coefficients and effect
sizes were very small and mostly at the margins of significance.

In sum, estimating the model with each initiative separately yielded the following major results:
- Largely, initiative *availability* favorably affected *strain-based WLC*: access
  to *reduced schedules, (long-term) flexible work hour arrangements, leaves
  of absence, office (Frid)day, childcare,* and *free choice of residence* appear to yield the potential to reduce strain-based WLC.
- Initiative *use* was only linked to reduced *strain-based WLC* in the case of
  free choice of residence.
- *Time-based work-life conflict* was *largely unaffected* by both initiative
  availability and use.
- *With regards to 'secondary' initiatives, access* to *individual coaching* and
  support for educational programs was reduced to experiencing lower levels of *strain-based WLC.*

---

45   The initiative 'eldercare' was also assessed but excluded from the analysis because it
     was only utilized by a tiny number of respondents.

Table 10.a/b Relationships of initiative use and availability with time- and strain-based work-life conflict (N=794)

	Reduced Schedule			Short-term Flexible Work Hours			Long-term Flexible Work Hours			Leave of Absence		
	γ	t	f^2	γ	t	f^2	γ	t	f^2	γ	t	f^2
Initiative availability → tWLC	-.043	1.501		.021	.805		.023	.883		-.023	.813	
Initiative availability → sWLC	-.053⁺	1.657	.003	-.011	.345	.005	-.069*	2.548	.005	-.099**	2.971	.011
Initiative use → tWLC	.027	.771		-.008	.252		-.043	1.317		.040	1.284	
Initiative use → sWLC	-.032	.883		-.043	1.284		-.027	.727		-.005	.129	
	N_{INIavl} = 334 (42.2%) N_{INIuse} = 67 (8.4%)			N_{INIavl} = 95 (12.0%) N_{INIuse} = 235 (29.6%)			N_{INIavl} = 70 (8.8%) N_{INIuse} = 49 (6.2%)			N_{INIavl} = 87 (11.0%) N_{INIuse} = 218 (27.5%)		

	Home Office			Office (Fri)Day			Childcare			Free Choice of Residence		
	γ	t	f^2	γ	t	f^2	γ	t	f^2	γ	t	f^2
Initiative availability → tWLC	-.034	1.459		-.022	.845		-.063*	2.178	.003	.001	.023	
Initiative availability → sWLC	-.044	1.439	.003	-.066*	2.375	.005	-.080*	2.505	.008	-.056*	2.026	.004
Initiative use → tWLC	.016	.511		.036	1.180		.047*	2.322	.007	-.043	1.418	
Initiative use → sWLC	-.051	1.166		-.030	.875		.012	.374		-.105**	3.081	.012
	N_{INIavl} = 132 (16.6%) N_{INIuse} = 270 (34.0%)			N_{INIavl} = 38 (12.0%) N_{INIuse} = 361 (45.5%)			N_{INIavl} = 132 (16.6%) N_{INIuse} = 15 (1.9%)			N_{INIavl} = 79 (9.9%) N_{INIuse} = 264 (33.2%)		

– *Use* of *health/recovery initiatives* as well as *support for educational programs* was related to lower levels of *sWLC*, using *supportive services* seemed to yield the potential for reducing *time-based WLC*.

2.2.4 Subgroup Results

In order to theoretically advance insights about the usefulness of work-life balance initiatives and at the same time provide applicable results for organizations a more detailed look was shed at the impact of formal and informal demands and resources in the subsequent paragraphs. Following theoretical and practical considerations, subgroups were contrasted according to subbranch, life role priority, gender, age, characteristics of personal life being relationship status, parental status and dual-career status, and job characteristics, i.e. tenure and job position. The following sections focus on results of the structural model estimation. Measurement model results were evaluated and monitored but are not further reported as they do not significantly diverge from the results reported in section 2.2.1.

2.2.4.1 Life Role Priority

A frequent assumption in existing work-life research is that the salience of life roles is associated with different work-life experiences, as outlined earlier in these writings. In the present sample, with regards to work (tenure, job level) and personal life characteristics (marital status etc.) the three groups were quite equally distributed concerning all characteristics. Parents' priorities ranged more strongly in the 'life' sphere but also almost half of the non-parents prioritized more in favor of personal life. There was an observable tendency towards prioritizing work with rising age. With regards to tenure and job level it must be remarked that those with 3.5 to 6 years of tenure and those at medium organizational levels comprised the largest percentage of 'life' types compared to those with higher/lower tenure and higher/lower organizational levels respectively. Results of the structural model estimation are presented in Table 12.

Informal organizational demands were related to the experience of work-life conflict largely independent of life role priority, the same was observed for the effect of work hours on time-based WLC and job-related travel on behavior-based WLC being the only notable effects with respect to formal organizational demands. Formal organizational support showed inconsistent results once more: Initiative availability had a decreasing effect on strain-based WLC for 'workers' and even more so 'balancers', not for the 'life' type however. The use of initiatives was negatively related to strain-based WLC for 'workers' only.

Table 11. Results of estimating the model contrasting subgroups according to life role priority

	Life Type[a]		Work Type[b]		Balance Type[c]	
	γ	t	γ	t	γ	t
Formal Demands						
Work Hours → tWLC	.158**	3.080	.151**	2.422	.142[†]	1.843
Work Hours → sWLC	.038	.787	.061	1.043	-.092	1.067
Work Hours → bWLC	.060	.977	.107[†]	1.824	.169[†]	1.730
Travel → tWLC	.094*	2.109	.018	.367	.118	1.358
Travel → sWLC	.027	.486	.041	.772	.106	1.187
Travel → bWLC	.199***	3.665	.158**	2.714	.176[†]	1.741
Informal Demands						
Org. Time Demands → tWLC	.437***	8.831	.421***	6.526	.210[†]	1.887
Org. Time Demands → sWLC	.264***	4.899	.339***	5.537	.315**	3.160
Org. Time Demands → bWLC	.302***	4.817	.305***	4.828	.190[†]	1.741
Neg. Career Cons. → INIuse	-.285***	5.753	-.234***	4.039	-.072	.837
Formal Resources						
Initiative availability → tWLC	-.042	1.019	-.060	.267	.000	.004
Initiative availability → sWLC	-.051	1.173	-.165**	3.029	-.265**	2.782
Initiative use → tWLC	.041	.946	.014	1.367	-.081	1.209
Initiative use → sWLC	.009	.157	-.168***	3.546	.009	.131
Informal Resources						
Management Support → tWLC	-.222***	4.027	-.178**	2.790	-.164	1.330
Management Supp. → sWLC	-.247***	4.244	-.121*	1.952	-.009	.118
Management Supp. → bWLC	-.144***	2.047	-.212**	3.120	-.054	.606
Supervisor Support → tWLC	-.026	.489	-.081	1.536	-.127	1.293
Supervisor Support → sWLC	-.047	.782	-.094	1.581	-.250*	2.157
Supervisor Support → bWLC	-.012	.210	-.008	.0149	-.218[†]	1.771
Co-worker Support → INIuse	.034	.745	.121*	2.022	.193*	2.199

[a] N = 388:
$R^2_{tWLC} = .417$, $R^2_{sWLC} = .234$,
$R^2_{bWLC} = .213$;
$Q^2_{tWLC} = .323$, $Q^2_{sWLC} = .190$,
$Q^2_{bWLC} = 138$;
GoF =.468;

[b] N = 310:
$R^2_{tWLC} = .438$, $R^2_{sWLC} = .367$,
$R^2_{bWLC} = .311$;
$Q^2_{tWLC} = .357$, $Q^2_{sWLC} = .311$,
$Q^2_{bWLC} = .215$;
GoF = .534;

[c] N = 93:
$R^2_{tWLC} = .250$, $R^2_{sWLC} = .282$,
$R^2_{bWLC} = .260$;
$Q^2_{tWLC} = .191$, $Q^2_{sWLC} = .249$,
$Q^2_{bWLC} = .208$;
GoF = .448;

[†] $p < .10$; * $p < .05$; ** $p < .01$; *** $p < .001$

An interesting finding is that for the 'life' type and the 'work' type alike management support played a major role in reducing all three dimensions of WLC, whereas for the balancers, if any, it was supervisor support that helped reduce their (strain- and behavior-based) work-to-life conflict. Co-worker support was not related to initiative use for the 'life' type suggesting that the impact of peer pressure may be higher if the work sphere plays a more important role for the individual.

Whereas other results might also be explained here with differences in sample size, remarkable findings with regards to life role priority are:

- Professionals of with *'work'* priority and those of *'balance'* type who had *access to work-life initiatives* experienced reduced levels of *strain-based work-to-life conflict*;
- *Initiative use* was only beneficial for professionals with *'work'* priority in terms of *strain-based work-to-life conflict*;
- *'Balancers' benefited from supervisor support in terms of reduced levels of strain-based and behavior-based work-life conflict, not so the 'life' and 'work' type, and*
- Professionals with *'work' priority* and even more so *'balancers'* were significantly more likely to make *use of initiatives* if they felt *supported by co-workers*.

In all three subsamples the model demonstrated predictive quality with Stone-Geisser criteria exceeding the zero threshold. *GoF* values were also satisfactory ($GoF_{life} = .468; GoF_{work} = .534; GoF_{balance} = .448$). The model explained considerably more variance (*R square*) of strain- and behavior-based WLC in the 'work' type subsample than in the 'life' type subsample. Lower *R square* values of the 'balancers' were most likely due to the small subsample size.

2.2.4.2 Management Consultants vs. Law Firm Professionals

Management consultants and law firm professionals both work in highly demanding environments predestining these two groups for the experience of problems in reconciling their work-life interface. The fact that management consultants faced considerably more travel in their daily work ($M_{MC} = 2.69; M_{LF} = 0.36$) was, however, expected to be a distinguishing factor for their work-life experiences. Moreover the management consultants in the sample worked significantly longer hours than law firm professionals ($M_{MC} = 58.42; M_{LF} = 53.38$). Therefore, the model was estimated separately for these two groups.

Respondents of the management consultant subsample held an average age of 31 years, the subsample consisted of 79 per cent males. Thirteen per cent were parents, 75 per cent reported being in a relationship or married with 51 per cent in a dual-career relationship. Average job experience was nearly six years, with a mean tenure of three years. 51 per cent rated themselves at entry to medium level organizational position, 29 per cent at medium level and 20 per cent at advanced to partner level. In the law firm sample 65 per cent were male, average age was 35.5. The majority of law firm professionals with a spouse were in a dual-career relationship, 17 per cent were without a partner. Also in this sample most respondents did not have children (63 per cent). Respondents indicated a mean tenure of four to five years, job experience (M = 7.21 years) was higher than in the MC subsample. Like in the management consultant subsample the largest group of respondents classified themselves among entry to medium organizational level (41.8 per cent), nearly 30 per cent categorized themselves into medium and advanced/top level positions respectively. With regards to the priorities assigned to work vs. personal life management consultants and law firm professionals did not differ significantly: in both subsamples the largest group was made up by 'life' types (MC = 50.8 per cent, LF = 48 per cent), followed by those who prioritized work (MC = 34.7 per cent, LF = 40.9 per cent) and the 'balancers' (MC = 14.7 per cent, LF = 10.5 per cent).

In the structural model estimation for law firm professionals work hours were significantly related to time- and behavior-based WLC, in the MC subsample however, only the work hours → tWLC relationship was significant ($p <$ .10)[46]. Whereas in the total sample travel demands also suggest a relationship towards tWLC and bWLC, a more differentiated look revealed that for management consultants the need to travel frequently was only related to behavior-based WLC ($p < .10$). Management consultants therefore did experience work-life conflict in the way that they must frequently change personal vacation plans or face unpredictable time off due to their extensive job-related travel. Interestingly, yet with a small path coefficient ($\gamma = .065, p < .05$), this effect also applied for law firm professionals whose work was associated with much less job-related travel. Effect sizes of formal organizational demands on time-based and behavior-based work-to-life conflict have to be considered rather small in both subsamples (MC: $f^2_{tWLC} = .016$, $f^2_{bWLC} = .014$; LF: $f^2_{tWLC} = .027$, $f^2_{bWLC} = .036$).

The high impact of informal organizational demands was found likewise in both subgroups, notably with higher path coefficients in the MC subsample. A culture where career advancement is associated with a 'work-first' attitude in

---

46   The reporting of results with an error margin as large as p < .10 is often viewed critically. The large difference in some subsample sizes within this study led to the decision to also report these results in order highlight tendencies towards significant results and to avoid mistakenly trenchant differentiations between samples that are only due to different group sizes.

terms of time demands and the consequences of making use of corporate policies was generally associated with high time-, strain-, and behavior-based work-
to-life conflict, even more so for management consultants. This may be because
a high-performance culture is even more pronounced in their occupational environment.

With regards to formal organizational resources, contrasting the two
subbranches largely reflected results obtained in the total sample estimation.
Under the assumption that management consultants and law firm professionals
differ in their access to work-life benefits as well as in terms of the usefulness of
initiatives for reducing work-life conflict, subbranch-specific model estimations
were conducted which only included one initiative at a time. This comparison
especially made sense under the expectation of differences concerning initiatives
that are available in certain branches. As reported earlier in this dissertation, the
assessment of available and used benefits was based on an investigation of
work-life initiatives advertised on the web sites of the top 25 German consulting
firms. In law firms most probably a number of these initiatives is not offered,
such as free choice of residence or office (Fri)day, because the structural character of their work differs from that of management consultants, i.e. by less job-
related travel days and other characteristics that render these initiatives irrele-
vant. It was thus decided to examine differences of the effects of initiative availability and use between these two subbranches of PSFs, always keeping an eye
on the number and percentage of respondents who did use the respective initiative and those who indicated access but no usage (cf. Appendix D).[47] Although
effect sizes were small some interesting results were found contrasting management consultants and law firm professionals. In sum, a number of major differences were found between these two PSF subbranches:

- Although law firm professionals work less hours (on average), they seem to
  be more strongly affected by their *work volume* in terms of time-based and
  even more so behavior-based work-life conflict than management consultants;
- Although law firm professionals travel significantly less frequently in their
  job, they were also affected by *job-related travel* in terms of *behavior-
  based WLC*;
- Whereas within the *MC sample* the impact of *informal organizational demands* (time demands, neg. career consequences) was more pronounced,
  LF professionals benefited more strongly from *informal organizational*

---

47   A similarly low participation in work-life programs in PSFs was reported by Johnson et
     al. (2008).

support (management, supervisor, co-worker support) than management consultants;
- *Initiative availability* was related *to lower levels of strain-based WLC in both subsamples*, yet only management consultants benefited from making use of WLB initiatives.

A separate look at WLB initiatives allows for more fine-grained results and these model estimations do indeed yield a number of interesting findings:
- *Management consultants* with *access* to reduced schedule arrangements, long-term flexible work hour arrangements, leave of absence, home office, and office day experienced lower work-life conflict;
- *Management consultants* who made *use* of short-term and long-term flexible work arrangements, office day and free choice of residence experienced lower work-life conflict in terms of *time*;
- *Law firm professionals* with *access* to long-term flexible work hours, leave of absence, office day, childcare, and free choice of residence experience lower work-life conflict in terms of *psychological strain*; Those with *access* to childcare arrangements experienced lower work-life conflict in terms of *time*, though making use of it was related to higher levels of tWLC;
- *Law firm professionals* who made *use* of free choice of residence experienced lower work-life conflict in terms of *psychological strain*.

For both subsamples effect sizes were small and results must therefore be interpreted cautiously. Findings indicated though that management consultants benefit from a set of work-life initiatives that differ in some respects from that of law firm professionals. Regarding 'secondary' initiatives it was found in the MC subsample that availability and use of support for further education was associated negatively with strain-based work-to-life conflict with a (small) effect size which was still considerably above all other effect sizes reported with regards to work-life initiatives. Indeed none of the other initiatives showed such a strong relationship with any of the work-to-life conflict dimensions. This effect was not found in the LF subsample. For law firm professionals it was found that making use of health/recovery initiatives and supportive services significantly reduced time-based work-to-life conflict. These unexpected results might suggest a trade-off attitude of management consultants towards their work-life interface taking the career in management consultancy as a step in their career ladder where they can 'make the most of it' before switching into a more predictable job situation.

Table 12. Results of estimating the model contrasting management consultants and law firm
professionals

	Management Consultants[a]		Law Firm Professionals[b]	
	γ	t	γ	t
Formal Demands				
Work Hours → tWLC	.106[†]	1.762	.139[**]	2.989
Work Hours → sWLC	.036	.628	.037	.871
Work Hours → bWLC	-.025	.324	.140[***]	3.409
Travel → tWLC	-.001	.020	-.005	.177
Travel → sWLC	.025	.411	-.009	.220
Travel → bWLC	.110[†]	1.734	.065[*]	2.052
Informal Demands				
Org. Time Demands → tWLC	.427[***]	6.332	.398[***]	9.108
Org. Time Demands → sWLC	.313[***]	4.493	.296[***]	6.782
Org. Time Demands → bWLC	.337[***]	5.437	.292[***]	5.929
Neg. Career Cons. → INIuse	-.200[*]	2.016	-.115[**]	2.674
Formal Resources				
Initiative availability → tWLC	-.073	1.337	-.046	1.486
Initiative availability → sWLC	-.146[*]	2.219	-.103[***]	3.049
Initiative use → tWLC	.066	1.384	.022	.639
Initiative use → sWLC	-.164[**]	2.569	.030	.739
Informal Resources				
Management Support → tWLC	-.188[*]	2.445	-.218[***]	4.626
Management Support → sWLC	-.007	.087	-.236[***]	4.735
Management Support → bWLC	-.122	1.482	-.181[***]	3.358
Supervisor Support → tWLC	-.023	.359	-.088[*]	2.097
Supervisor Support → sWLC	-.061	.840	-.125[**]	2.698
Supervisor Support → bWLC	-.013	.159	-.060	1.367
Co-worker Support → INIuse	.076	1.123	.120[**]	2.739

[a] N=242:
R^2_{tWLC} = .379, R^2_{sWLC} = .203,
R^2_{bWLC} = .186; R^2_{INIuse} = .058;
Q^2_{tWLC} = .323, Q^2_{sWLC} = .190,
Q^2_{bWLC} = .138; Q^2_{INIuse} = .059;
GoF =.443;

[b] N=552:
R^2_{tWLC} = .414, R^2_{sWLC} = .335,
R^2_{bWLC} = .268; R^2_{INIuse} = .038;
Q^2_{tWLC} = .302, Q^2_{sWLC} = .154,
Q^2_{bWLC} = .133; Q^2_{INIuse} = .038;
GoF = .524;

[†] $p < .10$; [*] $p < .05$; [**] $p < .01$; [***] $p < .001$

Different needs of these two groups were also reflected in the structure of initiatives that were 'not offered but needed' in consulting firms and law firms. Whereas management consultants called for stronger support for educational programs, many law firm professionals were in need for leave of absence policies and childcare initiatives. In both subsamples a considerable proportion would like to see more initiatives offered with regards to long-term flexible work hours, home office, supportive services, health and recovery programs and individual coaching. Whether respondents required these initiatives in order to specifically target their work-life reconciliation challenges cannot be answered in this study, this is an issue for further research projects. Results considering the role of informal social support on work-to-life conflict also differed with regards to subbranch. Whereas the data suggested that law firm professionals' time-based, strain-based and behavior-based WLC was associated with high management support this was only the case for time-based WLC in the MC subsample. Supervisor support was related to reduced time- and strain-based WLC in the LF subsample only and the co-worker support → initiative use relationship was only found in this group. Effect sizes of informal organizational support on time-based and strain-based WLC in the LF subsample were reasonable ($f^2_{tWLC} = .094$; $f^2_{sWLC} = .124$). The only significant effect of informal support within the MC subsample was the management support → time-based WLC relationship ($f^2 = .040$).

Regarding model fit, the two subsamples had similar determination coefficients with respect to time-based WLC, considerably more variance of strain-based and behavior-based WLC was explained by the constructs in the model in the case of law firm professionals. This may also be a matter of sample size as the LF subsample comprises more than twice as many respondents as the MC subsample. In both subsamples the model yielded predictive quality with Stone-Geisser criteria exceeding the zero margin by far (MC: $Q^2_{tWLC} = .323$, $Q^2_{sWLC} = .190$, $Q^2_{tWLC} = .138$; LF: $Q^2_{tWLC} = .302$, $Q^2_{sWLC} = .154$, $Q^2_{tWLC} = .133$). GoF values were also satisfactory ($GoF_{MC} = .443$; $GoF_{LF} = .524$).

2.2.4.3 Gender and Age

Gender and age are prominent demographic characteristics studied in work-life research though with mixed results. Women in the present sample were primarily employed in law firms (80 per cent), and on average 33 years old ($M_{male} = 34.6$). They worked on average 51 hours per week with less than one travel day. Men reported to work between 56 and 57 hours per week and spent one to two days per week traveling. With respect to job level, one fourth of the women were in advanced to top level positions compared to one third of the males in the sample (28.1 per cent). Concerning the tenure distribution both genders were

Table 13. Structural model results contrasting women and men

	Women[a]		Men[b]	
	γ	t	γ	t
Formal Demands				
Work Hours $\rightarrow$ tWLC	$.114^{\dagger}$	1.894	$.136^{**}$	2.673
Work Hours $\rightarrow$ sWLC	$.069$	1.175	$.034$	.774
Work Hours $\rightarrow$ bWLC	$.060$	.829	$.076$	1.613
Travel $\rightarrow$ tWLC	$.007$	.128	$.082^{*}$	2.080
Travel $\rightarrow$ sWLC	$-.009$	.172	$.076^{\dagger}$	1.661
Travel $\rightarrow$ bWLC	$.134^{\dagger}$	1.732	$.182^{***}$	4.291
Informal Demands				
Org. Time Demands $\rightarrow$ tWLC	$.504^{***}$	7.838	$.345^{***}$	7.208
Org. Time Demands $\rightarrow$ sWLC	$.392^{***}$	6.358	$.271^{***}$	6.045
Org. Time Demands $\rightarrow$ bWLC	$.267^{***}$	3.733	$.302^{***}$	6.254
Neg. Career Cons. $\rightarrow$ INIuse	$-.222^{**}$	3.282	$-.233^{***}$	5.221
Formal Resources				
Initiative availability $\rightarrow$ tWLC	$-.029$	.598	$-.061^{\dagger}$	1.822
Initiative availability $\rightarrow$ sWLC	$-.084$	.825	$-.079^{***}$	3.485
Initiative use $\rightarrow$ tWLC	$.031$	.598	$.009$	.253
Initiative use $\rightarrow$ sWLC	$-.050^{\dagger}$	1.733	$-.135^{\dagger}$	1.727
Informal Resources				
Management Support $\rightarrow$ tWLC	$-.108^{\dagger}$	1.545	$-.272^{***}$	5.511
Management Support $\rightarrow$ sWLC	$-.215^{**}$	3.043	$-.137^{***}$	2.641
Management Support $\rightarrow$ bWLC	$-.226^{**}$	2.728	$-.158^{*}$	2.908
Supervisor Support $\rightarrow$ tWLC	$-.094^{\dagger}$	1.634	$-.046$	1.093
Supervisor Support $\rightarrow$ sWLC	$.003$	.042	$-.151^{**}$	3.213
Supervisor Support $\rightarrow$ bWLC	$-.068$	1.028	$-.022$	.472
Co-worker Support $\rightarrow$ INIuse	$.156^{**}$	2.639	$.041$	.876

[a] $N = 241$:
$R^2_{tWLC} = .417$, $R^2_{sWLC} = .336$,
$R^2_{bWLC} = .276$; $R^2_{INIuse} = .097$;
$Q^2_{tWLC} = .340$, $Q^2_{sWLC} = .283$,
$Q^2_{bWLC} = .184$; $Q^2_{INIuse} = .095$;
GoF $= .442$;

[b] $N = 548$:
$R^2_{tWLC} = .402$, $R^2_{sWLC} = .261$,
$R^2_{bWLC} = .242$; $R^2_{INIuse} = .063$;
$Q^2_{tWLC} = .318$, $Q^2_{sWLC} = .217$,
$Q^2_{bWLC} = .166$; $Q^2_{INIuse} = .060$;
GoF $= .427$;

$^{\dagger} p < .10$; $^{*} p < .05$; $^{**} p < .01$; $^{***} p < .001$

close to equal. 78 per cent women and 82 per cent males were married / in a relationship, one fifth of the women in the sample were mothers versus 33 per cent fathers. 68 per cent of the female subsample reported being in a dual-career relationship versus 55 per cent in the male subsample. Although there were differences among women and men with regards to subbranch, parental status, dual-career relationship, organizational level, weekly work hours and travel, none of these differences were large. That the two genders are in tendency not so different sheds a picture on the study of the work-life interface other than it is usually the case.

Findings of the structural model estimation (Table 13) suggest that first of all, the effect of work hours on WLC is for both men and women only significant for the time-based conflict dimension (women $p < .10$). The fact that job-related travel largely only related to WLC for men was likely due to the fact that men were required to travel more frequently in their jobs. The striking impact of informal organizational time demands on all three conflict dimensions was also found in this subgroup comparison yet with a particularly high impact for women's experience of time-based WLC. With respect to formal organizational support initiative use and availability tended to be significant only for men. Although this may also be being due to sample size differences, it must be noted that males and females only differed substantially in their work-life initiative usage with respect to reduced schedules (more female users). Other than that differences regarding initiative use were small. From this perspective, it is an interesting finding that men benefit more strongly from initiative access and use than women, although a disturbing effect of different sample sizes cannot be ruled out here. Management support yielded similar results for women and men, all associations between MS and WLC were found to be significant and negative (i.e. favorable).

Another noticeable difference between men and women concerned the effect of supervisor support on WLC and co-worker support on initiative use. Whereas for men the perception of a supportive supervisor did play a significant role for their experience of strain-based WLC this was not the case for women. On the other hand for women co-worker support was found to be a promoter for making use of corporate WLB initiatives which was not the case for men. A closer look at the descriptive statistics of these two variables revealed that men in contrast to women perceived their supervisors and their co-workers to be more supportive. Although women and men used equal numbers of WLB initiatives, women made use of reduced schedules more frequently than men whereas men used home office and free choice of residence more frequently. The fact that reduced schedules potentially impact the work schedule of co-workers and thus requires their approval may be a valid explanation for the significant co-worker support

→ initiative use relationship found for women and not for their male counterparts. Besides the general result that male and female professionals are in the present study not substantially different in their work-life experiences, the gender comparison yielded a number of major findings:

- Informal organizational *time demands* particularly affected women's time-based WLC;
- *Men* benefited more strongly from initiative access and use in terms of reduced *strain-based WLC*;
- For men, *supervisor support* played an important role for reducing levels of strain-based WLC, not so for women, and
- For women, *co-worker support* played an important role for making use of WLB initiatives, not so for men.

With regards to *age* in the examination of Research Question 1 it was found that work-to-life conflict is highest for professionals in their thirties in the sample under examination. Concerning the structural model examination contrasting the four age groups informal time demands were, again, significantly related to all three conflict dimensions across all groups as well as negative career consequences associated with work-life issues were negatively related to initiative use. Other than that, results were inconsistent. No striking age-specific results were found concerning initiative availability and use on twLC, the impact of supervisor support on conflict and co-worker support on initiative use. The early thirties group was the only subsample where management support was significantly positively related to all three conflict dimensions, however, this could be due to the comparatively larger size of this subsample. Hence contrasting age groups no conclusive differential model effects were found. For both gender and age the model fit metrics were satisfactory. Notably, for women, who were shown to experience higher strain-based WLC (cf. section 2.1) the constructs in the model explained more variance of this variable than for men and generally for women *R squares* were higher despite the smaller size of this subsample.

2.2.4.4 Relationship Status, Parental Status, and DCC Status

The model was further examined with regards to differences between childless individuals versus parents, singles and individuals in a relationship, and individuals in a dual-career relationship versus in a non-dual career relationship.

To begin with, no differences were found between *parents and non-parents* with respect to the impact of organizational time demands and management support on WLC. With the exception of the MS → bWLC relationship all associations were found significant and in the direction hypothesized by the model. Time demands showed a particularly strong relationship with time-based WLC for parents ($\gamma = .464$, $p < .001$). Above and beyond, for non-parents all three conflict dimensions were significantly predicted by supervisor support, not so for parents. This might be because career advancement is probably more salient for non-parents than it is at the stage of starting a family. The finding that the impact of feared negative career consequences on (not) making use of initiatives is stronger for non-parents supports this notion. Differences with regards to travel were probably due to the fact that non-parents travel significantly more ($M = 1.29$) than parents ($M = 0.76$). Interestingly though parents' time-based and behavior-based WLC was affected by weekly work hours although they work significantly less ($M = 51.50$) than non-parents ($M = 56.32$). Knowing that WLB initiatives are available was associated with less strain-based WLC for non-parents. Not only did parents not benefit from using or having access to initiatives, making use of WLB initiatives was associated to higher time-based WLC for parents. Notably, the reported use of initiatives differed across the two subsamples. Parents were found more frequently than non-parents to make use of reduced schedule, home office, and childcare, whereas non-parents made use of office day and leave of absence more strongly. Together with the positive association between initiative use and conflict this indicates that parents must make substantially higher efforts in coordinating work and personal life. Findings might be interpreted in the direction that initiatives do not help parents because they are related to higher conflict, yet we do not know how parents' conflict levels would be without initiatives. It is more likely that initiatives offered in PSFs are not useful *enough* to assist parents with their needs regarding work-life integration. In sum, the most interesting findings within this comparison were the following:

- *Independent of parental status*, *management support* was favorably and *organizational time demands* were unfavorably linked to professionals' work-life conflict;
- *Supervisor support* played an important role as a buffer for *non-parents'* work-life conflict, not so for the parents in the sample;
- Initiative access alleviated strain-based WLC for non-parents;
- Using initiatives was associated with higher time-based WLC for parents;
- Parents used family-related work-life initiatives whereas non-parents made more use of leaves of absence and office day;

Regarding *relationship status*, individuals in a relationship and singles both profited from supportive management in terms of reduced conflict of all three dimensions and experienced higher conflict as a function of organizational time demands. The fear of negative career consequences as a result of making use of WLB initiatives was negatively related to initiative use in both groups. Due to the large sample size difference of these two groups, results must be interpreted cautiously, particularly as in several non-significant relationships in one group bootstrapping results nevertheless tended towards the direction of results which were significant in the larger group. The most noteworthy difference concerned the impact of formal organizational demands. For respondents in a relationship long work hours were positively associated with time-based WLC ($f^2 = .021$) and behavior-based WLC ($f^2 = .010$) although the groups did not differ in the amount of weekly work hours. For singles in turn work-related travel (which also did not differ in quantity among subsamples) was related to tWLC ($f^2 = .040$) and even more strongly to behavior-based WLC ($f^2 = .053$). Formal organizational demands thus exerted differential effects on these two groups.

Finally it was observed whether individuals in *dual-career relationships* differed in their work-life experiences from individuals not in dual-career relationships. Findings were presented (Part II, 2.1), that dual-career professionals experienced higher work-to-life conflict than individuals with a non-employed spouse or a partner in part-time employment. In the structural model estimation informal organizational demands were in both subgroups strong predictors of all three WLC dimensions, though to a stronger extent in the non dual-career sample. Long work hours were significantly related to time- and behavior-based WLC for respondents in non-dual career partnerships although this group worked significantly fewer hours per week ($M_{nonDCC} = 51.61$ vs. $M_{DCC} = 57.16$). For individuals in relationships were both partners work on a full-time schedule job-related travel was significantly related to higher tWLC and bWLC.[48] Availability of WLB initiatives was associated with reduced strain-based WLC for individuals with dual-career status only. Individuals without dual-career status, who made significantly more use of reduced work hours and home office, reported increased strain-based WLC associated with initiative use (!). As this result is similar to the parental status comparison, having children might be an underlying factor here. The management support → WLC association was much more pronounced for individuals with dual-career status. Finally, in tendency co-worker support played a more important role for non DC individuals' use of WLB initiatives and supervisor support also only had a negative impact on strain-based WLC for this group. With regards to (dual-career) relationship status, major findings were:

– Largely, *singles versus individuals in a relationship* did not differ substantially in their work-life dynamics in the present examination except for the

---

48   Individuals in dual-career relationships were shown to differ significantly in their travel
      volume: whereas non dual-career relationship individuals traveled less than one day per
      week those in a DC relationship traveled one to two days a week on average.

impact of *formal organizational demands*: *WLC of singles* is more strongly affected by *job-related travel* whereas *WLC of individuals in a partnership/marriage* is more strongly affected by *long work hours*;
- *Informal organizational time demands* affected *both individuals in a DC and in a non DC relationship* in terms of increasing WLC though the latter were affected more strongly;
- *Managerial support* affected *both individuals in a non DC and in a DC relationship* in terms of alleviating levels WLC though the latter were affected even more favorably;
- *Individuals in a non DC relationship were more strongly affected by long work hours in terms of higher WLC than individuals in a DC relationship;*
- Only *individuals with dual-career status* benefited from *access to WLB initiatives* in terms of reduced strain-based WLC;

2.2.4.5 Tenure and Job Position

Finally, group comparisons were conducted with respect to tenure and job position. The notion that the longer employees have prevailed within an organization, the more likely they are to know of available initiatives and have gained 'social allowance' for making use of them had been pronounced in previous papers, yet with inconsistent findings, also with regards to differences in WLC as a function of tenure or job level (cf. Part I, 3.3). ANOVA findings were already presented indicating that the highest levels of WLC are experienced among professionals with tenure of 3.5 to 6 years and at medium job level, i.e. rising responsibility within the job and a time that is likely to coincide with rising personal life responsibilities such as getting married or starting a family.

In terms of formal organizational demands it becomes visible from the results in Table 14 that work hours exerted an impact on time-based WLC for individuals in their earlier years within the organization. Job-related travel was only related to tWLC and bWLC for organizational newcomers. Informal demands consistently across all subsamples and all dimensions were related to increased WLC (time demands) and reduced use of initiatives (negative career consequences). Management support seemed to play a more or less equally important role among all tenure groups but co-worker support only had an impact on the use of initiatives for the newcomers. Making use of initiatives only made sense in reducing strain-based WLC for the 3.5 to 6 years tenure group, access to initiatives largely had positive effects on strain-based WLC for those who have been working in an organization more than three years.

Considering *job level* professionals at medium hierarchical level experienced the highest levels of time- and strain-based conflict associated with work hours, travel, and time demands. The perception of negative career

Table 14. Structural model results with respect to tenure

	0 to 3 years[a]		3.5 to 6 years[b]		6.5 years and longer[c]	
	γ	t	γ	t	γ	t
Formal Demands						
Work Hours → tWLC	.126*	2.435	.192**	2.661	.069	.758
Work Hours → sWLC	.017	.395	-.044	.674	.146	1.520
Work Hours → bWLC	.091†	1.760	.095	1.013	.115†	1.671
Travel → tWLC	.129**	3.272	-.054	.836	.015	.163
Travel → sWLC	.054	1.205	.068	.860	-.051	.581
Travel → bWLC	.229***	4.955	.082	.953	.095	1.089
Informal Demands						
Org. Time Demands → tWLC	.412***	7.825	.394***	4.850	.304***	3.457
Org. Time Demands → sWLC	.313***	6.155	.384***	5.506	.205**	2.660
Org. Time Demands → bWLC	.274***	4.650	.213**	2.852	.467***	5.811
Neg. Career Cons. → INIuse	-.248***	4.990	-.214**	2.770	-.202**	2.647
Formal Resources						
Initiative avail. → tWLC	-.044	1.208	-.068	1.169	.005	.070
Initiative avail. → sWLC	-.082†	1.946	-.139*	2.068	-.158*	2.080
Initiative use → tWLC	-.032	.784	-.007	.114	.151†	1.836
Initiative use → sWLC	-.075	1.511	-.143*	2.090	.055	.610
Informal Resources						
Management Supp. → tWLC	-.162**	2.924	-.302***	3.925	-.237*	2.127
Management Supp. → sWLC	-.153**	2.733	-.127	1.616	-.204*	1.960
Management Supp. → bWLC	-.148*	2.473	-.258**	2.851	-.041	.390
Supervisor Support → tWLC	-.077	1.771	-.004	.050	-.183*	2.010
Supervisor Support → sWLC	-.128**	2.562	-.067	.787	-.157†	1.813
Supervisor Support → bWLC	-.047	.887	-.044	.573	-.077	.844
Co-worker Support → INIuse	.102*	2.257	.073	.783	.063	.578

[a] N = 436:
$R^2_{tWLC} = .412$, $R^2_{sWLC} = .288$, $R^2_{bWLC} = .261$; $R^2_{INIuse} = .088$; $Q^2_{tWLC} = .327$, $Q^2_{sWLC} = .243$, $Q^2_{bWLC} = .180$; $Q^2_{INIuse} = .086$; GoF =.449;

[b] N = 190:
$R^2_{tWLC} = .451$, $R^2_{sWLC} = .296$, $R^2_{bWLC} = .219$; $R^2_{INIuse} = .063$; $Q^2_{tWLC} = .372$, $Q^2_{sWLC} = .247$, $Q^2_{bWLC} = .151$; $Q^2_{INIuse} = .062$; GoF = .445;

[c] N = 139:
$R^2_{tWLC} = .326$, $R^2_{sWLC} = .262$, $R^2_{bWLC} = .297$; $R^2_{INIuse} = .056$; $Q^2_{tWLC} = .244$, $Q^2_{sWLC} = .209$, $Q^2_{bWLC} = .204$; $Q^2_{INIuse} = .058$; GoF = .408;

† $p < .10$; * $p < .05$; ** $p < .01$; *** $p < .001$

consequences in the case of using work-life initiatives was in tendency also most pronounced at medium hierarchy levels though relationships were found at all levels. For professionals at medium hierarchical level using work-life benefits was associated with less strain-based WLC while in the case of lower or higher-level professionals only an association of initiative access with lower conflict was found. Interestingly, results indicate that professionals at higher organizational levels are more likely to experience behavior-based WLC as a function of time demands than the other two groups. The informal support dimension was found to matter most at the lower hierarchy levels, newcomers benefited from supervisor support and co-worker support, as well as a supportive management.To sum up, major results of contrasting tenure levels and job levels were the following:

– Formal organizational demands largely only played a role for *newcomers'* WLC;
– *Informal demands* impacted professionals' WLC largely independent of tenure and job level;
– Initiative access and use appeared to be particularly helpful for *professionals at tenure 3.5-6 years*, although access was also related to lower conflict levels of professionals with shorter and longer tenure;
– *Co-worker support* particularly impacted professionals' use of initiatives at lower hierarchy levels and short tenure respectively.

2.3 Summary of Empirical Results

The present study contributes a number of interesting findings that extend previous research regarding the impact of organizational demands and resources on the work-life interface of professionals (Table 15). Regarding the character of work-life conflict (Research Question 1) results indicate that particularly *time-based work-to-life conflict is an issue for professionals*. Strain-based and behavior-based conflict plays a smaller yet still considerable role. The majority of professionals experience *conflict between work and several life spheres*, indicating that the work-family dichotomy is not the only interaction of interest with regards to professionals' work-life interface. High conflict was experienced particularly with regards of *work vs. social engagement* and *work vs. self*. Moderate levels of conflict were reported particularly with regards to work vs. family, work vs. friends, and work vs. health/recovery. *Formal organizational initiatives* were found to have a small to moderate impact on professionals' work-life conflict. Both time- and behavior-based WLC were significantly impacted by work hours and job-related travel, not so however strain-based conflict. Most consistent finding concerned the association of implicitly endorsed time demands as a facet of organizational culture. In the total sample and across all subsamples *organizational time demands* were associated with higher time-based, strain-based, and behavior-based work-to-life conflict. Findings regarding the second informal demand were nearly as consistent. *Negative career consequences* were found in the total sample and in all but two subsamples to decrease the likeliness that professionals made use of work-life initiatives. Most inconsistent results were reported in the *area of formal organizational initiatives*. Model estimations do indicate that availability and use of corporate work-life benefits is associated with reduced levels of work-life conflict, primarily of the strain-based type. However, results are relatively inconsistent and likely are blurred by the high percentage of non-users in the sample. With regards to *informal organizational resources* again fairly steady results were reported on the dimension of management support. Supportive management was in the total sample and largely across subsamples found to be effective in reducing all three forms of WLC studied here. Results on behalf of supervisor support were less consistent. In the total sample supervisor support significantly predicted strain-based conflict but considering additional characteristics in the subsample analyses rendered the impact of supportive supervision highly changeable. Overall, co-worker support was found to be a predictor of professionals' use of WLB initiatives although negative career consequences were a much stronger predictor of non-use. In sum, a major finding within the total sample was that informal factors, both demands and resources, were much stronger and consistent predictors of work-life conflict than demands and resources that are based on some kind of formal agreement.

Results concerning Research Question 2 which examined the *impact of separate work-life initiatives*, are summarized in Table 16. *Access to all initiatives* but home office and short-term flexible schedule were related to lower levels of strain-based work-life conflict. Access to *childcare* seemed to yield the potential of reducing time- and strain-based WLC but at the same time users of childcare arrangements experienced higher time-based WLC. Overall, besides the fact that the effect sizes were all rather low, it was mostly *access* to a benefit that held an effect. Actual use of an initiative was only related to lower (strain-based) conflict in the case of *free choice of residence*. 'Secondary' initiatives were tested with some intriguing results. Availability of *individual coaching* and *support for educational programs* predicted lower levels of strain-based WLC. Additionally, users of educational support as well as *health and recovery initiatives* reported

Table 15. Summary of findings with regards to the total sample and all subsamples

| | N | Formal Demands | | | | | | Informal Demands | | | | Formal Resources | | | | Informal Resources | | | | | | |
| | | H1a Work Hours | | | H1b Job-related Travel | | | H3a Time Demands | | | H3b Neg Career Cons. | H2a Availability of Initiatives | | H2b Use of Initiatives | | H4a Management Support | | | Supervisor Support | | | H4b Co-Worker Support |
		tWLC	sWLC	bWLC	tWLC	sWLC	bWLC	tWLC	sWLC	bWLC	Initiative Use	tWLC	sWLC	tWLC	sWLC	tWLC	sWLC	bWLC	tWLC	sWLC	bWLC	Initiative Use
Overall Sample	**794**	✓	✗	✓	✓	✗	✓	✓	✓	✓	✓	✗	✓	✗	✓	✓	✓	✓	✗	✓	✗	✓
Subbranch																						
MC	242	✓*	✗	✗	✓*	✗	✗	✓	✓	✓	✓	✗	✗	✗	✗	✓	✗	✓	✗	✗	✗	✗
LF	552	✓	✗	✓	✓	✗	✓	✓	✓	✓	✓	✗	✓	✗	✓	✓	✓	✓	✓	✓	✗	✓
Life Role Prio.																						
'Life'	388	✓	✗	✗	✓	✗	✗	✓	✓	✓	✓	✗	✗	✗	✗	✓	✓	✓	✗	✗	✗	✗
'Work'	310	✓	✗*	✗	✗	✗	✗	✓	✓	✓	✓	✗	✗	✗	✗	✓	✓	✓	✓	✓	✗	✓
'Balance'	93	✓*	✗*	✗*	✗*	✗	✗*	✓	✓	✓*	✗	✗	✗	✗	✗	✗	✗	✗	✗	✓	✓*	✓
Gender																						
Male	548	✓	✗	✗	✓	✗	✓	✓	✓	✓	✓	✓*	✗	✗	✗	✓*	✗	✓	✗	✗	✗	✓*
Female	241	✓*	✗	✗	✓*	✗	✓*	✓	✓	✓	✓	✗	✓	✓*	✓*	✓*	✓	✓	✗	✓	✗	✓
Age																						
Under 30	181	✗	✗	✗	✗	✗	✓	✓	✓	✓	✓	✗	✗	✗	✗	✓	✗	✗	✓*	✗	✗	✓*
30-34	334	✓	✗	✗	✓	✗	✗	✓	✓	✓	✓	✗	✗	✗	✗	✓	✓	✓	✗	✗	✗	✗
35-39	135	✓	✗	✓	✓	✗	✗	✓	✓	✓	✗	✗	✓*	✓*	✗	✗	✓	✓	✗	✓*	✗	✗
40-49	112	✗	✗	✗	✓	✗	✓	✓	✓	✓	✓	✗	✓	✗	✓	✗	✓	✗	✓	✗	✗	✗
Marital Status																						
Single	153	✗	✗	✗	✓	✗	✗	✓	✓	✓	✓	✓*	✗	✓*	✗	✓*	✗	✓	✗	✓	✗	✓*
In a Rel./M.	639	✓	✗	✗	✓	✗	✓	✓	✓	✓	✓	✗	✓	✗	✗	✓	✓	✓	✗	✓	✗	✓
Parental Status																						
Childless	554	✓	✗	✗	✓	✗	✗	✓	✓	✓	✓	✗	✓	✓*	✗	✓	✓	✓	✓	✗	✗	✓*
Parent	181	✓	✗	✗	✗	✗	✗	✓	✓	✓	✓	✗	✓	✗	✗	✓	✓	✗	✗	✗	✓	✗
Dual-Career St.																						
Non-DC	375	✓	✗	✗	✗	✗	✗	✓	✓	✓	✓	✗	✗	☒	✗	✓*	✗	✓	✗	✗	✗	✓
DC	261	✗	✗	✗	✓	✗	✓	✓	✓	✓	✓	✗	✓	✗	✓*	✗	✓	✗	✓	✗	✓	✓
Tenure																						
0-3.5 yrs	436	✓	✗	✗	✓	✗	✗	✓	✓	✓	✓	✗	✗	✗	✗	✓	✓	✓	✓	✗	✗	✓
3.5-6 yrs	190	✓	✗*	✓	✓	✗	✗	✓	✓	✓	✓	✗	✓	✗	✓	✓	✗	✓	✗	✓	✗	✗
6 yrs +	139	✗	✗	✓	✗	✗	✓	✓	✓	✓	✓	✗	✓	☒	✗	✓	✗	✓	✓	✗	✗	✗
Job Level																						
Entry – Med.	436	✓	✗	✗	✗	✗	✗	✓	✓	✓	✓	✗	✓	✗	✗	✓	✓	✓	✓	✗	✗	✓
Medium Lvl	234	✓	✗	✓	✓	✗	✗	✓	✓	✓	✓	✗*	✓	✗	✓	✓	✗	✓	✗	✗	✗	✗
Med – Top	205	✓*	✗	✗	✗	✗	✗	✓	✓	✓	✓	✗	✓	✗	✓	✓	✓	✗	✓	✓	✗	✗

Note: ✓ hypothesis supported; ✗ hypothesis not supported; ✓* hypothesis supported at significance level p < .10, ☒ significant relationship in opposite direction

Table 16. Summary of findings with regards to the effects of individual work-life initiatives (Research Question 2)

	Availability						Use					
	tWLC			*sWLC*			*tWLC*			*sWLC*		
	Overall Sample	MC	LF	Overall Sample	MC	LF	Overall Sample	MC	LF	Overall Sample	MC	LF
Reduced Schedule[a]	✗	✓	✗	✓	✓	✗	✗	✗	✗	✗	✗	✗
Short-term Flex. Work Hours[b]	✗	✗	✗	✗	✗	✗	✗	✓	✗	✗	✗	✗
Long-term Flex. Work Hours[c]	✗	✗	✗	✓	✗	✓	✗	✓	✗	✗	✓	✗
Home Office	✗	✓*	✗	✗	✗	✗	✗	✗	✗	✗	✗	✗
Office (Fri)Day	✗	✓*	✗	✓	✗	✓	✗	✗	✗	✗	✓*	✗
Leave of Absence / Sabbatical	✗	✗	✗	✓	✓*	✓	✗	✗	✗	✗	✗	✗
Free Choice of Residence	✗	✗	✗	✓	✗	✓	✗	✗	✗	✓	✓	✓*
Childcare	✓	/	✓	✓	/	✓*	☒	/	☒	✗	/	✗
Supportive Services	✗	✗	✗	✗	✓*	✗	✓*	✗	✓	✗	✗	✗
Health and Recovery Programs	✗	✓	✗	✗	✗	✗	✗	✗	✓	✓*	✗	✓*
Individual Coaching	✗	✗	✗	✓	✗	✓*	✗	✗	✗	✗	✓*	✗
Support for Educational Programs	✗	✗	✗	✓	✓	✗	✗	✗	✗	✓	✓	✗

Note: ✓ hypothesis supported; ✗ not supported; / not tested due to small subsample size; ✓* significance level p < .10; ☒ significant, but in opposite direction as expected.

less strain-based WLC and users of *supportive services* reported experiencing less WLC in terms of time. Moderating effects were observed by means of group comparisons with a number of interesting findings. Despite their differing working patterns particularly with regards to travel requirements, *management consultants and law firm professionals* did not diverge largely in their work-life dynamics. The most striking difference between these two groups concerned the impact of organizational support. Whereas for law firm professionals management support, supervisor support and support from the co-worker were associated with the hypothesized outcomes, this was not the case for management consultants. Management support was related to lower time-based conflict which was the only significant finding in the arena of informal organizational resources in the MC sample. Long work hours affected law firm professionals more strongly than management consultants and they also experienced behavior-based conflict as a function of job-related travel which was surprising considering the much lower travel frequency in law firms. Comparative evaluation of initiative effects in the two subbranches revealed a number of interesting findings as well. Perceived access to initiatives in the case of reduced schedule, home office, office day, and health programs reduced levels of time-based conflict for management consultants, for law firm professionals in turn only the provision of childcare was attractive in that sense. However, availability of most initiatives reduced lawyers' strain-based conflict which was not the case for management consultants. Use of initiatives seemed to be more beneficial for the strain-based WLC of management consultants. Despite many similarities across the *life role priority* comparison groups differed notably in several respects. Initiative use was related to reduced levels of strain-based conflict only in the case of those who favor work over personal life. Additionally, overall the constructs in the model comparatively explained the highest variance of all conflict types for this group, R squares for the 'life type' and the 'balancers' were remarkably smaller. Above and beyond, an interesting finding is that 'work' professionals and 'balancers' feel more encouraged to make use of initiatives if they are supported by co-workers, an effect that was not supported in the 'life' type subsample. *Gender* differences were also found. Work hours and job-related travel were found stronger predictors of conflict among males who also reported working longer hours and travelling more frequently than the female professionals. Interestingly formal support was found to be more strongly associated with desirable outcomes (i.e. reduced conflict) for men. In the male subsample initiative use and access were related to lower strain-based and (in the case of availability) time-based conflict while females experienced less strain-based conflict as a function of initiative use, at the margins of significance though. Feeling supported by co-workers only encouraged initiative use in the case of females. A differentiated observation of the model concerning age groups did not yield illuminating results. There were notable differences which, nevertheless, are more likely due to further characteristics which are related to age, e.g. being married of being a parent. Being a *parent* or not was associated with equal harm in terms of time demand and equal benefit in terms of management support but a much stronger impact of work hours on work-life conflict. Childless respondents in turn reported higher work-life conflict as a function of job-related travel. Most interestingly, they also benefited from a supportive supervision, in contrast to the parents in the sample. While nonparents perceived lower levels of strain-based work-life conflict if they had access to work-life initiatives, parents' time-based work-life conflict was beneficially impacted by the use of work-life benefits. While most respondents in the sample were childless, the majority had a partner. Only those in a relationship cared for access to work-life initiatives in terms of reduced strain-based conflict. Being *in a relationship* meant a notably higher impact of work hours on conflict than in the case of singles. Travel requirements however were very strongly associated with time- and strain-based work-life conflict for individuals without a partner. When examining the dual-*career status* of respondents an interesting pattern emerged. Those not in a DC relationship were more strongly affected by long work hours and organizational time demands in terms of time- and behavior-based WLC and notably, for them the using initiatives was associated with higher levels of conflict, opposite to Hypothesis 2b.

Finally, two work characteristics were examined, *tenure* and *job level*. Work hours were found to particularly exert an impact on work-life conflict in earlier years within an organization, likewise job-related travel. Informal demands were consistently related to increased WLC (time demands) and reduced use of initiatives (negative career consequences). Management support seemed to play a more or less equally important role among all tenure groups but co-worker support only had an impact on the use of initiatives for the newcomers. Making use of initiatives only made sense in reducing strain-based WLC for the 3.5 to 6 years tenure group, the availability of initiatives largely had positive effects on strain-based WLC for those who worked for their organization more than three years. Additionally a somewhat curious finding was the negative association of supervisor support and strain- and behavior-based WLC in the advanced / top level group. Results may be blurred by the fact that members of this group are in the process of promotion to partner and support from the 'very top' is presumably highly salient regarding most aspects of these professionals' work.

In sum, the present study has come up with a number of interesting findings that are of relevance for further development of research in the work-life arena as well as for strategic human resource management of organizations, particularly PSFs. In the forthcoming sections previous research is linked with the findings of the present study critically discussing these results and deducing a set of implications for theory and practice.

III. DISCUSSION OF RESULTS AND IMPLICATIONS

The aim of the present empirical examination was to illuminate the work-life dynamics of professionals in PSFs who on the one hand face extreme working demands but on the other hand might be willing to do so because this job and their engagement in a high-performance environment is rewarding to them. Under the general assumption that professionals *are* affected by work-life conflict, the major objectives were to explore which demands particularly affect professionals' work-life conflict and clarify the scope of action of PSFs for alleviating conflict in order to maintain maximum productivity and performance of their employees. In other words, it was examined which role organizational demands play for professionals' work-life interface and how resources provided by the organization are able to buffer these demands. Above and beyond a question was raised which had so far largely been neglected in work-life research, about what is behind the 'life' component of work-life conflict.

1. Discussion of Empirical Results

In the forthcoming section the results obtained in an empirical examination comprising nearly 800 professionals of two subbranches of PSFs, management consulting and law firms are reviewed critically, with regards to the character of professionals' work-life conflict (1.1), the impact of formal and informal demands and resources as well as differential effects of altogether twelve work-life initiatives which are frequently available in the PSF context (1.2 and 1.3) with a brief look at the relevance of the hypothesized model for understanding professionals' work-life interface (1.4). Subgroup results concerning subbranch, life role values, gender, age, relationship and parental status as well as tenure and job position are evaluated taking into consideration results from previous research that were presented in Part I (1.5). Results are all discussed from a theoretical point of view also critically taking into consideration limitations and methodological issues which might have impacted certain results (1.6).

1.1 Professionals and the Experience of Work-Life Conflict

Before actually investigating antecedents of work-life conflict (WLC) the question was raised whether professionals perceive problems in reconciling their life spheres at all and if so, of what character exactly is the conflict they experience. It had previously been argued that 'work-life balance' is more than work and family, issues of leisure, health and recovery as well as individual development were raised in prior discussions and a broader scope of work-life benefits was claimed in order to address the needs of all employees in organizations as well as more inclusive populations in empirical studies (Kaiser et al., 2010).

In order to shed light on the type of conflict employees in PSFs experience descriptive data were examined concerning the three work-life conflict dimensions (time-based, strain-based, and behavior-based WLC), five types of work-'life' conflict (work vs. partnership/family, friends, social engagement, health and recovery, and self), as well as life role values expressed in terms of importance, priorities, and centrality of spheres in professional's lives. ANOVAs were further conducted to unravel differences among consulting professionals and law firm professionals, males and females, with respect to life role priority types, age groups, and several characteristics of work and family. A number of interesting findings and conclusions result from this examination and are discussed subsequently.

1.1.1 Life Role Values

Despite their willingness to engage in a demanding but doubtlessly also highly attractive job, the data obtained in this study strongly suggest that *work-life conflict is an issue for professionals,* specifically employees in professional service firms. This is consistent with results reported previously underscoring the conclusion that "work-life conflict matters" (Messersmith, 2007, p. 446). First and foremost this conclusion is in the present examination based upon observations of descriptive data regarding professionals' importance and priority assigned to life spheres as well as centrality of life roles. Life roles most central to the respondents were work and family, followed by friends, health and recovery and time for self. If average points attributed to all nonwork spheres would be counted together (also including social engagement) centrality of nonwork spheres would account for about 70 per cent in comparison to 30 per cent for the work role. Of course this perspective has its limitations and respondents' choice was probably impacted by the fact that five nonwork roles versus the (one) work role were presented for them to distribute their centrality points. Nevertheless this gives us a first hint that to hard-working professionals, spheres other than work *do* matter (cf. Jourdrey & Wallace, 2009). This is strengthened by the finding that about 30 per cent of the participants rated work very important while more than half of the sample considered personal life very important. Results regarding life role priority further support this notion: 40 per cent of the professionals' indicated that personal life was more important to them than work and the same percentage answered that both spheres were of equal importance in their view. Considering these findings and the requirement of a 'putting work first' attitude necessary to advance in a PSF that was pointed out previously (e.g. Williams,

2007), the assumption that professionals are particularly prone to the experience of WLC was supported by the data used here.

Notably, centrality ratings did not differ largely across subgroups. Interestingly, respondents of different gender and different age groups assigned on average similar centrality values to life domains. In previous research it has been argued that men and women diverge substantially in their work-life experiences with women being stronger advocates for the family domain (e.g. Barnett & Hyde, 2001). In the present sample both men and women assigned about 30 points out of 100 to work and the same to the family sphere. Consensus was also observed with respect to life role importance and priorities, where both men and women assigned high importance to both work and personal life and ranged between rating both spheres equally and prioritizing in favor of higher personal life importance. This finding might owe to the fact that, indicated by an average age of early thirties in both subsamples, the majority of respondents are at the beginning of their career and still share the same values until it comes to starting a family. Opposed to this idea however, results that compared four age groups were again characterized by very low disparity. This observation indicates that men and women and professionals at different ages do not differ dramatically with respect to their life role priorities, a finding that challenges previous research findings (Bagger et al., 2008; Matthews et al., 2009) and is highly relevant for PSFs' recruiting and retention strategies.

1.1.2 The Multi-Faceted Nature of Professionals' Work-Life Conflict

While results on professionals' life role values hold a meaningful message themselves, they were basically a means of putting more specific evidence in scope. With a self-created scale that was based on thoughts of Carlson and Kacmar (2000) and Friedman (2008b), the experience of different types of conflict between work and five nonwork spheres (family, friends, social engagement, health, self) was assessed. A number of interesting findings were attained.

About one third of the respondents indicated that they did not experience any of the conflict types. The remaining professionals largely experienced *moderate to high conflict* among four or all life spheres, i.e. nearly two thirds of the professionals examined here experienced conflict between work and several – up to five – nonwork spheres. It was further found that of those who indicated 'no conflict' in a category, the largest proportion was in the area work vs. family. At the same time in this category the percentage of professionals that indicated high conflict was considerably smaller than in the other four areas. This is a highly interesting finding considering the fact that most studies concentrate on the dichotomy of work vs. family, consciously excluding all individuals without family responsibilities. Respondents indicated moderate levels of conflict particularly in the areas of friends and health / recovery. The highest percentages of 'high conflict' ratings were found in the spheres of social engagement and self but results must be put in scope with findings concerning life role centrality, which indicate that social engagement ranges among less central life spheres. Despite this limitation, these findings strongly support what had been argued in previous work: studying work-nonwork conflict only in terms of work and family does not do justice to the complex dynamics of people's lives. From examining conflict types it has become clear that both research and practice should consider a more comprehensive work-life interface because areas beyond work also matter for achieving successful work-life reconciliation, which is also discussed by Lewis (2003). For the organization this again yields implications for recruiting and also for corporate work-life integration management (WLIM). As work-life integration not only matters for those in 'special' situations requiring 'extra' treatment but it matters for a very wide range of issues and people, organizations should change their often used 'marginalization' tactics (Williams, 2007) into a strategy that considers the whole individual or, as Ostendorp (2007) puts it, a culture of differences.

Concerning the *three conflict dimensions* pronounced by Greenhaus and Beutell (1985) that were studied in this examination, it turned out that in the total sample time-based WLC was experienced more strongly in comparison to strain-based and behavior-based conflict. Yet ranging between three and four on a 5-point Likert scale, all reported means were well above the midpoint of the scale, suggesting that considerable levels of conflict of all three qualities were strongly prevalent for professionals. Moreover, reported levels in the present data exceed conflict means attained in comparable studies such as Chen et al. (2009) who report means below three for time- and strain-based conflict and Lapierre et al. (2008) who likewise reported lower mean values for these conflict dimensions (cf. Appendix A, Table A.5). This finding gives further support to the assumption that professionals are affected by WLC. In the present sample work-life conflicts were perceived in terms of *time*, that is, time-consuming work volumes take away time dispensable for nonwork problems. Conflict was also experienced in terms of stress or *strain*, i.e. professionals perceived it as psychologically burdening that work takes so much time and energy forcing them cut down on personal life. Above and beyond these rather passive perceptions, professionals experienced conflict such that they, because of work-related matters, often have to *act* in ways which impede their engagement in nonwork roles, such as postponing or cancelling a vacation because of an important project in their firm. This result contributes to existing research in two ways. First, levels of conflict reported here give evidence to the notion that professionals working in 'extreme jobs' face work-life integration challenges. Secondly, the present study provides data on the third conflict dimension of Greenhaus and Beutell, behavior-based work-life conflict, which had been largely neglected in past research as for example pointed out by van Daalen and colleagues (2006). The present examination developed two items in order to assess behavior-based conflict and despite non-optimal metrics (cf. Part II, 2.2.1) results were obtained which suggest that professionals are also occupied with this kind of conflict. Hence, results are provided here on the far understudied third conflict dimension indicating that neglecting it draws an incomplete picture of individuals' work-life interface.

1.1.3 A More Differentiated Look: Work-Life Conflict in Several Subsamples

A number of additional examinations were made to detect differences as a function of individual characteristics in the type and intensity of conflicts experienced. *Management consultants versus law firm professionals* reported higher conflict levels of the types work vs. social engagement and work vs. health and recovery. Anecdotal evidence suggests that the notion that many management consultants want to see themselves as 'socially committed' and 'do gooders' and the related issue of social desirability puts the statement that heavy work volumes conflict with social engagement into perspective. Yet the perception of higher conflict of work with health issues might indeed be explained by the fact that management consultants work longer hours and spend more time traveling than law firm professionals. This goes in line with the finding that time-based and strain-based conflict was higher in the management consultant group.

Contrasting the experience of conflict types of individuals with different *life role values* by means of three groups revealed that those who prioritized personal life experience significantly higher conflict between work-family and work-friends compared to those who prioritize in favor of work and those with equal priority ('balancers'). 'Life' prioritizers also experienced the highest levels of work interfering with personal life in terms of time, followed by the balancers and lastly the 'work' type. Similar results were found in the case of strain-based conflict. Highest levels concerning work-related behaviors that interfered with personal life spheres (bWLC) were reported by the balancers, the 'work' type was again the group with lowest on WLC. Previous research in this area indicated different findings: Cinamon and Rich (2002a) found that work-family conflict was highest for the dual type (equal importance of domains) and lowest for the 'family type', who was found to spent less hours at work. Bourne et al. (2009) reported findings which indicate that the dual-centric type experiences high satisfaction with work-family balance, again indicating contradictory results. However, comparability of findings is questionable because measurements differed in the two studies mentioned and in the present examination. From the present study, the finding that those whose focus in life is more on their work sphere face lower WLC clearly indicates how the importance attributed to one's life spheres impacts the perception of conflict. For organizations these individuals are, at first sight, first-choice employees because they are more likely to put work matters first on their priority list. But these individuals are also on top of the list for being work addicts or workaholics, and it has been shown that an extremely high engagement in the work role can easily result in psychosomatic problems and burnout (Burke & Fiksenbaum, 2008). Ultimately, these employees might therefore cost the firm more than they contribute and relying on a potentially workaholic workforce is a risky strategy over time, not least because with the surfacing of personal problems, turnover of once overly committed employees might be abrupt. Taking into account the tendency that individual life role values shift towards leading a fulfilled life in all domains (cf. Part I, 3.3.2) PSFs should rather focus on providing options which address these desires.

Females and males did not differ in their experience of conflict types, which is in itself an interesting finding. It has been argued in previous research and in the public debate that in professional careers women are often disadvantaged facing a 'glass ceiling effect', their careers come to a halt before they reach the top (Cheung & Halpern, 2010; Kumra & Vinnicombe, 2008; Lyness & Thompson, 1997). Findings here do not support this notion. Females comprise 30 per cent of those at medium to top level and 20 per cent of those at top or partner level. Considering the fact that usually in PSFs women make up about 20 per cent of the whole workforce this is remarkable in itself. Taken together with the fact that female and male life role values and perceptions of conflict among life spheres largely go in line, this is clearly a hint towards a general change in young professionals' attitudes towards work and personal life in favor of a more balanced and gender-neutral attitude. Although it often seems that this convergence of values among men and women has not yet reached politics or the media, Galinsky and Matos (2011) report from a large-scale national survey in the U.S. that indeed the majority of U.S. citizens agree on an equal distribution of work-nonwork responsibilities instead of a traditional one (female homemaker – male breadwinner). Meanwhile, professional women in the sample were found to experience significantly higher WLC in terms of psychological strain which corresponds to previous findings (van Daalen et al., 2006).

Although *age groups* were similar in their life role values, as indicated above, they differed in some respects that deserve attention. Younger employees had a stronger feeling that work conflicted with their family, their temporal resources for meeting friends as well as their ability to engage socially. Above and beyond, early thirties professionals experienced higher time-based and strain-based WLC than professionals of age 40 and older. Explanations include the notion that personal life issues might become less acute at an advanced age, i.e. children are grown up or, just as likely, their working patterns change to less stressful. Indeed, the data also suggest that older employees work 'only' about 51 hours weekly with one or less days of travelling whereas younger professionals work on average 57 hours per week and travel at least two days a week. It might also be argued that professionals who prevail in such highly demanding work environments at an older age have concentrated their social life including friends at the workplace, as has been argued by Hewlett and Luce (2006). Largely, findings correspond to previous results (e.g. Golden, Veiga & Simsek, 2006; Pasewark & Viator, 2006; Taylor, Delcampo & Blanchero, 2009) which indicate that age is not a crucial factor for the experience of WLC. It appears to be life events which occur *at* a certain age that make the difference.

Examining *singles versus professionals in a relationship,* those with a partner felt that they had less time for themselves. Other than that no differences were found with regards to conflict types and dimensions. However, an interesting finding was reported concerning *parents and nonparents.* In the data, those who had no children experienced higher levels of conflict between work versus family and work versus friends. Nonparents also reported significantly higher time-, strain-, and behavior-based WLC. One explanation for this outcome is the more frequent use of reduced schedules, short-term flexible work hours, working from home, and childcare arrangements which seem to support parents in their work-life reconciliation. Additionally, this finding might be explained by the fact that most parents in the sample had non-employed spouses who potentially help manage nonwork concerns and thus support their partners' extreme jobs. Professionals without children were in most cases involved in relationships where their partner also works full-time, here referred to as dual-career couples. It has previously been discussed how dual-career couples face greater challenges in managing their work and nonwork spheres (Abele & Volmer, Berg et al., 2003; 2011; Grady & McCarthy, 2008). In the data, *dual-career status* was also tested for differences between conflict types and dimensions with confirmative results. Professionals in a dual-career relationship perceived stronger WLC of all three dimensions though regarding conflict types only work vs. friends was higher for them. This confirms previous findings that particularly professionals who are in a relationship where both partners pursue a high-level career have a hard time satisfying demands and needs on behalf their personal life. As such partnership constellations are generally on the rise, organizations are asked to support these challenges in order to maintain their professionals in the company. One such solution could be the implementation of a rarely referred to work-life

benefit type, one that is not directly addressing the professional workers themselves but their spouses or their family constellations as a whole. Such existing
benefits are relocation services which aim at supporting professionals and their
families (e.g. spousal job-finding assistance) when they relocate in order to start
a new job or shift because of a long-term project (Zedeck & Mosier, 1990).
Similar interventions that take into account the personal constellation of the
professional are called into action.

Last but not least, professionals of different years of *tenure* and three different *job levels* in the organizational hierarchy were compared concerning mean
differences of conflict types and dimensions. Highest levels of all five conflict
types were reported by professionals who had prevailed 3.5 to 6 years in the
organization. Time- and strain-based conflict was also highest for them and
lowest for the professionals of more than 6 years in the organization. Concerning *job level,* strain-based conflict was significantly higher from entry up to
medium level as compared to those advancing towards top level. Time-based
conflict was likewise higher at lower hierarchy levels. This is surprising considering the fact that higher-level jobs are often associated with higher pressure,
long work hours and intense emotional demands (Schieman, Glavin & Milkie,
2009). It may be that in PSFs a socialization and adaptation process takes place
where professionals either adapt to the high demands of the job or drop out at a
low to medium job level (cf. Lorsch & Tierney, 2002). The observation that
conflict levels decrease with rising job level and tenure is consistent with findings of Golden, Veiga and Simsek (2006) who found lower levels of WLC the
longer professionals stayed in an organization (cf. also Batt & Valcour, 2003).
Although mean levels are still considerable at longer tenure/higher job levels
this finding can also be explained by situational characteristics of personal life –
e.g. children are grown up to an age where they represent less time pressure than
newborns – and a more or less settled career where dedication and commitment
must not as strongly be demonstrated by weekly work hours of 60 and more. In
sum, a number of major conclusions can be drawn from this close-up of the
nature professionals' work-life conflict:

- Work-life conflict is *an issue that matters for professional employees in
  PSFs,*
- Work-life conflict consists of *more than work and family,*
- The present study provides evidence for the importance of including the
  third dimension of Greenhaus and Beutell, *behavior-based conflict,* in the
  study of the work-life interface.

Above and beyond previous research, the present study contributes insights regarding the impact of demographic, work and personal life characteristics on the experience of work-life conflict of professionals in PSFs:

- *Management consultants* are even more affected by WLC than law firm professionals;
- Those who *prioritize work* over personal life spheres face less conflict of every type and every dimension;
- *Females and males* converge in their life role priorities and conflict types they experience, yet women face stronger strain-based conflict;
- *Younger employees* face higher levels of conflict among life domains and in terms of conflict dimensions than employees of age 40 and older;
- *Non-parents* experienced higher conflict between work and several life domains than parents as well as higher work-life conflict in terms of time, strain and behavior;
- *Professionals in dual-career couples experience higher levels of time-, strain-, and behavior-based work-life conflict than professionals in non dual-career couples;*
- Highest levels in conflict types and dimensions in the tenure comparison experienced those who *were in their firm 3.5 to 6 years*, with similar results in the comparison of *job levels*.

Supported by the fact that the majority of studies in the work-life field use professional samples (Casper et al., 2007), it has often been taken as an obvious fact that professionals are *the* population for studying work-life conflict. The study presented here is the first to explicitly examine the nature and character of professionals' WLC in detail. Briefly summarized, results indicate that particularly the time-based dimension of work-life conflict is an issue for employees in professional service firms. This finding is not surprising considering the immense work-related time demands that professionals face. But they also experience conflict between work and personal life that originates in psychological strain and in terms of work-related behavior which collides with personal life interests. These results further strengthen the notion raised by Greenhaus and Beutell (1985) that conflict is a complex construct with (at least) three dimensions that deserve differential consideration.

No study has so far taken into account *conflict types*, i.e. whether work-'life' conflict reaches beyond work and family. The present study examined conflict between work, as the most demanding role in the lives of professionals, with five facets of the personal life sphere with the important finding that most respondents experienced conflict between work and several aspects of personal life, not only family. These findings contribute to work-life research enlightening the facets hidden behind the 'life' sphere and help us better understand the character of professionals' work-life conflict.

1.2 Formal and Informal Demands and the Work-Life Conflict of Professionals

The close-up examination of professionals' work-life conflict types and dimensions was meant to serve as a foundation for examining dynamics of WLC and its antecedents in the highly demanding field of professional service firms. Specifically, the central aim of the present study was to find out which demands negatively impact the work-life interface of professionals and which resources may act as buffers, i.e. reduce work-life interferences. As outlined previously (Part I, Section 3.) formal as well as informal demands and resources were investigated using quantitative data of management consultants and law firm professionals. Findings with regards to the research model will be discussed in the subsequent sections including the impact of work hours and travel (formal demands), work-life initiatives (formal resources), organizational time demands and negative career consequences (informal demands), and managerial, supervisor, and co-worker support (informal resources) on time-, strain-, and behavior-based work-to-life conflict.

1.2.1 Formal Organizational Demands: Work Hours and Job-related Travel

From the working pattern of professionals two highly salient work demands were identified (cf. Part I, 3.2.1): extremely long work hours and frequent job-related travel, the latter being an inherent characteristic of management consultants' job profile. The present study examined the impact of these two formal demands on professionals' time-, strain-, and behavior-based WLC.

1.2.1.1 Work Hours as a Predictor of Time-based Work-Life Conflict

Notably, average work hours which respondents indicated here exceeded mean work hours of almost all other professional samples reviewed in Part I. Mean work hours of participating consultants (58.42 hrs/week) and law firm professionals (53.38 hrs/week) were substantially higher than of most professionals examined in prior research which range around average weekly hours of 45 to 50, in some cases less (cf. Appendix A, Table A.5). This strengthens the notion that professionals examined here work in 'extreme jobs' according to characteristics outlined by Hewlett and Luce (2006). Consistent with previous research, support was provided in the total sample for the hypothesis that long work hours predict WLC. Work hours were indeed significantly related with temporal interference between work and nonwork spheres and to a lesser extent with behavior-based WLC. Respondents did have the feeling that due to their work volume, they had less *time* for nonwork spheres and had to act in ways that often restrict their personal life activities. Notably, the relationship with strain-based conflict was positive but considerably failed to reach any acceptable significance limit in the total dataset as well as in all subsample comparisons. The finding that actual work hours are a predictor of WLC is consistent with previous research (Aryee, 1992; Batt & Valcour, 2003; Kossek, Lautsch & Eaton, 2006; Jacobshagen et al., 2005; Judge, Boudreau & Bretz, 1994; Nielsen, Carlson & Lankau, 2001; Taris et al., 2006; Thompson et al., 1999; Wharton & Blair-Loy, 2006; Wallace, 2009). It extends previous research by showing that the impact of work volume on conflict not necessarily occurs in terms of psychological strain which highlights the requirement that such relationships must be regarded more differentially. First and foremost, professionals seemed to perceive their long work hours to be restrictive of their personal life in terms of time. This is concurrent with existing research in Fortune 500 firms which also found such an association (Major et al., 2002). That work volume interferes with personal time volume is easily explained by means of previously mentioned Conservation of Resources (COR) theory (Hobfoll, 1989, 2001). Because individuals "strive to retain, protect, and build resources and [...] what is threatening to them is the potential or actual loss of these valued resources" (Hobfoll, 1989, p. 513), the experience of WLC as a means of high work time volume is only natural.

It was further found that work hours were a significant, yet weaker predictor of *behavior-based WLC*. In other words, due to long working hours, professionals are more likely to exert behaviors which interfere with nonwork interests, such as postponing a personal vacation. This is interesting as to my knowledge, behavior-based WLC as an outcome of work hours was not examined in past research. Contrary to previous findings, where work hours were also associated with psychological distress (Major et al., 2002), present results did not support this evidence. The reasoning that among professionals, excessive work hours are not associated with *strain-based WLC* underscores the notion of the high intrinsic value of professional work. It was outlined previously that studying work-life dynamics of this occupational group requires a differential point of view in terms of meaning attached to work as an identity-creating factor. Thus, it is a highly intriguing finding that work hours affect professionals' time-based WLC and also predict levels of behavior-based WLC but are not meaningfully related to work-personal life interactions in terms of psychological strain. First and foremost, professionals in the sample perceived their long work hours to substantially take temporal resources off their personal life.

1.2.1.2 Job-Related Travel as a Predictor of Behavior-based Work-Life Conflict

A different pattern emerged for job-related travel: although the travel → tWLC relationship was also significant, frequent business travel was substantially more strongly associated with behavior-based WLC. Strain-based conflict was again not impacted by this type of formal demand. Professionals in the sample thus perceived the demand of traveling regularly to be associated with trade-offs on behalf of personal life, for example in terms of low schedule predictability and high likeliness of having to postpone private vacations (behavior-based WLC). These results complement O'Mahoney (2007), who illustrated extreme travel obligations in management consulting and their high costs on behalf of home life. Findings also add new knowledge to outcomes of Mayerhofer et al.'s (2008) qualitative study where professionals complained about the lack of recognition they get for their times spent on transport.

Overall, findings regarding hypotheses 1a and 1b summarize in the conclusion that formal organizational demands, namely work hours and job-related travel, affect professionals' work-life interface in terms of temporal availability for personal life matters and behavioral patterns that interfere with personal life interests. These formal demands do, however, *not create a* psychological burden in terms of wishing to spend more energy in personal life activities while being unable to do so, or feelings of guilt associated with insufficient time spent in personal life spheres (Greenhaus & Beutell, 1985). This is insofar an interesting finding that it increases our knowledge about the precise character of work-life conflict which employees in general and professionals specifically experience as a result of objective work pressures. An association between work volume and conflict was found in previous studies as outlined in Part I. Yet, inferring from operationalizations used, it seems that often studies implicitly assume 'WLC' is associated with psychological stress. In this specific sample, professionals did experience work-life conflict as a function of formal organizational demands but not in the sense of a psychological burden. It seems more as if respondents were saying, 'Yes, my work requirements take time off my personal activities, and yes, they sometimes make me act and decide in ways that interfere with personal life interests, yet my long work hours and frequent travel duties do not make me feel bad in terms of not being available for personal life responsibilities'. While PSFs do demand a lot from their professionals in terms of work volume and flexibility, these formal demands seem to have fairly little impact on psychological strain and seem to be seen as a factual necessity of the job. This indicates that in terms of work hours and travel requirements professionals are willing to make the necessary trade-offs in favor of their career, and it may be other factors which actually cause psychological strain.

In terms of research, these findings add another quality to the three-dimensional structure of work-life conflict suggested by Greenhaus and Beutell (1985). While in previous research work-life conflict is seen as a problem, the threefold taxonomy allows to view work-life dynamics from a more 'objective' angle: work hours might interfere with personal life in terms of available time, and flexibility requirements in terms of incompatible behavior but as long as individuals are willing to make this trade-off, there is no 'problem', it is a personal decision. Whether time-based and behavior-based WLC in turn lead to psychological distress as an outcome would be different story. The major conclusion here, with regards to *formal organizational demands*, is that these demands do indeed impact the work-life interface of professionals but obviously not in ways which create a psychological burden. In sum, the most important conclusions from hypotheses 1a and 1b are:

- *Work hours* were most strongly associated with *time-based work-to-life conflict* and to a lesser extent with behavior-based work-to-life conflict,
- *Job-related travel* was most strongly associated with *behavior-based work-to-life conflict* and to a lesser extent with time-based work-to-life conflict, and
- Neither of those formal organizational demands was associated with *strain-based work-to-life conflict* in the present professional sample.

1.2.2 Culturally Endorsed Pressures: The Role of Informal Demands

As compared to formal demands, informal or culturally endorsed demands act 'under the surface', for example in terms of practices that make long work hours an indicator for performance and thus a prerequisite for career advancement, or in terms of halted or slower career advancement if WLB initiatives are made use of. The current paragraph discusses findings with regards to this type of organizational pressures and its effect on professionals' work-life interface (Hypotheses 3a and 4a).

1.2.2.1 The Crucial Role of Implicit Time Expectations

Organizational time demands implicitly prevalent in an organization and rooted in its culture were the most consistent and most striking predictor of all three WLC dimensions in the total dataset and all subgroup comparisons. Significant evidence for Hypothesis 3a, which proposed a positive relationship between implicitly endorsed organizational time demands and WLC, was found without exception throughout the whole analysis. The largely consistent impact pattern was that time demands first and foremost affected time-based WLC (path coefficients ranged from .210 to .504) and secondly strain-based WLC, followed by behavioral conflict. While Smith and Gardner (2007) found time demands to be the strongest predictors of work-family conflict, present findings extend this by relating time norms to the more specific and yet more inclusive concept of work-personal life conflict in the dimensions of time, strain, and behavior.

Notably, in contrast to formal organizational demands, informal time demands affected strain-based conflict in considerable intensity, path coefficients ranged from .205 to .392. In other words, the work-life interface of professionals was in the present sample most substantially impacted by culturally rooted organizational time demands in terms of the temporal and behavioral as well as the psychological strain dimension of conflict. Feeling pressured to spend exceptional amounts of time at work, regardless of actual productivity, was associated with higher conflict in terms of time which would rather be spent with personal life activities, in terms of behavior that interferes with personal life and also in terms of psychological burden, i.e. feeling stressed by the fact that time and energy spent at work interfere with available personal resources in nonwork domains. This finding is consistent with previous research (Dikkers et al., 2007a; Frone, Yardley & Markel, 1997; Thompson et al., 1999) and gives further evidence for the extraordinarily high impact of implicitly expected time norms in the work environment of professional service firms. Results underscore the notion of 'time politics' in PSFs discussed by Williams (2007) and Wharton and Blair-Loy (2006), who argue that commitment and dedication for an employer is very frequently measured by time devoted to work. In this context, the 'ideal worker norm' raised by Williams (2007) describing employees that work full-time and dedicate most of their life to their career, is likely be prevalent in the working environments of many professionals studied here. In order to break with this culture of presenteeism it is necessary to establish objective and results-based methods and metrics of measuring performance as for example with assessment tools suggested by Thiehoff (2004) and Morris and colleagues (2009).

1.2.2.2 Career Damage Expected: How the Anticipation of Negative Career Consequences Impedes Initiative Use

A 'work first' culture is also manifested in potential negative career consequences that are associated with making use of corporate work-life initiatives. The second hypothesis which respect to the impact of informal organizational demands on the work-life interface linked fear of negative career consequences with professionals' use of corporate work-life arrangements (Hypothesis 3b). Previous research circles around questions of how using work-life benefits impacts career advancement, generally with findings that suggest benefit users are less likely to be promoted (Allen & Russell, 1999; Johnson, Lowe & Reckers, 2008; Judiesch & Lyness, 1999). In the present study, an opposite perspective was taken by investigating the idea that if professionals anticipate negative career consequences, they do not use work-life initiatives or use them less frequently.

Similar to the support given to Hypothesis 3a, in all but very few subgroups, anticipation of negative career consequences made professionals in this study refrain from making use of organizational work-life initiatives. That professionals feel restricted from using work-life benefits because they expect this might harm their career is consistent with findings of Smith and Gardner (2007) and results from public accountants studied by Johnson and colleagues (2008). Findings supporting the previously issued statement that negative career consequences were significantly and negatively related to making use of work-life initiatives supporting the previously issued statement, that organizational culture determines whether individuals use available benefits (Thompson et al., 1999). This is an important result for HR practitioners whose task is not only to implement but also to legitimize the implementation of work-life policies (Connor, Hooks & McGuire, 1999).

If corporate culture is not supportive and employees do not dare make use of work-life initiatives because they fear impacts on their career advancement potential, initiative implementation is largely a waste of effort and money. Even more striking findings suggest that informally endorsed time pressures, associated with them the phenomena of face time and presenteeism, are related substantially to all three dimensions of work-life conflict. This calls organizations into action to reflect their practices of measuring commitment and rather focus on productive outputs instead of time spent at the firm or answering e-mails late at night. In sum, the most important research findings concerning the impact of *informal organizational demands* on the work-life interface were:

- *Informal organizational time norms* significantly and substantially predicted all three forms of work-life conflict in the total dataset and all subsamples, and
- The anticipation of *informally rooted negative career outcomes* in the case of using work-life benefits was related to reduced levels of actual initiative usage in the total sample as well as all subgroups.

1.3 The Role of Formal and Informal Organizational Resources

Another major aim of the present thesis was to examine the actual role of formal and informal resources for professionals' work-life interface. Such insights are valuable for organizations in order to a) help them understand the resources they posses for dealing with employees' work-life conflicts, b) enable them to purposefully manage these resources and hence c) effectively control employees' work-life balance and avoid negative outcomes which occur as a result of work-life conflict. The present examination investigated the impact of formal organizational resources, work-life initiatives, and informal organizational resources, managerial, supervisor, and co-worker support. On the forthcoming pages, findings concerning hypotheses 2a and 2b as well as 3b and 4b are discussed

1.3.1 Use and Usefulness of Work-Life Initiatives

The present examination closely investigated the impact of formal organizational resources on professionals' work-life interface. For this purpose an analysis was conducted to find out which work-life initiatives are available in PSFs (cf. Part I, 3.2.2) resulting in a catalogue of thirteen benefits that relate more or less closely to the work-life interface. While it has been discussed vividly in the past whether to study *initiative availability* or *use*, the present investigation observed both options and their different dynamics. Access to and use of work-life initiatives were shown in the present study to yield beneficial results in terms of primarily *reduced strain-based WLC*. Model evaluations with the total dataset as well as subgroup comparisons quite consistently indicated an association of initiative availability and use with strain-based WLC while the majority of linkages with time-based WLC were not significant. In order to address Research Question 2, initiatives were distinguished into WLB initiatives in a more narrow sense and secondary initiatives which address work-life dynamics in a wider sense. The present empirical study conducted separate estimations of the PLS model which included only one initiative at a time. This procedure enabled tracking down effects of initiative use and availability to single initiatives and making inferences that contribute solid evidence to work-life research and enable clear implications for PSFs. Overall, the finding was that both, initiatives more closely aimed at reconciling life spheres and secondary initiatives imposed an effect on WLC. Furthermore, it was largely those initiatives that exerted an impact of which it would not have been expected so in the first place. Finally, more effects were found for strain-based conflict than for WLC in terms of time. The impact of work-life initiatives on management consultants versus law firm professionals also differed in some interesting respects.

1.3.1.1 Availability of Initiatives

Perceived access to initiatives (*availability*) was related to reduced levels of work-life conflict, which also had been found in previous examinations (e.g. Smith & Gardner, 2007). Note that initiatives most frequently offered (but not used) in the present data were reduced schedule and leave of absence, followed by home office and childcare. In the subgroup comparison *consultants and lawyers* likewise profited in terms of lower psychological strain from the knowledge that work-life initiatives were available in their firms. This finding contradicts previous research as Baltes et al. (1999) in their meta-analysis indicated that many work-life initiatives did not apply for professionals as a comparatively large amount of flexibility is inherent in their working patterns. Access to *reduced scheduling* was found to predict lower levels of strain-based conflict but in the subbranch comparison this finding turned out to be only significant for the consultants, who also experienced lower time-based conflict as a function of reduced schedule availability. Considering the missing effect of actual initiative use renders this finding contra intuitive at first sight, but a look at other frequently available benefits in consultancies might serve as an explanation. It is a common practice that consultants enter PSFs straight after their university degree and further educational support is usually inherent in the career of these young professionals. Firms usually support MBA programs or PhDs by granting a leave of absence to the professionals or by reducing their work hours (Deller, 2004). Therefore the prospect of this initiative might appeal to professionals in this field contributing to the feeling that the firm makes an investment in their career. The link towards 'work-life balance' seems yet rather distant under this perspective. The availability of *long-term flexible work hours* was attractive in terms of lower strain-based WLC, probably expressing the wish of consultants and lawyers to get their share of extra work hours paid by storing them in a time-savings account as indicated by Mayerhofer et al. (2008). Though its use had no effect on the work-life interface, for both management consultants and law firm professionals the prospect of a *leave of absence* or sabbatical appeared to reduce work-life conflict in terms of psychological strain. This is supported by the comparatively high (though still 'small') effect size of this relationship. Access to a leave of absence, often also for educational and developmental rather than family reasons, seems to be highly attractive. The missing link between reduced conflict and taking such a time-out might be explained with anticipated undesired career outcomes (cf. Judiesch & Lyness, 1999). This explanation is strengthened by the finding that nearly half of the management consultants and one third of lawyers indicated that leave of absence was available in their company but they did not use it (compared to still 32 per cent users in the MC subsample and 4.2 per cent users in the LF subsample). Nevertheless, this finding contributes to the scarce research evidence on the benefits of this arrangement and extends findings of Dikkers et al. (2004) who indicated that parental leave specifically was associated with lower work-home interference.

1.3.1.2 Use of Work-Life Initiatives

Initiative use in general was also, though less consistently, related to stronger strain-based WLC. Making use of *long-term flexible work hours* was only effective in reducing management consultants' time- and strain-based WLC. Probably the project-based structure in consultancies more strongly enables this working pattern compared to law firms, as consultants often have less pressing phases between projects and in turn work more when they are on a project. Such a structure of high work volume versus recovery periods may relieve professionals somewhat of their high demands. Whether this is an actual work-life benefit, however, or whether this is just the way 'how things work' is to be questioned. *Office day* was shown to yield the potential for reducing psychological strain in the case of management consultants. In light of these findings, it seems that consultants perceive their office day as less stressful than the rest of the week and thus beneficial for ameliorating work life conflict. Anecdotal evidence as well as empirical findings of Ahuja et al. (2007) supports the appealing character of working from the near firm's office rather than from the client site. Making use of *childcare* was related to higher work-life conflict in the total sample (and likewise in the LF subsample). This relationship opposite to expectations can be an indicator for two issues. It may be that using a childcare arrangement causes additional time pressure to individuals because they have to bring and pick up their child(ren) at certain times, which is likely to collide with work responsibilities and thus creates temporal work-life conflict. It may also be that individuals seek to use childcare because they experience high work-life conflict indicating a reverse causality of the hypothesized path (cf. 6., limitations). Meanwhile, strain-based WLC was not affected by childcare use. Lastly, interesting effects were found with respect to *free choice of residence*. The benefit that the firm pays expenses from professionals' preferred home location (usually within national scope) to the work location was shown to reduce professionals' (both law firm professionals' and consultants') experience of strain-based WLC. In fact, this relationship displayed the highest effect size of all initiatives under study. It has been shown that maintaining a strong social environment – which is very often tied to the place of residence – helps individuals cope with work-life conflict (Wiersma, 1994). Insofar, this result contributes to our knowledge about work-life initiatives as this is the first empirical examination that considers this type of benefit within the work-life dynamics. Findings emphasize the importance of looking beyond traditional initiatives and more into context- and branch-specific benefits as well as solutions tailored to individual needs.

1.3.1.3 Secondary Initiatives

Most frequently available secondary initiatives were support for educational programs and health programs. Interestingly, secondary initiatives were also associated with a number of positive work-life outcomes. Availability of *coaching* reduced levels of strain-based WLC and management consultants who *used* individual coaching actually experienced lower conflict in terms of strain. This links to research which previously emphasized the beneficial effect of having a mentor or coach (Almer & Kaplan, 2002; Bussell, 2008; Höher & Steenbuck, 2006; Nielson et al., 2001), also for work-life dynamics. The importance of *health and recovery* opportunities for reducing work-personal life interferences has also been pointed out in prior research (Frone et al., Frone et al., 1992; Netemeyer et al., 1996; Sonnentag & Niessen, 2008). Indeed the present data revealed beneficial effects of health programs in terms of lower strain-based WLC. Differential observation of the data suggested that *access* to such benefits was related to lower time-based WLC for management consultants, law firm professionals perceived reduced time- and strain-based WLC as a consequence of *using* health benefits. Availability and use of *support for educational programs* predicted lower levels of strain-based WLC as well. While at first sight this finding is not so intuitive it may be explained with leave policies often attached to educational programs in PSFs during which professionals complete their MBA, PhD, etc. Therefore, compared to the daily business such an educational program might very well be perceived as less stressful and leaving more time for personal life. Finally, professionals who made use of *supportive services* felt they had more time available for personal life, i.e. reported lower levels of time-based WLC, consistent with existing knowledge about the strains of housework (Kandel, Davies & Raveis, 1985). These four initiatives have so far been untested in work-life research, yet they increase insights about how and which benefits relate to work-life dynamics. Despite the fact that they do not necessarily support the work-life interface in a traditional sense, their study added valuable knowledge for further investigations of work-life benefits in professional environments and engage researchers and practitioners to think 'out of the box' concerning solutions that support work-life integration.

1.3.1.4 Organizational Practice or Work-Life Initiative?

Two types of initiatives did not affect work-life conflict in any relationship: *short-term flexible work hours* and *home office*. Existing literature does suggest that flexible schedules (O'Driscoll et al., 2003; Cinamon & Rich, 2002a) and telework arrangements (Golden et al., 2006) favorably impact the work-life interface of professionals. Other researchers yet concur with the results of the present study, that flexible work arrangements have no beneficial effect on work-life conflict (Dikkers et al., 2004; Taylor et al., 2009; Thompson et al., 1999). This finding is even more interesting considering the high availability and use in PSFs: in the present study 30 per cent of the respondents used flexible work arrangements on a short-term basis. Insignificant results with regards to arrangements of working from home were also found in the past (Kossek et al., 2006) and have been discussed critically. Dikkers et al. (2004) and Hyman and Baldry (2011) both pointed out that home office may not be useful for reconciling work and personal life better, but is used as a means of getting more work done in stressful times by *additionally* taking work home (cf. also Hooks & Higgs, 2002). This idea is strengthened by the fact that in the present study 34 per cent of the professionals under observation made use of home office without any effect on work-life conflict. Findings with respect to these two initiatives raise important conceptual questions: *which practice within an organization is really a work-life initiative?* While in some work environments making times of starting and finishing work more flexible might be a benefit for employees, in others, such as PSFs, a large amount of flexibility in time scheduling is commonplace and is not perceived as a benefit. This is consistent with meta-analytic findings of Baltes et al. (1999) who reported that flexible work arrangements had no effect for managers and professionals. Besides, as work hours in the present sample were extraordinarily long, there would be not much available scope for flexibilization. Concerning home office, the same question should be asked: professionals in the study indicated to 'make use of home office' probably meaning that they work from home *on top* of their work in the firm / at the client site. Holt and Thaulow (1996) argued along that line stating that flexible work time arrangements are often available options in more demanding jobs, indicating that they are only at first sight aimed at ameliorating work-life reconciliation. More likely, they are implemented as a means of dealing with changing workloads, connecting to with higher work pressure and stress instead of reduced strains. Likewise, working from home appears to be an established phenomenon in PSFs during typical but also atypical working times, i.e. on weekends or on vacation (Hooks & Higgs, 2002). Under this view, working flexibly in time and space is not a work-life benefit but an additional burden which is likely to increase work-life conflict. While changes in the culture and work structure of organizations are needed to overcome such practices, from a research perspective a more precise assessment of initiative access and use is needed in terms of 'I have the possibility of working from home instead of going to the office' or similar testing really whether professionals have the possibility of 'not working from home' when they finish their work day but switch off their computer, mobile devices, etc.

1.3.1.5 Not Offered but Needed – A Brief Look at Professionals' Desired Work-Life Benefits

While available and used initiatives were observed directly, the need for initiatives among PSF professionals was also assessed. Above all, professionals expressed a strong need for more benefits in the area of *health and recovery*. Pretty much regardless of characteristics of work and personal life, more than one third of the professionals under study wish for more initiatives of this type which is consistent with previous qualitative results where employees in management consulting firms voiced need for on-site gyms and similar benefits (Nord et al., 2002). Second in the row are *coaching* and *supportive services*, followed by *long-term flexible work hours* which are wished for by around a quarter of the participants. The desire for such flexible work hour arrangements is curious considering that short-term arrangements did not yield any benefits at all. Long-term flexible work hours were found to be positive for those who used them and the greater need in this area is probably a matter of desired compensation for overtime as also indicated by Mayerhofer et al. (2008). Professionals on time savings accounts work probably just as much as those without, but they know they will in the end receive a payback from it. Being able to go on a longer holiday after pulling a lot of hours seems naturally very attractive to a great number of employees. Fourth in the row of desired initiatives was *childcare*. Again about 25 per cent of the professionals claimed that this option was not available for them despite their need. Further, greater need was expressed concerning *leaves and sabbaticals*, which is likely to be associated with need for childcare (parental leave) but also long-term time savings options. A conclusion of this observation as compared to those options that are offered and used and among them, the effective ones for work-life dynamics, is that organizations should make efforts to meet more precisely the needs of their employees. This is suggested particularly by the great disparity of initiatives that were used and the ones that were needed but not available. Of course the issue of negative career consequences associated with initiative use should also be on the organizational work-life agenda.

In sum, although in the meta-analysis of Baltes and colleagues (1999) it was argued that professionals do not benefit from work-life initiatives, the present data suggest they do. Above and beyond, initiative use was largely related to reduced levels of strain-based conflict, which is probably the most crucial dimension of work-life conflict for individual well-being and feelings of 'work-life balance'. While it has been argued that major reasons for initiative implementation may be communicative reasons rather than making 'real' options available (Kelly, 1999; Ostendorp, 2007), the present findings showed that perceived access to initiatives does yield the potential to reduce work-life conflicts. Results obtained here concur with the previous finding that largely regardless of family or demographic characteristics, young professionals are more attracted by organizations which offer flexible work arrangements than those which offer only traditional sets of HR benefits (Honeycutt & Rosen, 1997). This further supports the notion that work-life initiatives can support both employee's goals (reduced WLC) and employer's goals (improved recruiting) and thus create a win-win situation (Friedman, Christensen & DeGroot, 1998; Halpern & Murphy, 2005; Lewis, Rapoport & Gambles, 2003).

The general finding, that the impact of work-life initiatives on reducing conflict was rather low, has been reported in previous findings, too. Yet, the results must be regarded with a number of thoughts in mind. Those who made use of work-life initiatives were also the ones in need for support. We do not know which results would have been obtained if professionals in need would not have used work-life initiatives. Work-life conflict levels might still have been found extensively higher, an issue that was also discussed by Dikkers et al. (2004). Secondly, the wider view in terms of work and personal life dynamics instead of work-family has also broadened the focus of work-life initiatives into directions of leisure, health and individual development. Thirdly, certain initiatives, such as home office, may not have been used to foster work-life integration but for other reasons (cf. also Dikkers et al., 2004), and thus not represent work-life initiatives as intended in the data collection. Working from home or work hour flexibility were in the literature discussed as classic work-life initiatives, yet in PSFs they might in fact have an opposite effect on the dynamics of work and personal life. It seems that professionals are taking work home because of the load, not for reasons of better work-life balance. Notably, findings are impacted by the fact that in the present study comparatively few of the professionals made use of work-life initiatives. Reluctant initiative use despite the obvious existence of work-life conflict might be explained with findings related to Hypothesis 3b: the respondents might have feared *negative impacts on their career* if they used work-life initiatives. A negative association between the use of initiatives and the perception of negative career consequences was indeed found in the data, as discussed previously. Considering the fact that initiative use was generally quite low and effect sizes of significant results were fairly small, findings discussed in the present section must be put in scope and not be overrated. Nevertheless, research findings also demonstrate: concluding that work-life initiatives are useless in PSFs is premature. Rather, research must develop measurements of these initiatives that are precise, e.g. by asking more directly whether a respective initiative is also perceived as improving work-life balance. Further, a coupling of *values* and *paradigms* in terms of supportive management and supervision with *artifacts* (Schein, 2004) in terms of useful and usable initiatives seems essential for really achieving beneficial work-life outcomes. Similar associations were proposed by Kaiser et al. (2010)[49] in the field of management consulting underscoring the importance of formal *and* informal organizational resources such as supervisor support. In sum, the most prominent findings with regards to formal organizational resources were:

- *Availability* of work-life initiatives was associated to lower levels of strain-based work-life conflict among professionals, particularly access to *long-term flexible work hours, leave of absence, childcare* as well as *health and recovery initiatives, coaching* and *support for educational programs* was associated with reduced work-life conflict. For management consultants access to *reduced schedules* was associated with reduced work-life conflict.
- *Making use* of work-life initiatives was, though to a weaker extent, associated primarily to lower levels of strain-based work-life conflict, use of *free choice of residence, health and recovery benefits, support for educational programs*, and *supportive services* were associated with reduced work-life conflict. For management consultants, using *office day, long-term flexible work hours*, and *coaching* were related to reduced levels of work-life conflict.
- Access to and use of *short-term flexible work hours* and *home office* had no effect on work-life conflict.
- Professionals' *need* for initiatives lies primarily in the area of *health and recovery* as well as *supportive services*. Further, more offers are needed with regards to *long-term flexible work hours, coaching, childcare* and *leave policies*.

---

49 Kaiser et al. (2010) evaluated data that consisted of participants of one large consulting firm and an additional set of data comprising participants of a large variety of firms. From analyzing the effect of initiatives from the large consulting firm separately, the authors conclude that for these consultants, initiative use predicted lower work-life conflict substantially more strongly than in the rest of the sample. While this may also be an issue of data consistency, this result perhaps indicates that in contrast to the mixed portion of the data, this specific consultancy had a particularly effective work-life integration management in terms of effective initiatives and supportive supervision.

1.3.2 Informal Organizational Support

Finally, the impact of informal organizational resources on the work-life interface was examined. Specifically, Hypothesis 4a postulated a positive relationship between management and supervisor support towards the three dimensions of work-life conflict, and Hypothesis 4b predicted that co-worker support would be positively associated with making use of formal initiatives. Largely, the impact of management support and support from co-workers was confirmed in the data, supervisor support yielded less convincing results.

Management support was overall substantially negatively associated with work-life conflict. High levels of perceived support from the management were related to lower work-life conflict, primarily in the temporal and the strain dimension but also with regards to behavior. In general, professionals rated their management quite favorably in supporting their work-life concerns (M = 3.14). That the perception of an overall work-life friendly management reduces levels of work-life conflict complements the finding that benefit availability – regardless of actual use – predicted lower levels of conflict. It seems that the perception alone, that in the case of a need situation, professionals can hope for formal and informal organizational support solves a proportion of their work-life interference. In their recent meta-analysis Mesmer-Magnus and Visveswaran (2007) observed that work-family culture was the strongest predictor of work-family conflict suggesting it is a critical precondition to the effectiveness and utilization of other work-family benefits. Specifically, previous evidence did suggest a strong association among supportive management and time- and strain-based work-to-family conflict among financial consultants (Dikkers et al., 2004) and managers (Lapierre et al., 2008).[50] The findings of the present study replicate existing research about the crucial role of management support for time-, strain- and behavior-based conflict in the context of PSFs and extend knowledge towards conflict beyond work-family.

Supervisor support significantly predicted lower amounts of time- and even more so strain-based work-life conflict, the association with behavior-based conflict failed to show significant results though. Interestingly, the effect of supervisor support was considerably smaller than the impact of management support despite the fact that professionals considered their direct supervisors generally more supportive in work-life concerns (M = 3.41) than overall management. The lower consistency of results may be due to an issue raised in the pretest of this study: primarily consultants indicated that reporting on supervisor

---

50   In the Lapierre et al. study lower behavior-based conflict was also associated with management support.

support might be difficult for professionals because it was questionable which supervisor should be referred to. Contrary to industrial companies, PSFs work strongly project-based. Projects are staffed to suit the requirements of the assignment and thus supervision is likely to change regularly, particularly in the consulting area (Lorsch & Tierney, 2002). On behalf of law firms it was further indicated that hierarchies tend to be flat with the implication that professionals perceive themselves as working in a team of equal characters and supervisors do not become as visible. These considerations might indeed have weakened results of supervisor support on work-life conflict despite the obvious alternative, that management support, i.e. the feeling of working in a work-life friendly firm, just exerts a much stronger impact on work-life dynamics. Allen (2001) presented respective findings which underscore the superior role of managerial support compared to supervisor support that also became obvious in the present study. Above and beyond, findings complement previously found associations of supervisor support with work-life dynamics in PSFs, e.g. management consultancies (Kaiser et al., 2010; Peper et al., 2011). Moreover, the work-life conflict measure includes more strongly those employees without family responsibilities making a unique contribution to existing research.

Co-worker support, as predicted in Hypothesis 4b, was significantly associated with making use of work-life initiatives emphasizing the crucial role of peers in the context of PSFs. The more strongly respondents felt supported by their colleagues in terms of work-life concerns, the more likely they were to make use of work-life initiatives. Kossek, Barber and Winters (1999) outlined in their managerial sample how the social environment and its composition affect initiative use. They found that peer gender, age and responsibility of co-workers for dependents were important for individuals to feel supported if they made use of an arrangement themselves. Above and beyond, professionals in their study were more likely to use initiatives, such as leave policies or part-time if their co-workers had also used or were using them. Though likewise anticipated, such a relationship stayed without supportive evidence in a sample of managers and professionals of a global high-commitment firm (Blair-Loy & Wharton, 2004). The present study yet strengthens the notion that making use of corporate work-life initiatives is substantially impacted by co-worker support. Explanations for this relationship according to my insights concern two issues. From a *social justice* point of view, in cohesive and cooperative environments, it is much likelier that professionals make use of initiatives if co-workers are supportive (Litrico & Lee, 2008). If coordination and cooperation, regular meetings, a chat on the office floor are a central part of the working pattern, unsupported professionals will have a hard time working from home or flexibilizing their hours. Their special situation is likely to be stigmatized (Williams, 2007) and if co-workers feel they must cover up for the home-working colleague, this creates an undesired situation for both sides and the employer as well. From a *social identity* perspective, which postulates that employees define themselves among other factors through social groups they want to belong to (Alvesson, 2000), co-workers transport this set of values and behaviors to which an employee accommodates in the attempt to belong to this group. If these values consist entirely of an 'always-on' ethic accompanied by 'jokes' for those who deviate from this behavioral norm (Fuchs-Epstein et al., 1999; Williams, 2007), i.e. if co-worker support is low, likeliness that out-of-the-box solutions like work-life initiatives are used is likewise very low. This notion is particularly salient in a culture dominated by male values and behaviors and a lack of role models with regards to work-life balancing, which is likely the case in many PSFs (Kaiser & Ringlstetter, 2011).

In sum, major findings with regards to the role of *informal organizational resources* are summarized as follows:

– *Management support* acts as an essential resource in ameliorating professionals' time-, strain-, and behavior-based work-life conflict,
– *Supervisor support*, though less convincingly, was identified as a predictor of professionals' time-based and strain-based work-life conflict, and
– *Co-worker support* was shown to play a crucial role for the decision of professionals to make use of work-life initiatives.

1.4 Relevance of the Research Model for Understanding the Work-Life Dynamics of Professionals

Making use of the partial least squares methodology, it was examined how formal and informal demands and resources impact the work-life conflict of professionals. After discussing the individual linkages of the model separately, here a brief critical look is shed at the research model as a whole. The model aimed at testing the effects of interacting organizational demands and resources, formal and informal in their character, on dimensions of professionals' WLC. Major findings of the model can be summarized as follows: while *formal organizational demands* played a relatively small role, they did predict a proportion of time-based (work hours) and behavior-based (travel) work-life conflict. Overall, the impact of formal demands was not large, judging from an effect size of $f^2 = .038$ for time-based WLC and $f^2 = .065$ for behavior-based WLC. With an effect size below .02, strain-based WLC was literally not affected by formal organizational demands. *Informal organizational demands* as operationalized by time norms where the strongest predictor of all forms of work-life conflict in the model with effect sizes of $f^2 = .181$ for time-based WLC, $f^2 = .088$ for strain-based WLC and $f^2 = .079$ for behavior-based WLC. *Formal organizational resources*, first and foremost initiative availability, had a small effect on strain-based WLC ($f^2 = .022$). Last but not least, *informal organizational resources* again largely exceeded effect sizes of formal resources with $f^2 = .075$ for time-based WLC, $f^2 = .060$ for strain-based WLC and $f^2 = .032$ for behavior-based WLC. While the impact of co-worker support was not substantial in terms of effect size, negative career consequences exerted a 'small' effect on initiative use ($f^2 = .048$). The bottom line is that for the work-life dynamics of the professionals under study *informal organizational demands and resources exerted a far greater impact than formal organizational demands and resources*.

With respect to further quality criteria of the structural model the Stone-Geisser criteria obtained here all ranged well above the threshold of zero attributing predictive relevance to the research model. *GoF* indices further attested the model a good fit of the data. The constructs in the model predicted nearly 40 per cent of the variance in time-based WLC, 28 per cent in strain-based WLC and 25 per cent of behavior-based WLC. Under the awareness that work-life conflict is subject to a complex set of antecedents which differ by means of individual characteristics, the result that at least one fourth of these dynamics could be explained by the variables under study is a considerable result. Only in the case of initiative use, the determination coefficient did not exceed 10 per cent explained variance, which is a rather small amount. It must also be noted that only organizational antecedents were observed in the present examination and it has been shown previously that situational characteristics related to personal life and internal individual characteristics, e.g. personality dimensions as suggested by Bruck and Allen (2003), considerably impact work-life dynamics as well (Byron, 2005; Michel et al., 2010). In sum, all model parameters were satisfactory and the model could be considered useful for achieving a better understanding of how formal and informal demands and resources interact in impacting professionals' work-life interface.

1.5 Work-Life 'Diversity': Insights from Subsample Examinations

In order to also shed a look at personal life dynamics and individual characteristics, several subsample comparisons were conducted in Part II. While results with respect to these separate model estimations were to some extent already discussed in the previous section, a number of peculiarities that emerged in the subgroup comparisons are outlined.

1.5.1 PSF Subsector – Perspectives of Management Consultants and Law Firm Professionals

It was discussed that subsectors of PSFs, despite their similarities, may differ with respect to structural work characteristics such as the amount of travel or the professional ethos and related cultural norms. Also the availability of HR benefits may differ among subsectors. Comparison of participants with respect to PSF subsector membership in management consultancy or law firms contributes some intriguing insights to existing research. Frequent business *travel* affected management consultants' behavioral work-life conflict and surprisingly, despite their much lower travel frequency, this effect was also found for law firm professionals. It may be that the latter perceive travel even more of a hassle as they are not as accommodated to it as consultants who travel weekly to and from clients may be. While management consultants' *initiative use* resulted in less strain-based work-life conflict, for law firm professionals this effect was not found. Actual initiative use differed substantially in that the consultants made more use of home office, office day, leaves of absence, free choice of residence, health programs and coaching. Particularly the latter four initiatives are associated with relatively high costs for the organization, but they seem effective in improving the professionals' perception of work-life balance. Another interesting observation was that for management consultants *informal resources* played a substantially smaller role for their work-life dynamics than they did for the law firm professionals. While this may be a function of sample size, it must be noted that the groups did not differ in their perception of organizational demands and support. The missing association with informal resources might be explained by the fact that management consultants, more than law firm professionals, spend their daily work not within the context of their firm but in the organizational and cultural context of the client (Lorsch & Tierney, 2002). Therefore, support from their management and supervision might just play a minor role and other factors which were not investigated here, such as career prospects provided by the firm or cultural similarity with the client firm are important. The fact that the model explained substantially more variance in work-life conflict dimensions of law firm professionals might be meaningful as well, but due to the smaller MC sample cannot necessarily be interpreted as such. Conversely, it was the management consultants who experienced significantly higher levels of time- and behavior-based WLC. In sum, from these findings we learn that taking a closer look at structural characteristics of a specific branch is worthwhile for practitioners in order to tailor initiatives to employees' needs. For researchers findings show the worthiness of a context-specific assessment of work-life dynamics and initiatives that was undertaken in the present thesis by scrutinizing consultancies' web sites for their work-life issues. This procedure can certainly be refined and generalized in order to be used within other branches.

1.5.2 Life Role Values – Perspectives of Life Types, Work Types, and Balancers

The present research design also examined the perspective of different life role value patterns. Three groups were examined, 'life' prioritizers, 'work' types and 'balancers'. Concurrent with previous research (Carlson & Kacmar, 2000; Cinamon & Rich, 2002a; Honeycutt & Rosen, 1997) these groups differed in some meaningful respects in their work-life experiences. The 'life' type reported substantially higher levels of time-based WLC compared to the work type and for the balancers, conflict in terms of incompatible behavior was highest. Surprisingly, for individuals with 'life' priorities the impediment of initiative use by negative career consequences was highest. Therefore, for individuals whose central focus is their life beyond work, slower or halted career advancement seems to be an issue, too. As indicated by Cinamon and Rich (2002a) those who attach high importance to family will not necessarily devote little time and energy to work, but could also have an opposite effect so that individuals invest more in work to provide for the family income. Management support played an important role for the 'life' and the 'work' prioritizers, whereas supervisor support seemed to matter mostly for the balancers. The balancer group also profited most from initiative availability in terms of reduced sWLC. This association is not surprising as initiatives should be aimed at helping individuals reconcile their work and nonwork responsibilities and for those who 'want it all' available initiatives seemed to help achieve a feeling that this is made possible. The finding, that work-oriented participants were the only subgroup which profited from initiative use ($\rightarrow$ sWLC) complements and extends previous findings. Honeycutt and Rosen (1997) reported that besides family- oriented and balance-oriented individuals, also career-oriented individuals (MBA students) were more attracted to firms which offer flexible career paths and policies. The likeliness that balancers and the 'work' priority group made use of initiatives was furthermore dependent on co-worker support, not so for the 'life' priority group. Hence, as was previously shown in the study of Cinamon and Rich (2002a), incorporating different importance profiles adds important insights to the study of the work-life interface. Yet the question of these authors, whether job pressures affect the work-life interface differently depending on an individual's importance profile, cannot be confirmed in the present data. Neither formal nor informal demands demonstrated a substantially different impact on the three types of work-life conflict among the professionals studied here. Bearing in mind that results are based on differing sample sizes and thus must be interpreted with caution, they nevertheless have implications for further work-life outcomes. Carlson and Kacmar (2000) pointed out that for individuals who attach high importance to both work and family, conflict at work is strongly associated with reduced job satisfaction. Findings emphasize the potential of examining different life role priority profiles for the study of work-life dynamics and also for corporate HR policy departments.

1.5.3 Gender – Work-Life Dynamics of Female and Male Professionals

It has traditionally been assumed that men and women differ in their work-life dynamics (Barnett & Hyde, 2001). However in present research, some unexpected findings could be extracted from the comparison of male and female professionals. First and foremost, as already outlined previously, neither did men and women have fundamentally different ideas about their life role values, nor did they differ largely in terms of conflict experience. McElwain et al. (2005) argued that studying both gender full-time employees within the same industry, such similar perceptions are not a surprise. Yet research evidence suggests that women are usually affected by higher work-family / work-life conflict and lower career prospects (Batt & Valcour, 2003; Duxbury & Higgins, 1991; Nielson et al., 2001; Taylor et al., 2009). The present study found both similarities and disparities under the gender perspective. Men experienced conflict more strongly as a function of formal demands while they also worked longer and traveled more frequently. Work-life conflict of both male and female professionals was impacted by organizational time expectations, yet path coefficients for women were substantially larger ($\gamma_{iWLC} = .504$; $\gamma_{sWLC} = .392$; $\gamma_{bWLC} = .267$) than men's ($\gamma_{iWLC} = .345$; $\gamma_{sWLC} = .271$; $\gamma_{bWLC} = .302$). This finding can be discussed in terms three explanations. First of all, women are usually the ones who take more responsibility within nonwork spheres, particularly family, and thus may experience higher conflict as a function of organizational time demands. Related to gender-specific life role values, it was for example found by Cinamon and Rich (2002b) that women tend to attribute equal importance to work and family or more importance to family, whereas men are quite equally distributed among work prioritizers, family prioritizers and balancers. Female professional's attribution of importance and centrality to life roles in the present study corresponded almost 1:1 to that of the male subgroup, which speaks against this explanation. Williams (2007) discusses how professional women often are stereotyped into being less committed towards the organization and their profession because of their potential maternity. It is therefore often argued that women, in order to advance their career, must not only be exceptionally good but exceptionally better than their male competitors because employers expect their career commitment and dedication towards the firm to be 'naturally' lower. Time demands which collide with other life interests might therefore be particularly salient for women. A third explanation lies in the proactive character of career advancement in PSFs. Temporal commitment is one way of showing high engagement towards the firm and maybe men are better at 'playing the game'. Women, as shown by Kumra and Vinnicombe (2008), are less self-promoting of their achievements and are thus maybe less willing to show their dedication towards the firm in terms of temporal presence at the workplace:

> "It is nothing to do with quality of work, [...] it is a very male culture, and the people that do get into the partnership tend to be like the existing partners" (Male director at an international consulting firm, cited by Kumra and Vinnicombe, 2008; p. 70).

Women's weaker skills in 'impression management' (Parris et al., 2008, p. 112) might further explain results of the high association between work-life conflict and organizational time demands.

Support from the management played an important role for both men and women despite the fact that women perceived managerial, supervisor and co-worker support significantly less favorably.[51] This might have to do with an issue raised by Dikkers et al. (2004) who argue that individuals who are interested in actual initiative use, perceive their culture less favorably.[52] Indeed, female professionals indicated substantially more need for initiatives in the area of working pattern adjustment (reduced schedule, flexibility arrangements, home office), dependent care (childcare and eldercare), as well as for leaves, health interventions, coaching and supportive services, thus signaling interest in WLB initiative use. Taking this as an indicator for greater likeliness of using initiatives, the explanation voiced by Dikkers et al. (2004) might apply here too. Furthermore, women did not benefit from initiative availability in terms of reduced conflict, whereas for males access to work-life initiatives seemed to reduce strain-based conflict successfully, again undermining the notion that those who do not initially intend to make use of initiatives have a more work-life friendly perception of their firm and benefit from it in terms of lower work-life conflict. Further supportive of this notion is the greater importance of co-worker support

---

51   In Dikkers et al. (2007b) women perceived their work-home culture more favorably than men.

52   Dikkers et al. (2004) argue that employees who intend to use initiatives are at risk of being confronted with resistance from supervisors and colleagues. Those who do not intend to use WLB initiatives thus perceive their culture as more supportive (than it actually is).

for initiative use in the case of women. Initiative use was found to reduce strain-based work-life conflict of both *genders* which is interesting as the only striking difference in their utilization behavior is that women make substantially more use of part-time, consistent with previous findings (Dikkers et al., 2007b; Fuchs-Epstein et al., 1999; Hill et al., 2006; Kossek et al., 1999). Beyond that, initiatives most frequently used by both men and women were office day, followed by home office, free choice of residence and short-term schedule flexibility. What puts these results into perspective is the notion of male-dominated versus female-dominated organizational cultures. According to Holt and Thaulow (1996)

> "male-dominated workplaces are characterized by inherently greater latitude for adjustment than female-dominated workplaces owing to the differences in work type and organization" (p. 87).

However they argue that this greater latitude is largely manifested in terms of compensation, not in terms of initiatives that reduce pressure or workload. The fact that work cultures in professional service firms are to a large extent male-dominated (Kaiser & Ringlstetter, 2011) may further explain the general finding that initiatives are only used by a small percentage of respondents in the present study.

1.5.4 Age – Perspectives of 'Youngsters' and 'Old Hands'

While the majority of prior research does not find age-specific differences in the experience of work-life conflict, life course perspective suggests that individuals differ in their work-life dynamics at certain life stages, for example putting aside work-life balance in favor of career advancement at a younger age (Sturges & Guest, 2004). Although the present study did not reveal outstanding differences, a number of issues are worth mentioning. Travel was most prominently an issue for bWLC of younger professionals which could indicate that a certain socialization process occurs where the newcomers get adjusted to the work demands of their environment (cf. Poulter & Land, 2008). Rising *age* was associated with increasing importance of initiative availability as a means of reducing work-life conflict. That may be explained by increasing levels of legitimacy of making use of initiatives at a certain age (or tenure). However, expectations of negative effects on career advancement as an impediment for making use of WLB initiatives that are still salient at age 40 plus. Management support's impact on WLC was highest at 30 to 39, presumably the life stage where for one thing important career steps are taken by professionals and yet professionals usually start a family at that age. To a limited extent, present findings support what had been discussed before, "taking one-size-fits-all approaches to helping workers manage work and family demands may not always be effective and workers in different age groups may experience work-family demands in different ways" (Matthews et al., 2009, p. 89). This is expressed by the stronger need for further initiatives voiced by professionals in their thirties, e.g. for more health benefits and child-care arrangements as well as flexible work arrangements. With rising age, leave policies seem to gain attractiveness. From an age-specific comparison among professionals in the present research we can draw the conclusion that work-life conflict is also an issue during early years as well as later years of employment. However, likely a great share of differences is not attributable to age directly but rather to other variables that *occur* at a certain age.

1.5.5 Perspectives of Parents and Professionals in a (Dual-Career) Relationship

One area of such age-related characteristics is parenthood but also the presence or absence of a full-time employed partner may impact work-life dynamics differentially. Results of the present study indicated that *marital or relationship status* is not clearly predictive of lower work-life conflict levels. Consistent with meta-analytic results (Mesmer-Magnus & Viswesvaran, 2007) which suggest that a (supportive) spouse can be related to higher levels of work-family conflict, professionals in a relationship are more strongly harmed by long work hours, than single professionals. However, the previously voiced assumption that this is due to lower flexibility within a partnership was not reflected in the results: job-related travel impacted single professionals' (time- and behavior-based) WLC substantially more strongly than professionals in a partnership. Particularly professionals in relationships where both partners pursue a career as well as those who were parents of young children experienced higher levels of work-life conflict in past research (Aryee, 1992; Aryee & Luk, 1996; Higgins & Duxbury, 1992; Judge et al., 1994; Wallace, 2009; Wharton & Blair-Loy, 2006). *Non dual-career professionals* experienced higher temporal WLC as a result of making use of initiatives in the present examination. These professionals used reduced schedules and home office substantially more frequently. Although the effect cannot directly be attributed to one of these arrangements, it is likely that working from home made work interfere with personal life, e.g. due to feelings of having to invest more time in work to show productivity towards the firm. Despite existing evidence of the success of home work arrangements (Hill et al., 2003; Madsen, 2003), it had also been indicated previously that working from home can cause role overload (Duxbury et al., 1996) or not be associated with work-family conflict at all (Kossek et al., 2006). Findings with regards to non dual-career professionals in the sample might indicate that their working from home is more harmful than beneficial for them. It was found in the present examination that for dual-career professionals the impact of informal organizational demands on WLC was lower and at the same time support from the management was a greater buffer for WLC. This finding suggests that for those individuals the work role is more salient[53] indicating that dual-career professionals might be better accustomed to the demands of their job. In dual-career relationships there is also potentially more mutual understanding and respect for the work sphere of the partner (Abele & Volmer, 2011), which could explain their lower impact of informal demands on WLC. Nevertheless, dual-career professionals in the present study benefited substantially from organizational support, which logically complements the picture: in order to be able to cope with their challenging situation, dual-career professionals even more than non dual-career professionals experience lower levels of WLC if they are supported by their organization. Hence, as dual-career professionals might be more committed to their careers, organizations should support their work-life concerns in order to provide relief for the 'double burden' these workers face (Kasper et al., 2005). This is complemented by the finding that respondents in a *dual-career relationship* perceived initiative access as conflict-reducing although they used significantly less initiatives.

A number of interesting findings were also reported concerning *parental status*. Results confirm the previously found moderating effect of the presence/number of (young) children in the family (cf. Aryee, 1992; Judge, Boudreau & Bretz, 1994; Kossek, Lautsch & Eaton, 2006; Wallace, 2009) and support the intuitive notion that parents, due to their more immediate nonwork responsibilities, are more vulnerable to organizational demands (work hours, informal time demands) and benefit more strongly from organizational resources (informal support). Notably, the model explained substantially more variance in the strain-based WLC of parents as compared to non-parents. The finding that implicit time norms impact parents' WLC more strongly confirms previously voiced concerns that a culture where performance and dedication is measured in terms of presence at the workplace is particularly problematic for parents. Williams (2007) describes this problem as a clash of ideals, as "an all-or-nothing workplace disadvantages most women […] and an increasing number of men who want to participate in child rearing, by forcing them to 'choose' between being either a bad worker or a bad parent" (p. 383). The result that parents, who made use of WLB initiatives was related to higher levels of WLC further sup-

---

53   Comparison of DC and non DC professionals' life role priorities supported this notion: the larger share of non DC professionals were found in the 'life' type group, whereas in the 'work' type group and among the 'balancers', professionals in dual-career relationships made up the larger share.

port the idea of a huge discrepancy between their demands as compared to the nonwork responsibilities of non parents: as discussed in section 3.1 in the present part, their use of (short-term) flexible work hours, home office, and childcare probably caused additional time pressure to them instead of relieving conflict. There might also be an alternative explanation for this finding: parents might just have much higher levels of WLC than non parents, which in fact is their motivation for making use of initiatives. The positive relationship could therefore also explained with a) high conflict levels despite WLB initiative use, or b) use of initiatives because of high conflict levels, the latter indicating reversed causality (cf. 1.6, Limitations). As Dikkers et al. (2004) note, only longitudinal research that studies professionals' WLC before and after/during initiative use (and controls for further changes in their lives) would be able to finally confirm or disconfirm the usefulness of WLB initiatives.

1.5.6 Tenure and Job Level – Perspectives of Newcomers versus Seniors

Finally, work-life dynamics of professionals with different tenure and job levels were evaluated. Formal organizational demands played the largest role for newcomers' work-life conflict arguing in favor of an accommodation to demands and an incorporation of professional norms (Alvesson, 2000). The finding that those with longer tenure and higher job levels were less affected by formal and informal demands also speaks in favor of the 'strong cultures' hypothesis raised in Part I (section 3.3.5), i.e. the idea that cultures with markedly performance-oriented values have a strong potential for shaping individuals' personal values (cf. Kristof-Brown & Jansen, 2007; Lorsch & Tierney, 2002). Another intriguing finding emerged for Hypothesis 3b: with rising tenure, the negative relationship of negative career consequences with initiative use declined, although it was still significant at tenure six years and longer. That brings up two ideas: it may be that with rising tenure and job level, it becomes more legitimate to make use of initiatives because intense dedication and commitment towards the firm had been shown in preceding years. It may, however, also indicate that the interest in taking up initiatives changes. Indeed a look at initiative use and availability as well as need for unavailable initiatives in the tenure groups reveals a decline in need for and use of initiatives concerning almost the whole set of the thirteen benefits under observation, speaking in favor of the second explanation. Making use of reduced schedule, short-term and long-term flexible work hours, and home office substantially increased with rising tenure and higher job level, whereas office day and leave of absence use substantially decreased. Yet, only those in the middle range of tenure and at medium organizational level felt reduced stress as a function of *initiative use*, although their usage pattern is not particularly exceptional. A possible explanation is that at this point in their career professionals face the decision of whether to remain in the PSF or quit in favor of a less demanding job pattern and this is where the possibility of using benefits becomes particularly salient. Moreover, of course, it may also play a role that these individuals are in their mid- to end thirties which is the age where professionals in high-level jobs usually start a family. The positive relationship between making use of initiatives and WLC for professionals of 6 years tenure and more can be explained by their exceptionally high use of home office, which in PSFs more than elsewhere, might not aim at reducing WLC but represent an option of getting more work done (cf. Dikkers et al., 2004).

With respect to job level, a peculiar finding was the supervisor support → WLC relationship at higher job levels. Results may be blurred by the fact that members of this group are in the process of promotion to partner and support from 'the very top' is highly salient at this stage. In general, the informal support dimension was found to matter most at the lower hierarchy levels, newcomers benefited from supervisor support and co-worker support, as well as from supportive management. The evaluation of the model within subgroups revealed a number of important insights of which the major findings are:

- Both *management consultants and law firm professionals* were affected by travel. For management consultants, managerial and supervisor support hardly played a role for predicting conflict, but they experienced higher levels of work-life conflict than law firm professionals.
- Individuals with different *life role priorities* experienced work-life dynamics differently, e.g. 'balancers' benefited most from initiative access. For both 'balancers' and 'work' types support from co-workers was important.
- Despite their similar life role value profiles, *men and women* differed in their work-life dynamics: the impact of formal demands was stronger for the work-life conflict of male professionals and initiative access reduced conflict levels for them only. Initiative use was beneficial for both genders in terms of lower strain-based work-life conflict, yet support from co-workers was more important for women.
- *Age* differences were found, yet these are largely traceable to issues that occur at a certain age, such as starting a family or promotion to partner.
- Important differences with regards to characteristics of personal life were found: *singles* were also strongly affected by work-life conflict and while the impact of organizational demands was lower for professionals in a *dual-career relationship*, the impact of management support was higher for them.
- Newcomers experienced the highest impact of organizational demands in the *tenure* comparison, while negative career consequences impeded initi-

ative use at all tenure levels. With increasing tenure the need for initiatives declined. Particularly at lower *job levels*, informal support mattered for reducing work-life conflict.

In sum, the subgroup comparison underscored the importance of fine-grained analyses in order to draw useful conclusions. Findings that would have remained undetected in examining the total sample show once more that generalizing of results must be done with caution and organizations should not be too enthusiastic about targeting work-life dynamics of all employees with a one-size-fits-all set of initiatives.

1.6 Limitations

While research presented here is informative about the work-life dynamics of business professionals, it is also subject to a number of conceptual and methodological limitations. Concerning conceptual limitations, it is discussed whether stress is an underlying variable, how distinct conflict types and life domains are and can be, the minor consideration of individual in contrast to organizational antecedents, and the missing integration of a 'positive' work-life interaction in the sense of work-life enrichment. With regards to methodological limitations, the data collection procedure is discussed critically as well as the issue of single source bias / common method bias, several limitations concerning the sample and respective generalizability of results, subgroup evaluations and the issue of causality in the present cross-sectional study.

1.6.1 Conceptual Limitations

The model underlying this research is based on postulates that were born from insights of previous work on the work-life dynamics of professionals. However, a number of issues may be raised with regards to the conceptual design of the study.

1.6.1.1 Stress as the Underlying Variable?

It may be argued that it is not a lack of balance between work and personal life that was 'really' impacted by the predictors in the framework but it may actually be 'stress'. Particularly a number of the less intuitive results may raise this suspicion together with the substantial need for more health and recovery benefits expressed by participants. This guess is not entirely wrong considering the fact that stress is a complex and multi-facetted concept. Yet, if stress is described in terms of "situations that can result in negative physical and psychological consequences" (Ford et al., 2007, p. 61), the individual challenge associated with balancing one's responsibilities and needs across life domains can be considered a very specific kind of stress. Accordingly, low levels of within-role stress were found to be related to a balanced life (Greenhaus et al., 2003). Work-life conflict has above and beyond also been conceptualized as a stressor itself (Mauno et al., 2006). In the understanding underlying the present thesis, work-life conflict is a specific type of stress that is experienced as a result of incompatibilities of life role demands and interests with a temporal, a strain-, and a behavioral dimension according to the Greenhaus and Beutell model (1985).

1.6.1.2 Life Domains

Another major issue concerns the distinctiveness of the conflict types in the present analysis. Examination and measurement of types of work-life conflict may be viewed critically and the spheres under examination– work, family, friends, health / recovery, social engagement, self – are not trenchantly distinct. This is also indicated in the data by high correlations among these types. Additionally, certainly work also constitutes a 'life' domain (cf. Eikhof et al., 2007). However, the fact that life domains overlap is exactly the case in most individuals' lives and addresses a fundamental problem of measuring work-life conflict. In the attempt to overcome previous criticism about the exclusion of all employees without family responsibilities and in order to understand what it is about work vs. 'life' that affects professionals, this typology was created. Preliminary categories were drawn from existing research (Carlson & Kacmar, 2000; Friedman et al., 1998) and after taking into account results from the pre-test of the questionnaire they were adjusted to the specific context of professionals. Future research about work-'life' interactions should follow this example and evaluate more closely which domains are hidden behind the term life, yet for specific populations the spheres under study might have to be adjusted. Health and recovery as an area of life was included because of the presumably high physical and psychological pressure professionals face, for other populations other facets of life might be more salient. It did seem worthwhile to examine both the type of work-life interaction as well as the centrality of spheres in order to put results in scope.[54]

1.6.1.3 Minor Consideration of Individual Antecedents

Although individual characteristics were considered in subsample analyses, the focus of the present study was on organizational predictors of conflict. Recently, the necessity to incorporate personality characteristics in the study of work-life

---

54   High conflict level of work vs. social engagement were for example being put in scope
       by the (small) centrality across overall life that professionals attached to the sphere of
       social engagement.

dynamics was voiced by Michel and Clark (2011), particularly under the assumption that professionals might share certain personality characteristics. Individual differences were accounted for in the investigation of life role values, however further personality dimensions are of interest. As for Big 5 personality traits (McCrae & Costa, 1997), neuroticism might predispose for high conflict levels (cf. Schneewind & Kupsch, 2007) and conscientiousness was associated positively with career success (Judge et al., 1999) and might also promote individuals' ability to time- and self-manage their work-life interfaces. Michel and Clark (2011) suggest that personality is a driving force behind work-to-life and also life-to-work conflict impacting the perception of conflict as well as behaviors related to integrating work and personal life. According to Friede and Ryan (2005) individuals may also self-select into environments that make work-life integration management easier or more challenging (e.g. career-oriented versus 9-5 jobs) as a function of their personality structure, an issue that would be particularly worthwhile to investigate in high-performance environments such as PSFs.

1.6.1.4 Work-Life Conflict as the Major Criterion

A final conceptual limitation is the fact that only the conflict perspective of work-life integration was examined in the present study. This was motivated by the impression that work plays such a dominant role in professionals' lives that there is hardly any space for anything else, which is also substance to extensive discussions in the literature (Anderson et al., 2010; Fu & Shaffer, 2001; Lyness & Judiesch, 2008). Additionally, Friedman (2000) argued that the direction work-to-life is more strongly influenced by organizational practices and policies. That findings were obtained with regards to the three dimensional concept of work-family conflict by Greenhaus and Beutell (1985) is a major contribution and extension of existing work-life research which largely neglected the behavior dimension. The active character of behavioral conflict in contrast to the more passive component of time- and strain-based conflict makes this aspect an important element to observe because behavior could be changed more easily than perceptions or passive experiences. Nevertheless it is suggested for future research to include positive work-life interactions more strongly. Considering the intrinsic nature of professional work it is likely that dynamics of work-life enrichment (Carlson et al., 2006) also play a role for employees in PSFs.

1.6.2 Methodological Limitations

The present empirical examination is subject to a number of methodological limitations.

1.6.2.1 Data Collection

One potential limitation concerns the collection of data on management consultants in the present study. As establishing contact with PSFs proved difficult, about one third of the data were obtained with snowballing method. This is a common procedure in the social sciences, yet awareness of the existing danger of uncontrollable selectivity that is associated with this method is necessary (Scott, 1991). Personal and professional contacts used for the snowballing process were widespread which to some extent reduced the likeliness of 'bundled' datasets. The data were evaluated with regards to distributions of demographics and descriptive results did not display any unexpected similarities. The fact that it is unknown how many consultants worked at the same firm is, however, indeed a limitation to the present study. Nevertheless, the snowballing procedure enabled access to professionals whose organizations were not willing to provide access to 'sensitive' data such as feelings about work-life balance and, first and foremost, actual work hour volumes of their employees. Thus, the data collection procedure contributed a highly interesting population to the study of work-life balance, exactly because obtaining such data proved so challenging.

1.6.2.2 Self-Report Data and Single Source Bias

The data were obtained by self-reported measures. That means, a) the answers are all based on the subjective perception of professionals rather than objective facts, and b) all data are based on the same questionnaire answered by the same person raising the issue of common method variance (Temme et al., 2009). Due to the difficulty of obtaining multi-source and objective data in the social sciences, this is a universal limitation the majority of work-life research can be taunted with. With regards to the first issue, it has often been argued that the subjective perception of phenomena is exactly what social scientists are interested in. Edwards and Rothbard (1999) in this context referred to an objective versus a subjective person or environment and whether an individual experiences conflict between life domains is an entirely subjective issue. Further, it is not the objective work-life friendliness of organizations which matters but employees' personal *perception* of, for example, how appropriate it is to make use of work-life benefits within the organizational environment. Therefore, it is exactly the subjective view of professionals which also makes the present study interesting. Concerning b), it must be noted that common method bias can never be ruled out completely in studies where all constructs under examination are measured with the same instrument (Söhnchen, 2007). The relative absence of multicollinearity and non-intuitive relationships indicate that common method variance is not a major concern in the present study. However, the subjective measures have potentially added effects of social desirability, i.e. the dependence on self-report measures could lead to a socially desirable response by the participants, an issue that was also discussed by McElwain et al. (2005). Further research should follow the example of Grant-Vallone and Donaldson (2001), who suggested examining self-ratings together with co-worker ratings and including a social desirability measure in the instrument.[55] Even though it is the individuals' perception of phenomena that are of interest, additional data sources could further undermine the findings obtained from individuals.

1.6.2.3 Sample

The professionals sample used in this study is at the same time a strength and a weakness. It contributes to existing research results from a German PSF context, data which have rarely been presented in work-life research that is generally very U.S. centered.[56] Application and adaptation of existing scales and observing work-life dynamics in a non U.S. cultural context extends our methodological and conceptual knowledge about underlying constructs and their generalizability. However, characteristics of the sample as well as postulated relationships might be different in other organizational and cultural contexts, even within the same branch. Anecdotal evidence suggests that certain demands characterize primarily the German PSF context but vary by cultural context. It was for example suggested that extreme work hours as they were found in the present data may not occur in other countries' consulting or PSF industry. That cultural values might also play a role was illustrated for example by Wharton and Blair-Loy (2006) in their examination of Asian versus U.S. professionals: for those with Chinese cultural background were far more likely to express concerns about their long work hours pointing to the higher value of family life in this cultural context. Therefore, more cross-national research is needed to determine the dynamics of work demands and resources for professionals in their specific social and cultural environment. While the total sample was of satisfactory *volume*, in subsample examinations sample sizes soon became rather small. From the statistical point of view, the PLS methodology is the method of choice in the case of small sample sizes. Yet it becomes clear, for example from the life role type examinations, that differences in sample size of the subsamples may distort results. For this reason in the subgroup model estimations also findings with an

---

55 The authors measured social desirability with the Marlowe-Crowne Social Desirability Scale (SDS) which measures the degree to which employees respond in ways that make them look more favorable (Grant-Vallone & Donaldson, 2001).

56 Casper et al. (2007) reported in their review of research methods in work-life research that 75 per cent of all studies under consideration were within samples based in the United States.

error probability of p < .10 were considered meaningful. However, larger sample sizes in these analyses would have granted greater validity of conclusions. Further, although subgroups with respect to each characteristic were formed following clear-cut criteria, there is still opportunity for heterogeneity which, as discussed by Matthews et al. (2009), might influence the nature of dynamics under study. Therefore, it would have been interesting to conduct more fine-grained analyses of these subgroups, i.e. how individual work-life initiatives affect certain subgroups beyond subsector membership or explore gender-specific effects within the life role value typology. Unfortunately, this again was restricted by sample size.

1.6.2.4 Subgroup Evaluations

Evaluating the model with respect to specific characteristics was done by creating subgroups. It may be criticized that comparatively large weight was given to the subgroup evaluations in the present study. Additionally, these comparisons may have created the expression of 'more' results. Therefore two things must be noted. Subgroup model estimations were conducted in order to draw a differential and fine-grained picture of the work-life dynamics of the population under study. When total samples are observed many effects are just averaged out. Instead of dealing with individual characteristics in a 'demographics-controlled-for' manner, the present examination paid attention to a number of individual characteristics, which are important for grasping a more comprehensive picture of professionals' work-life interactions. Nevertheless these subgroup comparisons must not be viewed as providing knowledge on top of the whole model but each subgroup evaluation is a *change of perspective*. Naturally, all groups from the subsample comparisons were part of the same sample, the separate analysis just put the spot on one special characteristic at a time. Results may definitely not be interpreted across subgroups (i.e. 'For women the effect was found but not so for Newcomers'), they must be interpreted within subgroups in statements like 'from a tenure perspective, newcomers experienced a higher impact of formal demands'.

1.6.2.5 Generalizability of Findings

The present study focused on the specific occupational environment of professional service firms, more specifically on management consulting and law firms as two subbranches of PSFs. Therefore, the findings are first and foremost to be regarded within this context. Potential incompatibilities with other populations and occupations became obvious within the present study, for example the application of the set of initiatives that had been extracted from an analysis in the consulting environment also within the law firm context where some initiatives are just not as common. However, it is generally assumed that the majority of findings could be replicated in similarly demanding work environments which can be characterized as 'extreme jobs'. With the rather young age of participants and the gender ratio, demographic characteristics were largely representative of PSFs (cf. Kaiser et al., 2010). Therefore, findings of the present study may presumably be extended towards the broader context of PSFs and towards business professionals in highly demanding, knowledge-based jobs in general.

1.6.2.6 Causality

Partial least squares analysis is a powerful methodology for testing causal models. Nevertheless, the cross-sectional character of the present data limits inferences about causality of linkages. As argued in Thompson et al. (1999), a supportive management might be the consequence of many employees' experience of work-life conflict, an issue that was also raised by Batt and Valcour (2003). The finding that childcare use was significantly related to higher time-based work-to-life conflict may point to a general methodological criticism that in cross-sectional research each 'causal' relationship may also operate in the opposite direction. However it may also be that individuals who make use of childcare offered by the organization experience higher time-based conflict because they feel they 'owe' their firm even more extraordinary engagement in exchange for the support they receive. Nevertheless causality is an issue in every cross-sectional design and interpretations of the presented results should be treated with the thought in mind, that reversed causality might be a potential flaw. The only reliable source of causal inferences is longitudinal research for cross-sectional designs can always just represent a snapshot of reality.

1.7 Summary of the Discussion of Empirical Results

In the present dissertation, a framework of organizational demands and resources was proposed and tested describing three dimensions of work-life conflict in a sample of professionals, specifically PSF employees. Despite the high salience of their work, professionals under study experienced substantial amounts of work-life conflict of all three dimensions. Moreover, testing types of conflict between work and several life spheres gave evidence to often voiced concerns about the narrow focus of previous work-family studies. These effects were differentially examined among subgroups with findings that further challenge the notion that only individuals with family responsibilities are prone to experiencing work-life conflict. Using PLS methodology a model of organizational demands and resources representing major antecedents of work-life conflict was estimated. The central objective of the model was to provide insights about how organizational antecedents impact professionals' work-life conflict in order to provide strategies of better managing this conflict. Overall, the model represented the data well and the majority of expectations were confirmed in the empirical study. It was shown that

- *Formal organizational time demands*, i.e. work hours and business travel, did impact work-life conflict but in relatively small intensity,
- *Formal organizational resources*, i.e. use and availability of work-life initiatives and secondary initiatives yield the potential of reducing levels of work-life conflict of professionals although results were relatively small, and

Informal practices and conditions rooted in *organizational culture* impacted professionals' work-life dynamics above and beyond formal practices:

- Professionals' work-life conflict is impacted negatively (i.e. favorably) by informal organizational resources, particularly *managerial support*;
- Professionals' work-life conflict is impacted positively (i.e. in terms of higher conflict) by informal organizational demands, particularly *time demands;*
- While *support from peers* at the workplace encouraged professionals to make use of work-life initiatives, anticipation of *negative career consequences* in the case of using these benefits kept them from utilizing them.

These results underscore the unfavorable impact of implicit organizational demands and the beneficial impact of informal organizational resources. In accordance with ideas of person-organization fit theory, subgroup comparisons showed that individuals in different situations and with different characteristics experienced the dynamics of the demands and resources framework differently. Bearing in mind conceptual and methodological considerations the following last section presents a number of implications for work-life research as well as for the management of work-life issues from an organizational point of view.

2. Implications for Theory and Practice

The previous part critically discussed empirical findings on organizational demands and resources of professionals taking into account previous research. It was shown how the present results contribute theoretically and methodologically to existing research on human resource management and work-life dynamics. The aim of this last section is to pull together major findings and contributions from insights gained in Part I, II, and III, in order translate them into a number of directions for further research in the work-life field and implications for a strategic 'work-life integration management' (WLIM) in organizations, particularly in the PSF context. Findings of how organizational demands and resources impact professionals' work-life interface should inspire future research in further branches and cultures. Questions and quests for further research are suggested with regards to the character of work-life conflict, current deficits and subsequent open questions for the study of work-life initiatives, as well as ideas for further research on work-life dynamics in professional service firms (2.1.1). Methodological suggestions are voiced concerning the operationalization of conflict types, further research on the three dimensions of conflict proposed by Greenhaus and Beutell (1985), the study of life role values, and lastly, a call for more multisource and objective measures (2.1.2). Current results should also inspire professional service firms to take action towards engraining WLIM in their corporate culture enabling the unsanctioned use of initiatives and thus leverage performance at the individual, the interpersonal and the organizational level. Insights gained in the present empirical examination of professionals underline the importance of taking work-life concerns of professionals seriously (2.2.1), of closely monitoring informal organizational demands (2.2.2) and expanding formal and informal resources (2.2.3). Above and beyond, successful work-life integration management – not only in PSFs – is about the creation and evaluation of the need of employees, the organization and its clients in order to achieve a state of fit between these needs and subsequently maximize individual and organizational performance (2.2.4 and 2.2.5).

2.1 Implications for Further Research on Work-Life Dynamics

The present thesis answered a number of questions which complement work-life research, yet new issues were raised and open questions remain unanswered. This concerns theoretical aspects as well as methodological issues.

2.1.1 Further Research Issues

A number of insights can be drawn from the empirical examination of law firm professionals and consultants and their work-life dynamics. Meanwhile, also several questions remain for further research attempts in this area.

2.1.1.1 Work-Life Conflict is More Than Work and Family

Results from the investigation of conflict types and measures of life role values strongly undermine previously discussed concerns about the narrow focus of work-life research on the spheres of work versus family, e.g. by Casper et al. (2007). The present study showed that professionals experience conflict between work and family but also other life domains and their feeling of difficulty with handling different role responsibilities is not limited to one sphere only. This goes in line with previously voiced propositions to extend the focus of work-family research into one of work-life research (Guest, 2001; Lewis, 2003). Alike the approach taken by Bourne et al. (2009) researchers should pay tribute to the complexity and multi-facetedness of individuals' lives and study the interaction of life spheres in a broader view. In a similar vein, further research should more strongly pay attention to the priorities of individuals with regards to their life spheres. Carlson and Kacmar (2000) pioneered research in this arena underscoring additional insights gained by considering life role importance, centrality, and priorities of individuals, yet comparatively little research followed this direction. Future studies should consider life roles beyond work and family more strongly.

2.1.1.2 Further Research on Work-Life Initiatives

The present study raised a few issues for the future investigation of work-life initiatives. First and foremost, differential effects of initiative use and availability must be considered more strongly. Kelly et al. (2008) previously criticized the fact that examinations focus on either use of initiatives or on access to initiatives. Yet we can only understand effects of work-life initiatives if we observe both individual's access to them and their use of benefits. That work-life dynamics are clearly distinct comparing the impact of initiative access and initiative use was shown in the present investigation. Furthermore, researchers should pay closer attention to the character of benefits as being supportive of work-life issues. The present data showed that particularly wide-spread and often researched initiatives such as flexible work hours and home office were without effect on work-life conflict. In line with recommendations of Blair-Loy and Wharton (2004), not only initiative use and availability should be studied but also employees' perception of them as useful or not useful for fostering work-life balance. Findings further contribute to existing research by testing an innovative set of work-life initiatives which were directly assessed within the field they are offered in. This fills a gap in research which was raised by Eikhof, Warhurst and Haunschild (2007) who criticized that most WLB policies address the issue of dependent care (directly by care initiatives or indirectly by providing flexibility policies which enable employees to organize care responsibilities better). Additionally, as in the present study, examining which work-life initiatives are needed by employees adds further important knowledge about the discrepancy between available benefits and those which would be needed.

2.1.1.3 Work-Life Dynamics in Professional Service Firms

The present study examined dynamics of organizational resources and demands and their impact on the work-life interface of professionals in two PSF subbranches: management consulting and law firms. In order to replicate and strengthen findings, further research should expand into other branches of PSFs and knowledge-intensive firms. While it is likely that demands are equally high, structural characteristics as well as cultural norms may vary among PSF subsectors, for instance more innovative and creative subbranches, e.g. marketing or media, may tend to be more open towards innovative HR strategies than more traditional subbranches such as accounting. Furthermore, the present framework only examined a limited set of antecedents to professionals' work-life conflict. Future research should extend the present approach by incorporating further demands, such as speed of project delivery, and resources, such as job autonomy in terms of self-determined working time and time spent at work that is determined by external forces. Deeper insights are also necessary on the role of the supervisor in PSFs as it has been argued here that due to flat hierarchies and the strong cooperation with client firms, the role of the supervisor is often not strongly perceived as such. In line with Litrico and Lee's concerns (2008), it is recommended to put a stronger focus on the work group context with regards to formal and informal resources as well as demands. The impact of co-workers was shown in the present examination, yet due to the project-team structure in PSFs this unit of analysis should be considered more strongly. Depending on the group composition, values at team level and respective demands and resources may vary. This is particularly important in the PSF context because project teams usually operate relatively isolated from the rest of the firm at the client's premises over longer periods of time. Above and beyond, future research should directly study antecedents as well as outcomes of work-life dynamics of professionals to give evidence to the negative effects of high work-life conflict on professionals' health, motivation, firm loyalty and performance, aspects which in the present thesis only were derived from existing research (Part I, 1.).

2.1.2 Methodological Suggestions

The current study took an innovative approach concerning the investigation of a number of constructs, particularly with regards to the assessment of conflict types and of work-life initiative use and access. While these rather novel approaches represent a valuable contribution to existing work-life research, some methodological suggestions are made in order to refine these assessment strategies in future studies.

2.1.2.1 Conflict Types

The study of conflict types in the present examination added important insights about the work-life dynamics of professionals. Yet, as outlined in the limitations section, types tested in the present examination are for one thing not trenchantly distinct and additionally, were tailored to the context of the present study by including the health area and changing the religious sphere suggested by Carlson and Kacmar (2000) into time for self. The measurement of centrality of life roles additionally to measuring conflict types added important background knowledge to the present findings because it helped put the conflict results in scope and not overestimate respective results, as for example conflict of work vs. social engagement. Further research is needed with regards to life spheres of different groups of individuals and their measurement. Future quantitative and qualitative research approaches should further enlighten life spheres and conflict types and try to develop more trenchant operationalizations in order to pay tribute to the complexity and richness of individuals' life roles.

2.1.2.2 Further Research on the Three Conflict Dimensions

The present study provides insightful results on the three dimensions of work-life conflict proposed by Greenhaus and Beutell (1985). While previous research frequently neglected the role of behavior-based WLC (Allen et al. 2000; Chen et al., 2009; Rotondo, Carlson & Kincaid, 2003; van Daalen et al., 2006; Wallace, 1997), this dimension was included in the current study with a self-developed measure. In future studies, behavior-based conflict should be a more flexible set of items as previous research might frequently have refrained from applying this measure because of missing suitability of items for the population under study. This was also the case at the start of the present examination: items developed by Carlson et al. (2000) did just not fit to potential behaviors exerted in a PSF environment. Thus, two items were included in the questionnaire, which represent two behaviors that are very common in PSFs and are likely to interfere with nonwork interests: difficulty in predicting times of returning from work as a function of heavy workload and unpredictable schedules, and having to postpone or cancel a personal vacation due to work volume. Further research should follow this example and study the behavior-based dimension of conflict but adjust items to the context of the population under examination because behavior is highly context-specific.

2.1.2.3 Life Role Values

Alvesson (2000) underscored the particular importance of social identity for loyalty in knowledge-intensive firms, which lets the study of life role priorities continue to be a highly interesting area of study. Further research may incorporate life role perspectives in the study of intent to leave the firm as well as organizational and professional commitment. Additionally, prior approaches to the study of life role values and priorities are highly ambiguous. While a number of studies directly examine individuals' priorities attached to certain life spheres (e.g. Cinamon & Rich, 2002a), others examine these priorities in terms of active involvement in a role (e.g. Adams et al., 1996; Brummelhuis et al., 2008; Carlson & Frone, 2003). This diversity of operationalizations regarding individual's values attached to life spheres and related needs calls for a meta-analytical examination which systematically investigates what we know about different levels of priority setting (e.g. active in the sense of actual behavior versus passive in terms of desires, aspirations and goals), and how these different priorities affect work-life dynamics.

2.1.2.4 Objective Measures that Allow Causal Inferences

Besides using measures that are based on an individual's perception of a phenomenon, more objective data should be applied in the future and studies should use multiple data sources in order to allow conclusions about causality. Scientists operating in this field often use supervisor or peer ratings and compare them with self-reported answers. For example Lyness and Judiesch (2008) collected self-ratings and peer ratings on employees' work-life balance and related career advancement potential. For replications and extensions of the present study, for example an analysis of corporate websites as it was conducted in the present study could serve as an indicator of work-life friendliness of firms. They should in that case however be accompanied by interviews or other sources of data to verify the perception that arises from looking at corporate communications on the web. Furthermore, work-life research largely lacks studies with longitudinal designs. Compared to the striking number of cross-sectional studies longitudinal research remains scarce in the area of research on the work-life interface.[57] Last but not least, future research should follow examples such as Deelstra et al. (2003) who experimentally confirmed that social support among co-workers can also be undesirable if it is not voluntary but imposed: imposed instrumental support was in this study related to stress instead of appreciation of relief.. Further studies should incorporate experimental and quasi-experimental designs more strongly in order to enable 'real' causal inferences.

2.2 Implications for Human Resource Management

In Part I the relevance of the work-life debate for organizations was discussed pointing out individual, interpersonal and organizational benefits of successful work-life integration. The empirical examination in Part II showed that professionals in PSFs experience work-life conflict as a function of organizational demands. Resources on behalf the organization were shown to ameliorate these

---

57   Explicitly, only the following studies examined work-life dynamics under a repeated-measure or longitudinal design: Dikkers et al. (2007b), Giardini and Kabst (2008), Grant-Vallone and Donaldson (2001), Ilies, Schwind and Wagner (2009), Kinnunen et al. (2010) as well as van Steenbergen and Ellemers (2009).

conflicts. Additionally, professionals differ in their work-life dynamics, for example depending on subbranch, gender, or life role priority. Findings from the present study have implications for strategic HRM, including the necessity to take work-life concerns of professionals seriously (2.2.1), closely monitor informal organizational demands (2.2.2) and expand formal as well as informal organizational support (2.2.3). In order to maximize employee productivity, satisfaction and commitment and at the same time sustain and maximize organizational performance and success, organizational HRM should aim at achieving fit between individuals and the organization by closely evaluating both sides' needs, demands and resources (2.2.4). A comprehensive process of developing, implementing and evaluating work-life integration management (WLIM) could serve organizations as a guideline for considering all important aspects of such an endeavor (2.2.5).

2.2.1 Taking Work-Life Concerns of Professionals Seriously

As results showed, professionals attach high importance to areas outside work. Thus, relying on a workforce that puts full-speed full-force into their job is a risky strategy for firms on the long run (cf. Løwendahl, 2005). Besides, it is unlikely that in the future, organizations will be able to rely on such employees as shown by the finding that life roles beyond work are highly important to both male and female professionals and in all age groups in the present examination. PSFs are today among the most attractive employers for young professionals but exactly for this reason firms must pay close attention to applicants' needs and values. Despite their attractiveness, PSFs are also well-known for their high demands and a firm that is successful in signaling concern about employees' nonwork interests has a recruiting advantage compared to those who neglect this issue. In their recruitment and retention strategy, PSFs should therefore take into consideration the fact that the majority of young professionals have an interest in pursuing a career *and* leading a fulfilled life outside work. Priorities in this respect might also change over time. As Honeycutt and Rosen (1997) pointed out, salient identity is a predictor of individuals' attraction to an organization's career path and benefits.

2.2.2 Monitoring Informal Organizational Demands

It was shown in the present study that informal demands above and beyond formal demands impact professionals' work-life conflict as illustrated in Figure 10. While the character of PSFs as highly demanding work environments is unlikely to change entirely, based on the present findings two demands should be weakened in favor of a more productive firm with better interpersonal climate. While formal organizational demands are unlikely to decrease substantially informal demands could be ameliorated creating improvements for both the firm and its workforce. Therefore, PSFs should monitor the implicit demands they impose on their workforce and try to ameliorate them.

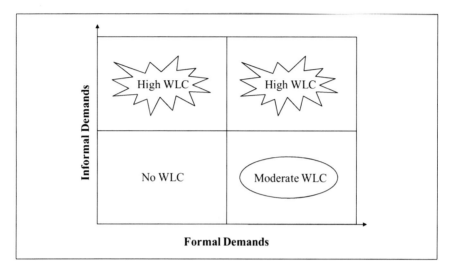

Figure 12. The impact of informal and formal demands on the work-life conflict of professionals

The present study indicated that the strongest predictor of professionals' work-life conflict in the present examination were implicit organizational time demands necessary to advance in a firm, i.e. organizational time demands and negative career consequences resulting from using WLB initiatives. Kaiser and Ringlstetter (2011) discuss the need for performance measurement systems which enable differentiated *evaluation of individual contributions to the company's performance*. These evaluation systems should be objective and productivity-oriented rather than based on time devoted to the firm, which seemed to be the case though for most of the participants in the present study. Performance should be more strongly measured in terms of output and this must also be engrained into organizational culture. While both employee and organization benefit from such a measure's objectivity, measuring performance in terms of output instead of in terms of time spent at work would also lever out cultures of 'face time' and 'presenteeism'. Furthermore, employees should not be sanctioned for making use of organizational benefits by slower or halted career advancement. The present examination showed that this impediment is very powerful across all job levels within PSFs. Yet, if objective performance measures were implemented successfully, there is a chance that *professionals who take a leave or reduce their work hour volumes are not marginalized*. But if a firm rewards employees who live the culture of presenteeism, using formal initiatives will not be consistent with corporate culture (cf. also Perlow, 1995). Consequently, initiatives are in vain and professionals are in danger of facing impairments as a consequence of work-life conflict, which may result in sickness absence and turnover. These outcomes cost the organization more and are less predictable than granting its professionals effective interventions to handle their work and nonwork responsibilities adequately.

To name an example of successful realization of these ideas, Connor, Hooks and McGuire (1999) report of a newly implemented career model at the management consulting unit of Price Waterhouse LLP which highlights competencies and skills rather than tenure and presence. Promotion thus depends on the attainment of a certain predefined skill level which offers the opportunity for employees to choose their own pace of career advancement. This strategy also yields the benefit that individual accountability for results must be established and clarified. In a similar vein, Hill, Ferris and Märtinson (2003) argued that work-life initiatives can support corporate strategic business needs by stimulating a reevaluation of employee productivity. Flexibility policies such as working from home require performance evaluations that are output-oriented. Besides increased productivity, a more objective performance evaluation also increases social justice at the workplace because all employees are evaluated by the same standards. In practice this means to develop solutions how to objectify performance measurement as it has been pointed out previously, that productivity in PSFs is something that is hard to measure (cf. Ringlstetter & Kaiser, 2007).

Actual work demands, such as long work hours and frequent travel requirements, do not harm professionals as much as an unsupportive culture. As work hour volumes are unlikely to decrease, organizations must therefore *reconsider their implicitly communicated practices* with regards to the sensitive issue of work-personal life reconciliation and *provide informal support* in order to retain a healthy and productive workforce.

2.2.3 Expanding Formal and Informal Organizational Resources

The present thesis showed that formal initiatives – their availability as well as their use – have some potential for reducing work-life conflicts of professionals. Yet overall, the impact of informal resources, particularly of managerial support, was much stronger and consistent in predicting lower levels of work-life conflict. As argued before, organizations are therefore particularly effective in supporting their employees' work-life issues if they consider these in terms of formal arrangements as well as a supportive organizational culture.

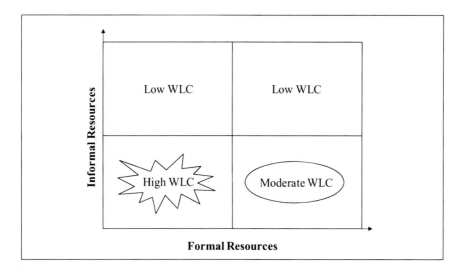

Figure 13. The impact of informal and formal resources on the work-life conflict of profes-
sionals

Effects of management and supervisor support as well as of the availability
of formal initiatives, being an indicator for being responsive for these concerns
as well, indicated that a supportive climate is more effective in dealing with
work-life conflicts than formal initiatives alone (cf. Figure 11).

Informal support in the present study was described in terms of support from
the management, supervisors and co-workers. Previous research argued that
supervisors should more strongly act as role models promoting a work-life supportive culture. If supervisors use alternative work arrangements themselves,
they communicate

> "that it's acceptable to place personal time demands on an equal footing with work
> time demands. [...] if more managers 'walked the talk' (used flexible schedules), al-
> ternative work schedule implementation would be enhanced for all employees"
> (Kossek et al., 1999, p. 34).

The present study supports this idea showing that supervisor support primarily
favorably affected (lower) strain-based work-life conflict. Accordingly, making
use of alternative arrangements should not be sanctioned by negative career
consequences as was the case in the present dataset. Particularly in 'strong cultures' such as in most PSFs (Lorsch & Tierney, 2002), positive role models and
flagships representing positive examples of successful work-life reconciliation
should be communicated via organizational channels within the firm and also

outwardly for recruiting purposes by telling more 'success stories' (Connor, Hooks and McGuire, 1999).

Work-life initiatives offered in organizations and in PSFs should be revised and tailored more strongly to the needs of professionals. It was indicated that some initiatives such as short-term flexible work hours and home office may not have the primary aim of reducing work-life interferences but are just working practices which are communicated as initiatives. Among others Hooks and Higgs (2002) argued that completing a certain amount of work volume from home is common in PSFs and can therefore not be regarded as a work-life initiative. Likewise, in the case of flexible work arrangements Trinczek (2006) argued that those practices enable firms to demand more hours from their professionals than they would under a more fixed schedule. Firms should therefore implement an evaluation system which assesses employees' needs and use respective insights for tailoring work-life benefits to these needs. This serves the individual in terms of access to useful initiatives and the firm as well in terms of meaningful and goal-directed efforts instead of money spent on one-size-fits-all sets of benefits. Along that line Perry-Smith and Blum (2000) argue in favor of strategically bundled organizational work-life interventions that are incorporated into the strategic HR of an organization in order to make them a competitive advantage. If messages of informal culture concur with available work-life initiatives,

> "work-life programs may help companies protect and leverage their general investments in human assets" (Konrad & Mangel, 2000, p. 1225).

2.2.4 Evaluation and Monitoring Needs and Resources: Creating Fit between the Professional, the Firm and the Client

Cooperation of the organization and the individual and mutual compliance are required for finding the right solutions for the right persons. The present research has shown that all types of professionals are affected by work-life conflict. Demands increase conflict, while resources ameliorate it. Yet, different individuals face different needs and different work-life dynamics which organizations should consider. In order to do so, organizations and particularly PSFs should first find out what their employees need in order to provide tailor-made solutions for their primary assets instead of offering one-size-fits-all solutions which are not used and not useful. The assessment and monitoring of professionals' needs might reveal unexpected insights which are of central concern to organizations, such as the finding here that male and female professionals, contrary to previous findings, not differ substantially in their life role priorities and experience of conflict types. As values of both genders seem to largely converge, PSFs must address these needs more strongly, for example by granting parental leave policies for fathers and mothers without negative career consequences, a concern that was also critically discussed by Burnett et al. (2011). As professionals in dual-career relationships are increasingly becoming more typical organizations should also address this concern by providing benefits which address specific needs of dual-career constellations. These could be options which take the employment situation of the partner into consideration, too, for example by enabling the coordination of a dual-earner 60 hour workweek (Hill et al., 2006). The finding that with increasing tenure work-life conflict decreases underscores the importance of offering attractive work-life options in earlier years of tenure in order to retain young professionals. While there seems to be a silent agreement that work-life benefits must be earned by collecting tenure years, present results show that work-life issues are also important in early years of tenure and organizations can use this knowledge for improving employee' loyalty, commitment and satisfaction by addressing these needs. Attentiveness to issues of work-life integration can after all be a strategy for winning the 'war for talent' (Barnett & Hall, 2001).

Insights from subgroup differentiations in Part II unite in the obvious need of putting into focus individual needs and resources and their fit with organizational demands and resources linking to previously mentioned theoretical reasonings about person-organization fit (e.g. Edwards & Rothbard, 2005). Honeycutt and Rosen (1997) conclude that *people perform best in situations that are personally compatible*. In order to maintain a healthy and motivated workforce and maximize firm productivity, fit between organizational needs and resources with individual needs and resources should be attempted at different levels. Professionals' values should fit to those of their project team in order to enable smooth cooperation and maximize team performance. It was pointed out by Poelmans and Beham (2008b) that effective work-life programs that are used by those in need and accepted by co-workers are related to higher coverage and better scheduling for all team members. Congruence between individual work-life needs and organizational resources can manifest itself regarding both formal and informal resources. Organizations should monitor the needs of its professional workforce and address them adequately, but these answers must also be incorporated into implicit culture of organizations in order to be effective. From the individual point of view, professionals also self-select into environments which are perceived as meeting their needs. In this respect, prior research results indicate that congruence between individual work values and organizational values (as for example expressed in work-life supportiveness) predict job choice better than pay or promotion opportunities (Judge & Bretz, 1992).

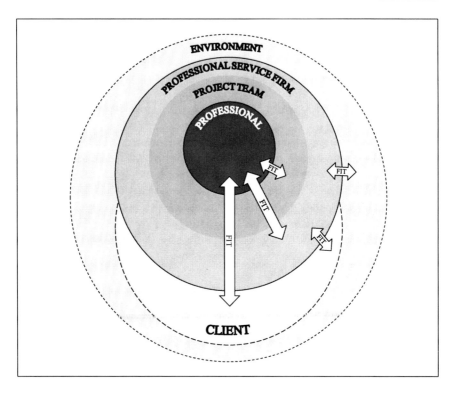

Figure 14. Illustration of person-organization fit at different levels in order to improve work-life dynamics of professionals

The notion that individual life role values play a role for the impact of organizational demands and resources on work-life interactions was also confirmed in the present investigation among professionals. Hence, besides considering value congruence among organization and employee, also fit between environmental developments and organizational practices should be considered (Figure 12). It was outlined in previously in this thesis that one of the developments which are observable in the organizational environment, also of PSFs, are changes of employees' and potential employees' values towards higher priorities in nonwork spheres as compared to previous generations. As Judge and Bretz (1992) pointed out, job seekers evaluate recruitment material such as web sites for cues of whether an organization fits with their salient identity. If PSFs want to remain top employers of young high potentials they should, beyond communication on web sites, incorporate work-life supportiveness in their set of corporate values. Organizations will be rewarded with higher employee satisfaction and commitment (Da Silva, Hutcheson & Wahl, 2010; Kristof, 1996; O'Reilly et al., 1991). Another important issue with regards to fit of the individual and the organization in the PSF context is a third party, the *client*. Clients as primary stakeholders of the professional service firm should be consciously and strategically integrated in corporate work-life integration management (WLIM). Serving clients' needs is the primary goal of PSFs and clients first and foremost have an interest in motivated and productive professionals (Lorsch & Tierney, 2002). Fit between an organization and its client could furthermore be addressed in terms of improved performance measurement of the professionals. There are companies which in the past were successful at changing a culture based on 'face-time' into one that is results-based as for example suggested by Galinsky and Matos (2011) who report experiences from a U.S. corporate tax firm that implemented an output-based system of measuring performance:

> "It's a results-based environment that says, if you meet financial results and you meet client service scores – we take those through independent surveys on an ongoing basis – you can work whenever you want ... Work when you're most productive, when you're most engaged. And we'll change the culture to where what really matters are results. Hours don't matter. [...] We spent a lot of time developing a dashboard that all of our people can see everyday when they come into the office to find out where they're at. The beauty of that is – although it's difficult – that focus on measuring results crystallizes your thinking and makes people focus and concentrate on what's important. [...] I have learned that workplace flexibility is much more than an employee benefit – it's not like pizza on Fridays for the employees – it is an incredibly powerful business strategy" (Brint Ryan, Co-Founder and CEO of Ryan LLC, cited in Galinsky and Matos, 2011, p. 271).

It is an interest of the client to make firm outputs visible and if firms are also interested in measuring professionals' productivity more objectively, both parties profit from respective changes. Additionally, evaluations of clients' work-life culture and congruence with the PSF's culture have implications for staffing projects. Clients which are more open to innovative working patterns may not resist to having their project staffed with two professionals sharing a job. Additionally, flexible clients might not object to reducing travel requirements to and from the client site if the professional service firm openly communicates its operating strategy and if solutions and processes which are worked out off-site are transparent for the client. This strategy of creating fit between needs of the organization, the professional and the client has been referred to as "modern patchwork consulting" (Kaiser et al., 2011, p. 287) which is characterized by flexibility of the work-location as well as innovative work hour arrangements such as part-time or job-sharing. If PSFs develop strategies to successfully communicate to the client that performance is not measurable by presence and makes output more visible, the firm, the client, and the professionals will benefit by creating a *win-win outcome* (Halpern & Murphy, 2005). From an experiment of introducing more predictable work schedules and overall reducing work hour volumes in a large international consulting organization, Perlow and Porter (2009) reported that "the process creates efficiencies and promotes work/life balance – without sacrificing anything on the client side" (p. 106). Additionally to these aspects, PSFs together with their clients could also reconsider their project portfolios and create innovative approaches to selling projects. It is imaginable that projects about processes and solutions which are not characterized by extreme time pressure may be staffed with reduced load professionals. A larger time frame might be needed but clients could be won over for such an approach by making clear that longer temporal cooperation, during which besides identifying problems and finding solutions also accompaniment of the implementation process is included, may be more effective than short-term full-time project teams. Therefore clients benefit in terms of high quality consulting, organizations retain highly qualified professionals and the professionals themselves can continue to pursue their challenging jobs on reduced-load without disappearing in an internal back-office position of the PSF.

2.2.5 A Process Model of Developing, Implementing and Evaluating 'Work-Life Integration Management' in Professional Service Firms

While the majority of practical implications derived from empirical work-life research continue to be vague and generic a number of authors provided checklists and guidelines for implementing effective work-life integration management (Friede et al., 2008; Hill & Weiner, 2003; Lewis & Cooper, 2005; Poelmans et al., 2008; Thompson, 2008). As a final step of this thesis major conclusions are pulled together from such guidelines with particular attention to PSFs as well as incorporate findings from the present empirical examination of lawyers and consultants in order to suggest a set of implications for developing, implementing and evaluating an effective work-life integration management (WLIM) (cf. Figure 13).

2.2.5.1 Analysis of the Current Situation

In order to pay tribute to employee diversity and consider characteristics and situation of all employees, PSFs attempting to develop and implement work-life integration management (WLIM) should spend reasonable efforts in analyzing the needs and resources of their professional workforce, the firm itself, its client(s), and the organizational environment.

Assessment of individual preconditions, characteristics and needs. Individual characteristics and resources that enable successful coping with work-life challenges should be taken into consideration, as it is suggested that individuals most successful at integrating work and personal life are those "with self-regulated work habits and 'proactive' personalities and flexible attitudes, who [are] also highly committed and tended to put forth extra effort" (Friede et al., 2008, p. 721). As shown in the present examination, it is worthwhile to assess whether *professionals are affected by work-life conflict* in the first place and subsequently their *need and use of work-life initiatives* in order to tailor benefits to the requirements of the workforce. Particular attention should be paid to the assessment of time-based, strain-based and behavior-based WLC as these conflict types also require different types of initiatives (i.e. addressing temporal issues, relieving strain from professionals or enabling work-related behavior which does not interfere with nonwork concerns). That is, if the PSF's aim really is to improve their professionals' health and satisfaction and not merely use the work-life issue for marketing purposes (Ostendorp, 2007). Multiple sources of information should be used, e.g. also from employees that are leaving or have left the firm in order to identify their reasons (Center for Ethical Business Cultures, 1997). As pointed out by Barnett and Hall (2001), "to win the war for talent, ask the talent what it wants!" (p. 206).

Assessment of organizational needs and resources. On behalf of the organization three aspects should be considered before defining the goal of work-life integration management:

- *Why do we need WLIM?* Reasons could include all aspects raised in Part I (1.1), for example to reduce absenteeism and maintain employee health, to improve employee productivity or to improve recruiting success.
- *What are the specific demands we put upon our professionals?* As shown in the present study, informal demands have a much stronger impact on professionals' work-life dynamics than formal demands such as work hours. PSFs should clarify what they demand from their workforce and whether there is a way of alleviating a number of these demands, for example culturally engrained 'presenteeism' by implementing results-based performance measurements.
- *What resources do we dispose of for dealing with professionals' work-life concerns?* PSFs should furthermore evaluate their resources including formal and informal resources in order to strengthen resources which already successfully support professionals and find out which resources are crucial yet missing in their organization, for example by evaluating employee needs.

Assessment of clients' needs. Clients' needs should be evaluated and monitored as well. A first step towards effective WLIM that involves clients' needs is to *start dialogue* about this issue with the client. It may turn out that if clients are not as reluctant towards employee-friendly work arrangements as firms often think if both parties communicate openly (Perlow & Porter, 2009). Furthermore, clients' need for 24/7 service should be evaluated and discussed as every organization today works with innovative communication technology and presence at the client site 4-5 days a week might not prove necessary in all cases (Kaiser et al., 2011). Within a law firm context, Williams (2007) points out another important aspect of clients' interest in successful WLIM of PSFs: besides accessibility, clients need stability and thus high turnover rates are not at all in the interests of clients.

Demands and resources from the organizational environment. The social environment of the PSF further puts a number of demands on the organization such as legal regulations concerning (parental) leave arrangements or flextime. These demands must be taken into consideration as well as opportunities to integrate resources into WLIM which could be the cooperation with a nearby childcare institution or fitness and recreation center.

2.2.5.2 Definition of Goals

Goals associated with developing and implementing a WLIM strategy can be manifold ranging from focus on outward communication and 'improved employer branding' to a comprehensive 'strategy of individual differences' as outlined by Ostendorp (2007). Hence, goals organizations associated with their efforts to support employees' work-life integration may be to improve individual and organizational performance, sharpen recruiting and employee selection in order to attain a competitive advantage on the talent market, improve employee retention, improve health management of employees to minimize absenteeism, and increase shareholder value, only naming a few (cf. Part I, 1.1). Whichever strategy is in the focus of an organization, aims of should be clarified and operationalized in accordance with corporate culture as well as the organizational mission and vision (Friedman, 2006). In a similar vein, guidelines for WLIM implementations suggest that

> "work/life is not charity [...]. Strategies should be designed to solve definable issues in ways that strengthen the business" (Center for Ethical Business Culture, 1997, p. 18).

2.2.5.3 Choice and Development of a Strategy

A strategy of successful WLIM could address areas of WLB benefits, an organization's recruiting and selection strategy, innovative work organization, performance measurement beyond 'presenteeism' and overall cultural change in favor of a work-life integration responsive corporate culture. When developing a strategy not only the scope of action must be determined but firms must decide whether to undergo a comprehensive change process or whether it is sufficient to start with a step-by-step strategy, for example by first tackling the most pressing issues or by implementing certain policies in one operating area of the firm to see how things go (Center for Ethical Business Culture, 1997). Possible strategies which organizations pursue when deciding to develop and implement WLIM include cultural change processes, the development of a WLB benefit system, recruiting and personnel selection strategies, organizing daily work innovatively and empowering employees.

Culture change has in the present study been shown a crucial aspect of effective WLIM. Changing organizational work-life culture includes clear communication about career consequences and eradication of stigmatization and 'jokes' (Williams, 2007). Above and beyond, implicit organizational time demands should be overcome by developing outcome-based cultures of performance measurement (Thiehoff, 2004; Morris et al., 2009).

WLB benefit system: Clear planning of technical aspects of WLB (hours, salary, specific design) and clarification of the handling of ambiguous and exceptional situations (e.g. meetings scheduled on nonwork days of part-timers) is crucial in order to transport authentic messages about the possibilities and limitations of WLB initiatives (Friede et al., 2008).

Recruiting and selection strategy: Recruiting strategies which 'use' work-life issues for attracting talent should not only address women or young parents but be based on the notion that total focus on work is not healthy and on the long run neither serves the individual nor the organization (Williams, 2007). Selection strategies should be transparent and clear about their benefits and their expectations. That work-life issues matter for recruitment purposes was for example shown by Carless and Wintle (2007) (cf. also Part I, 1.1).

Innovative work organization: Although it appears difficult at first sight to implement flexible and reduced-load arrangements in PSFs, innovative consulting projects which use communication technology and are bureaucratically flexible and which first and foremost integrate the client in the consulting process could enable an innovative work organization where working from 'everywhere' and on flextime schedules is possible (Kaiser et al., 2011). Nord et al. (2002)

suggest to staff consulting teams which operate at the client site 4 days per week with changing team compositons in order to grant full coverage for the client.

Empower employees: Responsibility for effective WLIM lays not only on behalf the organization, first and foremost of course employees are asked to find solutions to their challenges in integrating nonwork concerns with their work and vice versa. Besides providing assistance in terms of WLB initiatives organizations can empower their employees in several other ways. Gibson and Campbell Quick (2008) suggest 'stress matching' (p. 92) as a way of dealing with critical stress incidents. In this innovative concept, workers who have to deal with critical stress issues are matched with workers who have successfully gone through the same critical stress situations. This approach could be particularly valuable for professionals in PSFs to manage their work-life integration better, as in these firms encounter and exchange of professionals in similar situations is not necessarily self-evident due to work at remote and frequently changing (client) sites. Besides, the relevance of training employees in time management, self-management and stress management is frequently pointed out (e.g. Schabracq, 2003a). Barnett and Hall (2001) propose that "if we enable the employee to find a way […] to produce good work and to find personal work-life integration, the employee will probably find a way" (p. 205).

It is usually recommended to *pilot* intended solution in order to increase sense of control of those in charge as well as provide opportunities for readjustment before widespread implementation (Center for Ethical Business Culture, 1997). Whichever strategy is chosen *fit* among professionals, their team, the employing firm as well as the client and the social environment (Figure 12) should be actively pursued and monitored in order to ensure long-term success of organizational WLIM (cf. also Edwards & Rothbard, 2005). Those with decision latitude and managers and partners with representative function have a crucial role in creating fit between the firm's goals and client expectations – particularly in PSFs:

> "To achieve these dual objectives of serving clients while giving high priority to employees' life-balance goals, a major part of the burden would appear to fall to high-level executives (e.g. the partners in these settings) in negotiating client expectations" (Nord et al., 2002, p. 236).

2.2.5.4 Implementation of Solutions

Issues which matter most at the implementation stage but are in fact critical at all stages of the process of developing effective WLIM include involvement of all stakeholders, accurate and clear communication, training of managers and supervisors as well as networking and collaboration. Besides, of course tracking and monitoring costs, outcomes and acceptance of the process as well as client satisfaction matter particularly at the implementation stage in order to provide data for the stage of measuring outcomes.

That *involvement of all stakeholders* is crucial for managing work-life integration was pointed out previously (Hyland & Jackson 2006; Perlow & Porter 2009) and especially in PSFs where clients expect 24/7 availability of the professionals, it is important to take into consideration the needs and resources of all relevant parties. *Professional employees* of course must be involved in the creation of useful benefits but also as active change agents on the way to an organizational culture which is results-based and performance-promoting while respecting individual nonwork needs and responsibilities. *Clients* should also be involved in order to enable out-of-the-box solutions such as staffing consulting projects with job sharers (cf. Kaiser et al., 2011). As pointed out by Litrico and Lee (2008) it is crucial to involve *co-workers and team members* as they are often skeptical towards those who use WLB benefits because they may cause them extra-work or leave it to them to 'pick up the slack' (p. 1007). In order to promote social justice in the organization (cf. Part I, 1.1.2) co-workers should not 'suffer' from their colleagues' WLB initiative use. It is further imperative that *top management* supports and promotes the strategy of effective WLIM and cultural change in order to guarantee long-term success of these efforts as shown in the present study by the high importance of management support for reducing WLC (cf. Friede et al., 2008).

Communication. As underscored by the Center for Ethical Business Culture (1997), firms should from the very beginning communicate their vision of change regarding WLIM and make clear that change is expected from all stakeholders and will be rewarded. Meanwhile, Edmondson and Detert (2005) underscore that employees have to speak up in order to find consideration for their work-life integration concerns. Additionally, in order to make initiatives usable they must be communicated clearly (Nord et al., 2002; Reindl, Kaiser & Stolz, 2011) together with fair and transparent communication of advantages and also drawbacks and challenges so that individuals as well as supervisors and the management have realistic expectations and perceptions (Friede et al., 2008). Nord et al. (2002), inferring from examining work-life policies in two management consulting firms, highlight the importance of communicating WLIM strategies to clients in order to reconcile their needs with the firm's commitment to promoting work-life integration.

Training of management, supervisors, and decision makers. As underscored by Friede, Kossek and MacDermid (2008) it is important to train supervisors on advantages and challenges of alternative work arrangements such as part-time, and finding ways of adjusting 'unsuitable' jobs such as project work so that work-life integration is possible (e.g. by giving fewer projects to the profession-al). Furthermore, managers and supervisors need practical guidelines and tools that enable them to make clear decisions, track progress and measure outcomes (Center for Ethical Business Culture, 1997). Kossek and Hammer (2008) suggest that supervisor training includes four scopes of action: providing emotional support, providing structural support, modeling healthful behavior and partnering with other managers to strategically address work/life issues. From a comparison of supervisors who participated in 30-to-45-minute computer tutorials followed by 75-minute face-to-face discussions with a control group that did not receive such training the authors conclude that subordinates of the first group of managers perceived their supervisors as being substantially more supportive. Additionally employees were more satisfied with their jobs and had lower turnover intentions leading Kossek and Hammer to the conclusion that "small interventions can have a big impact throughout an organization" (p. 36).

Networking and communication. As every organization and even more so the professional service firm operates in a social network of other organizations, insights from those who already have an effective WLIM up and running should be sought by those still in the development process (Center of Ethical Business Cultures, 1997). Networking and collaboration should reach the individual level for example by using 'stress matching' suggested by Gibson and Campbell Quick (2008).

2.2.5.5 Monitoring and Measurement of Outcomes

While during the implementation processes and costs should be closely monitored, organizations should also define a point in time where the implementation process is evaluated and outcomes are measured (Barnett & Hall, 2001). Work-life literature suggests evaluating the 'business case' for WLIM. This may be done using a balanced scorecard approach (Thiehoff, 2004) or with another type of measurement system as for example the Organizational Development Human-Capital Accounting System (ODHCAS) developed by Morris, Storberg-Walker and McMillan (2009). In the measurement of success 'hard', i.e. tangible returns such as less employee turnover, lower recruiting costs, and fewer health-related absenteeism should be included as well as 'soft' factors such as employee commitment and satisfaction. Additionally, an analysis of effectiveness of work-life integration management should include organizational success as well as effectiveness at the individual level and on behalf the client (and other potential stakeholders). Furthermore, changing shareholder value before and after implementation of work-life integration management can be evaluated (Arthur & Cook, 2004).

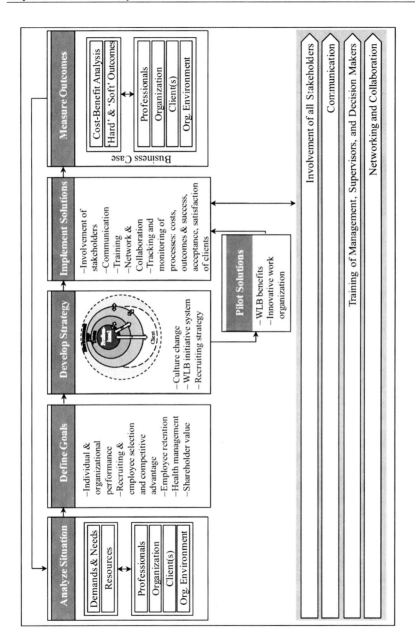

Figure 15. Developing, implementing and evaluating an effective work-life integration management (WLIM)

Organizational support efforts regarding employees' work-life integration should further be integrated in organizational reporting as recommended by Galinsky and Matos (2011):

> "The goal is not to provide a laundry list of employee benefit programs, but to present a human capital management strategy that will leverage the organization's human resources toward greater success. [...] These reports would expand the currently available information on the effects of organizational activities, such as carbon footprints and corporate social responsibility efforts. If we monitor the health and wellbeing of our human resources the way we monitor the health of our environmental resources, we could create more and more workplaces that promote the engagement, job satisfaction, retention, health and work-life fit of employees" (p. 278).

3. Conclusion

The aim of the present dissertation was to gain insights on the work-life interface of professionals and the specific interaction of organizational demands and resources and their impact on work-life dynamics. Based on a review of existing evidence, a framework of organizational demands and resources was proposed and tested describing three dimensions of work-life conflict in a sample of professionals, specifically PSF employees. Despite the high salience of their work, professionals under study experienced substantial amounts of work-life conflict of all three dimensions. Moreover, testing types of conflict between work and several life spheres gave evidence to the often voiced concerns about the narrow focus of previous work-family studies. These effects were differentially examined among subgroups with findings that further challenge the notion that only individuals with family responsibilities are prone to the experience of work-life conflicts. Using PLS methodology a model of organizational demands and resources was estimated representing major antecedents of work-life conflict was estimated. Overall the model represented the data well and for the majority of expectations evidence was found in the data. It was shown that formal organizational time demands, i.e. work hours and business travel, did impact work-life conflict but in relatively small intensity, use and availability of work-life initiatives and secondary initiatives yield the potential for reducing levels of work-life conflict of professionals but results were relatively small, and first and foremost, professionals' work-life conflict is impacted negatively (i.e. favorably) by informal organizational resources, particularly managerial support, and impacted positively (i.e. in terms of higher conflict) by informal organizational demands, particularly time demands. Further, while support from peers at the workplace encouraged professionals to make use of work-life initiatives, the anticipation of negative career consequences in the case of using these benefits kept them from utilizing them. These results underscore the unfavorable impact of organizational demands and the beneficial impact of organizational resources. In accordance with ideas of person-organization fit theory, subgroup comparisons showed that individuals in different situations and with different characteristics experienced the dynamics of the demands and resources framework differently.

Findings obtained in the current study extend existing work-life research in the context of PSFs in several ways. Contrary to many existing studies, the antecedents under study are not composed in a 'laundry-list approach' (Bakker & Demerouti, 2007), but are meaningfully comprised representing major demands and resources which professionals in PSFs face in their jobs. At the same time availability and use of a distinct set of work-life initiatives in PSFs were investigated as well as the distinctive effects of singular initiatives allowing for statements about the usefulness of specific initiatives. The current study also incorporated psychological and social characteristics of employees, such as life role salience and dual versus single earner status, as well as employees at different career stages as recommended by Thompson et al. (1999). Another contribution of this study is the expansion of knowledge about the dynamics between formal and informal factors, and demands and resources. It was shown that informal factors are much stronger predictors of all three types of work-life conflict, time-, strain-, and behavior-based work-life conflict, than formal demands such as work hours or travel and formal resources, i.e. work-life initiatives. This strongly calls organizations into action with regards to really taking the challenge of organizational change instead of *pro forma* implementing a set of work-life benefits for recruiting purposes only. Exploring the dynamics of demands and resources around the work-life interface contributed to a better understanding of the complex interactions between work and personal life in the challenging context of professional service firms.

The present thesis made a number of important theoretical and methodological contributions to current management science and the study of work-life dynamics. Findings of how organizational demands and resources impact professionals' work-life interface should inspire future research in further branches and cultures and inspire professional service firms to take action towards ingraining work-life management in their corporate culture enabling the unsanctioned use of initiatives and thus leverage performance at the individual, the interpersonal and the organizational level with a comprehensive work-life integration management (WLIM). After all, individuals who are satisfied with their work-life dynamics contribute crucially to the success of firms. In other words, a 'positive' human resource management (Kaiser & Ringlstetter, 2006) which fosters professionals' work-life integration at the same time promotes organizational success creating a win-win-situation.

REFERENCES

Abele, A. E., & Volmer, J. 2011. Dual-Career Couples: Specific Challenges for Work-Life Integration. In S. Kaiser, M. Ringlstetter, D. R. Eikhof & M. Pina e Cunha (Eds.), Creating balance? International perspectives on the work-life integration of professionals: 173–189. Berlin: Springer.

Adams, G. A., King, L. A., & King, D. W. 1996. Relationships of job and family involvement, family social support, and work-family conflict with job and life satisfaction. Journal of Applied Psychology, 81(4): 411–420.

Ahuja, M. K., McKnight, D. H., Chudoba, K. M., George, J. F., & Kacmar, C. J. 2007. IT road warriors: Balancing work-family conflict, job autonomy, and work overload to mitigate turnover intentions. MIS Quarterly, 31(1): 1–17.

Albers, S., Klapper, D., Konradt, U., Walter, A., & Wolf, J. (Eds.) 2007. Methodik der empirischen Forschung (2nd ed.). Wiesbaden: Gabler.

Allen, T. D. 2001. Family-supportive work environments. The role of organizational perceptions. Journal of Vocational Behavior, 58(3): 414–435.

Allen, T. D., & Russell, J. E. A. 1999. Parental leave of absence. Some not so family-friendly implications. Journal of Applied Social Psychology, 29(1): 166–191.

Allen, T. D., Herst, D., Bruck, C. S., & Sutton, M. 2000. Consequences associated with work-to-family conflict: A review and agenda for future research. Journal of Occupational Health Psychology, 5(2): 278–308.

Almer, E. D., & Kaplan, S. E. 2002. The effects of flexible work arrangements on stressors, burnout, and behavioral job outcomes in public accounting. Behavioral Research in Accounting, 14: 1.

Alvesson, M. 2000. Social identity and the problem of loyalty in knowledge-intensive companies. Journal of Management Studies, 37(8): 1101–1124.

Amatea, E. S., Cross, E. G., Clark, J. E., & Bobby, C. L. 1986. Assessing the work and family role expectations of career-oriented men and women: The life role salience scales. Journal of Marriage and the Family, 48(4): 831–838.

Amos, E. A., & Weathington, B. L. 2008. An analysis of the relation between employee-organization value congruence and employee attitudes. Journal of Psychology: Interdisciplinary and Applied, 142(6): 615–631.

Anderson, D., & Kelliher, C. 2009. Flexible working and engagement. The importance of choice. Strategic HR Review, 8(2): 13–18.

Anderson, D., Vinnicombe, S., & Singh, V. 2010. Women partners leaving the firm: Choice, what choice? Gender in Management: An International Journal, 25(10): 170–183.

Anderson, N., Ones, D. S., Kepir Sinangil, H., & Viswesvaran, C. (Eds.) 2005. Handbook of Industrial, Work and Organizational Psychology: Volume 2, Organizational Psychology. London: Sage.

Anderson, S. E., Coffey, B. S., & Byerly, R. T. 2002. Formal organizational initiatives and informal workplace practices. Links to work-family conflict and job-related outcomes. Journal of Management, 28(6): 787–810.

Arthur, M. M. 2003. Share price reactions to work-family initiatives. An institutional perspective. Academy of Management Journal, 46(4): 497–505.

Arthur, M. M., & Cook, A. 2004. Taking stock of work-family initiatives. How announcements of "family friendly" human resource decisions affect shareholder value. Industrial & Labor Relations Review, 57(4): 599–613.

Aryee, S. 1992. Antecedents and outcomes of work-family conflict among married professional women. Evidence from Singapore. Human Relations, 45(8): 813–837.

Aryee, S., & Luk, V. 1996. Balancing two major parts of adult life experience: Work and family identity among dual-earner couples. Human Relations, 49: 465–487.

Aryee, S., Luk, V., Leung, A., & Lo, S. 1999. Role stressors, interrole conflict, and well-being: The moderating influence of spousal support and coping behaviors among employed parents in Hong Kong. Journal of Vocational Behavior, 54(2): 259–278.

Aryee, S., Srinivas, E., & Tan, H. H. 2005. Rhythms of life. Antecedents and outcomes of work-family balance in employed parents. Journal of Applied Psychology, 90(1): 132–146.

Ashforth, B. E., Kreiner, G. E., & Fugate, M. 2000. All in a day's work. Boundaries and micro role transitions. Academy of Management Review, 25(3): 472–491.

Ashkanasy, N. M., & Jackson, C. R. A. 2005. Organizational culture and climate. In N. Anderson, D. S. Ones, H. Kepir Sinangil & C. Viswesvaran (Eds.), Handbook of Industrial, Work and Organizational Psychology: Volume 2 Organizational Psychology: 398–415. London: SAGE.

Bacik, I., & Drew, E. 2006. Struggling with juggling: Gender and work/life balance in the legal professions. Women's Studies International Forum, 29(2): 136–146.

Backhaus, K., Erichson, B., Plinke, W., & Weiber, R. 2003. Multivariate Analysemethoden: Eine anwendungsorientierte Einführung (10th ed.). Berlin: Springer.

Badura, B., & Vetter, C. 2004a. „Work-Life-Balance" – Herausforderung für die betriebliche Gesundheitspolitik und den Staat. In B. Badura, H. Schellschmidt, C. Vetter & G. Bäcker (Eds.), Wettbewerbsfaktor Work-Life-Balance. Betriebliche Strategien zur Vereinbarkeit von Beruf, Familie und Privatleben: 5–17. Berlin: Springer.

Badura, B., Schellschmidt, H., Vetter, C., & Bäcker, G. (Eds.) 2004b. Wettbewerbsfaktor Work-Life-Balance: Betriebliche Strategien zur Vereinbarkeit von Beruf, Familie und Privatleben. Berlin: Springer.

Bagger, J., Li, A., & Gutek, B. A. 2008. How much do you value your family and does it matter? The joint effects of family identity salience, family-interference-with-work, and gender. Human Relations, 61(2): 187–211.

Bailyn, L. 1993. Breaking the mold. Women, men, and time in the new corporate world. New York: Maxwell Macmillan International.

Bakker, A. B., & Demerouti, E. 2007. The Job Demands-Resources model: state of the art. Journal of Managerial Psychology, 22(3): 309–328.

Bakker, A. B., Demerouti, E., & Euwema, M. C. 2005. Job resources buffer the impact of job demands on burnout. Journal of Occupational Health Psychology, 10(2): 170–180.

Bakker, A. B., Demerouti, E., & Schaufeli, W. B. 2005. The crossover of burnout and work engagement among working couples. Human Relations, 58(5): 661–689.

Baltes, B. B., Briggs, T. E., Huff, J. W., Wright, J. A., & Neuman, G. A. 1999. Flexible and compressed workweek schedules. A meta-analysis of their effects on work-related criteria. Journal of Applied Psychology, 84(4): 496–913.

Barnett, R. C. 2004. Women and work. Where are we, where did we come from, and where are we going? Journal of Social Issues, 60(4): 667-664.

Barnett, R. C., & Gareis, K. C. 2006. Role theory perspectives on work and family. In M. Pitt-Catsouphes, E. E. Kossek & S. A. Sweet (Eds.), The work and family handbook. Multi-disciplinary perspectives, methods, and approaches: 209–221. Mahwah, NJ: Lawrence Erlbaum Associates.

Barnett, R. C., & Hall, D. T. 2001. How to use reduced hours to win the war for talent. Organizational Dynamics, 29(3): 192–210.

Barnett, R., & Hyde, J. S. 2001. Women, men, work and family. An expansionist theory. American Psychologist, 56(10): 781–796.

Baron, R. M., & Kenny, D. A. 1986. The moderator-mediator variable distinction in social psychological research: Conceptual, strategic, and statistical considerations. Journal of Personality and Social Psychology, 51(6): 1173–1182.

Batt, R., & Valcour, M. P. 2003. Human resources practices as predictors of work-family outcomes and employee turnover. Industrial Relations, 42(2): 189–220.

Beatty, C. A. 1996. The stress of managerial and professional women: Is the price too high? Journal of Organizational Behavior, 17(3): 233–251.

Beauregard, T. A. 2006. Predicting interference between work and home. A comparison of dispositional and situational antecedents. Journal of Managerial Psychology, 21(3): 244–264.

Bedeian, A. G., Burke, B. G., & Moffett, R. G. 1988. Outcomes of work-family conflict among married male and female professionals. Journal of Management, 14(3): 475–491.

Berg, P., Kalleberg, A. L., & Appelbaum, E. 2003. Balancing work and family: The role of high-commitment environments. Industrial Relations, 42(2): 168–188.

Bianchi, S. M., Casper, L. M., & Berkowitz King, R. (Eds.) 2005. Work, family, health, and well-being. Mahwah, NJ: Lawrence Erlbaum Assoc.

Blair, S. L. 1996. Work roles, domestic roles and marital quality. Perceptions of fairness among dual-earner couples. Social Justice Research, 11(3): 313–335.

Blair-Loy, M. 2009. Work without end?: Scheduling flexibility and work-to-family conflict among stockbrokers. Work and Occupations, 36(4): 279–317.

Blair-Loy, M., & Wharton, A. S. 2004. Organizational commitment and constraints on work-family policy use: Corporate flexibility policies in a global firm. Sociological Perspectives, 47(3): 243–267.

Bliemel, F., Eggert, A., Fassott, G., & Henseler, J. (Eds.) 2005. Handbuch PLS-Pfadfmodellierung: Methode, Anwendung, Praxisbeispiele. Stuttgart: Schäffer-Poeschel.

Bloom, N., & van Reenen, J. 2006. Management practices, work-life balance, and productivity. A review of some recent evidence. Oxford Review of Economic Policy, 22(4): 457–482.

Blyton, P. (Ed.) 2006. Work-life integration. International perspectives on the balancing of multiple roles. Basingstoke: Palgrave Macmillan.

Blyton, P., & Dastmalchian, A. 2006. Work-life integration and the changing context of work. In P. Blyton (Ed.), Work-life integration. International perspectives on the balancing of multiple roles: 17–27. Basingstoke: Palgrave Macmillan.

BMFSFJ (Federal Ministry for Family Affairs) 2010a. European Company Survey on Reconciliation of Work and Family Life. Berlin.

BMFSFJ (Federal Ministry for Family Affairs) 2010b. Ausbildung, Studium und Elternschaft. Analysen und Empfehlungen zu einem Problemfeld im Schnittpunkt von Familien- und Bildungspolitik. Berlin.

Bolton, S. C., & Houlihan, M. (Eds.) 2007. Searching for the human in human resource management: Theory, practice and workplace contexts. Basingstoke: Palgrave Macmillan.

Bond, J. T., & Galinsky, E. 2006. Using survey research to address work-life issues. In M. Pitt-Catsouphes, E. E. Kossek & S. A. Sweet (Eds.), The work and family handbook. Multi-disciplinary perspectives, methods, and approaches: 411–433. Mahwah, NJ: Lawrence Erlbaum Associates; Lawrence Erlbaum.

Bonebright, C. A., Clay, D. L., & Ankenmann, R. D. 2000. The relationship of workaholism with work-life conflict, life satisfaction, and purpose in life. Journal of Counseling Psychology, 47(4): 469–477.

Bourne, K. A., Wilson, F., Lester, S. W., & Kickul, J. 2009. Embracing the whole individual: Advantages of a dual-centric perspective of work and life. Business Horizons, 52(4): 387–398.

Boyar, S. L., & Mosley, D. C. 2007. The relationship between core self-evaluations and work and family satisfaction. The mediating role of work-family conflict and facilitation. Journal of Vocational Behavior, 71(2): 265–281.

Boyar, S. L., Maertz Jr., C. P., & Pearson, A. W. 2005. The effects of work-family conflict and family–work conflict on nonattendance behaviors. Journal of Business Research, 58: 919–925.

Brett, J. M., & Stroh, L. K. 2003. Working 61 plus hours a week: Why do managers do it? Journal of Applied Psychology, 88(1): 67–78.

Bretz Jr., R. D., & Judge, T. A. 1994. Person-Organization Fit and the Theory of Work Adjustment: Implications for Satisfaction, Tenure, and Career Success. Journal of Vocational Behavior, 44(1): 32–54.

Brough, P., O'Driscoll, M. P., & Kalliath, T. J. 2005. The ability of 'family friendly' organizational resources to predict work-family conflict and job and family satisfaction. Stress and Health, 21(4): 223–234.

Bruck, C. S., & Allen, T. D. 2003. The relationship between big five personality traits, negative affectivity, type A behavior, and work-family conflict. Journal of Vocational Behavior, 63: 457–472.

Bruck, C. S., Allen, T. D., & Spector, P. E. 2002. The relation between work-family conflict and job satisfaction: A finer-grained analysis. Journal of Vocational Behavior, 60(3): 336–353.

Bruhn, M., & Stauss, B. (Eds.) 2003. Dienstleistungsnetzwerke: Dienstleistungsmanagement. Wiesbaden: Gabler.

Brummelhuis, L. L. ten, van der Lippe, T., Kluwer, E. S., & Flap, H. 2008. Positive and negative effects of family involvement on work-related burnout. Journal of Vocational Behavior, 73(3): 387–396.

Buck, M. L., Lee, M. D., MacDermid, S. M., & Smith, S. 2000. Reduced-load work and the experience of time among professionals and managers. Implications for personal and organizational life. In C. L. Cooper & D. M. Rousseau (Eds.), Time in organizational behavior: 13–35. Chichester: Wiley.

Bunting, M. 2004. Willing slaves. How the overwork culture is ruling our lives. London: HarperCollins.

Bürger, B. 2005. Aspekte der Führung und der strategischen Entwicklung von Professional Service Firms: Der Leverage von Ressourcen als Ausgangspunkt einer differenzierten Betrachtung. Wiesbaden: Gabler.

Burgess, J., Henderson, L., & Strachan, G. 2007. Work and family balance through equal employment opportunity programmes and agreement making in Australia. Employee Relations, 29(4): 415–430.

Burke, R. 2009. Working to live or living to work. Should individuals and organizations care? Journal of Business Ethics, 84(0): 167–172.

Burke, R. J. 2003. Work experiences, stress and health among managerial women. Research and practice. In M. J. Schabracq, J. A. M. Winnubst & C. L. Cooper (Eds.), The handbook of work and health psychology: 259–278 (2nd ed.). Chichester: John Wiley & Sons.

Burke, R. J. 2004. Work and personal life integration. International Journal of Stress Management, 11(4): 299–304.

Burke, R. J., & Cooper, C. L. (Eds.) 2008a. Building more effective organizations: HR management and performance in practice. Cambridge: Cambridge University Press.

Burke, R. J., & Cooper, C. L. (Eds.) 2008b. The long work hours culture. Causes, consequences and choices. Bingley: Emerald.

Burke, R. J., & Fiksenbaum, L. 2008. Work hours, work intensity, and work addiction: Costs and benefits. In R. J. Burke & C. L. Cooper (Eds.), The long work hours culture. Causes, consequences and choices: 3–36. Bingley: Emerald.

Burnett, S., Gatrell, C., Cooper, C. L., & Sparrow, P. 2011. Fatherhood and Flexible Working: A Contradiction in Terms? In S. Kaiser, M. Ringlstetter, D. R. Eikhof & M. Pina e Cunha (Eds.), Creating balance? International perspectives on the work-life integration of professionals: 151–171. Berlin: Springer.

Burwell, R., & Chen, C. P. 2008. Positive psychology for work-life balance: A new approach in treating workaholism. In R. J. Burke & C. L. Cooper

(Eds.), Building more effective organizations. HR management and performance in practice: 295–313. Cambridge: Cambridge University Press; Cambridge Univ. Press.

Bussell, J. 2008. Great expectations: Can maternity coaching affect the retention of professional women? International Journal of Evidence Based Coaching and Mentoring: 14–26.

Byron, K. 2005. A meta-analytic review of work-family conflict and its antecedents. Journal of Vocational Behavior, 67: 169–198.

Cameron, K. S., Dutton, J. E., & Quinn, R. E. 2003a. Foundations of Positive Organizational Scholarship. In K. S. Cameron, J. E. Dutton & R. E. Quinn (Eds.), Positive organizational scholarship. Foundations of a new discipline: 3–13. San Francisco, CA: Berrett-Koehler.

Cameron, K. S., Dutton, J. E., & Quinn, R. E. (Eds.) 2003b. Positive organizational scholarship. Foundations of a new discipline. San Francisco, CA: Berrett-Koehler.

Caplan, R. D. 1987. Person-environment fit theory and organizations: Commensurate dimensions, time perspectives, and mechanisms. Journal of Vocational Behavior, 31(3): 248–267.

Carless, S. A., & Wintle, J. 2007. Applicant attraction. The role of recruiter function, work-life balance policies and career salience. International Journal of Selection and Assessment, 15(4): 394–404.

Carlson, D. S. 1999. Personality and role variables as predictors of three forms of work–family conflict. Journal of Vocational Behavior, 55: 236–253.

Carlson, D. S., & Frone, M. R. 2003. Relation of behavioral and psychological involvement to a new four-factor conceptualization of work-family interference. Journal of Business and Psychology, 17(4): 515–535.

Carlson, D. S., & Kacmar, K. M. 2000. Work-family conflict in the organization. Do life role values make a difference? Journal of Management, 26(5): 1031–1054.

Carlson, D. S., & Perrewe, P. L. 1999. The role of social support in the stressor-strain relationship: An examination of work-family conflict. Journal of Management, 25(4): 513–540.

Carlson, D. S., Kacmar, K. M., Wayne, J. H., & Grzywacz, J. G. 2006. Measuring the positive side of the work-family interface. Development and validation of a work-family enrichment scale. Journal of Vocational Behavior, 68(1): 131–164.

Carlson, D. S., Kacmar, K. M., & Williams, L. J. 2000. Construction and initial validation of a multidimensional measure of work-family conflict. Journal of Vocational Behavior, 56(2): 249–276.

Carr, A. E., & Li-Ping Tang, T. 2005. Sabbaticals and employee motivation: Benefits, concerns, and implications. Journal of Education for Business, 80(3): 160–164.

Carr, J. C., Boyar, S. L., & Gregory, B. T. 2008. The moderating effect of work-family centrality on work-family conflict, organizational attitudes, and turnover behavior. Journal of Management, 34(2): 244–262.

Cascio, W. F., & Young, C. E. 2005. Work-family balance: Does the market reward firms that respect it. In D. F. Halpern (Ed.), From work-family balance to work-family interaction. Changing the metaphor: 49–63. Mahwah, NJ: Lawrence Erlbaum Assoc.

Casper, W. J., & Buffardi, L.C. 2004. Work-life benefits and job pursuit intentions. The role of anticipated organizational support. Journal of Vocational Behavior, 65: 391–410.

Casper, W. J., Eby, L., Bordeaux, C., Lockwood, A., & Lambert, D. 2007. A review of research methods in IO/OB work-family research. Journal of Applied Psychology, 92(1): 28–43.

Casper, W. J., Martin, J. A., Buffardi, L. C., & Erdwins, C. J. 2002. Work-family conflict, perceived organizational support, and organizational commitment among employed mothers. Journal of Occupational Health Psychology, 7(2): 99–108.

Casper, W. J., Weltman, D., & Kwesiga, E. 2007. Beyond family-friendly. The construct and measurement of singles-friendly work culture. Journal of Vocational Behavior, 70(3): 478–501.

Chambers, E. G., Foulton, M., Handfield-Jones, H., Hankin, S., & Michaels Ill, E. G. 1998. The war for talent. McKinsey Quarterly(3): 44–57.

Chang, S.-I. 2008. Work role stressors and turnover intentions: A study of IT personnel in South Korea. Zeitschrift für Personalforschung, 22(3): 272–290.

Chatman, J. A. 1989. Improving interactional organizational research: A model of person-organization fit. Academy of Management Review, 14: 333–349.

Chen, Z., Powell, G. N., & Greenhaus, J. H. 2009. Work-to-family conflict, positive spillover, and boundary management: A person-environment fit approach. Journal of Vocational Behavior, 74(1): 82–93.

Chesley, N. 2006. Families in a high-tech age: Technology usage patterns, work and family correlates, and gender. Journal of Family Issues, 27(5): 587–608.

Cheung, F. M., & Halpern, D. F. 2010. Women at the top: Powerful leaders define success as work and family in a culture of gender. American Psychologist, 65(3): 182–193.

Chin, W. W. 1998a. Issues and opinion on structural equation modeling. MIS Quarterly, 22(1): vii-xvi.

Chin, W. W. 1998b. The partial least squares approach to structural equation modeling. In G. A. Marcoulides (Ed.), Modern methods for business research: 295–336. Mahwah, N.J.: Lawrence Erlbaum Assoc.

Chin, W. W. 2010. How to write up and report PLS analyses. In V. Esposito Vinzi, W. W. Chin, J. Henseler & H. Wang (Eds.), Handbook of Partial Least Squares. Concepts, Methods and Applications: 655–690. Berlin, Heidelberg: Springer.

Christophersen, T., & Grape, C. 2007. Die Erfassung latenter Konstrukte mit Hilfe formativer und reflektiver Messmodelle. In S. Albers, D. Klapper, U. Konradt, A. Walter & J. Wolf (Eds.), Methodik der empirischen Forschung: 103–118 (2nd ed.). Wiesbaden: Gabler.

Cinamon, R. G., & Rich, Y. 2002a. Profiles of attribution of importance to life roles and their implications for the work-family conflict. Journal of counseling psychology, 49(2): 212–220.

Cinamon, R. G., & Rich, Y. 2002b. Gender differences in the importance of work and family roles: Implications for work-family conflict. Sex Roles, 47(11): 531–541.

Clark, S. C. 2000. Work-family border theory. A new theory of work-family balance. Human Relations, 53(6): 747–770.

Cohen, J. W. 1988. Statistical power analysis for the behavioral sciences (2nd ed.). Hillsdale, NJ: Erlbaum.

Collier, P. J., & Callero, P. J. 2005. Role theory and social cognition. Learning to think like a recycler. Self and Identity, 4: 45–58.

Connor, M., Hooks, K., & McGuire, T. 1999. Gaining legitimacy for flexible work arrangements and career paths. The business case for public accounting and professional service firms. In S. Parasuraman & J. H. Greenhaus (Eds.), Integrating work and family. Challenges and choices for a changing world: 154–166. Westport Conn. u.a.: Praeger.

Crompton, R., & Lyonette, C. 2006. Work-life 'balance' in Europe. Acta Sociologica, 49(4): 379–393.

Cronbach, L. J. 2004. My current thoughts on coefficient alpha and successor procedures. Educational and Psychological Measurement, 64(3): 391–418.

Da Silva, N., Hutcheson, J., & Wahl, G. D. 2010. Organizational Strategy and Employee Outcomes: A Person-Organization Fit Perspective. The Journal of Psychology: Interdisciplinary and Applied, 144(2): 145–161.

Day, A. L., & Chamberlain, T. C. 2006. Committing to your work, spouse and children. Implications for work-family conflict. Journal of Vocational Behavior, 68(1): 116–130.

Deelstra, J. T., Peeters, M. C. W., Schaufeli, W. B., Stroebe, W., van Doornen, L. P., & Zijlstra, F. R. H. 2003. Receiving instrumental support at work. When help is not welcome. Journal of Applied Psychology, 88(2): 324–331.

DeGraat, E. 2007. Kennzahlen und Kosten-Nutzen-Relationen zur Bewertung familienfreundlicher Maßnahmen in Unternehmen. In A. S. Esslinger & D. B. Schobert (Eds.), Erfolgreiche Umsetzung von Work-Life Balance in Organisationen. Strategien, Konzepte, Maßnahmen: 231–242. Wiesbaden: Deutscher Universitäts-Verlag.

Deller, C. 2004. Evaluation flexibler Arbeitszeitmodelle am Beispiel einer Unternehmensberatung: Die motivationalen Auswirkungen verschiedener Sabbatical- und Teilzeitprogramme aus Teilnehmersicht. München: Hampp.

Demerouti, E., Nachreiner, F., Bakker, A. B., & Schaufeli, W. B. 2001. The Job Demands-Resources model of burnout. Journal of Applied Psychology, 86(3): 499–512.

Dex, S., & Scheibl, F. 2001. Flexible and family-friendly working arrangements in UK-based SMEs: Business cases. British Journal of Industrial Relations, 39(3): 411.

Diener, E., Suh, E. M., Lucas, R. E. & Smith, H. L. (1999). Subjective wellbeing: Three decades of progress. Psychological Bulletin, 125(2): 276-302.

Dievernich, F. E. P., & Endrissat, N. 2010. Work-Life Balance im Demographie-Kontext. Neue Herausforderungen für die Rekrutierung und Bindung von High Potentials. In S. Kaiser & M. Ringlstetter (Eds.), Work-Life Balance: Erfolgversprechende Konzepte und Instrumente für Extremjobber: 83–99. Berlin, Heidelberg: Springer.

Dikkers, J., Geurts, S. A., den Dulk, L., Kompier, M., & Peper, B. 2004. Relations among work-home culture, the utilization of work-home arrangements, and work-home interference. International Journal of Stress Management, 11(4): 323–345.

Dikkers, J. S., Geurts, S. A., Dulk, L. d., Peper, B., Taris, T. W., & Kompier, M. A. 2007a. Dimensions of work-home culture and their relations with the use of work-home arrangements and work-home interaction. Work & Stress, 21(2): 155–172.

Dikkers, J., Geurts, S. A., Kompier, M. A. J., Taris, T. W., Houtman, I. L., & van den Heuvel, F. 2007b. Does workload cause work-home interference or is it the other way around? Stress & Health, 23(5): 303–314.

Dinger, M., Thatcher, J. B., & Stepina, L. P. 2010. A study of work-family conflict among IT Professionals: Job characteristics, individual values, and management practices. Journal of Organizational Computing & Electronic Commerce, 20(1): 91–121.

DiRenzo, M. S., Greenhaus, J. H., & Weer, C. H. 2011. Job level, demands, and resources as antecedents of work-family conflict. Journal of Vocational Behavior, 78(2): 305–314.

Drago, R., & Golden, R. 2006. The role of economics in work-family research. In M. Pitt-Catsouphes, E. E. Kossek & S. A. Sweet (Eds.), The work and family handbook. Multi-disciplinary perspectives, methods, and approaches: 267–282. Mahwah, NJ: Lawrence Erlbaum Associates.

Dulebohn, J. H., Molloy, J. C., Pichler, S. M., & Murray, B. 2009. Employee benefits: Literature review and emerging issues. Emerging trends in human resource management theory and research. Human Resource Management Review, 19(2): 86–103.

Duxbury, L. E., & Higgins, C. A. 1991. Gender differences in work-family conflict. Journal of Applied Psychology, 76(1): 60–74.

Duxbury, L. E., & Smart, R. 2011. The "myth of separate worlds": An exploration of how mobile technology has redefined work-life balance. In S. Kaiser, M. Ringlstetter, D. R. Eikhof & M. Pina e Cunha (Eds.), Creating balance? International perspectives on the work-life integration of professionals: 269–284. Berlin, Heidelberg: Springer.

Duxbury, L. E., Higgins, C. A., & Thomas, D. R. 1996. Work and family environments and the adoption of computer-supported supplemental work-at-home. Journal of Vocational Behavior, 49(1): 1–23.

Eberl, M. 2006. Formative und reflektive Konstrukte und die Wahl des Strukturgleichungsverfahren. Eine statistische Entscheidungshilfe. DBW, Die Betriebswirtschaft, 66(6): 651–668.

Eby, L., Casper, W. J., Lockwood, A., Bordeaux C., & Brinley, A. 2005. Work and family research in IO/OB. Content analysis and review of the literature (1980-2002). Journal of Vocational Behavior, 66(1): 124–197.

Eddleston, K. A., Veiga, J. F., & Powell, G. N. 2006. Explaining sex differences in managerial career satisfier preference: The role of gender self-schema. Journal of Applied Psychology, 91: 437–445.

Edmondson, A. C., & Detert, J. R. 2005. The role of speaking up in work-life balancing. In E. E. Kossek & S. J. Lambert (Eds.), Work and life integration. Organizational, cultural, and individual perspectives: 401–427. Mahwah, NJ: Lawrence Erlbaum Associates.

Edwards, J. R., & Harrison, R. V. 1993. Job demands and worker health: Three-dimensional reexamination of the relationship between person - environment fit and strain. Journal of Applied Psychology, 78(4): 628–648.

Edwards, J. R., & Rothbard, N. P. 1999. Work and family stress and well-being: An examination of person-environment fit in the work and family domains. Organizational Behavior and Human Decision Processes, 77(2): 85–129.

Edwards, J. R., & Rothbard, N. P. 2000. Mechanisms linking work and family. Clarifying the relationship between work and family constructs. Academy of Management Review, 25(1): 178–199.

Edwards, J. R., & Rothbard, N. P. 2005. Work and family stress and well-being. An integrative model of person-environment fit within and between the work and family domains. In E. E. Kossek & S. J. Lambert (Eds.), Work and life integration. Organizational, cultural, and individual perspectives: 211–242. Mahwah, NJ: Lawrence Erlbaum Associates.

Edwards, J. R., & Shipp, A. J. 2007. The relationship between person-environment fit and outcomes: An integrative theoretical framework. In C. Ostroff & C. L. Cooper (Eds.), Perspectives on organizational fit: 209–258. New York: Taylor & Francis Group.

Edwards, J. R., Scott, J. C., & Raju, N. S. (Eds.) 2003. The human resources program-evaluation handbook. Thousand Oaks, Calif.: Sage.

Eikhof, D. R., Warhurst, C., & Haunschild, A. 2007. Introduction: What work? What life? What balance? Critical reflections on the work-life balance debate. Employee Relations, 29(4): 325–333.

Esposito Vinzi, V., Chin, W. W., Henseler, J., & Wang, H. (Eds.) 2010. Handbook of Partial Least Squares. Concepts, Methods and Applications. Berlin, Heidelberg: Springer.

Esslinger, A. S., & Schobert, D. B. (Eds.) 2007. Erfolgreiche Umsetzung von Work-Life Balance in Organisationen: Strategien, Konzepte, Maßnahmen. Wiesbaden: Deutscher Universitäts-Verlag.

Ezzedeen, S. R., & Ritchey, K. G. 2009. Career and family strategies of executive women: Revisiting the quest to "Have it all". Organizational Dynamics, 38(4): 270–280.

Farnsworth-Riche, M. 2006. Demographic implications for work-family research. In M. Pitt-Catsouphes, E. E. Kossek & S. A. Sweet (Eds.), The work and family handbook. Multi-disciplinary perspectives, methods, and approaches: 125–140. Mahwah, NJ: Lawrence Erlbaum Associates.

Fassott, G., & Eggert, A. 2005. Zur Verwendung formativer und reflektiver Indikatoren in Strukturgleichungsmodellen. Bestandsaufnahme und Anwendungsempfehlungen. In F. Bliemel, A. Eggert, G. Fassott & J. Henseler (Eds.), Handbuch PLS-Pfadmodellierung. Methode, Anwendung, Praxisbeispiele: 31–47 (1st ed.). Stuttgart: Schäffer-Poeschel.

Fisher, G. G., Bulger, C. A., & Smith, C. S. 2009. Beyond work and family: A measure of work/nonwork interference and enhancement. Journal of Occupational Health Psychology, 14(4): 441–456.

Ford, M. T., Heinen, B. A., & Langkamer, K. L. 2007. Work and family satisfaction and conflict. A meta-analysis of cross-domain relations. Journal of Applied Psychology, 92(1): 57–80.

Fornell, C., & Bookstein, F. 1982. Two structural equation models: LISREL and PLS applied to consumer exit-voice theory. Journal of Marketing Research, 19(4): 440–452.

Fornell, C., & Cha, J. 1994. Partial least squares. In R. P. Bagozzi (Ed.), Advanced methods of marketing research: 52–78. Malden, Mass.: Blackwell.

Fornell, C., & Larcker, D. F. 1981. Evaluating structural equation models with unobservable variables and measurement error. Journal of Marketing Research, 18(1): 39–50.

Forsberg, L. 2009. Managing time and childcare in dual-earner families: Unforeseen consequences of household strategies. Acta Sociologica, 52(2): 162–175.

Frazier, P. A., Tix, A. P., & Barron, K. E. 2004. Testing moderator and mediator effects in counseling psychology research. Journal of counseling psychology, 51(1): 115–134.

Freidson, E. 1987. The future of the profession. Journal of Dental Education, 51(3): 140–144.

Frey, D., Oßwald, S., Peus, C., & Fischer, P. 2006. Positives Management, ethikorientierte Führung und Center of Excellence - Wie Unternehmenserfolg und Entfaltung der Mitarbeiter durch neue Unternehmens- und Führungskulturen gefördert werden können. In M. Ringlstetter, S. Kaiser & G. Müller-Seitz (Eds.), Positives Management. Zentrale Konzepte und Ideen des Positive Organizational Scholarship: 239–270. Wiesbaden: Gabler.

Friede, A., Kossek, E. E., Lee, M. D., & Macdermid, S. 2008. Human resource manager insights on creating and sustaining successful reduced-load work arrangements. Human Resource Management, 47(4): 707–727.

Friede, A., & Ryan, A. M. 2005. The importance of the indvidual. How self-evaluations influence the work-family interface. In E. E. Kossek & S. J. Lambert (Eds.), Work and life integration. Organizational, cultural, and individual perspectives: 193–209. Mahwah, NJ: Lawrence Erlbaum Associates.

Friedman, S. D. 2006. Learning to lead in all domains of life. American Behavioral Scientist, 49(9): 1270–1297.

Friedman, S. D. 2008a. Be a better leader, have a richer life. Harvard Business Review, 86(4): 112–118.

Friedman, S. D. 2008b. Total leadership. Be a better leader. Have a richer life. Boston, MA: Harvard Business Press.

Friedman, S. D., Christensen, P., & DeGroot, J. 1998. Work and life: The end of the zero-sum game. Harvard Business Review, 76(6): 119-129.

Friedman, S. D., & Greenhaus, J. H. 2000. Work and family - Allies or enemies? What happens when business professionals confront life choices. Oxford: Oxford Univ. Press.

Frone, M. R. 2003. Work-family balance. In J. C. Quick & L. E. Tetrick (Eds.), Handbook of occupational health psychology: 143–162. Washington, DC: American Psychological Assoc.

Frone, M. R., Russell, M., & Cooper, M. 1992. Antecedents and outcomes of work-family conflict: Testing a model of the work-family interface. Journal of Applied Psychology, 77(1): 65–78.

Frone, M. R., Russell, M., & Cooper, M. 1993. Relationship of work-family conflict, gender, and alcohol expectancies to alcohol use/abuse. Journal of Organizational Behavior, 14(6): 545–558.

Frone, M. R., Russell, M., & Cooper, M. 1997. Relation of work-family conflict to health outcomes. A four-year longitudinal study of employed parents. Journal of Occupational and Organizational Psychology, 70: 325–335.

Frone, M. R., Yardley, J. K., & Markel, K. S. 1997. Developing and testing an integrative model of the work-family interface. Journal of Vocational Behavior, 50(2): 145–167.

Frye, N. K., & Breaugh, J. A. 2004. Family-friendly policies, supervisor support, work-family conflict, family-work conflict, and satisfaction: A test of a conceptual model. Journal of Business and Psychology, 19(2): 197–220.

Fu, C. K., & Shaffer, M. A. 2001. The tug of work and family. Direct and indirect domain-specific determinants of work-family conflict. Personnel Review, 31(5): 502–522.

Fuchs Epstein, C., Seron, C., Oglensky, B., & Sauté, R. 1999. The part-time paradox. Time norms, professional lives, family, and gender. New York: Routledge.

Galinsky, E., & Matos, K. 2011. The future of work-life fit. Organizational Dynamics, 40(267-280).

Galinsky, E., & Stein, P. J. 1990. The impact of human resource policies on employees. Balancing work/family life. Journal of Family Issues, 11(4): 368–383.

Gardner, T. M. 2002. In the trenches at the talent wars. Competitive interaction for scarce human resources. Human Resource Management, 41(2): 225.

Gault, B., & Lovell, V. 2006. The costs and benefits of policies to advance work/life integration. American Behavioral Scientist, 49(9): 1152–1164.

German Federal Statistical Office 2006. Leben und Arbeiten in Deutschland, Sonderheft 2: Vereinbarkeit von Familie und Beruf – Ergebnisse des Mikrozensus 2005. Wiesbaden.

German Federal Statistical Office. 2010. Bevölkerungs- und Haushaltsentwicklung im Bund und in den Ländern. Ausgabe 2011. Wiesbaden

Gerstel, N., & Sarkisian, N. 2006. Sociological perspectives on families and work. The import of gender, class and race. In M. Pitt-Catsouphes, E. E. Kossek & S. A. Sweet (Eds.), The work and family handbook. Multidisciplinary perspectives, methods, and approaches: 237–266. Mahwah, NJ: Lawrence Erlbaum Associates.

Geurts, S. A., & Demerouti, E. 2003. Work/non-work interface: a review of theories and findings. In M. J. Schabracq, J. A. M. Winnubst & C. L. Cooper (Eds.), The handbook of work and health psychology: 279–312. Chichester: John Wiley & Sons.

Geurts, S. A., Beckers, D. G. J., Taris, T. W., Kompier, M. A., & Smulders, P. G. W. 2008. Worktime demands and work-family interference: Does worktime control buffer the adverse effects of high demands? Journal of Business Ethics, 84: 229–241.

Giardini, A., & Kabst, R. 2008. Effects of work-family human resource practices. A longitudinal perspective. International Journal of Human Resource Management, 19(11): 2079–2094.

Gibson, A. L., & Quick, J. C. 2008. Best practices for work stress and well-being. Solutions for human dilemmas in organizations. In R. J. Burke & C. L. Cooper (Eds.), Building more effective organizations. HR management and performance in practice: 84–109. Cambridge: Cambridge University Press; Cambridge Univ. Press.

Gmür, M., Kaiser, S., & Kampe, T. 2009. Leistungsorientiertes Personalmanagement in Wirtschaftskanzleien - Auswirkungen auf HRM Effektivität und Commitment. Die Unternehmung(4): 395–421.

Goff, S. J., Mount, M. K., & Jamison, R. L. 1990. Employer supported child care, work/family conflict, and absenteeism. A field study. Personnel Psychology, 43(4): 793–809.

Golden, T. 2007. Co-workers who telework and the impact on those in the office: Understanding the implications of virtual work for co-worker satisfaction and turnover intentions. Human Relations, 60(11): 1641–1667.

Golden, L. 2009. A brief history of long work time and the contemporary sources of overwork. Journal of Business Ethics, 84(0): 217–227.

Golden, T., Veiga, J., & Simsek, Z. 2006. Telecommuting's differential impact on work-family conflict. Is there no place like home? Journal of Applied Psychology, 91(6): 1340–1350.

Goode, W. J. 1960. A theory of role strain. American Sociological Review, 25: 483–496.

Götz, O., Liehr-Gobbers, K., & Krafft, M. 2010. Evaluation of structural equation models using the partial least squares (PLS) approach. In V. Esposito Vinzi, W. W. Chin, J. Henseler & H. Wang (Eds.), Handbook of Partial Least Squares. Concepts, Methods and Applications: 691–712. Berlin, Heidelberg: Springer.

Gouthier, M. H. J., Coenen, C., Schulze, H., & Wegmann, C. (Eds.) 2007. Service Excellence als Impulsgeber: Strategien, Management, Innovationen, Branchen. Wiesbaden: Gabler.

Grady, G., & McCarthy, A. M. 2008. Work-life integration: Experiences of mid-career professional working mothers. Journal of Managerial Psychology, 23(5): 599–622.

Grant-Vallone, E. J., & Donaldson, S. I. 2001. Consequences of work-family conflict on employee well-being over time. Work & Stress, 15(3): 214–226.

Greenhaus, J. H., & Beutell, N. J. 1985. Sources and conflict between work and family roles. Academy of Management Review, 10(1): 76–88.

Greenhaus, J. H., Collins, K., & Shaw, J. D. 2003. The relation between work-family balance and quality of life. Journal of Vocational Behavior, 63: 510–531.

Greenhaus, J. H., & Powell, G. N. 2006. When work and family are allies. A theory of work-family enrichment. Academy of Management Review, 31(1): 72–92.

Greenhaus, J. H., Collins, K. M., Singh, R., & Parasuraman, S. 1997. Work and family influences on departure from public accounting. Journal of Vocational Behavior, 50(2): 249–270.

Greenhaus, J. H., Parasuraman, S., & Collins, K. 2001. Career involvement and family involvement as moderators of relationships between work-family conflict and withdrawal from a profession. Journal of Occupational Health Psychology, 6(2): 91–100.

Greenwood, R., & Empson, L. 2003. The professional partnership: Relic or exemplary form of governance? Organization Studies, 24(6): 909–933.

Greenwood, R., Li, S. X., Prakash, R., & Deephouse, D. L. 2005. Reputation, diversification, and organizational explanations of performance in Professional Service Firms. Organization Science, 16(6): 661–673.

Greguras, G. J., & Diefendorff, J. M. 2009. Different fits satisfy different needs: Linking person-environment fit to employee commitment and performance using self-determination theory. Journal of Applied Psychology, 94(2): 465–477.

Greiner, L. E., & Ennsfellner, I. 2010. Management consultants as professionals, or are they? Organizational Dynamics, 39(72-83).

Gröpel, P., & Kuhl, J. 2006. Having time for life activities. Life balance and selfregulation. Zeitschrift für Gesundheitspsychologie, 14(2): 54–63.

Grzywacz, J. G., & Marks, N. F. 2000. Reconceptualizing the work-family interface. An ecological perspective on the correlates of positive and negative spillover between work and family. Journal of Occupational Health Psychology, 5(1): 111–126.

Guest, D. E. 2002. Perspectives on the study of work-life balance. Social Science Information, 41(2): 255–279.

Guillaume, C., & Pochic, S. 2009. What would you sacrifice? Access to top management and the work-life balance. Gender, Work & Organization, 16(1): 14–36.

Gutek, B. A., Searle, S., & Klepa, L. 1991. Rational versus gender role explanations for work-family conflict. Journal of Applied Psychology, 76(4): 560–568.

Haar, J. M. 2004. Work-family conflict and turnover intention: Exploring the moderation effects of perceived work-family support. New Zealand Journal of Psychology, 33(1): 35–39.

Hall, M., Smith, D., & Langfield-Smith, K. 2005. Accountants' commitment to their profession: Multiple dimensions of professional commitment and opportunities for future research. Behavioral Research in Accounting, 17: 89–109.

Halpern, D. F. 2005a. How time-flexible work policies can reduce stress, improve health, and save money. Stress and Health: Journal of the International Society for the Investigation of Stress, 21(3): 157–168.

Halpern, D. F. (Ed.) 2005b. From work-family balance to work-family interaction: Changing the metaphor. Mahwah, NJ: Lawrence Erlbaum Assoc.

Halpern, D. F., & Murphy, S. E. 2005. From balance to interaction: why the metaphor is important. In D. F. Halpern (Ed.), From work-family balance to work-family interaction. Changing the metaphor: 3–9. Mahwah, NJ: Lawrence Erlbaum Assoc.

Hardy, S. T., & Adnett, N. 2002. The parental leave directive. Towards a 'family-friendly' social Europe? European Journal of Industrial Relations, 8(2): 157.

Harrington, B., & James, J. B. 2006. The standards of excellence in work-life integration. From changing policies to changing organizations. In M. Pitt-Catsouphes, E. E. Kossek & S. A. Sweet (Eds.), The work and family handbook. Multi-disciplinary perspectives, methods, and approaches: 665–683. Mahwah, NJ: Lawrence Erlbaum Assoc.

Harrington, B., & Ladge, J. J. 2009. Work-life integration: Present dynamics and future directions for organizations. Organizational Dynamics, 38(2): 148–157.

Hayman, J. R. 2009. Flexible work arrangements: Exploring the linkages between perceived usability of flexible work schedules and work/life balance. Community, Work & Family, 12(3): 327–338.

Henseler, J., & Fassott, G. 2010. Testing moderating effects in PLS path models: An illustration of available procedures. In V. Esposito Vinzi, W. W. Chin, J. Henseler & H. Wang (Eds.), Handbook of Partial Least Squares. Concepts, Methods and Applications: 713–736. Berlin, Heidelberg: Springer.

Henseler, J., Ringle, C. M., & Sinkovics, R. R. 2009. The use of partial least squares path modeling in international marketing. Advances in International Marketing, 20: 277-319.

Hewlett, S. A., & Luce, C. B. 2005. Off-ramps and on-ramps: Keeping talented women on the road to success. Harvard Business Review, 83(3): 43–54.

Hewlett, S. A., & Luce, C. B. 2006. Extreme jobs. The dangerous allure of the 70-hour workweek. Harvard Business Review: 49–59.

Higgins, C., & Duxbury, L. 2005. Saying "No" in a culture of hours, money and non-support. Ivey Business Journal, 69(6): 1–5.

Higgins, C. A., & Duxbury, L. E. 1992. Work-family conflict: A comparison of dual-career and traditional-career men. Journal of Organizational Behavior, 13(4): 389–411.

Hill, E. J., & Weiner, S. P. 2003. Work/life balance policies and programs. In J. E. Edwards, J. C. Scott & N. S. Raju (Eds.), The human resources program-evaluation handbook: 447–468. Thousand Oaks, Calif.: SAGE.

Hill, E. J., Allen, S., Jacob, J., Bair, A. F., Bikhazi, S. L., van Langeveld, A., Martinengo, G., Parker, T. T., & Walker, E. 2007. Work-family facilitation. Expanding theoretical understanding through qualitative exploration. Advances in Developing Human Resources, 9(4): 507–526.

Hill, E. J., Ferris, M., & Märtinson, V. 2003. Does it matter where you work? A comparison of how three work venues (traditional office, virtual office, and home office) influence aspects of work and personal/family life. Journal of Vocational Behavior, 63: 220–241.

Hill, E. J., Hawkins, A. J., Ferris, M. S., & Weitzman, M. 2001. Finding an extra day a week: The positive influence of perceived job flexibility on work and family life balance. Family Relations, 50(1): 49–54.

Hill, E. J., Märtinson, V., & Ferris, M. 2004. New-concept part-time employment: A work-family adaptive strategy for women professionals with small children. Family Relations, 53: 282–292.

Hill, E. J., Mead, N. T., Dean, L. R., Hafen, D. M., Gadd, R., Palmer, A. A., & Ferris, M. S. 2006. Researching the 60-hour dual-earner workweek. An alternative to the 'opt-out revolution'. American Behavioral Scientist, 49(9): 1184–1203.

Hobfoll, S. E. 1989. Conservation of resources: A new attempt at conceptualizing stress. American Psychologist, 44(3): 513–524.

Hobfoll, S. E. 2001. Conservation of resources: A rejoinder to the commentaries. Applied Psychology: An International Review, 50(3): 419–421.

Hochschild, A. R. 2000. The time bind: When work becomes home and home becomes work. New York: Holt.

Höher, F., & Steenbuck, G. 2006. Personenbezogene Beratung und regionale Strukturpolitik. Ein integratives Beratungskonzept der Work-Life-Balance. Gesprächspsychotherapie und personenzentrierte Beratung, 2: 94–99.

Holt, H., & Thaulow, I. 1996. Formal and informal flexibility in the workplace. In S. Lewis & J. Lewis (Eds.), The work-family challenge. Rethinking employment: 79–92. London: Sage.

Honeycutt, T. L., & Rosen, B. 1997. Family friendly human resource policies, salary levels, and salient identity as predictors of organizational attraction. Journal of Vocational Behavior, 50(2): 271–290.

Hooks, K. L., & Higgs, J. L. 2002. Workplace environment in a professional services firm. Behavioral Research in Accounting, 14(1): 105–127.

Hoyt, W. T., Leierer, S., & Millington, M. J. 2006. Analysis and interpretation of findings using multiple regression techniques. RCB, 49(4): 223–233.

Hulland, J. 1999. Use of partial least squares (PLS) in strategic management research: a review of four recent studies. Strategic Management Journal, 20(2): 195–204.

Hyland, M. A., & Jackson, S. E. 2006. A multiple stakeholder perspective. Implications for measuring work-family outcomes. In M. Pitt-Catsouphes, E. E. Kossek & S. A. Sweet (Eds.), The work and family handbook. Multidisciplinary perspectives, methods, and approaches: 527–549. Mahwah, NJ: Lawrence Erlbaum Associates.

Hyman, J., & Baldry, C. 2011. The pressures of commitment: Taking software home. In S. Kaiser, M. Ringlstetter, D. R. Eikhof & M. Pina e Cunha (Eds.), Creating balance? International perspectives on the work-life integration of professionals: 253–268. Berlin: Springer.

Ilies, R., Schwind W. K., & Wagner, D. T. 2009. The spillover of daily job satisfaction onto employee's family lives. The facilitating role of work-family integration. Academy of Management Journal, 52(1): 87–102.

IPOB (Ed.) 2010. The future of knowledge-intensive service work. Theory and practice of managing human and organizational resources (1st ed.). Marburg: Metropolis.

Izzo, J., & Withers, P. 2001. Balance and synergy: The greatest benefit? How companies are responding to changing employee values. Compensation & Benefits Management, 17(3): 23.

Jackson, M. 2005. The limits of connectivity: Technology and 21st-century life. In D. F. Halpern (Ed.), From work-family balance to work-family interaction. Changing the metaphor: 135–150. Mahwah, NJ: Lawrence Erlbaum Assoc.

Jacobshagen, N., Amstad, F. T., Semmer, N. K., & Kuster, M. 2005. Work-Family Balance im Topmanagement. Zeitschrift für Arbeits- und Organisationspsychologie A&O, 49(4): 208–219.

Jacobsen, H., & Schallock, B. (Eds.) 2010. Innovationsstrategien jenseits traditionellen Managements. Stuttgart: Fraunhofer Verlag.

Jahn, S. 2007. Strukturgleichungsmodellierung mit LISREL, AMOS und SmartPLS. Eine Einführung. Discussion Paper (WWDP 86/07), Fakultät für Wirtschaftswissenschaften, Technische Universität Chemnitz.

Janssen, J., & Laatz, W. 2007. Statistische Datenanalyse mit SPSS für Windows. Eine anwendungsorientierte Einführung in das Basissystem und das Modul Exakte Tests (6th ed.). Berlin, Heidelberg: Springer.

Jarvis, C. B., Mackenzie, S. B., Podsakoff, P. M., Mick, D. G., & Bearden, W. O. 2003. A Critical Review of Construct Indicators and Measurement Model Misspecification in Marketing and Consumer Research. Journal of Consumer Research, 30(2): 199–218.

Johnson, E. M., Lowe, D. J., & Reckers, P. M. J. 2008. Alternative work arrangements and perceived career success: Current evidence from the big four firms in the US. Accounting, Organizations & Society, 33(1): 48–72.

Jones, F., Burke, R. J., & Westman, M. (Eds.) 2006. Work-life balance: A psychological perspective. Hove: Psychology Press.

Jöreskog, K. G. W. H. (Ed.) 1982. Systems under indirect observation. Causality, structure, prediction. Amsterdam, New York: North-Holland Publ.

Joudrey, A. D., & Wallace, J. E. 2009. Leisure as a coping resource: A test of the job demand-control-support model. Human Relations, 62(2): 195–217.

Judge, T. A., & Bretz, R. D. 1992. The effects of work values on job choice decision. Journal of Applied Psychology, 77: 261–271.

Judge, T. A., Boudreau, J. W., & Bretz, R. D., Jr. 1994. Job and life attitudes of male executives. Journal of Applied Psychology, 79(5): 767–782.

Judge, T. A., Higgins, C. A., Thoresen, C. J., & Barrick, M. R. 1999. The big five personality traits, general mental ability, and career success across the life span. Personnel Psychology, 52(3): 621–652.

Judiesch, M. K., & Lyness, K. S. 1999. Left behind? The impact of leaves of absence on managers' career success. Academy of Management Journal, 42(6): 641–651.

Kahn, R. L., Wolfe D. M., Quinn R. P., Snoek J. D., & Rosenthal R. A. 1964. Organizational stress. Studies in role conflict and ambiguity. New York: John Wiley & Sons.

Kaiser, S. & Ringlstetter, M. 2006. Individuell-subjektives Glücksempfinden als unternehmerischer Erfolgsfaktor. In M. Ringlstetter, S. Kaiser & G. Müller-Seitz (Eds.), Positives Management. Zentrale Konzepte und Ideen des Positive Organizational Scholarship: 3-10 Wiesbaden: Gabler.

Kaiser, S., & Ringlstetter, M. (Eds.) 2010. Work-Life Balance: Erfolgversprechende Konzepte und Instrumente für Extremjobber. Berlin, Heidelberg: Springer.

Kaiser, S., & Ringlstetter, M. 2011. Strategic Management of Professional Service Firms. Theory and Practice. Berlin, Heidelberg: Springer.

Kaiser, S., Reindl, C. Stolz, M. & Ringlstetter, J. 2011. Managing work-life balance in consulting organizations: Issues and results. In IPOB (Ed.), The future of knowledge-intensive service work. Theory and practice of managing human and organizational resources: 243–294. Marburg: Metropolis.

Kaiser, S., Ringlstetter, M., Reindl, C. U., & Stolz, M. 2010. Die Wirkung von Work-Life Balance Initiativen auf das Mitarbeitercommitment: Eine empirische Untersuchung in der Unternehmensberatungsbranche. Zeitschrift für Personalforschung, 24(3): 231–265.

Kaiser, S., Ringlstetter, M., Eikhof, D. R., & Pina e Cunha, M. (Eds.) 2011. Creating balance? International perspectives on the work-life integration of professionals. Berlin: Springer.

Kandel, D. B., Davies, M., & Raveis, V. H. 1985. The stressfulness of daily social roles for women: Marital, occupational and household roles. Journal of Health and Social Behavior, 26: 64–78.

Kasper, H., Meyer, M., & Schmidt, A. 2005. Managers dealing with work-family-conflict. An explorative analysis. Journal of Managerial Psychology, 20(5): 440–461.

Kastner, M. 2004a. Verschiedene Zugänge zur Work Life Balance. In M. Kastner (Ed.), Die Zukunft der Work Life Balance. Wie lassen sich Beruf und Familie, Arbeit und Freizeit miteinander vereinbaren?: 67–105. Kröning: Asanger.

Kastner, M. (Ed.) 2004b. Die Zukunft der Work Life Balance: Wie lassen sich Beruf und Familie, Arbeit und Freizeit miteinander vereinbaren? Kröning: Asanger.

Kelloway, E. K., Gottlieb, B. H., & Barham, L. 1999. The source, nature, and direction of work and family conflict: A longitudinal investigation. Journal of Occupational Health Psychology, 4(4): 337–346.

Kelly, E. L. 1999. Theorizing corporate family policies: How advocates built "the business case" for "family-friendly" programs. Research in the Sociology of Work, 7: 169–202.

Kelly, E. L., Kossek, E. E., Hammer, L. B., Durham, M., Bray, J., Chermack, K., Murphy, L. A., & Kaskubar, D. 2008. Chapter 7: Getting there from here: Research on the effects of work-family initiatives on work-family conflict and business outcomes. Academy of Management Annals, 2(1): 305–349.

Kettler, B. von 2010. (R)evolution der Arbeit – Warum Work-Life Balance zum Megathema wird und sich trotzdem verändert. Wie konkrete Handlungsempfehlungen und gezielte Projekte aussehen. In S. Kaiser & M. Ringlstetter (Eds.), Work-Life Balance: Erfolgverprechende Konzepte und Instrumente für Extremjobber: 139–153. Berlin, Heidelberg: Springer.

Kinnunen, U., & Mauno, S. 1998. Antecedents and outcomes of work-family conflict among employed women and men in Finland. Human Relations, 51(2): 157–177.

Kinnunen, U., Feldt, T., Geurts, S., & Pulkkinen, L. 2006. Types of work-family interface: Well-being correlates of negative and positive spillover between work and family. Scandinavian Journal of Psychology, 47: 149–162.

Kinnunen, U., Feldt, T., Mauno, S., & Rantanen, J. 2010. Interface between work and family: A longitudinal individual and crossover perspective. Journal of Occupational & Organizational Psychology, 83(1): 119–137.

Kinnunen, U., Mauno, S., Geurts, S. A. E., & Dikkers, J. 2005. Work-family culture in organizations: theoretical and empirical approaches. In S. A. Y. Poelmans (Ed.), Work and family. An international research perspective: 87–120 (1st ed.). Mahwah, NJ: Lawrence Erlbaum Assoc.

Kirchmeyer, C. 1993. Nonwork-to-work spillover: A more balanced view of the experiences and coping of professional women and men. Sex Roles, 28: 531–552.

Klein, H. J., Becker, T. E., & Meyer, J. P. (Eds.) 2009. Commitment in organizations. Accumulated wisdom and new directions. New York, NY: Routledge.

Kofodimos, J. R. 1990. Why executives lose their balance. Organizational Dynamics, 19(1): 58–73.

Konrad, A. M., & Mangel, R. 2000. The impact of work-life programs on firm productivity. Strategic Management Journal, 21(12): 1225–1237.

Kor, Y. Y., & Leblebici, H. 2005. How Do Interdependencies Among Human-Capital Deployment, Development, and Diversification Strategies Affect Firms' Financial Performance? Strategic Management Journal, 26(10): 967–985.

Kossek, E. E., & Friede, A. 2006. The business case: Managerial perspectives on work and the family. In M. Pitt-Catsouphes, E. E. Kossek & S. A. Sweet (Eds.), The work and family handbook. Multi-disciplinary perspectives, methods, and approaches: 611–626. Mahwah, NJ: Lawrence Erlbaum Assoc.

Kossek, E. E., & Hammer, L. B. 2008. Supervisor work/life training gets results. Harvard Business Review, November 2008: 36.

Kossek, E. E., & Lambert, S. J. (Eds.) 2005. Work and life integration. Organizational, cultural, and individual perspectives. Mahwah, NJ: Lawrence Erlbaum Assoc.

Kossek, E. E., & Ozeki, C. 1998. Work-family conflict, policies, and the job-life satisfaction relationship. A review and directions for organizational behavior-human resources research. Journal of Applied Psychology, 83(2): 139–149.

Kossek, E. E., & Ozeki, C. 1999. Bridging the work-family policy and productivity gap. A literature review. Community, Work & Family, 2(1): 7–32.

Kossek, E. E., Barber, A. E., & Winters, D. 1999. Using flexible schedules in the managerial world: The power of peers. Human Resource Management, 38(1): 33–46.

Kossek, E. E., Lautsch, B. A., & Eaton, S. C. 2006. Telecommuting, control, and boundary management: Correlates of policy use and practice, job control, and work-family effectiveness. Journal of Vocational Behavior, 68(2): 347–367.

Kothes, P. J. 2010. Balance liegt in der Natur des Menschseins. Warum Authentizität eine Work-Life Balance überflüssig macht. In S. Kaiser & M. Ringlstetter (Eds.), Work-Life Balance: Erfolgversprechende Konzepte und Instrumente für Extremjobber: 243–255. Berlin, Heidelberg: Springer.

Kreiner, G. E. 2006. Consequences of work-home segmentation or integration: A person-environment fit perspective. Journal of Organizational Behavior, 27(4): 485–507.

Kristof, A. L. 1996. Person-organization fit: An integrative review of its conceptualizations, measurement and implications. Personnel Psychology, 49(1): 1–49.

Kristof-Brown, A. L., & Jansen, K. J. 2007. Issues of person-organization fit. In C. Ostroff & C. L. Cooper (Eds.), Perspectives on organizational fit: 123–153. New York, NY: Taylor & Francis Group.

Kumra, S., & Vinnicombe, S. 2008. A study of the promotion to partner process in a professional services firm: How women are disadvantaged. British Journal of Management, 19: 65–74.

Ladge, J. J., Greenberg, D., & Clair, J. 2011. What to expect when she's expecting: Work-family and identity integration challenges and opportunities of "soon-to-be" working professional mothers. In S. Kaiser, M. Ringlstetter, D. R. Eikhof & M. Pina e Cunha (Eds.), Creating balance? International perspectives on the work-life integration of professionals: 143–155. Berlin: Springer.

Lambert, S. J. 2000. Added benefits: The link between work-life benefits and organizational citizenship behavior. Academy of Management Journal, 43(5): 801–815.

Lambert, S. J., & Haley-Lock, A. 2004. The organizational stratification of opportunities for work-life balance: Addressing issues of equality and social justice in the workplace. Community, Work & Family, 7(2): 179–195.

Lambert, A. D., Marler, J. H., & Gueutal, H. G. 2008. Individual differences: Factors affecting employee utilization of flexible work arrangements. Journal of Vocational Behavior, 73(1): 107–117.

Lapierre, L. M., & Allen, T. D. 2006. Work-supportive family, family-supportive supervision, use of organizational benefits, and problem-focused coping: Implications for work-family conflict and employee well-being. Journal of Occupational Health Psychology, 11(2): 169–181.

Lapierre, L. M., Spector, P. E., Allen, T. D., Poelmans, S., Cooper, C. L., O'Driscoll, M. P., Sanchez, J. I., Brough, P., & Kinnunen, U. 2008. Family-supportive organization perceptions, multiple dimensions of work-family conflict, and employee satisfaction: A test of model across five samples. Journal of Vocational Behavior, 73(1): 92–106.

Lee, M. D., MacDermid, S. M., & Buck, M. L. 2000. Organizational paradigms of reduced-load work: Accommodation, elaboration, transformation. Academy of Management Journal, 43(6): 1221–1226.

Lee, M. D., MacDermid, S. M., Williams, M. L., Buck, M. L., & Leiba-O'Sullivan, S. 2002. Contextual factors in the success of reduced-load work arrangements among managers and professionals. Human Resource Management, 41(2): 209–223.

Lewis, S. 1997. 'Family friendly' employment policies: A route to changing organizational culture or playing about at the margins? Gender, Work & Organization, 4(1): 13–23.

Lewis, S. 2003. The integration of paid work and the rest of life. Is post-industrial work the new leisure? Leisure Studies, 22: 343–355.

Lewis, S., & Cooper, C. L. 2005. Work-life integration: Case studies of organizational change. Chichester: Wiley.

Lewis, S., & Taylor, K. 1996. Evaluating the impact of family-friendly employer policies: A case study. In S. Lewis & J. Lewis (Eds.), The work-family challenge. Rethinking employment: 112–127. London: Sage.

Lewis, S., Gambles, R., & Rapoport, R. 2007. The constraints of a 'work-life balance' approach: An international perspective. International Journal of Human Resource Management, 18(3): 360–373.

Lewis, S., Rapoport, R., & Gambles, R. 2003. Reflections on the integration of paid work and the rest of life. Journal of Managerial Psychology, 18(8): 824–841.

Lirio, P., Lee, M. D., Williams, M. L., Haugen, L. K., & Kossek, E. E. 2008. The inclusion challenge with reduced-load professionals. The role of the manager. Human Resource Management, 47(3): 443–461.

Litrico, J.-B., & Lee, M. D. 2008. Balancing exploration and exploitation in alternative work arrangements. A multiple case study in the professional and management services industry. Journal of Organizational Behavior, 29(8): 995–1020.

Lobel, S. A. 1992. A value-laden approach to integrating work and family life. Human Resource Management, 31(3): 249–265.

Lorsch, J. W. & Tierney, T. 2002. Aligning the stars: How to succeed when professionals drive results. Boston, Mass.: Harvard Business School Press.

Loughlin, C. & Barling, J. 2001. Young workers' work values, attitudes and behaviors. Journal of Occupational and Organizational Psychology, 74: 543–558.

Løwendahl, B. R. 2005. Strategic management of professional service firms (3rd ed.). Copenhagen: CBS Press.

Lu, J.-F., Siu, O.-L., Spector, P. E., & Shi, K. 2009. Antecedents and outcomes of a fourfold taxonomy of work-family balance in Chinese employed parents. Journal of Occupational Health Psychology, 14(2): 182–192.

Lu, L., Kao, S.-F., Cooper, C., Allen, T., Lapierre, L., O'Driscoll, M., Poelmans, S., Sanchez, J., & Spector, P. E. 2009. Work resources, work-to-family conflict, and its consequences: A Taiwanese-British cross-cultural comparison. International Journal of Stress Management, 16(1): 25–44.

Lyness, K. S., & Judiesch, M. K. 2008. Can a manager have a life and a career? International and multisource perspectives on work-life balance and career advancement potential. Journal of Applied Psychology, 93(4): 789–805.

Lyness, K. S., & Thompson, D. E. 1997. Above the glass ceiling? A comparison of matched samples of female and male executives. Journal of Applied Psychology, 82(3): 359–375.

Madsen, S. R. 2003. The effects of home-based teleworking on work-family conflict. Human Resource Development Quarterly, 14(1): 35–58.

Maister, D. (1993). Managing the Professional Service Firm. New York: Free Press.

Major, D. A., & Germano, L. M. 2006. The changing nature of work and its impact on the work-home interface. In F. Jones, R. J. Burke & M. Westman (Eds.), Work-life balance: A psychological perspective: 13–38. Hove: Psychology Press.

Major, D. A., Fletcher, T. D., Davis, D. D., & Germano, L. M. 2008. The influence of work-family culture and workplace relationships on work interference with family: A multilevel model. Journal of Organizational Behavior, 29(7): 881–897.

Major, V. S., Klein, K. J., & Ehrhart, M. G. 2002. Work time, work interference with family, and psychological distress. Journal of Applied Psychology, 87(3): 427–436.

Marks, S. R. 2006. Understanding diversity of families in the 21st century and its impact on the work-family area of study. In M. Pitt-Catsouphes, E. E. Kossek & S. A. Sweet (Eds.), The work and family handbook. Multidisciplinary perspectives, methods, and approaches: 41–65. Mahwah, NJ: Lawrence Erlbaum Assoc.

Marks, S. R., & MacDermid, S. M. 1996. Multiple roles and the self. A theory of role balance. Journal of Marriage and the Family, 58(2): 417–432.

Matthews, R. A., Bulger, C. A., & Barnes-Farrell, J. L. 2009. Work social supports, role stressors, and work-family conflict: The moderating effect of age. Journal of Vocational Behavior, 76(1): 78–90.

Mauno, S., & Kinnunen, U. 1999. The effects of job stressors on marital satisfaction in Finnish dual-earner couples. Journal of Organizational Behavior, 20(6): 879–895.

Mauno, S., Kinnunen, U., & Ruokolainen, M. 2006. Exploring work- and organization-based resources as moderators between work-family conflict, well-being, and job attitudes. Work & Stress, 20(3): 210–233.

May, T. Y.-M., Korczynski, M., & Frenkel, S. J. 2002. Organizational and occupational commitment: Knowledge workers in large corporations. Journal of Management Studies, 39(6): 775–801.

Mayerhofer, H., Müller, B., & Schmidt, A. 2008. Working everytime and everywhere. Herausforderungen für Führungskräfte. In J. Mühlbacher & H. Kasper (Eds.), Management Development. Wandel der Anforderungen an Führungskräfte. Festschrift für Helmut Kasper zum 60. Geburtstag: 103–121. Wien: Linde.

Mayerhofer, H., Müller, B., & Schmidt, A. 2011. Working in polycontextual environments: An empirical analysis of flexpatriates' lifestyles. In S. Kaiser, M. Ringlstetter, D. R. Eikhof & M. Pina e Cunha (Eds.), Creating balance? International perspectives on the work-life integration of professionals: 285–302. Berlin: Springer.

Mayring, P. 2000. Qualitative Inhaltsanalyse. Grundlagen und Techniken. Weinheim: Beltz.

McCrae, R. R., & Costa Jr., P. T. 1997. Personality trait structure as a human universal. American Psychologist, 52(5): 509–516.

McDonald, K. S., & Hite, L. M. 2008. The next generation of career success: Implications for HRD. Advances in Developing Human Resources, 10(1): 86–103.

McElwain, A. K., Korabik, K., & Rosin, H. M. 2005. An examination of gender differences in work-family conflict. Canadian Journal of Behavioral Science/Revue canadienne des sciences du comportement, 37(4): 283–298.

McKenna, S., & Richardson, J. 2007. The increasing complexity of the internationally mobile professional: Issues for research and practice. Cross Cultural Management, 14(4): 307–320.

Mescher, S., Benschop, Y., & Doorewaard, H. 2010. Representations of work-life balance support. Human Relations, 63(1): 21–39.

Mesmer-Magnus, J. R., & Viswesvaran, C. 2007. How family-friendly work environments affect work/family conflict: A meta-analytic examination. Journal of Labor Research, 27(4): 555–574.

Mesmer-Magnus, J., & Viswesvaran, C. 2009. The role of the coworker in reducing work-family conflict: A review and directions for future research. Pratiques Psychologiques, 15(2): 213–224.

Messersmith, J. 2007. Managing work-life conflict among information technology workers. Human Resource Management, 46(3): 429–451.

Meyer, J. P., Becker, T. E., & van Dick, R. 2006. Social identities and commitments at work: Toward an integrative model. Journal of Organizational Behavior, 27(5): 665–683.

Meyer, J. P., Stanley, D. J., Herscovitch, L., & Topolnytsky, L. 2002. Affective, continuance, and normative commitment to the organization: A meta-analysis of antecedents, correlates, and consequences. Journal of Vocational Behavior, 61(1): 20–52.

Michaels, E., Handfield-Jones, H., & Axelrod, B. 2009. The war for talent. Boston, Mass.: Harvard Business School Press.

Michalk, S., & Nieder, P. 2007. Erfolgsfaktor Work-Life-Balance. Weinheim: Wiley.

Michel, J. S., & Clark, M. A. 2011. Personality and work-life integration. In S. Kaiser, M. Ringlstetter, D. R. Eikhof & M. Pina e Cunha (Eds.), Creating balance? International perspectives on the work-life integration of professionals: 81–99. Berlin: Springer.

Michel, J. S., Kotrba, L. M., Mitchelson, J. K., Clark, M. A., & Baltes, B. B. 2010. Antecedents of work-family conflict: A meta-analytic review. Journal of Organizational Behavior.

Milliken, F. J., & Dunn-Jensen, L. M. 2005. The changing time demands of managerial and professional work. Implications for managing the work-life boundary. In E. E. Kossek & S. J. Lambert (Eds.), Work and life integration. Organizational, cultural, and individual perspectives: 43–59. Mahwah, NJ: Lawrence Erlbaum Assoc.

Mohe, M., Gruber, H., Kaiser, S., Mulder, R., Birner, K., Dorniok, D., Reindl, C., Rupprecht, M., Stolz, M., Sieweke, J., & Stollfuss, M. 2010. Rhetorik und Realität in der Unternehmensberatung. In H. Jacobsen & B. Schallock (Eds.), Innovationsstrategien jenseits traditionellen Managements: 307–317. Stuttgart: Fraunhofer.

Mohe, M., Dorniok, D., & Kaiser, S. 2010. Auswirkungen von betrieblichen Work-Life Balance Maßnahmen auf Unternehmen: Stand der empirischen Forschung. Zeitschrift für Management, 5(2): 105–139.

Moldaschl, M., & Voß, G. (Eds.) 2002. Subjektivierung von Arbeit. München: Hampp.

Morris, M. L., & Madsen, S. R. 2007. Advancing work-life integration in individuals, organizations, and communities. Advances in Developing Human Resources, 9(4): 439–454.

Morris, M. L., Storberg-Walker, J., & McMillan, H. S. 2009. Developing an OD-intervention metric system with the use of applied theory-building methodology: A work/life-intervention example. Human Resource Development Quarterly, 20(4): 419–449.

Munck, B. 2001. Changing a Culture of Face Time. Harvard Business Review, 79(10): 125–131.

Na Ayudhya, U. C., & Lewis, S. 2011. From 'Balancers' to 'Integrators'? Young professionals' talk about 'Work' and the rest of 'Life' in the UK. In S. Kaiser, M. Ringlstetter, D. R. Eikhof & M. Pina e Cunha (Eds.), Creating balance? International perspectives on the work-life integration of professionals: 47–63. Berlin: Springer.

Neault, R. A., & Pickerell, D. A. 2005. Dual-career couples: The juggling act. Canadian Journal of Counselling, 39(3): 187–198.

Nelson, D. L., Quick, J. C., Hitt, M. A., & Moesel, D. 1990. Politics, lack of career progress, and work/home conflict: Stress and strain for working women. Sex Roles, 23(3-4): 169–185.

Netemeyer, R. G., Boles, J. S., & McMurrian, R. 1996. Development and validation of work-family conflict and family-work conflict scales. Journal of Applied Psychology, 81(4): 400–410.

Nielson, T. R., Carlson, D. S., & Lankau, M. J. 2001. The supportive mentor as a means of reducing work-family conflict. Journal of Vocational Behavior, 59(3): 364–381.

Nikandrou, I., Panayotopoulou, L., & Apospori, E. 2008. The impact of individual and organizational characteristics on work-family conflict and career outcomes. Journal of Managerial Psychology, 23(5): 576–598.

Nippert-Eng, C. E. 1996. Home and work. Negotiating boundaries through everyday life. Chicago, Ill.: University of Chicago Press.

Nord, W. R., Fox, S., Phoenix, A., & Viano, K. 2002. Real-world reactions to work-life balance programs: Lessons for effective implementation. Organizational Dynamics, 30(3): 223–238.

Nordenflycht, A. von 2010. What is a Professional Service Firm? Toward a theory and taxonomy of knowledge-intensive firms. Academy of Management Review, 35(1): 155–174.

Nunnally, J. C., & Bernstein, I. H. 1994. Psychometric theory (2nd ed.). New York: McGraw-Hill.

O'Driscoll, M. P., Poelmans, S., Spector, P. E., Kalliath, T., Allen, T. D., Cooper, C. L., & Sanchez, J. I. 2003. Family-responsive interventions, perceived organizational and supervisor support, work-family conflict, and psychological strain. International Journal of Stress Management, 10(4): 326–344.

O'Mahoney, J. 2007. Disrupting trust and angst in management consulting. In S. C. Bolton & M. Houlihan (Eds.), Searching for the human in human resource management. Theory, practice and workplace contexts: 281–302. Basingstoke: Palgrave Macmillan.

O'Reilly, C. A., Chatman, J., & Caldwell, D. F. 1991. People and organizational culture: A profile comparison approach assessing person-organization fit. Academy of Management Journal, 34(3): 487–516.

Organisation for Economic Co-operation and Development (OECD) 2010. Moving beyond the jobs crisis. Employment Outlook. Paris: OECD.

Ostendorp, A. 2007. Möglichkeiten für KMU und Großunternehmen bei der Umsetzung eines Trends. Life Balance als Beitrag zu einer Kultur der Unterschiede. In A. S. Esslinger & D. B. Schobert (Eds.), Erfolgreiche Umsetzung von Work-Life Balance in Organisationen. Strategien, Konzepte, Maßnahmen: 187–211. Wiesbaden: Deutscher Universitäts-Verlag.

Osterman, P. 1995. Work/family programs and the employment relationship. Administrative Science Quarterly, 40: 681–700.

Ostroff, C., & Cooper, C. L. (Eds.) 2007. Perspectives on organizational fit. New York, NY: Taylor & Francis Group.

Parasuraman, S., & Greenhaus, J. H. (Eds.) 1999. Integrating work and family: Challenges and choices for a changing world. Westport, Conn.: Praeger.

Parasuraman, S., & Greenhaus, J. H. 2002. Toward reducing some critical gaps in work-family research. Human Resource Management Review, 12(3): 299.

Parris, M., Vickers, M., & Wilkes, L. 2008. Caught in the middle. Organizational impediments to middle managers' work-life balance. Employee Responsibilities & Rights Journal, 20(2): 101–117.

Pasewark, W. R., & Viator, R. E. 2006. Sources of work-family conflict in the accounting profession. Behavioral Research in Accounting, 18: 147–165.

Peake, A., & Harris, K. L. 2002. Young adults' attitudes toward multiple role planning. The influence of gender, career traditionality and marriage plans. Journal of Vocational Behavior, 60(3): 405–421.

Peeters, M. C., Montgomery, A. J., Bakker, A. B., & Schaufeli, W. B. 2005. Balancing work and home: How job and home demands are related to burnout. International Journal of Stress Management, 12(1): 43–61.

Peper, B., Dikkers, J., Vinkenburg, C. J., & van Engen, M. L. 2011. Causes and consequences of the utilization of work-life policies by professionals: "Unconditional supervisor support required". In S. Kaiser, M. Ringlstetter, D. R. Eikhof & M. Pina e Cunha (Eds.), Creating balance? International perspectives on the work-life integration of professionals: 225–250. Berlin: Springer.

Perlow, L. A. 1995. Putting the work back into work/family. Group & Organization Management, 20(2): 227–239.

Perlow, L. A., & Porter, J. L. 2009. Making time off predictable & required. Harvard Business Review, 87(10): 102–109.

Perry-Smith, J. E., & Blum, T. C. 2000. Work-family human resource bundles and perceived organizational performance. Academy of Management Journal, 43(6): 1107–1117.

Pitt-Catsouphes, M., Kossek, E. E., & Sweet, S. A. (Eds.) 2006. The work and family handbook. Multi-disciplinary perspectives, methods, and approaches. Mahwah, NJ: Lawrence Erlbaum Associates.

Poelmans, S. A. Y. (Ed.) 2005. Work and family: An international research perspective). Mahwah, NJ: Lawrence Erlbaum Assoc.

Poelmans, S. A. Y., & Caligiuri, P. (Eds.) 2008. Harmonizing work, family, and personal life: From policy to practice. Cambridge: Cambridge University Press.

Poelmans, S., & Beham, B. 2008a. The moment of truth: Conceptualizing managerial work-life policy allowance decisions. Journal of Occupational and Organizational Psychology, 81(3): 393–410.

Poelmans, S. A. Y., & Beham, B. 2008b. Reviewing policies for harmonizing work, family and personal life. In S. A. Y. Poelmans & P. Caligiuri (Eds.), Harmonizing work, family, and personal life: From policy to practice: 39–77. Cambridge: Cambridge University Press.

Poelmans, S. A. Y., Patel, S., & Beham, B. 2008. Stages in the implementation of work-life policies. In S. A. Y. Poelmans & P. Caligiuri (Eds.), Harmonizing work, family, and personal life: From policy to practice: 133–165. Cambridge: Cambridge University Press.

Porter, G., & Perry, J. L. 2008. Animal farm, baby boom and crackberry addicts. In R. J. Burke & C. L. Cooper (Eds.), The long work hours culture. Causes, consequences and choices: 255–274. Bingley: Emerald.

Poulter, D., & Land, C. 2008. Preparing to work: Dramaturgy, cynicism and normative 'remote' control in the socialization of graduate recruits in management consulting. Culture and Organization, 14(1): 65–78.

Quick, J. C., & Tetrick, L. E. (Eds.) 2003. Handbook of occupational health psychology. Washington, DC: American Psychological Assoc.

Rapoport, R., & Rapoport, R. N. 1969. The dual career family: A variant pattern and social change. Human Relations, 22(1): 3–30.

Reindl, C. U., Kaiser, S., & Stolz, M. 2011. Integrating Professional Work and Life: Conditions, Outcomes and Resources. In S. Kaiser, M. Ringlstetter, D. R. Eikhof & M. Pina e Cunha (Eds.), Creating balance? International perspectives on the work-life integration of professionals: 3–26. Berlin: Springer.

Reynolds, J. 2005. In the face of conflict: Work-life conflict and desired work hour adjustments. Journal of Marriage and the Family, 67(5): 1313–1331.

Rice, R. W., Frone, M. R., & McFarlin, D. B. 1992. Work-nonwork conflict and the perceived quality of life. Journal of Organizational Behavior, 13(2): 155–168.

Riester, B., & Dern, A. 2010. Work-Life Choice bei PricewaterhouseCoopers. Erfolgsversprechende Konzepte und Instrumente. In S. Kaiser & M. Ringlstetter (Eds.), Work-Life Balance: Erfolgversprechende Konzepte und Instrumente für Extremjobber: 154–166. Berlin, Heidelberg: Springer.

Ringle, C. M. 2004. Gütemaße für den Partial Least Squares-Ansatz zur Bestimmung von Kausalmodellen. Industrielles Management, Arbeitspapier Nr. 16. Universität Hamburg; Institut für Industriebetriebs-lehre und Organisation.

Ringle, C. M., Boysen, N., Wende, S., & Will, A. 2006. Messung von Kausalmodellen mit dem Partial-Least-Suqares-Verfahren. WISU, 35(1): 81–88.

Ringlstetter, M., & Bürger, B. 2003. Bedeutung netzwerkartiger Strukturen bei der strategischen Entwicklung von Professional Firms. In M. Bruhn & B. Stauss (Eds.), Dienstleistungsnetzwerke. Dienstleistungsmanagement: 113–130. Wiesbaden: Gabler.

Ringlstetter, M., & Kaiser, S. 2007. Positives Personalmanagement in wissensintensiven Dienstleistungsunternehmen. In M. H. J. Gouthier, C. Coenen, H. Schulze & C. Wegmann (Eds.), Service Excellence als Impulsgeber: Strategien, Management, Innovationen, Branchen: 347–362. Wiesbaden: Gabler.

Ringlstetter, M., & Kaiser, S. 2008. Humanressourcen-Management. München: Oldenbourg.

Ringlstetter, M., Kaiser, S. & Bürger, B. 2004. Professional Service Firms: Geschäftstypen, Vergütungsformen und Teilbranchen. In M. Ringlstetter, B. Bürger & S. Kaiser, (Eds.), Strategien und Management für Professional Service Firms: 39-61. Weinheim: Wiley.

Ringlstetter, M., Bürger, B. & Kaiser, S. (Eds.) 2004. Strategien und Management für Professional Service Firms. Weinheim: Wiley.

Ringlstetter, M., Kaiser, S., & Müller-Seitz, G. (Eds.) 2006. Positives Management: Zentrale Konzepte und Ideen des Positive Organizational Scholarship. Wiesbaden: Gabler.

Ringlstetter, M., Kaiser, S., & Müller-Seitz, G. 2006. Positives Management. Ein Ansatz zur Neuausrichtung und Erweiterung bisheriger Managementforschung und -praxis. In M. Ringlstetter, S. Kaiser & G. Müller-Seitz

(Eds.), Positives Management. Zentrale Konzepte und Ideen des Positive Organizational Scholarship: 3-10 Wiesbaden: Gabler.

Roth, W. L., & Zakrzewski, B. M. 2006. Work Life Balance jenseits der 50-Stunden-Woche: Motive, Visionen und Lebensgestaltung junger High-Potentials; eine qualitative Untersuchung. Kröning: Asanger.

Rothbard, N. P. 2001. Enriching or depleting? The dynamics of engagement in work and family roles. Administrative Science Quarterly, 44(4): 655–684.

Rothbard, N. P., & Dumas, T. L. 2006. Research perspectives: Managing the work-home interface. In F. Jones, R. J. Burke & M. Westman (Eds.), Work-life balance: A psychological perspective: 73–89. Hove: Psychology Press.

Rothbard, N. P., Phillips, K. W., & Dumas, T. L. 2005. Managing multiple roles. Work-family policies and individuals' desires for segmentation. Organization Science, 16(3): 243–258.

Rotondo, D. M., Carlson, D. S., & Kincaid, J. F. 2003. Coping with multiple dimensions of work-family conflict. Personnel Review, 32(3): 275–296.

Russell, H., O'Connell, P. J., & McGinnity, F. 2009. The impact of flexible working arrangements on work-life conflict and work pressure in Ireland. Gender, Work & Organization, 16(1): 73–97.

Rustemeyer, H., & Buchmann, C. 2010. Erfolgsfaktor Work-Life Balance bei der Unternehmensberatung A.T. Kearney. In S. Kaiser & M. Ringlstetter (Eds.), Work-Life Balance: Erfolgversprechende Konzepte und Instrumente für Extremjobber: 165–179. Berlin, Heidelberg: Springer.

Saltzstein, A. L., Ting, Y., & Saltzstein, G. H. 2001. Work-family balance and job satisfaction: The impact of family-friendly policies on attitudes of federal government employees. Public Administration Review, 61(4): 452–467.

Sanders, M. M., Lengnick-Hall, M. L., Lengnick-Hall, C. A., & Steele-Clapp, L. 1998. Love and work: Career-family attitudes of new entrants into the labor force. Journal of Organizational Behavior, 19(6): 603.

Schabracq, M. J. 2003a. What an organization can do about its employees' well-being and health: an overview. In M. J. Schabracq, J. A. M. Winnubst & C. L. Cooper (Eds.), The handbook of work and health psychology: 585–600 (2nd ed.). Chichester: John Wiley & Sons.

Schabracq, M. J., Winnubst, J. A. M., & Cooper, C. L. (Eds.) 2003b. The handbook of work and health psychology (2nd ed.). Chichester: John Wiley & Sons.

Schein, E. H. 2004. Organizational culture and leadership (3rd ed.). San Francisco, Calif.: Jossey-Bass.

Schepers, J., Wetzels, M., & Ruyter, K. de 2005. Leadership styles in technology acceptance: Do followers practice what leaders preach? Managing Service Quality, 15(6): 496–508.

Schieman, S., Glavin, P., & Milkie, M. A. 2009. When work interferes with life: Work-nonwork interference and the influence of work-related demands and resources. American Sociological Review, 74(6): 966–988.

Schneewind, K., & Kupsch, M. 2007. Patterns of neuroticism, work-family stress, and resources as determinants of personal distress: A cluster analysis of young, dual-earner families at the individual and couple level. Journal of Individual Differences, 28(3): 150–160.

Scholderer, J., & Balderjahn, I. 2005. PLS versus LISREL: Ein Methodenvergleich. In F. Bliemel, A. Eggert, G. Fassott & J. Henseler (Eds.), Handbuch PLS-Pfadfmodellierung. Methode, Anwendung, Praxisbeispiele: 87–98. Stuttgart: Schäffer-Poeschel.

Schor, J. B. 1998. The overworked American: The unexpected decline of leisure. New York, NY: Basic Books.

Scott, J. 1991. Social network analysis. A handbook. London: Sage.

Scott, M. C. 2001. The professional service firm: The manager's guide to maximizing profit and value. Chichester: Wiley.

Seligman, M. E. P., & Csikszentmihalyi, M. 2000. Positive Psychology: An introduction. American Psychologist, 55(1): 5–14.

Shaffer, M. A., & Joplin, J. R. W. 2001. Work-family conflict on international assignments: Time- and strain-based determinants and performance effort consequences. Academy of Management Proceedings, 2001: 1–6.

Shaffer, M. A., Harrison, D. A., Gilley, K., & Luk, D. M. 2001. Struggling for balance amid turbulence on international assignments: Work-family conflict, support and commitment. Journal of Management, 27(1): 99.

Shelton, B. A., & John, D. 1996. The division of household labor. Annual Review of Sociology, 22(1): 299.

Shockley, K. M., & Allen, T. D. 2007. When flexibility helps: Another look at the availability of flexible work arrangements and work-family conflict. Journal of Vocational Behavior, 71(3): 479–493.

Simpson, R. 1998. Presenteeism, power and organizational change: Long hours as a career barrier and the impact on the working lives of women managers. British Journal of Management, 9(s1): 37–50.

Smith, J., & Gardner, D. 2007. Factors affecting employee use of work-life balance initiatives. New Zealand Journal of Psychology, 36(1): 3–12.

Söhnchen, F. 2007. Common method variance und Single source bias. In S. Albers, D. Klapper, U. Konradt, A. Walter & J. Wolf (Eds.), Methodik der empirischen Forschung: 135–149. Wiesbaden: Gabler.

Sonnentag, S. 2001. Work, recovery activities, and individual well-being: A diary study. Journal of Occupational Health Psychology, 6(3): 196–210.

Sonnentag, S., & Bayer, U.-V. 2005. Switching off mentally: Predictors and consequences of psychological detachment from work during off-job time. Journal of Occupational Health Psychology, 10(4): 393–414.

Sonnentag, S., & Kruel, U. 2006. Psychological detachment from work during off-job time: The role of job stressors, job involvement, and recovery-related self-efficacy. European Journal of Work and Organizational Psychology, 15(2): 197–217.

Sonnentag, S., & Niessen, C. 2008. Staying vigorous until work is over: The role of trait vigor, day-specific work experiences and recovery. Journal of Occupational and Organizational Psychology, 81: 435–458.

Sparks, K., Cooper, C. L., Fried, Y., & Shirom, A. 1997. The effects of hours of work on health: A meta-analytic review. Journal of Occupational and Organizational Psychology, 70(4): 391–408.

Staines, G. L., Fudge, D. A., & Pottick, K. J. 1986. Wives' employment and husbands' attitudes toward work and life. Journal of Applied Psychology, 71(1): 118–128.

Starbuck, W. H. 1992. Learning by knowledge-intensive firms. Journal of Management Studies, 29(6): 713–740.

Stahl, G. K., & Björkman, I. (Eds.) 2006. Handbook of research in international human resource management. Cheltenham: E. Elgar.

Still, M. C., & Williams, J. C. 2006. A legal perspective on family issues at work. In M. Pitt-Catsouphes, E. E. Kossek & S. A. Sweet (Eds.), The work and family handbook. Multi-disciplinary perspectives, methods, and approaches: 309–326. Mahwah, NJ: Lawrence Erlbaum Assoc.

Stock-Homburg, R., & Bauer, E.-M. 2007. Work-Life-Balance im Topmanagement. Aus Politik und Zeitgeschichte, 34: 25–32.

Strauss, A. L. 1987. Qualitative analysis for social scientists. Cambridge: Cambridge University Press.

Sturges, J., & Guest, D. 2004. Working to live or living to work? Work/life balance early in the career. Human Resource Management Journal, 14(4): 5–20.

Sullivan, S. E., & Mainiero, L. A. 2007. The changing nature of gender roles, alpha/beta careers and work-life issues. Theory-driven implications for human resource management. Career Development International, 12(3): 238–263.

Sutton, K. L., & Noe, R. A. 2005. Family- friendly programs and work-life integration: more myth than magic? In E. E. Kossek & S. J. Lambert (Eds.),

Work and life integration. Organizational, cultural, and individual perspectives: 151–169. Mahwah, NJ: Lawrence Erlbaum Associates.

Taris, T. W., Beckers, D. G. J., Verhoeven, L. C., Geurts, S. A. E., Kompier, M. A. J., & van den Linden, D. 2006. Recovery opportunities, work-home interference and well-being among managers. European Journal of Work and Organizational Psychology, 15(2): 139–157.

Taylor, B. L., Delcampo, R. G., & Blancero, D. M. 2009. Work-family conflict/facilitation and the role of workplace supports for U.S. Hispanic professionals. Journal of Organizational Behavior, 30(5): 643–664.

Temme, D., Paulssen, M., & Hildebrandt, L. 2009. Common Method Variance. Ursachen, Auswirkungen und Kontrollmöglichkeiten. DBW, Die Betriebswirtschaft, 2/2009(2): 123–146.

Tenenhaus, M., Vinzi, V., Chatelin, Y., & Lauro, C. 2005. PLS path modeling. Computational Statistics & Data Analysis, 48(1): 159–205.

Thiehoff, R. 2004. Work Life Balance mit Balanced Scorecard: Die wirtschaftliche Sicht der Prävention. In M. Kastner (Ed.), Die Zukunft der Work Life Balance. Wie lassen sich Beruf und Familie, Arbeit und Freizeit miteinander vereinbaren?: 409–436. Kröning: Asanger.

Thomas, L. T., & Ganster, D. C. 1995. Impact of family-supportive work variables on work-family conflict and strain: A control perspective. Journal of Applied Psychology, 80(1): 6–15.

Thompson, C. A. 2008. Barriers to the implementation and usage of work-life policies. In S. A. Y. Poelmans & P. Caligiuri (Eds.), Harmonizing work, family, and personal life: From policy to practice: 209–234. Cambridge: Cambridge University Press.

Thompson, C. A., & Prottas, D. 2005. Relationships among organizational family support, job autonomy, perceived control, and employee well-being. Journal of Occupational Health Psychology, 10(4): 100–118.

Thompson, C. A., Beauvais, L. L., & Allen, T. A. 2006. Work and family from an industrial/organizational psychology perspective. In M. Pitt-Catsouphes, E. E. Kossek & S. A. Sweet (Eds.), The work and family handbook. Multi-disciplinary perspectives, methods, and approaches: 283–307. Mahwah, NJ: Lawrence Erlbaum Assoc.

Thompson, C. A., Beauvais, L. L., & Lyness, K. S. 1999. When work-family benefits are not enough. The influence of work-family culture on benefit utilization, organizational attachment, and work-family conflict. Journal of Vocational Behavior, 54(3): 392–415.

Ton, M.-T. N., & Hansen, J.-I. C. 2001. Using a person-environment fit framework to predict satisfaction and motivation in work and marital roles. Journal of Career Assessment, 9(4): 315–331.

Trinczek, R. 2006. Work-life balance and flexible working hours. The German experience. In P. Blyton (Ed.), Work-life integration. International perspectives on the balancing of multiple roles: 113–134. Basingstoke: Palgrave Macmillan.

Ulich, E., & Wiese, B. S. 2011. Life Domain Balance. Konzepte zur Verbesserung der Lebensqualität. Wiesbaden: Gabler.

Valcour, M. P. 2007. Work-based resources as moderators of the relationship between work hours and satisfaction with work-family balance. Journal of Applied Psychology, 92(6): 1512–1523.

Valcour, M. P., & Hunter, L. W. 2005. Technology, organizations, and work-life integration. In E. E. Kossek & S. J. Lambert (Eds.), Work and life integration. Organizational, cultural, and individual perspectives: 61–84. Mahwah, NJ: Lawrence Erlbaum Assoc.

van Knippenberg, D., & Sleebos, E. 2006. Organizational identification versus organizational commitment: Self-definition, social exchange, and job attitudes. Journal of Organizational Behavior, 27(5): 571–584.

van Daalen, G., Willemsen, T. M., & Sanders, K. 2006. Reducing work-family conflict through different sources of social support. Journal of Vocational Behavior, 69(3): 462–476.

van Rijswijk, K., Bekker, M. H. J., Rutte, C. G., & Croon, M. A. 2004. The relationships among part-time work, work-family interference, and well-being. Journal of Occupational Health Psychology, 9(4): 286–295.

van Steenbergen, E. F., & Ellemers, N. 2009. Is managing the work-family interface worthwhile? Benefits for employee health and performance. Journal of Organizational Behavior, 30(5): 617–642.

Verquer, M. L., Beehr, T. A., & Wagner, S. H. 2003. A meta-analysis of relations between person-organization fit and work attitudes. Journal of Vocational Behavior, 63(3): 473–489.

Voydanoff, P. 2004. Implications of work and community demands and resources for work-to-family conflict and facilitation. Journal of Occupational Health Psychology, 9(4): 275–285.

Voydanoff, P. 2005a. Work demands and work-to-family and family-to-work conflict: Direct and indirect relationships. Journal of Family Issues, 26(6): 707–726.

Voydanoff, P. 2005b. Consequences of boundary-spanning demands and resources for work-to-family conflict and perceived stress. Journal of Occupational Health Psychology, 10(4): 491–503.

Voydanoff, P. 2005c. Toward a conceptualization of perceived work-family fit and balance: A demands and resources approach. Journal of Marriage and the Family, 67(4): 822–836.

Wallace, J. E. 1995. Organizational and professional commitment in professional and nonprofessional organizations. Administrative Science Quarterly, 40(2): 228–255.

Wallace, J. E. 1997. It's about time: A study of hours worked and work spillover among law firm lawyers. Journal of Vocational Behavior, 50(2): 227–248.

Wallace, J. E. 2006. Work commitment in the legal profession. A study of Baby Boomers and Generation Xers. International Journal of the Legal Profession, 13(2): 137–151.

Wallace, J. E. 2009. Job stress, depression and work-to-family conflict. A test of the strain and buffer hypothesis. Industrial Relations, 60(3): 510–539.

Wallace, J. E., & Young, M. C. 2008. Parenthood and productivity: A study of demands, resources and family-friendly firms. Journal of Vocational Behavior, 72(1): 110–122.

Welch, D. E., & Worm, V. 2006. International business travelers: A challenge for IHRM. In G. K. Stahl & I. Björkman (Eds.), Handbook of research in international human resource management: 279–298. Cheltenham: E. Elgar.

Werr, A., & Schilling, A. 2010. "Talent factories" and "expert houses": Patterns of human resource practices in professional service firms. In IPOB (Ed.), The future of knowledge-intensive service work. Theory and practice of managing human and organizational resources: 127–150 (1st ed.). Marburg: Metropolis.

Westman, M., Etzion, D., & Gattenio, E. 2008. International business travels and the work-family interface: A longitudinal study. Journal of Occupational and Organizational Psychology, 81(3): 459–480.

Wharton, A. S. 2006. Understanding diversity of work in the 21st century and its impact on the work-family area of study. In M. Pitt-Catsouphes, E. E. Kossek & S. A. Sweet (Eds.), The work and family handbook. Multidisciplinary perspectives, methods, and approaches: 17–39. Mahwah, NJ: Lawrence Erlbaum Assoc.

Wharton, A. S., & Blair-Loy, M. 2006. Long work hours and family life: A cross-national study of employees' concerns. Journal of Family Issues, 27(3): 415–436.

White, M., Hill, S., McGovern, P., Mills, C., & Smeaton, D. 2003. 'High-performance' management practices, working hours and work-life balance. British Journal of Industrial Relations, 41(2): 175–195.

Whitely, W., & England, G. W. 1977. Managerial values as a reflection of culture and the process of industrialization. Academy of Management Journal, 20(3): 439–453.

Whittington, J. L., Maellaro, R., & Galpin, T. 2011. Redefining success: The foundation for creating work-life balance. In S. Kaiser, M. Ringlstetter, D. R. Eikhof & M. Pina e Cunha (Eds.), Creating balance? International perspectives on the work-life integration of professionals: 65–77. Berlin: Springer.

Wiersma, U. J. 1994. A taxonomy of behavioral strategies for coping with work-home role conflict. Human Relations, 47(2): 211–221.

Williams, J. C. 2007. The politics of time in the legal profession. University of St. Thomas Law Journal, 4(3): 379–404.

Williams, K. J., & Alliger, G. M. 1994. Role stressors, mood spillover, and perceptions of work-family conflict in employed parents. Academy of Management Journal, 34(4): 837–868.

Winkel, D. E., & Clayton, R. W. 2010. Transitioning between work and family roles as a function of boundary flexibility and role salience. Journal of Vocational Behavior, 76(2): 336–343.

Wold, H. 1982. Soft modeling: the basic design and some extensions. In K. G. W. H. Jöreskog (Ed.), Systems under indirect observation. Causality, structure, prediction: 1–54. Amsterdam, New York: North-Holland Publ.

Wright, P., & Kehoe, R. 2009. Organizational-level antecedents and consequences of commitment. In H. J. Klein, T. E. Becker & J. P. Meyer (Eds.), Commitment in organizations. Accumulated wisdom and new directions: 285–307. New York, NY: Routledge.

Zedeck, S., & Mosier, K. L. 1990. Work in the family and employing organization. American Psychologist, 45(2): 240–251.

Zijlstra, F. R. H., & Cropley, M. 2008. Recovery after work. In R. J. Burke & C. L. Cooper (Eds.), The long work hours culture. Causes, consequences and choices: 219–234. Bingley: Emerald.

Sources Retrieved from the World Wide Web

Booz & Company 2011. Wer nach oben will muss nach oben denken, [Recruiting brochure]. Retrieved at: http://www.booz-enough.de/downloads /booz-enough_Broschure.pdf, last access: 2011-05-19.

Capgemini 2010. Die innere Mitte, der ganze Mensch, [‚Career‘ Section of Capgemini Website]. Retrieved at: http://www.de.capgemini.com/ karriere/technology/einblicken/balance, last access: 2011-05-04.

Center for Ethical Business Cultures (1997). Creating high performance organizations. The bottom line value of work/life strategies, [Report]. Retrieved at:

http://www.cebcglobal.org/KnowledgeCenter/Publications/WorkLife/Cre
atinghighPerformanceOrganizations.htm, last access: 2011-12-06.

Coffman, J., & Hagey, R. 2010. Flexible work models: How to bring sustaina-
bility to a 24/7 world, [Brochure of Bain & Company]. Retrieved at:
http://www.bain.com/publications/articles/flexible-work-models-how-to-
bring-sustainability-to-24-7-world.aspx, last access: 2011-05-12.

Kienbaum 2010. High Potentials 2010/2011 [Press Release]. Retrieved at:
http://www.kienbaum.de/desktop devault.aspx/tabid-501/649_read-10221,
last access: 2011-07-11.

N.N. 2010. Arbeitgeber-Ranking: Studenten träumen von PwC und Google
[News Article]. Retrieved at: http://www.focus.de/finanzen/karriere
/perspektiven/arbeitgeber-ranking-studenten-traeumen-von-pwc-und-
google_aid_518850.html, last access: 2011-05-04.

PricewaterhouseCoopers 2010. Employee morale and loyalty are vulnerable as
companies ask over-stretched employees to do more with less [Press Re-
lease]. Retrieved at: http://www.pwc.com/gx/en/press-room/2010/
Employee-morale-loyality-vulnerable-as-emp.do-more.jhtml, last access:
2011-07-11.

Ringle, C. M., Wende, S., & Will, A. 2006 SmartPLS 2.0 (beta):
http://www.smartpls.de.

APPENDIX

Appendix A: Literature Review

Table A.1. Selection of major studies that examined the direct link between work demands and work-life outcomes in professional samples

Predictor	Work-Life Measure	Major Findings	Sample & Source
(Weekly) Work Hours	Work-family conflict	Work hours were related to increased work-family conflict ($\beta = .067$, $p < .05$)	277 Elite employees of a high-commitment, global financial services firm in the U.S., London, and Hong Kong (Wharton & Blair-Loy, 2006)
	Work-family conflict	Work hours were related to increased work-family conflict for women ($\beta = .136$, $p < .05$)	557 Employees of different professions with 71% of the sample being professionals and managers (Batt & Valcour, 2003) (Summed scores of a total of four types of care policies / five types of flexible working policies)
	Work-family conflict	Work hours were positively related to work-family conflict ($r = .354$, $p < .001$)	143 Swiss top managers of one large-sized company (Jacobshagen et al., 2005)
	Work-family conflict	Number of hours worked according to contract was not associated with work-home interference. High levels of overtime related to increased time-based work-to-home interference ($\gamma = .16$, $p < .05$)	117 Male and 82 female managers (Taris et al., 2006)
	Work-family conflict	Work hours were not related to work-family conflict	213 Israeli married computer workers and lawyers (Cinamon & Rich, 2002a)
	Work-to-family conflict	Hours spent at work were related to increased work-to-family conflict ($r_{psychologists} = .40$, $p < .01$ and $r_{sen. managers} = .56$, $p < .01$)	530 U.S. psychologists and 209 senior managers (Gutek, Searle & Klepa, 1991)
	Work-to-family conflict	Work hours significantly predicted increased work-to-family conflict	513 Employees of Fortune 500 companies (Major, Klein & Ehrhart, 2002)
	Work-family conflict (Job-spouse conflict, job-parent conflict, job-homemaker conflict)	Weekly work hours were significantly related to higher job-spouse, job-parent and job-homemaker types of work-family conflict ($r = .11$, $r = .16$, $r = .12$, $p < .05$)	354 Married professional women from dual-career families in Singapore (Aryee, 1992)
	Work-to-family conflict	Work hours were related to increased work-family conflict ($\beta = .205$, $p < .01$)	276 U.S. managers and professionals (Thompson, Beauvais & Lyness, 1999)
	Work-to-family conflict	Work hours related to increased work-to-family conflict ($\beta = .011$; $p < .001$)	1201 Lawyers who were married and working full-time (law firms, corporate offices, government) (Wallace, 2009)

Predictor	Work-Life Measure	Major Findings	Sample & Source
	Work-to-family conflict Family-to-work conflict	Work hours were significantly related to increased work-to-family conflict ($\beta = .36$, $p < .001$)	245 Professionals in two Fortune 500 firms with telework policies (Kossek, Lautsch & Eaton, 2006)
	Work-to-family conflict Family-to-work conflict	Work hours were significantly related to increased work-to-family conflict ($r = .30$, $p < .05$)	1,062 Male U.S. executives (Judge, Boudreau & Bretz, 1994)
	Work-to-family interference Family-to-work interference	Work hours were significantly related to increased work-to-family conflict ($\beta = .44$, $p < .01$)	272 Professionals (university alumni who earned a BA in business management) (Nielson, Carlson & Lankau, 2001)
Work (Over)Load	Work-family conflict	Perceived work overload related to increased work-family conflict ($\gamma = .46$, $p < .001$)	171 IT road warriors (Ahuja et al., 2007)
	Work-family conflict	Work overload related to increased to work-family conflict ($r = .484$, $p < .001$)	143 Swiss top managers of one large-sized company (Jacobshagen et al., 2005)
	Work-to-family conflict	Tight deadlines related to increased work-family conflict ($\beta = -.698$, $p < .01$) (Td measure reverse coded)	277 Elite employees of a high-commitment, global financial services firm in the U.S., London, and Hong Kong (Wharton & Blair-Loy, 2006)
	Work-home conflict	Work overload related to increased work-home conflict ($\gamma = .58$, $p < .05$)	310 U.S. public accountants who were married and/or with at least one child (Greenhaus et al., 1997)
	Work-to-family conflict	Work overload related to increased work-to-family conflict ($\beta = .348$; $p < .001$) but effect is completely buffered (moderated) by co-worker support ($\beta = -.125$; $p < .001$)	1201 Lawyers who were married and working full-time (law firms, corporate offices, government) (Wallace, 2009)
	Work-to-nonwork spillover	Work overload related to work-to-nonwork spillover ($\beta = .53$, $p < .001$)	253 Law firm lawyers (US) (Wallace, 1997)
Job-related Travel	Work-family conflict	Travel was not related to work-family conflict	557 Employees of different professions with 71% of the sample being professionals and managers (Batt & Valcour, 2003) (Summed scores of a total of four types of care policies / five types of flexible working policies)
	Work-family conflict Family-work conflict	Job-related travel was significantly related to increased work-to-family conflict ($\beta = -.17$, $p < .05$).	102 Expatriates in professional jobs who live and work in Hong Kong (Shaffer and Joplin, 2001)

Table A.2. Selection of major studies that examined the direct link between formal organizational resources (work-life initiatives) and work-life outcomes

Source	Work-Life Initiative(s)	WLC Measure	Sample	Main Findings
Allen (2001)	Use and availability of Flexible work arrangements Dependent care supports	Work-family conflict	522 participants employed in a variety of occupations and organizations	Using flexible work arrangements was significantly negatively correlated with work-family conflict (dependent care not so) Considering the perception of one's employer as family-friendly, the relationship between benefit availability and reduced work-family conflict became insignificant
Anderson, Coffey & Byerly (2002)	Availability of Flexible schedule Dependent care benefits	Work-to-family conflict Family-to-work conflict	2877 U.S. wage and salaried workers who either had at least one cohabiting child under age 18 or were involved in a dual-career relationship or were currently providing care for s.o. aged 65 or older	Schedule flexibility was negatively related to work-to-family conflict. Dependent care benefits were not significantly related to either family-to-work conflict or work-to-family conflict.
Aryee (1992)	Availability of Flexible schedule	Work-family conflict (Job-spouse conflict, job-parent conflict, job-homemaker conflict)	354 Married professional women from dual-career families in Singapore	Work schedule inflexibility was positively correlated with work-family conflict (job-homemaker type)
Batt & Valcour (2003)	Availability of Dependent care policies (dependent care referral services, parenting seminars, childcare center and sick childcare center) Flexible schedule (paid family leave, personal / dependent care time, flextime, telecommuting, time off for volunteering) (summed score)	Work-family conflict	557 Employees of different professions with 71% of the sample being professionals and managers	Access to work-life initiatives did not predict work-home interference.
Berg, Kalleberg & Appelbaum	Availability of Childcare	Work-family balance	Nearly 4000 workers across three manu-	Access to childcare referral services was positively associated with work-family balance

Source	Work-Life Initiative(s)	WLC Measure	Sample	Main Findings
(2003)			facturing industries in the U.S.	
Brough, O'Driscoll & Kalliath (2005)	Use of Workplace crèche facility Flexible working hours Family-friendly policies Job sharing Assistance with child-care/eldercare Family insurance/ savings plan, General support to meet family needs	Work-to-family conflict Family-to-work conflict	398 Employed men and women	'Family-friendly' resources were significantly positively related to family-to-work conflict, not work-to-family conflict
Cinamon & Rich (2002a)	Use of Flexible Working Hours	Work-to-family conflict Family-to-work conflict	213 Israeli married computer workers and lawyers	Making use of flexible work hours was negatively correlated with work-to-family conflict
Dikkers, Geurts, Den Dulk, Peper, Taris & Kompier (2004)	Use of 6 WLB initiatives: flexible schedule, telecommuting, working from home occasionally, working part time, financial support for child-care costs, parental leave (summed score)	Time-based work-home interference Strain-based work-home interference	638 Dutch financial consultants	Work-life initiative use was not related to work-family conflict.
Dikkers, Geurts, Den Dulk, Peper, Taris & Kompier (2007a)	Use of Flextime Part-time work Subsidized childcare Parental leave	Work-home interference Home-work interference	503 Dutch employees from three organizations (governmental service institute, manufacturing company, financial consultancy)	Work-home interference was negatively related to the use of part-time work, subsidized childcare, and parental leave. Home-work interference was positively related to the use of all four initiatives. (Correlations ranged only between -.14 and .18!)
Duxbury, Higgins & Thomas (1996)	Use of Home office (computer-supported supplemental work at home	Role overload Interference	547 dual-career employees in managerial or professional positions who did or did not use computer supported supp. work at home	Individuals who adopt computer-supported supplemental work at home are significantly more likely to perceive high levels of role overload and interference.

Source	Work-Life Initiative(s)	WLC Measure	Sample	Main Findings
Frye & Breaugh (2004)	3-item scale asking for general availability of useful policies	Work-to-family conflict Family-to-work conflict	135 U.S. employees who had a supervisor and at least one child	The perceived usefulness of family-friendly policies was significantly negatively related to work-to-family conflict.
Goff, Mount & Jamison (1990)	Use of and satisfaction with Employer-supported childcare	Work-family conflict	253 U.S. employees of a large electronics and communications firm (62 of them being users of childcare)	Use of a childcare center at work was not related to work-family conflict. Satisfaction with childcare arrangements were related to reduced work-life conflict.
Golden, Veiga & Simsek (2006)	Use of Telework	Work-to-family conflict Family-to-work conflict	454 Full-time professionals of a high-tech firm that telecommuted regularly	Use of telework was associated with reduced work-to-family conflict ($\beta = .-27\ p < .001$) but higher family-to-work conflict ($\beta = .19;\ p < .001$)
Hayman (2009)	Flexible schedule (perceived usability)	Work-personal life interference Personal life-work interference	710 Australian university administration employees (64% female)	Perceived usability of flexible schedules significantly predicted (lower) work-personal life interference and to a smaller extent personal life-work interference.
Hill, Märtinson & Ferris (2003)	Use of Telework (virtual office and home office vs. traditional work)	Work-life balance	5,524 U.S. IBM employees in primarily professional positons (14% virtual office users and 8% home office users)	Individuals that used home office arrangements reported a higher level of work-life balance, as well as higher job motivation and intent to stay in the organization. They were as productive as employees in the traditional office venue
Hill et al., (2006)	Use of Dual-earner 60 hour workweek	Work-family fit Work-to-family conflict	3,097 U.S. IBM employees with the majority in professional positions	Sixty-hour couples report significantly greater work-family fit and lower levels of work-to-family conflict
Judge, Boudreau & Bretz (1994)	5-item scale asking about the availability of adequate policies	Work-to-family conflict Family-to-work conflict	1,062 Male U.S. executives	The availability of perceived adequate work-life policies was related to reduced work-to-family conflict ($\gamma = .12,\ p > .001$)
Kossek, Lautsch & Eaton (2006)	Telework (working from home)	Work-to-family conflict Family-to-work conflict	245 professionals in two Fortune 500 firms with telework policies	The use of telework was not significantly related to work-family conflict

Source	Work-Life Initiative(s)	WLC Measure	Sample	Main Findings
Lapierre & Allen (2006)	Use of flexible schedule Use of telework	Time-based work-family interference Strain-based work-family interference Time-based family-work interference Strain-based family-work interference	230 U.S. employees from multiple organizations and industries	Only the use of telework was significantly negatively related to time-based family-work interference
Madsen (2003)	Use of Home-based teleworking	Time-based, strain-based, behavior-based work-to-family conflict Time-based, strain-based, behavior-based family-to-work conflict	221 U.S. full-time teleworkers and nonteleworkers in seven corporate organizations.	Teleworkers experienced significantly lower time-based FWC, strain-based WFC, strain-based FWC and behavior-based WFC than nonteleworkers
Nielson, Carlson & Lankau (2001)	Use of Mentoring	Work-to-family interference Family-to-work interference	272 Professionals (university alumni who earned a BA in business management)	Mentor supportiveness was significantly related to lower work-to-family interference ($\beta = -.22; p. < .01$) and family-to-work interference ($\beta = -.23; p. < .01$)
O'Driscoll, Poelmans, Spector, Kalliath, Allen, Cooper & Sanchez (2003)	Use and availability of Flextime Compressed work schedules Telecommuting Part-time work On-site childcare centers Subsidized local childcare Childcare information /referral services Paid maternity leave Paid paternity leave Eldercare	Work-to-family interference Family-to-work interference	355 Managers in New Zealand (100 women)	Benefit availability was not associated with work-family interference. Benefit use was significantly associated with reduced work-to-family interference
Pasewark & Viator (2006)	Availability and use of Flexible work hours	Work-family interference Family-work interference	552 U.S. public accountants	Availability and use of flexible work arrangements lower the relationship between work-family interference and job satisfaction and between family-work interference and turnover intention
Russell,	Use of	Work-life	5198 Irish	Part-time work and flextime

Source	Work-Life Initiative(s)	WLC Measure	Sample	Main Findings
O'Connell & *McGinnity* *(Russell et al.,* *2009)*	Flextime Part-time hours Home office Job sharing	conflict	Employees from the National Survey of Employees	are related to reduced work-life conflict Home office is related to increased work-life conflict Job sharing is related to increased work-life conflict for men
Shockley & *Allen (2007)*	Availability of Flexible schedule Flexible work location (possibility to work from home)	Work-to-family interference Family-to-work interference	230 Women of different occupations (criteria: work min 20 hrs/week, at least one child or an employed spouse)	Both forms of arrangements were significantly related to reduced work-to-family interference, more than to family-to-work interference
Smith & *Gardner* *(2007)*	Availability and use of 13 work-life initiatives[58] (summed score)	Work-to-family conflict Family-to-work conflict	153 Employees in a large New Zealand organization	Availability and use were negatively correlated with work-to-life conflict Use of work-life initiatives did not play a significant role for work-family conflict if variables of informal support were taken into consideration
Taylor, *Delcampo &* *Blancero* *(2009)*	Availability of Alternative work arrangements Dependent care supports (summed score)	Work-to-family conflict	1165 U.S. Hispanic business professionals	Availability of work-life initiatives was not significantly related to reduced work-to-family conflict
Thompson, *Beauvais &* *Lyness (1999)*	Availability of 19 work-family programs (summed score, areas: family care leave, absence autonomy, flextime, job sharing, and sick childcare)	Work-to-family conflict	276 U.S. managers and professionals	Availability of benefits was negatively associated with work-to-family conflict but this relationship became insignificant when work-family culture variables were entered in the equation
Van Rijswijk, *Bekker, Rutte* *& Croon* *(2004)*	Use of Part-time employment	Work-to-family interference	160 part-time and 29 full-time employed mothers (with a partner)	Working part-time was associated with a lower level of work-to-family interference

---

58   Paid special leave to care for dependents, Unpaid special leave to care for dependents, Paid special leave for other purposes, Unpaid special leave for other purposes, Flextime, Compressed work schedules, Telecommuting, Part-time work, On-site childcare, Job sharing, Paid maternity leave, Paid paternity leave, Eldercare, Study assistance - time off for study, Study assistance - financial assistance, and Time off to attend non-work events (making up the time elsewhere).

Source	Work-Life Initiative(s)	WLC Measure	Sample	Main Findings
			working at 2 insurance companies in the Nether- lands	

Table A.3.   Selection of major studies that examined the direct link between informal organizational demands and resources (organizational work-life culture) and work-life outcomes

Source	Work-Life Culture Dimension	WLC Measure	Sample	Main Findings
Allen (2001)	Family-supportive organizational perception Supervisor support	Work-family conflict	522 participants employed in a variety of occupations and organizations	Family-supportive organizational perception (FSOP) significantly predicted (lower) work-family conflict (β= -.50, p < .001) Supervisor support significantly predicted (lower) work-family conflict but became insignificant if FSOP was considered
Anderson, Coffey & Byerly (2002)	Managerial Support Negative Career Consequences	Work-to-family conflict Family-to-work conflict	2877 U.S. wage and salaried workers who either had at least one cohabiting child under age 18 or were involved in a dual-career relationship or were currently providing care for s.o. aged 65 or older	Management support was negatively related to work-to-family conflict (γ = -.11, p<.05) Career consequences were positively related to Work-to-family conflict (γ = .16, p<.01)
Batt & Valcour (2003)	Supervisor support	Work-family conflict	557 Employees of different professions with 71% of the sample being professionals and managers	Supervisor support was significantly related to reduced work-family conflict (β= -.103, p < .01)
Berg, Kalleberg & Appelbaum (2003)	Conflict with co-workers Understanding supervisor	Work-family balance	Nearly 4000 workers across three manufacturing industries in the U.S.	An understanding supervisor was positively associated with work-family balance (β= .556, p < .001) Conflict with co-workers was negatively associated with work-family balance (β= -.117, p < .05)

Source	Work-Life Culture Dimension	WLC Measure	Sample	Main Findings
Cinamon & Rich (2002a)	Managerial support	Work-to-family conflict Family-to-work conflict	213 Israeli married computer workers and lawyers	Managerial support not related to work-family/family-work conflict
Dikkers, Geurts, den Dulk, Peper, Kompier (2004)	Supportive work-life culture	Time-based work-home interference Strain-based work-home interference	638 Dutch financial consultants	Supportive culture is related to decreased time- and strain-based work-home interference ($F(2, 638)$ = 9.34, p < .001, and F(2, 638) = 13.47, p < .001)
Dikkers, Geurts, Den Dulk, Peper, Taris & Kompier (2007a)	Support (organizational, supervisor, and co-worker support) Hindrance (career consequences, time demands)	Work-home interference Home-work interference	503 Dutch employees from three organizations (governmental service institute, manufacturing company, financial consultancy)	A supportive organizational culture was associated with reduced work-home interference (β= -.20, p < .001) A hindering organizational culture was associated with increased work-home interference (β= .27, p < .001)
Dinger, Thatcher & Stepina (2010)	Supervisor support	Work-family conflict	130 U.S. IT professionals in public sector agencies	Supervisor support related to reduced work-family conflict (γ = −.25, p < .01)
Frye & Breaugh (2004)	Supervisor support	Work-to-family conflict Family-to-work conflict	135 U.S. employees who had a supervisor and at least one child	Supervisor support was significantly negatively related to work-to-family and family-to-work conflict (γ = -.43, p < .05)
Higgins & Duxbury (1992)	Implicitly expected engagement for the organization	Work-family conflict	220 Employees in professional or managerial jobs, who were married to a full-time employed spouse, parents of children living at home	Work expectations related to increased work-family conflict (γ = .131, p < .001)
Jacobshagen et al. (2005)	Workplace support regarding work-life issues	Work-family conflict	143 Swiss top managers of one large-sized company	Workplace support regarding work-life issues was negatively related to work-family conflict (r= −.338, p < .001)
Judge, Boudreau & Bretz (1994)	Workplace support	Work-family conflict	1,062 Male U.S. executives	Workplace support regarding work-life issues was related to increased work-family conflict (γ = −.12, p < .01)

Source	Work-Life Culture Dimension	WLC Measure	Sample	Main Findings
Lapierre & Allen (2006)	Supervisor support	Time-based work-family interference Strain-based work-family interference Time-based family-work interference Strain-based family-work interference	230 Employees from multiple organizations and industries	Supervisor support was significantly negatively related to time-based and strain-based work-family interference $(\beta_{tWFI} = -.18, p < .05; \beta_{sWFI} = -.26, p < .001)$
Lapierre, Spector, Allen, Poelmans, Cooper, O'Driscoll, Sanchez, Brough & Kinnunen(2008)	Supportive work-life culture	Time-based work-to-family conflict Strain-based work-to-family conflict Behavior-based work-to family conflict Time-based family-to-work conflict Strain-based family-to-work conflict Behavior-based family-to-work conflict	1,533 Managers from different countries and branches	Supportive culture related to decreased time-based work-to-family interference $(\gamma = -.47, p < .001)$, strain-based work-to-family interference $(\gamma = -.46, p < .001)$ and behavior-based work-to-family interference $(\gamma = -.28, p < .001)$ Supportive culture related to decreased Time-based family-to-work interference $(\gamma = -.15, p < .001)$, strain-based family-to-work interference $(\gamma = -.13, p < .001)$ and behavior-based family-to-work interference $(\gamma = -.30, p < .001)$
Major, Klein & Ehrhart (2002)	Organizational norms for time spent at work	Work-to-family interference	513 employees of Fortune 500 companies	Organizational time expectations were significantly related to high work-to-family interference $(r = .44, p < .01)$
Major et al. (2008)	Managerial Support Supervisor Support Co-Worker Support	Work-to-family conflict	792 IT employees from 10 organizations	Management support not related to work-family conflict $(\gamma = .02, ns)$, however indirectly affects work-family conflict through its effects on leader-member exchange and co-worker support Supervisor support (Leader-member exchange) related to reduced work-to-family conflict $(\gamma = -.22, p < .01)$ Co-worker support related to reduced work-family conflict $(\gamma = -.12, p < .01)$

Source	Work-Life Culture Dimension	WLC Measure	Sample	Main Findings
McElwain, Korabik & Rosin (2005)	Informal work demands	Work-to-family conflict	320 Full-time professional employees of Canadian organizations (banking, accounting, telecommunications and engineering)	Work demands (including informal demands and work hours) related to increased work-to-family conflict ($\gamma = .29, p < .001$)
Nikandrou, Panayotopoulou & Apospori (2008)	Humane orientation of the organization	Work-family conflict	399 Greek managerial women	Humane orientation of the organization (i.e. support) was negatively related to work-family conflict ($\gamma = -.12, p < .05$)
O'Driscoll, Poelmans, Spector, Kalliath, Allen, Cooper & Sanchez (2003)	Family-supportive organizational perception Supervisor support	Work-to-family interference Family-to-work interference	355 Managers in New Zealand (100 women)	Family-supportive organizational perception and supervisor support were both significantly related to reduced work-to-family and family-to-work interference ($r = -.36, r = -.31, p < .01$)
Shockley & Allen (2007)	Perception of organization as family-friendly	Work-to-family interference Family-to-work interference	230 Women of different occupations (criteria: work min 20 hrs/week, at least one child or an employed spouse)	Family-supportive perception of the organization was significantly related to reduced work-to-family and family-to-work interference ($\beta = -.360; p < .01$)
Smith & Gardner (2007)	Managerial Support Supervisor Support Co-Worker Support Organizational Time Demands Negative Career Consequences	Work-to-family conflict Family-to-work conflict	153 Employees in a large New Zealand organization	Managerial and supervisor support but not co-worker support were significantly negatively correlated with work-to-family conflict ($r = .22, r = .42, p < .01$) Organizational time demands and career damage were significantly positively correlated with work-to-family conflict ($r = .34, r = .46, p < .01$) Neither of the informal dimensions significantly predicted work-life benefit use Management support and time demands most strongly associated with work-family conflict of all variables
Taylor, Delcampo & Blancero (2009)	Supportive work climate Supervisor support	Work-to-family conflict	1165 U.S. Hispanic business professionals	Work climate for family related to decreased work-to-family conflict ($\beta = -.293; p < .001$) Supervisor support related to decreased work-to-family conflict ($\beta = -.230; p < .001$)

Source	Work-Life Culture Dimension	WLC Measure	Sample	Main Findings
Thomas & Ganster (1995)	Supervisor support	Work-family conflict	398 Health professionals with children aged 16 or younger	Supervisor support significantly predicted reduced work-family conflict ($\gamma = -.23, p < .01$)
Thompson, Beauvais & Lyness (1999)	Management support Organizational time demands Negative career consequences	Work-to-family conflict	276 U.S. managers and professionals	Management support not related to work-to-family conflict ($\beta = -.156$, *n.s.*) Lower organizational time demands related to decreased work-to-family conflict ($\beta = -.254, p<.01$) Fewer negative career consequences related to decreased work-to-family conflict ($\beta = -.181, p < .01$)
Thompson & Prottas (2005)	Supervisor support Co-worker support Supportive work-life culture	Work-to-family conflict Family-to-work conflict	3,504 U.S. employees of various occupations	Supervisor support, co-worker support and a supportive organizational culture significantly negatively predicted work-to-life conflict ($\beta = -.09; \beta = -.12; \beta = -.09, p < .001$) (in the case of FWC only overall culture)
Wallace (2009)	Organizational support Co-worker support	Work-to-family conflict	1201 Lawyers who were married and working full-time (law firms, corporate offices, government)	Organizational support related to decreased work-to-family conflict ($\beta = -.162; p<.01$) Co-worker support not directly related to work-to-family conflict but moderates the negative effect of work overload on work-to-family conflict ($\beta = -.125; p<.001$)

Table A.4. Selection of studies that examined work-life experiences of subgroups with respect to differential characteristics

Predictor	Work-Life Measure	Main Findings	Sample & Source
Life Role Values			
Importance of Life Roles	Work-to-family conflict Family-to-work conflict	High work importance individuals and high importance of work *and* family individuals experienced higher work-to-family conflict compared to high family importance individuals	213 Israeli married computer workers and lawyers (Cinamon & Rich, 2002a)
		High family importance individuals did not experience higher levels of family-to-work conflict than high work importance individuals and high importance	

Predictor	Work-Life Measure	Main Findings	Sample & Source
		of work *and* family individuals	
	Work-family conflict	Work ethic related to increased work-family conflict ($\gamma = .15$, $p<.01$)	130 U.S. IT professionals in public sector agencies (Dinger, Thatcher & Stepina, 2010)
		Leisure ethic related to decreased work-family conflict ($\gamma = -.33$, $p<.01$)	
Role Involvement	Work-family conflict	Work involvement related to increased work-family conflict ($\gamma_{men} = .260$, $p<.01$ and ($\gamma_{women} = .322$, $p<.01$)	240 Employees in professional or managerial jobs, who were married to a full-time employed spouse, parents of children living at home (Duxbury & Higgins, 1991)
		Family involvement related to increased work-family conflict for men ($\gamma = .054$, $p<.01$) and decreased work-family conflict for women ($\gamma = -.042$, $p<.01$)	
	Work-family conflict	Job involvement related to increased work-family conflict ($\gamma = .320$, $p<.001$)	220 Employees in professional or managerial jobs, who were married to a full-time employed spouse, parents of children living at home (Higgins & Duxbury, 1992)
	Work-home conflict	Family involvement related to decreased work-home conflict ($\gamma = -.16$, $p<.05$)	310 U.S. public accountants who were married and/or with at least one child (Greenhaus et al., 1997)
Role commitment	Work-family conflict	Commitment to friends related to decreased work-family conflict ($\beta = -.24$); Commitment to spouse related to increased work-family conflict ($\beta = .45$); Commitment to children related to increased work-family conflict ($\beta = .64$)	399 Greek managerial women (Nikandrou et al., 2008)
	Work-to-nonwork spillover	Measures of work salience (work and professional commitment) not related to work-to-nonwork spillover	253 Law firm lawyers (US) (Wallace, 1997)
Role Salience	Work-to-family interference	Career identity salience was not significantly related to work-to-family interference but to actual work time ($r = .14$, $p < .01$)	513 Fortune 500 employees (Major, Klein & Ehrhart, 2002)
Demographic Characteristics			
Gender	Work-to-family conflict	Gender not related to work-to-family conflict	276 U.S. managers and professionals (Thompson, Beauvais & Lyness, 1999)
	Work-to-family conflict	Women experienced higher work-to-family conflict than men	277 Elite employees of a high-commitment, global financial services firm in the U.S., London, and Hong Kong (Wharton & Blair-Loy, 2006)

Predictor	Work-Life Measure	Main Findings	Sample & Source
	Work-to-family conflict	Women experienced higher work-to-family conflict than men ($M_{men}=3.02$ vs. $M_{women}=3.51$)	320 Full-time professional employees of Canadian organizations (banking, accounting, telecommunications and engineering) (McElwain, Korabik & Rosin, 2005)
	Work-to-family conflict	Women experienced higher work-to-family conflict than men ($r = .067, p < .05$)	1165 U.S. Hispanic business professionals (Taylor, Delcampo & Blancero, 2009)
	Work-to-family interference Family-to-work interference	Women experienced significantly higher work-to-family conflict than men ($\beta = .20, p < .01$)	272 Professionals (university alumni who earned a BA in business management) (Nielson, Carlson & Lankau, 2001)
	Work-to-nonwork spillover	Gender not related to work-to-nonwork spillover	253 Law firm lawyers (US) (Wallace, 1997)
	Time-based work-home conflict Strain-based work-home conflict	Men experienced more time-based work-home interference than women ($M_{men}=2.09$ vs. $M_{women}=1.86$) Women perceived work-home culture as more supportive and less hindering (time demands, career consequences	638 Dutch financial consultants (Dikkers, Geurts, den Dulk, Peper, Kompier, 2004)
	Work-family conflict	Women reported higher work-family conflict ($\beta=.165, p.<.001$) SS is related to lower work-family conflict for women ($\beta= -.178, p<.001$)	557 Employees of different professions with 71% of the sample being professionals and managers (Batt & Valcour, 2003)
	Work-family conflict	No gender differences related to work-family conflict	143 Swiss top managers of one large-sized company (Jacobshagen et al., 2005)
	Work-personal life / Personal life-work interference	No gender differences	710 Australian university administration employees (64% female) (Hayman, 2009)
	Work-to-family conflict Family-to-work conflict	No gender differences	245 professionals in two Fortune 500 firms with telework policies (Kossek, Lautsch & Eaton, 2006)
	Work-to-family conflict Family-to-work conflict	No gender differences	454 Full-time professionals of a high-tech firm that telecommuted regularly (Golden, Veiga & Simsek, 2006)
Age	Work-to-family conflict	No age differences related to work-to-family conflict	276 U.S. managers and professionals (Thompson, Beauvais & Lyness, 1999)
	Work-to-family conflict	No age differences related to work-to-family conflict	1165 U.S. Hispanic business professionals (Taylor, Delcampo & Blancero, 2009)
	Work-family conflict	No age differences related to work-family conflict	557 Employees of different professions with 71% of the sample being professionals and

Predictor	Work-Life Measure	Main Findings	Sample & Source
			managers (Batt & Valcour, 2003)
	Work-family conflict	No age differences related to work-family conflict	143 Swiss top managers of one large-sized company (Jacobshagen et al., 2005)
	Work-to-family conflict Family-to-work conflict	No age differences related to work-family conflict	230 Women of different occupations (criteria: work min 20 hrs/week, at least one child or an employed spouse) (Shockley & Allen, 2007)
	Work-to-family conflict Family-to-work conflict	No age differences related to work-family conflict	153 Employees in a large New Zealand organization (Smith & Gardner, 2007)
	Work-family conflict	No age differences related to work-family conflict	522 participants employed in a variety of occupations and organizations (Allen, 2001)
	Work-to-family conflict Family-to-work conflict	No age differences related to work-family conflict	454 Full-time professionals of a high-tech firm that telecommuted regularly (Golden, Veiga & Simsek, 2006)
Parental status	Work-to-family conflict	Parental status not related to increased work-to-family conflict	276 U.S. managers and professionals (Thompson, Beauvais & Lyness, 1999)
	Work-to-family conflict	Parental status related to increased work-to-family conflict	277 Elite employees of a high-commitment, global financial services firm in the U.S., London, and Hong Kong (Wharton & Blair-Loy, 2006)
	Work-to-family conflict	No of children related to increased work-to-family conflict ($\beta = .108;$ $p < .001$)	1201 Lawyers who were married and working full-time (law firms, corporate offices, government) (Wallace, 2009)
	Work-to-nonwork spillover	Parental status (preschool children) not related to work-to-nonwork spillover (but negatively related to hours worked)	253 Law firm lawyers (US) (Wallace, 1997)
	Work-family conflict Family-work conflict	Parental status was related to increased work-family conflict ($\gamma = .09, p < .01$)	1,062 Male U.S. executives (Judge, Boudreau & Bretz, 1994)
	Time-based work-home conflict Strain-based work-home conflict	Parental status related to increased work-home interference Parents vs. nonparents did not differ in their perception of the employer as work-family friendly	638 Dutch financial consultants (Dikkers, Geurts, den Dulk, Peper, Kompier, 2004)
	Work-family conflict	Parental status was significantly related to the experience of higher work-family conflict	522 participants employed in a variety of occupations and organizations (Allen, 2001)
	Work-to-family interference	Parental demands were not significantly related to work-to-family interference	513 Fortune 500 employees (Major, Klein & Ehrhart, 2002)

Predictor	Work-Life Measure	Main Findings	Sample & Source
	Work-personal life interference Personal life-work interference	Parental status related to increased work-personal life interference and personal life-work interference	710 Australian university administration employees (64% female) (Hayman, 2009)
	Work-family conflict (Job-spouse conflict, job-parent conflict, job-homemaker conflict)	Parental demands was significantly related to the experience of job-parent conflict	354 Married professional women from dual-career families in Singapore (Aryee, 1992)
	Work-to-family conflict Family-to-work conflict	Parental status not related to increased work-to-family conflict	153 Employees in a large New Zealand organization (Smith & Gardner, 2007)
	Work-family balance	Parental status (together with being married and single-earner status) was significantly related to reduced work-family balance	Nearly 4000 workers across three manufacturing industries in the U.S. (Berg, Kalleberg & Appelbaum, 2003)
	Work-to-family conflict Family-to-work conflict	Parental status not related to increased work-family conflict	245 professionals in two Fortune 500 firms with telework policies (Kossek, Lautsch & Eaton, 2006)
Marital status	Work-to-family conflict	Marital status not related to work-to-family conflict	276 U.S. managers and professionals (Thompson, Beauvais & Lyness, 1999)
	Work-to-nonwork spillover	Marital status not related to work-to-nonwork spillover	253 Law firm lawyers (US) (Wallace, 1997)
	Work-to-family interference Family-to-work interference	Marital status not related to work-to-family conflict	230 Women of different occupations (criteria: work min 20 hrs/week, at least one child or an employed spouse) (Shockley & Allen, 2007)
	Time-based work-family interference Strain-based work-family interference Time-based family-work interference Strain-based family-work interference	Marital status not related to any of the interference dimensions	230 Employees from multiple organizations and industries (Lapierre & Allen, 2006)
	Work-family conflict	Marital status not related to work-to-family conflict	522 participants employed in a variety of occupations and organizations (Allen, 2001)
	Work-family balance	Marital status (together with being a parent and single-earner status) was significantly related to reduced work-family balance	Nearly 4000 workers across three manufacturing industries in the U.S. (Berg, Kalleberg & Appelbaum, 2003)
	Work-to-family conflict	Marital status not related to increased work-family conflict	245 professionals in two Fortune 500 firms with telework policies

Predictor	Work-Life Measure	Main Findings	Sample & Source
	Family-to-work conflict		(Kossek, Lautsch & Eaton, 2006)
Dual-career status	Work-family conflict	Dual-career status men experienced significantly higher work-family conflict than single-earner male professionals.	273 Male professionals (Higgins & Duxbury, 1992)
	Work-family balance	Dual-earner status was not significantly related to reduced work-family balance, whereas single earner status in association with being married and having children was	Nearly 4000 workers across three manufacturing industries in the U.S. (Berg, Kalleberg & Appelbaum, 2003)
Tenure	Work-family conflict	Tenure only related to reduced work-family conflict for men ($\beta = -.115, p < .05$)	557 Employees of different professions with 71% of the sample being professionals and managers (Batt & Valcour, 2003)
	Work-to-family conflict	Tenure not related to work-to-family conflict	276 U.S. managers and professionals (Thompson, Beauvais & Lyness, 1999)
	Work-to-family conflict	Tenure not related to work-to-family conflict	1165 U.S. Hispanic business professionals (Taylor, Delcampo & Blancero, 2009)
	Work-to-nonwork spillover	Tenure not related to work-to-nonwork spillover	253 Law firm lawyers (US) (Wallace, 1997)
	Work-family conflict Family-work conflict	Tenure not related to work-to-family conflict neither to family-to-work conflict	1,062 Male U.S. executives (Judge, Boudreau & Bretz, 1994)
	Time-based work-family interference Strain-based work-family interference Time-based family-work interference Strain-based family-work interference	Tenure not related to any of the interference dimensions	230 Employees from multiple organizations and industries (Lapierre & Allen, 2006)
	Work-to-family conflict Family-to-work conflict	Tenure not related to increased work-to-family conflict	153 Employees in a large New Zealand organization (Smith & Gardner, 2007)
	Work-family conflict	Tenure not related to increased work-family conflict	522 participants employed in a variety of occupations and organizations (Allen, 2001)
	Work-to-family conflict Family-to-work conflict	Tenure was significantly negatively related to work-to-family conflict ($\beta = -.22; p < .001$)	454 Full-time professionals of a high-tech firm that telecommuted regularly (Golden, Veiga & Simsek, 2006)
Job level (Hierarchy)	Time-based work-family interference	(Higher) Job level was significantly negatively related to time-	230 Employees from multiple organizations and industries

Predictor	Work-Life Measure	Main Findings	Sample & Source
	Strain-based work-family interference	based work-family interference (β = -.17; p < .05)	(Lapierre & Allen, 2006)
	Time-based family-work interference		
	Strain-based family-work interference		
	Work-to-family conflict	Management level was significantly positively related to work-to-family conflict (β = .25; p < .001)	454 Full-time professionals of a high-tech firm that telecommuted regularly (Golden, Veiga & Simsek, 2006)
	Family-to-work conflict		
	Work-to-family conflict	Job level not related to work-to-family conflict	276 U.S. managers and professionals (Thompson, Beauvais & Lyness, 1999)

Table A.5. Characteristics, methodology, work-life conflict metrics and average weekly work hours of the reviewed studies using professional samples

Source	Sample	Methodology	Work-Life Conflict Measure(s) and Explained Variance of WLC	Working Hours (M;SD)
Ahuja et al. (2007)	171 IT road warriors	Covariance-based SEM (LISREL)	Work-family conflict (M = 5.04; SD = 1.37) (1-7 scale) R^2_{WFC} = .24	-
Aryee (1992)	354 Married professional women from dual-career families in Singapore	Hierarchical linear regression	Job-spouse conflict (M = 2.45; SD = .80) R^2 = .36 Job-parent conflict (M = 2.67; SD = .90) R^2 = .31 Job-homemaker conflict (M = 2.01; .83) R^2 = .25 (1-5 scale)	M = 45.00
Batt & Valcour (2003)	557 Employees of different professions with 71% of the sample being professionals and managers	Hierarchical linear regression	Work-family conflict (M = 2.75; SD = .62) (1-5 scale) R^2_{WFC} = .291	M = 42.27 (SD = 11.35)
Chen, Powell & Greenhaus (2009)	528 Professional employees of different functional backgrounds	Latent congruence modelling	Time-based work-to-family conflict (M = 2.67; SD = .97) Strain-based work-to-family conflict (M = 2.60; SD = 1.03) (1-5 scale)	-
Cinamon & Rich (2002a)	213 married computer workers and lawyers	Cluster analysis and	Work-family conflict (M = 3.01; SD = .79)	M = 48.80 (SD = 8.60)

Source	Sample	Methodology	Work-Life Conflict Measure(s) and Explained Variance of WLC	Working Hours (M;SD)
	(Israel)	MANOVA	Family-work conflict (M = 2.02; SD = .68) $R^2_{WFC} = .14$	
Dikkers, Geurts, den Dulk, Peper, Kompier (2004)	638 Dutch financial consultants	ANOVA and MANOVA	Time-based work-home interference (M = 1.98; SD = .53) Strain-based work-home interference (M = 1.86; SD = .49) (1-4 scale)	-
Dinger, Thatcher & Stepina (2010)	130 U.S. IT professionals in public sector agencies	SEM with partial least squares (PLS)	Work-family conflict (M = 3.45; SD = 1.66) (1-5 scale) $R^2_{WFC} = .454$	-
Duxbury & Higgins (1991)	240 Employees in professional or managerial jobs, who were married to a full-time employed spouse, parents of children living at home	SEM with partial least squares (PLS)	Work-family conflict ($M_{men} = 2.63$; SD = .59) ($M_{women} = 2.68$; SD = .66) (1-5 scale) R^2_{WFC} Men = .56 R^2_{WFC} Women = .60	-
Greenhaus et al. (1997)	310 U.S. public accountants who were married and/or with at least one child	Hierarchical multiple regression analysis and path analysis	Work-home conflict ($M_{men} = 3.70$; SD = .83) ($M_{women} = 3.67$; SD = .85) (1-5 scale)	-
Gutek, Searle & Klepa (1991)	530 U.S. psychologists and 209 senior managers	T-tests, regression analysis and analysis of covariance (ANCOVA)	Work-to-family interference $M_{PSYwomen} = 3.39/M_{PSYmen} = 2.93$ $M_{SMwomen} = 3.67/M_{SMmen} = 3.31$ Family-to-work interference $M_{PSYwomen} = 1.82/M_{PSYmen} = 1.80$ $M_{SMwomen} = 1.71$ $M_{SMmen} = 1.69$ (1-5 scale) $R^2_{WFC} = .21$ $R^2_{FWC} = .10$	$M_{PSYwomen} = 41.3$ (SD = 15.6) $M_{PSYmen} = 41.5$ (SD = 15.7) $M_{SMwomen} = 52.6$ (SD = 8.5) $M_{SMmen} = 51.3$ (SD = 9.2)
Hill, Hawkins, Ferris & Weitzman (2001)	6541 IBM employees in the U.S.	Hierarchical regression analysis	Work-family balance (M = 2.98; SD = .80) (1-5 scale) $R^2 = .39$	M = 55.23 (SD = 9.14)
Jacobshagen et al. (2005)	143 Swiss top managers of one large-sized company	Hierarchical regression analysis	Work-family conflict M = 3.36; SD = 1.01 (1-5 scale)	M = 59.68 (SD = 8.15)
Judge, Boudreau & Bretz (1994)	1,062 Male U.S. executives	Covariance-based SEM (LISREL)	Work-family conflict M = 3.78; SD = 1.34 Family-work conflict M = 1.86; SD = .73 (1-5 scale)	M = 55.81
Kossek, Lautsch & Eaton (2006)	245 professionals in two Fortune 500 firms with telework policies	Ordinary least squares regression	Work-family conflict M = 2.81; SD=.75 Family-work conflict M = 1.78;	M = 45.11 (SD = 8.25)

Source	Sample	Methodology	Work-Life Conflict Measure(s) and Explained Variance of WLC	Working Hours (M;SD)
			SD=.47 (1-5 scale)	
Lapierre et al. (2008)	1,533 Managers from different countries and branches	Covariance-based SEM	Time-based work-to-family interference M = 2.97; SD = .96 Strain-based work-to-family interference M = 2.95; SD = .86 Behavior-based work-to-family interference M = 2.96; SD = .79 Time-based family-to-work interference M = 2.25; SD = .85 Strain-based family-to-work interference M = 1.83; SD = .72 Behavior-based family-to-work interference M = 2.75; SD = .78 (1-5 scale)	-
Major, Klein & Ehrhart (2002)	513 Employees of Fortune 500 companies	Covariance-based SEM	Work-to-family interference M = 3.13, SD = .87 (1-5 scale)	M = 47.14 (SD = 7.29) (Min = 28.5, Max = 82.5)
Major et al. (2008)	792 IT employees from 10 organizations	Path modelling	Work-family conflict M = 2.95; SD = 1.00	
McElwain, Korabik & Rosin (2005)	320 Full-time professional employees of Canadian organizations (banking, accounting, telecommunications and engineering)	Path modelling (AMOS)	Work-to-family conflict M = 3.26; SD = .95 Family-to-work conflict M = 1.86; SD = .70 (1-5 scale)	-
Nielson, Carlson & Lankau (2001)	272 Professionals (university alumni who earned a BA in business management)	Hierarchical regression analysis	Work-to-family interference M = 3.08; SD = .98 Family-to-work interference M = 1.80; SD = .69 (1-5 scale)	M = 50.21 (SD = 10.75)
Nikandrou et al. (2008)	399 Greek managerial women	Multiple Regression and covariance-based SEM	Work-family conflict	-
O'Driscoll et al. (2003)	355 Male and female managers in New Zealand	Correlation, Moderator and Mediator Analysis	Work-to-family interference Family-to-work interference	45.6%: 41–50 hr per week 32.1%: 51–60 hrs per week
Taris et al. (2006)	199 Male and female managers	Covariance-based SEM and regression analysis	Time-based work-to-family conflict M = 1.91; SD = .59 Strain-based work-to-family conflict M = 1.90; SD = .50 (1-4 scale)	M = 37.90 (SD = 4.08); $M_{overtime}$ = 7.98 (SD = 5.63)

Source	Sample	Methodology	Work-Life Conflict Measure(s) and Explained Variance of WLC	Working Hours (M;SD)
Taylor, Delcampo & Blancero (2009)	1165 U.S. Hispanic business professionals	Hierarchical regression analysis	Work-to-family conflict $M = 2.94$; $SD = .69$ (1-5 scale)	-
Thompson, Beauvais & Lyness (1999)	276 U.S. managers and professionals	Hierarchical regression analysis	Work-to-family conflict $M = 14.32$; $SD = 5.74$ (1-7 scale) $R^2_{WFC} = .334$	$M = 47.41$ ($SD = 9.95$)
Wallace (1997)	253 Law firm lawyers (US)	Ordinary least squares regression	Work-to-nonwork spillover $M = 3.28$; $SD = .91$ (1-5 scale) $R^2_{Work\text{-}nonwork\ spilloverr} = .51$	$M = 51.23$ ($SD = 9.83$)
Wallace (2009)	1201 Lawyers who were married and working full-time (law firms, corporate offices, government)	Linear regression and mediation analysis	Work-to-family conflict $M = 3.04$; $SD = .90$ (1-5 scale) $R^2_{WFC} = .573$	$M = 48.50$ ($SD = 9.66$)
Wharton & Blair-Loy (2006)	277 Elite employees of a high-commitment, global financial services firm in the U.S., London, and Hong Kong	Logistic regression	Work-to-family conflict[59] $M = .46$	$M = 49.98$ ($SD = 8.25$)

---

59   In the Wharton & Blair-Loy study, work-to-family conflict was measured in terms of "employees' concerns about negative effects of their long work hours on those in their personal life" (p. 423) with one single item.

Appendix B: Data Collection

Table B.1 Original items

Construct	Items
Work-to-life conflict (Carlson, Kacmar & Wiliams, 2000)	
Time-based Work-to-Life Conflict	(1) The time I must devote to my job keeps me from participating equally in household responsibilities and activities.
	(2) My work keeps me from my family activities more than I would like.
	(3) I have to miss family activities due to the amount of time I must spend on work responsibilities.
Strain-based Work-to-Life Conflict	(1) When I get home from work I am often too frazzled to participate in family activities/responsibilities.
	(2) I am often so emotionally drained when I get home from work that it prevents me from contributing to my family.
	(3) Due to all the pressures at work, sometimes when I come home I am too stressed to do the things I enjoy.
Organizational Work-Life Culture (Thompson, Beauvais & Lyness, 1999)	
Management Support	(1) Managers in this organization are generally considerate towards the private life of employees.
	(2) In this organization, people are sympathetic towards care responsibilities of employees.
	(3) In this organization it is considered important that, beyond their work, employees have sufficient time left for their private life.
Supervisor Support	(1) My superior supports employees who (temporarily) want to reduce their working hours for private reasons
	(2) My supervisor support employees who want to switch to less demanding jobs for private reasons.
	(3) I am comfortable in discussing my private life with my superior.
Co-worker Support	(1) My colleagues help me out when I am (temporarily) preoccupied with my care responsibilities.
	(2) My colleagues support employees who (temporarily) want to reduce their working hours for private reasons.
	(3) My colleagues support employees who want to switch to less demanding jobs for private reasons.
Negative Career Conse-	(1) Employees who (temporarily) reduce their working hours for private reasons are considered less ambitious in this organization.

Construct	Items
quences	(2) Employees who (temporarily) reduce their working hours for private reasons are less likely to advance their career in this organization.
	(3) In this organization, it is more acceptable for women to (temporarily) reduce their working hours for private reasons than for men.
Organizational Time Demands	(1) To get ahead in this organization, employees are expected to work overtime on a regular basis.
	(2) In order to be taken seriously in this organization, employees should work long days and be available all of the time.
	(3) In this organization, employees are expected to put their job before their private life when necessary.

Appendix C: Descriptive Statistics

Table C.1. Type and intensity of work-personal life conflict experienced (N = 794)

	No Conflict	Small Conflict	Moderate Conflict	High Conflict
	%	%	%	%
Work vs. Partner & Family	8.1	27.1	37.5	24.8
Work vs. Friends	6.3	24.2	40.4	27.7
Work vs. Social Engagement	5.3	18.1	28.6	43.1
Work vs. Health & Recovery	5.2	22.4	43.2	28.5
Work vs. Self	3.5	19.8	36.0	40.5

Table C.2. Number of conflict types experienced (N = 794)

Number of conflicts experienced	Moderate and high levels of conflict		Moderate levels of conflict		High levels of conflict	
	N	%	N	%	N	%
One type of conflict	49	6.2	121	15.2	249	31.4
Two types of conflict	62	7.8	206	25.9	164	20.7
Three types of conflict	88	11.1	230	29.0	156	19.6
Four types of conflict	125	15.7	162	20.4	117	14.7
Five types of conflict	284	23.4	54	6.8	63	7.9

Table C.3. Means, standard deviations and correlations of the three work-to-life conflict subscales and type of conflict

	M	SD	1	2	3	4	5	6	7	8	9	10	11	12	13	14	15
1 Time-based WLC	3.83	.853															
2 Strain-based WLC	3.21	.977	.593**														
3 Behavior-based WLC	3.14	.915	.453**	.383**													
4 Conflict Work vs. Partner & Family	2.81	.910	.476**	.392**	.306**												
5 Conflict Work vs. Friends	2.91	.880	.409**	.472**	.317**	.460**											
6 Conflict Work vs. Social Engagement	3.15	.919	.438**	.400**	.260**	.261**	.539**										
7 Conflict Work vs. Health & Recovery	2.96	.848	.529**	.499**	.288**	.334**	.460**	.391**									
8 Conflict Work vs. Self	3.13	.854	.079*	.497**	.263**	.372**	.484**	.427**	.618**								
9 Subbranch (MC vs. LF)	1.30	.460	.011	-.028	.161**	.036	.032	.104**	.076*	.012							
10 Gender	1.31	.461	-.131**	.111**	-.063	.018	-.036	.026	.034	.052	-.147**						
11 Age	34.15	6.704	.012	-.129**	-.117**	-.117**	-.148**	-.203**	-.020	-.040	-.302**	-.097**					
12 Relationship Status	1.81	.395	-.115**	-.001	-.035	.032	.054	.035	.051	.092**	-.099**	-.036	.124**				
13 No of Children (Parental Status)	.50	.889	-.103**	-.148**	-.139**	-.014	-.128**	-.148**	-.076*	-.044	-.177**	-.167**	.579**	.210**			
14 Tenure	4.10	3.882	-.048	-.119**	-.059	-.028	-.062	-.125**	.017	.019	-.126**	-.040	.635**	.102**	.406**		
15 Job Position (Hierarchy)	2.75	1.266	-.071*	-.115**	-.049	-.043	-.060	-.133**	.053	.011	-.077*	-.107**	.698**	.125**	.482**	.609**	
16 Priority Work vs. Personal Life	2.57	.824	-.143**	-.089*	-.002	-.097**	-.029	-.076*	-.078*	-.103**	.003	-.041	.093**	-.150**	-.066	.072*	.058

$^*p < .05, ^{**}p < .01$

Appendix D: Initiative Use and Availability

Table D.1. Availability and use of WLB initiatives (N = 794)

		Not offered and not needed		Not offered but needed		Offered, but not used		Offered and used	
		N	%	N	%	N	%	N	%
'Primary' WLB Initiatives	Reduced Schedule[a]	159	20.0	123	15.5	334	42.1	67	8.4
	Short-term Flexible Work Hours[b]	186	23.4	128	16.1	95	12.0	235	29.6
	Long-term Flexible Work Hours[c]	296	37.3	213	26.8	70	8.8	49	6.2
	Home Office	120	15.1	175	22.2	132	16.6	270	34.0
	Office (Fri)Day	91	11.5	35	4.4	38	4.8	361	45.5
	Leave of Absence / Sabbatical	123	15.5	194	24.4	218	27.5	87	11.0
	Free Choice of Residence	154	6.8	54	6.8	79	9.9	264	33.2
	Childcare	320	40.3	202	25.4	132	16.6	15	1.9
	Eldercare	503	63.4	94	11.8	32	4.0	4	0.5
'Secondary' Initiatives	Supportive Services	272	34.4	270	34.0	77	9.7	87	11.0
	Health and Recovery Programs	231	29.1	298	37.5	108	13.6	84	10.6
	Individual Coaching	125	15.7	249	31.4	90	11.3	200	25.2
	Support for Educational Programs (MBA etc.)	40	5.0	91	11.5	264	33.2	317	39.9

[a] 35h per week, part-time, job sharing, etc.
[b] Flextime, trust-based working time, etc.
[c] Work time accounts, etc.

Table D.2. Availability and use of WLB initiatives comparing management consultants and law firm professionals

	Not offered and not needed		Not offered but needed		Offered, but not used		Offered and used	
	MC	LF	MC	LF	MC	LF	MC	LF
Reduced Schedule[a]	27.5	21.1	16.6	18.7	49.3	48.7	6.6	11.5
Short-term Flexible Work Hours[b]	29.8	28.4	14.9	22.4	17.2	13.5	38.1	35.7
Long-term Flexible Work Hours[c]	42.9	49.3	31.4	35.2	15.7	8.9	10.0	6.7
Home Office	9.6	20.9	19.3	27.9	14.9	20.9	56.1	30.3
Office (Fri)Day	4.8	27.0	7.0	6.4	5.2	8.8	83.0	57.8
Leave of Absence / Sabbatical	7.3	26.6	12.8	41.2	47.9	28.0	32.0	4.2
Free Choice of Residence	11.2	38.6	7.9	11.0	16.8	12.8	64.0	37.7
Childcare	50.2	46.7	17.2	36.1	30.1	15.0	2.4	2.2
Eldercare	74.3	81.6	15.5	14.6	9.1	3.4	1.1	0.4
Supportive Services	28.5	43.1	43.9	35.7	15.4	8.9	12.2	12.4
Health and Recovery Programs	18.8	38.0	35.0	44.2	26.9	9.6	19.3	8.2
Individual Coaching	7.7	26.6	23.5	41.2	20.4	28.0	48.4	4.2
Support for Educational Programs (MBA etc.)	3.2	6.7	19.9	9.6	38.5	36.5	38.5	47.3

Row groups (left margin): 'Primary' WLB Initiatives (Reduced Schedule through Eldercare); 'Secondary' Initiatives (Supportive Services through Support for Educational Programs).

[a] 35h per week, part-time, job sharing, etc.
[b] Flextime, trust-based working time, etc.
[c] Work time accounts, etc.

Note: Values represent percentages of the respective subsamples (N_{MC} = 242 and N_{LF} = 552).

Table D.3. Availability and use of WLB initiatives (Males vs. Females)

		Not offered and not needed		Not offered but needed		Offered, but not used		Offered and used	
		Male	Female	Male	Female	Male	Female	Male	Female
'Primary' WLB Initiatives	Reduced Schedule[a]	25.5	8.3	14.2	18.7	43.6	38.2	3.1	20.7
	Short-term Flexible Work Hours[b]	26.6	15.4	11.9	25.7	13.9	7.9	29.7	29.9
	Long-term Flexible Work Hours[c]	40.9	29.0	24.1	32.8	9.9	6.6	6.0	6.6
	Home Office	15.5	13.7	20.3	25.3	15.1	20.3	37.2	27.4
	Office (Fri)Day	10.9	12.9	4.2	5.0	5.3	3.7	46.5	43.2
	Leave of Absence / Sabbatical	15.7	15.4	23.4	27.4	29.7	22.8	12.4	7.5
	Free Choice of Residence	18.2	22.4	7.7	5.0	11.5	6.6	35.9	27.4
	Childcare	42.0	36.1	21.9	33.6	16.4	17.0	2.4	0.8
	Eldercare	63.7	62.2	10.2	15.4	4.4	3.3	0.4	0.8
'Secondary' Initiatives	Supportive Services	36.9	28.2	31.4	40.2	9.3	10.4	10.2	12.4
	Health and Recovery Programs	30.8	24.5	34.3	44.8	13.1	14.9	11.5	8.7
	Individual Coaching	16.6	14.1	28.1	39.0	12.4	8.7	28.1	19.1
	Support for Educational Programs (MBA etc.)	4.2	7.1	12.2	10.0	33.6	32.0	40.7	39.0

[a] 35h per week, part-time, job sharing, etc.

[b] Flextime, trust-based working time, etc.

[c] Work time accounts, etc.

Note: Values represent percentages of the respective subsamples (N_{Male} = 548 and N_{Female} = 241).

Forschung und Praxis zukunftsfähiger Unternehmensführung

Herausgegeben von Stephan Kaiser

Band 1 Arjan M. F. Kozica: Personalethik. Die ethische Dimension personalwissenschaftlicher Forschung. 2011.

Band 2 Stephan Kaiser / Stefan Süß / Ingrid Josephs (Hrsg.): Freelancer als Forschungsgegenstand und Praxisphänomen. Betriebswirtschaftliche und psychologische Perspektiven. 2012.

Band 3 Martin Lothar Stolz: Work-Life-Balance in Professional Service Firms. Eine empirische Untersuchung der Wirkung von Work-Life-Balance-Initiativen und der arbeitsbezogenen Konsequenzen des Work-Life-Konflikts. 2012.

Band 4 Cornelia Ulrike Reindl: Managing Work and 'The Rest of Life'. The Role of Formal and Informal Demands and Resources for the Work-Life Conflict of Professionals. 2013.

www.peterlang.de